The Nature of Confession

Evangelicals & Postliberals in Conversation

Essays by

George Lindbeck

Alister McGrath

George Hunsinger

Gabriel Fackre

& others

Edited by Timothy R. Phillips
& Dennis L. Okholm

InterVarsity Press
Downers Grove, Illinois

InterVarsity Press® is the book-publishing division of InterVarsity Christian Fellowship®, a student movement active on campus at hundreds of universities, colleges and schools of nursing in the United States of America, and a member movement of the International Fellowship of Evangelical Students. For information about local and regional activities, write Public Relations Dept., InterVarsity Christian Fellowship, 6400 Schroeder Rd., P.O. Box 7895, Madison, WI 53707-7895.

All Scripture quotations, unless otherwise indicated, are taken from the HOLY BIBLE, NEW INTERNATIONAL VERSION®. NIV®. Copyright © 1973, 1978, 1984 by International Bible Society. Used by permission of Zondervan Publishing House. All rights reserved.

ISBN 0-8308-1869-3

Printed in the United States of America ♾

Library of Congress Cataloging-in-Publication Data

The nature of confession: evangelicals & postliberals in conversation
  /edited by Timothy R. Phillips and Dennis L. Okholm.
      p.   cm.
    Includes bibliographical references.
    ISBN 0-8308-1869-3 (pbk.: alk. paper)
    1. Theology—Methodology.   2. Theology, Doctrinal—History—20th
century.   3. Hermeneutics—Religious aspects—Christianity—History
of doctrines—20th century.   4. Frei, Hans W.   5. Lindbeck, George
A.   6. Liberalism (Religion)—Protestant churches.   7. Liberalism
(Religion)—United States.   8. Evangelicalism.   I. Phillips,
Timothy R. (Timothy Ross), 1950-   .   II. Okholm, Dennis L.
  BR118.N28   1996
  230'.01—dc20   96-13028
                                                        CIP

18	17	16	15	14	13	12	11	10	9	8	7	6	5	4	3	2	1
11	10	09	08	07	06	05	04	03	02	01	00	99	98	97	96		

This work is dedicated to
the multitude of lay Christians
who practice a "premodern hermeneutic"
—where the Bible is their primary world—
and to
George Lindbeck and the late Hans Frei
who uncovered and defended this strategy in the academy.
We pray that their efforts will help
invigorate the church
for the twenty-first century.

Part I
INTRODUCTION

1

THE NATURE
OF CONFESSION

Evangelicals &
Postliberals

Timothy R. Phillips &
Dennis L. Okholm

W ho do people say that I am?"
Who is Jesus? The question is posed to church and world alike.
When Jesus put this question to his disciples, they suggested a range
of answers: Elijah, John the Baptizer, Jeremiah, an emissary of Beelzebub, Messiah,
Son of God.

The answers vary today. John Dominic Crossan uncovers a "Jewish—though not
so very Jewish—version of a wandering Cynic philosopher."[1] Betty Eadie encountered Jesus as a tour guide and advice giver whose insights included the announce-
ment that all religions are roads to God and whose central exhortation was to love
everyone.[2] The Way International repackages a brand of Arianism and teaches that
Jesus is not God the Son but the son of God. As Jaroslav Pelikan eloquently illustrated, Jesus has been depicted in many different ways through the centuries, often
depending on the culture in which the confessors live.[3] What makes the contemporary situation unique, as several contributors to the present volume indicate, is
that our culture has witnessed the emergence of pluralism so that there is no single
dominant answer to the question, Who is Jesus? It seems that the answers of all the
centuries—and then some—are well represented in the last few decades of this
millennium.

Even among traditionally orthodox groups diversity reigns. Diversity also characterizes the responses to this question provided by contemporary evangelicalism, reflecting its dissolution and loss of identity. What relationship exists between God's revelation in Jesus Christ through Scripture and our confession in this world? How should Christians answer Jesus' question? What is our answer?

While acclaimed as a success, evangelicalism, according to key observers, is fragmenting and collapsing. Popular indicators suggest that evangelicalism's unique moral and theological inheritance has been traded for a bowlful of spiritual junk food that feeds the contemporary appetite. American culture now carries more weight than revelation on a broad range of issues from ethics to beliefs. The prevalence of adultery and divorce—even among nationally known figures—no longer startles. Consumer research and related techniques increasingly supplant Scripture's analysis of the church's and believers' responsibilities.

Similarly, evangelicalism's answers to society's ills echo American ideologies and party politics.[4] Therapy is confused with salvation. The politics of the New Right are identified as the "Christian" coalition. Certainly evangelicals remain "people of the book." But the displays that greet customers entering a religious bookstore often indicate that the focus has shifted away from the gospel narrative to exotic dimensions that assume their own autonomy or sustain these American ideologies. For evangelicals on both the right and the left of the spectrum, American culture has dissipated the central benchmark of the faith, the christological center of Scripture.

The impact of American culture and the diminution of belief are even clearer among evangelical academics. The old theological standards have collapsed. Theologically central beliefs—such as God's judgment on sin, the unity and sole authority of Scripture, and salvation only through personal trust in Christ—are no longer defining.[5] Some evangelical theologians now bluntly assert that the world is an important *norm* for theology.[6] Many evangelical biblical scholars have thoroughly embraced the historical-critical method; whether the corresponding drive toward liberalism can be resisted is now an open question. The incessant refrains of our contemporary ideology, "everyone is entitled to his opinion" and "let's not judge," fill the evangelical academy. The Augustinian insight that all truth is God's truth guided evangelical academics in the 1960s and 1970s. Today it has been deconstructed to mean that any sincere religious person's perception of truth is probably God's truth.

Even more disturbing is the growing estrangement between the evangelical academy and the church. Evangelical scholarship is more directed to the academy than to the upbuilding of the laity. Not only do many scholars ignore the priority and indispensability of the community life of the church, but works targeting the laity are denigrated as intellectually vacuous.[7]

With the growing loss of identity and the splicing of the gospel narrative with foreign stories from U.S. cultural and intellectual history, evangelicals can no longer ignore the question of confession. What is *our* answer to Jesus' question, "Who do you say that I am?" More than anything else, our response to this question will define the future of evangelicalism.

This predicament is ironic. As descendants of American revival movements, evangelicals highlighted the supernatural regenerating work of Jesus Christ in their own lives while firmly adhering to the ecumenical creeds and Reformation distinctives. At the turn of the twentieth century this coalition led the reaction to the modernist attempt to desupernaturalize Christianity by focusing attention on the qualitative difference between nature and grace. J. Gresham Machen brilliantly defined the benchmark: "No product of sinful humanity could have redeemed humanity from its dreadful guilt or lifted a sinful race from the slough of sin. But a Saviour has come from God. There is the reason why the supernatural is the very ground and substance of the Christian faith."[8]

But a well documented anti-intellectualism bolstered fundamentalism's reaction against modernism. The fundamentalists' loyalty to Jesus Christ often implied an uncritical adherence to their own confessions and a censorious stance toward contemporary intellectual challenges. During the 1940s key fundamentalists questioned this separatistic, anti-intellectual stance and called for Christians to engage culture. Evangelicalism emerged from the isolated cocoon of fundamentalism with a strikingly different strategy and mission in the world. For the last five decades evangelicalism worked through the intellectual and social structures of American life to engage and transform it from within. Across the disciplines evangelical scholars mustered great intellectual vigor in emphasizing the congruence of nature and grace, reason and revelation (since all truth is God's truth), thus presenting Christianity as *the* truth.

Similarly, many evangelicals are now at the center of key occupations. If all truth is God's truth and all vocations can be callings of God, aren't the politicians, the businesspeople and the scientists glorifying God in their professions? During the last forty years evangelicals have adjusted Christian values to the American cultural framework as well as the academic one. At the end of the twentieth century evangelicalism appears to have succeeded in some respects. At least they are recognized— and maybe even respected—as a significant voice in American society.

The original evangelical strategy for bringing the gospel to America by emphasizing the commonality between reason and revelation has resulted in the accolades that it currently enjoys. But has this strategy actually worked to subvert the mission? Have evangelicalism's confidence in reason and delight with American culture become its quagmire? So it seems. Fifty years later the question no longer concerns the trivialization of reason but the trivialization of revelation![9] This concern is crucial. For this same strategy of transforming the world by translating and conforming the gospel to the culture is what drives the discussion of evangelicals like Miroslav Volf in this volume.

A Parallel Narrative
This historical narrative is not new. Others, much earlier, pursued a parallel strategy

with a comparable compromise, and evangelicals should have learned from them. Two hundred years ago a brilliant Christian pastor was similarly concerned that the cultural elite in his day repudiated the Christian community as obscurantist and irrelevant to life. He used public grounds to demonstrate the plausibility and even necessity of the Christian faith for all human life. This figure was Friedrich Schleiermacher. His strategy initiated the liberal experiment in theology, which includes some of the most creative Christian thinkers the church has ever known.

These brilliant theologians vigorously defended and presented Christianity as the truth by correlating nature and grace, reason and revelation—for "all truth comes from the one God and is his revelation."[10] Their strategy was simple. Shaped by the Enlightenment's demand for a ground common to all rational beings, they identified a universal human structure that Christianity and Jesus fulfill as its highest expectation. Jesus was reinterpreted as the most insightful moral teacher, or the one who always acknowledges his total dependence on God, or the founder of an earthly kingdom of God built on brotherly love. Whatever was not pertinent to this universal experience or ground became secondary or irrelevant and was rejected. In this way, the claims of Christianity were made acceptable to the modern world.

Two hundred years later this noble experiment is coming to an end. Historicism's discovery that all our thoughts are shaped by culture has called into question the possibility of a universal common ground. Religious pluralism has exploded the strategy of correlation. If all our criteria for truth are intrahistorical, how can there be any final or universal basis for judging the truth claims of another religion or another culture? As one self-proclaimed Christian revisionist concedes, "Arguments for the absoluteness, superiority or uniqueness of Christianity [have] become difficult if not impossible."[11] The emergence of religious pluralism forces one to affirm either that other religions are equally valid and Jesus is not the definitive revelation of God or that Christianity is not simply one of many valid ways of naming God because Jesus is the incarnate Son of God and Lord over all. The liberal strategy, with its correlation of reason and revelation, confesses the former option, assuming that the contemporary cultural understanding of reason, not Jesus Christ, is our primary access to truth.

Liberalism, now better known as revisionism, held reign during the late 1970s and early 1980s in mainline ecclesial and academic circles. To many evangelicals during this period, the future of classical orthodoxy appeared bleak. But the increasing support for religious pluralism eventually forced a confrontation with the decisive issue—Jesus' question, "Who do you say that I am?" Two successive quests for the historical Jesus have died trying to answer this question, and it has suddenly become viable again to confess Jesus as Lord and pursue a christocentric theology. Confessional groups are active in all the major denominations and are assuming leadership positions. New organizations, such as Carl Braaten's Center for Catholic and Evangelical Theology and Lesslie Newbigin's American wing of the Gospel and Our Culture Network, are making themselves felt, as well as many worship renewal groups.

Renewal movements in the mainline denominations—from the PCUSA and United Methodist to the Episcopal Church—are invigorated. Now the national magazine taking seriously theological discussions of the Trinity and the church is *The Christian Century!* A new theological coalition is developing that confesses Jesus Christ and the core biblical framework of salvation history as the norm for the Christian's life.

Instead of conforming the confession of Christ to American culture or to Enlightenment epistemology, this coalition insists that Jesus Christ is not subject to some higher authority. Compromise on this point—even for mission strategy—would ensure the dilution, even the distortion, of Christianity. These theologians confess that Jesus Christ is primary and all other reality needs to be construed in relation to him. What is at issue here is our identity as Christians. To acknowledge Jesus as the Truth in "whom are hidden all the treasures of wisdom and knowledge" (Col 2:3) means that he alone is our norm and judges every other aspect of reality. Either Christ confronts us with his exclusive claim as Lord over all, or he does not confront us at all.[12]

The Postliberals

At the center of this resurgence of confessional Christianity are the postliberals. *Postliberalism* refers to a theological movement most commonly linked with Yale Divinity School. It seeks to reverse the trend in modern Christianity of accommodation to culture. While significantly influenced by the thought of Ludwig Wittgenstein, Karl Barth, Clifford Geertz, Peter Berger and others, the originators of the distinctive "postliberal" agenda and label were Hans Frei and George Lindbeck. Their students, creative and provocative theologians like William Placher, Stanley Hauerwas and George Hunsinger, have further developed these key ideas.

Postliberalism includes a theory that explains the loss of Scripture's formative authority and the church's correlative accommodation to culture as well as a strategy for cultivating Christian identity. As Hans Frei's pathbreaking *The Eclipse of Biblical Narrative* (1974) showed, modern theories of biblical interpretation find the meaning of the text in something more basic and foundational than Scripture—a universally accessible reality. Whether meaning was found in eternal truths that the text symbolized (as for liberals) or identified exclusively with the story's factual reference (as for conservatives), both displaced the priority of Scripture.[13] Scripture no longer defined the church's social world in a normative way. "The great reversal had taken place: interpretation was a matter of fitting the biblical story into another world with another story rather than incorporating that world into the biblical story."[14] When another authority was found, Scripture's world-forming narrative was fragmented and eventually dispersed.

This shift in understanding—the loss of Scripture's grand narrative as well as its christological center and unity—impeded the biblical narrative from shaping the community of disciples. Increasingly, Scripture became a strange book that was closed to the laity and under the control of the academic elite. Accommodation to that culture was inevitable.

The postliberal repudiates these attempts to ground interpretation in a universally accessible ground as an ahistorical quest. A totally neutral and objective point of view does not exist. The language and tradition in which we live shape our experience and understanding of even the most basic components of reality. Even science, with its so-called objective standpoint, is not a purely rational, ahistorical enterprise. It involves a specific social and communal world that can be acquired only by submitting to the authority of a particular scientific tradition.[15] Uncovering the social roots grounding every vision of reality allows the postliberal to embrace Christianity's unique and historical particularity.

In place of these modern theories of interpretation, postliberals propose a "classical" hermeneutic in which the scriptural world structures the church's cosmos and identity. It has some affinities with what is sometimes called a "premodern" approach. Scripture "is the only real world" for the community.[16] More precisely, the biblical narrative that culminates in Jesus the Messiah is the most basic and normative story and cannot be interpreted into something else.

It is not that Scripture is first objectively understood by the academic elite and then applied to life. As Curtis Freeman reminds us in this book, readers are invited to enter the strange *new* world of the Bible, not merely to study the strange *old* world of the ancient Near East. Scripture through the Spirit's work constitutes the community's world, so that all believers actively understand and interpret it. Scripture is understood as a single interglossing whole that focuses on Jesus. In other words, Scripture is world-creating. It shapes the primary world of believers—the practice of worship, life and thought. Only through the life and practice of the church can the grammar of faith be understood. This scriptural vision creates a "followable" world that supplies the categories for understanding all of life. Through this process the biblical world "absorbs" the universe.

This is not a naive, ahistorical view of Scripture. Postliberals acknowledge that our understanding of Scripture is always shaped by a wider cultural context. This is one reason that they reject an ahistorical, propositionalist view of religion, in which doctrinal statements directly or "literally" refer to reality. Language is irreducibly shaped by history. They also reject the revisionist option, in which religious language expresses a universal human experience. Lindbeck's *The Nature of Doctrine: Religion and Theology in a Postliberal Age* (1984) contrasts these dominant theories of religion and doctrine, the cognitive-propositional and the experiential-expressive, with his cultural-linguistic theory. Here the biblical narrative forms the cultural-linguistic world for the church. Like rules of grammar that govern our use of language to describe the world, theological doctrines identify the rules for using confessional language in defining this social world. When taken together as a whole, they make ontological claims regarding reality.

In contrast to experiential-expressive claims, Christians worship God in a distinctive manner as the Trinity, which cannot be homogenized with other religions. And contrary to cognitive-propositional theorists, the church's understanding—like all cultures and languages—has changed, for better or worse, through crises and external influences.

Rather than translating Scripture into an external and alien frame of reference, which devalues and undermines its normative position and eventually produces an accommodation to culture, the postliberals call for an intratextual theology that finds the meaning of the Christian language within the text.[17] Then relevance follows: "Religious communities are likely to be practically relevant in the long run to the degree that they do not first ask what is either practical or relevant, but instead concentrate on their own intratextual outlooks and forms of life."[18] The encroachment of modernity is addressed not through the translation and subsequent diminution of theological belief, but by an intentional catechization. Throughout the centuries pagan converts have "submitted themselves to prolonged catechetical instruction in which they practiced new modes of behavior and learned the stories of Israel and their fulfillment in Christ" so that they "acquired proficiency in the alien Christian language and form of life" and were able to confess the faith "intelligently and responsibly." Through "an intimate and imaginatively vivid familiarity with the world of biblical narrative" these converts were able to "experience the whole of life in religious terms."[19]

The performance of the text by the faithful community is of central concern to the postliberal. "Faith and love wither despite purity of doctrine when worship, life and action are corrupt."[20] The elitist role of academics as the determiners of objective meaning and truth is removed. Meaning is given within the praxis of the church. The task for theological and biblical scholars becomes primarily practical: to discern deficiencies and distortions in the community's action and thought in order to build up the body of believers.

This view of language means that Christian beliefs are fallible and reformable, so that a sharply defined system of theological understanding cannot ensue. Certainly there are standards for identifying Christian doctrine, including intratextual and christological criteria. But they will not adjudicate many controversies. So the postliberal also includes a pragmatic criterion—an interpretation is preferred that serves the upbuilding of the church. The result is a hermeneutic that acknowledges diverse interpretations and unity at the same time.[21]

But as Lindbeck has repeatedly noted, postliberalism belongs in a formal rather than a material category. It is primarily a research program for those affirming the church's christological and trinitarian confessions. Thus it can accommodate diverse theological traditions and, in fact, includes theologians from across the spectrum.

Evangelicals and Postliberals
It might appear that postliberals and evangelicals should view each other as bedfellows and make common cause in reversing Christianity's conformity to modern-

ism.[22] Could postmodernist theory explain evangelicalism's present fragmentation and help cultivate a distinctively Christian identity while resisting the onslaught of modernity? After all, evangelicalism and postmodernism share an emphasis on the particularity of Christ, the normativity of Scripture and the distinctiveness of the Christian faith vis-à-vis the prevailing culture (as McGrath, Fackre and others observe in this volume).

But establishing a link between evangelicals and postliberals has not been easy. Evangelicalism's first dialogue with postliberals, the encounter between Carl F. H. Henry and Hans Frei at Yale, was abortive. Reflecting his long-standing defense of a universally accessible objective truth and a correlative suspicion of any Barthian turn, Henry summarily dismissed Frei's proposal as "an enchantment with the affective, a flight from history to the perspectival that enjoins no universal truth claims, a reflection of the revolt against reason."[23]

Frei protested, "Of course I believe in the 'historical reality' of Christ's death and resurrection, if those are the categories which we employ." Reflecting his repudiation of foundationalism, Frei tellingly adds that the reference and truth of the gospel narrative cannot be affirmed on any grounds other than faith.[24] But Frei was not understood—a fact that unintentionally illustrated his point that a universally comprehensive and neutral language does not exist.[25]

In recent years some of the fragmented groups within evangelicalism have linked their proposals with the postliberals. Roger Olson draws strong parallels between the postliberal proposal and some important evangelicals who stand opposite to Henry on the theological spectrum. Appropriately labeled postconservatives, these theologians include Stanley Grenz and Clark Pinnock.[26] They employ the language of narrative in order to correct an ahistorical view of doctrinal propositions that is common in some evangelical circles.[27]

But some observers find discordant themes among members of this group. Reflecting the experiential-expressive paradigm, their theology has a consciously strong apologetic cast that even employs the contemporary scene as a norm alongside the biblical narrative.[28] Contrary to the postliberal attempt to reverse the direction of conformity, Grenz defends a theological strategy wherein the academic guild translates Scripture into a contemporary "cognitive framework." "The theologian seeks to . . . help fashion the church's message in accordance to the categories of the recipients."[29] Pinnock's dismissive attitude toward key theological figures within the evangelical heritage, particularly Augustine and Calvin, is counterfactual.[30] The postliberal's regulative view of doctrine treats theological propositions as a second-order enterprise and values other enduring theological positions. The continuing conversation between postconservatives and postliberals should focus on theological method (whether Scripture should absorb the world) as well as the importance of the classic grammars of faith.

Standing between these two ends of the evangelical spectrum is a group of moderates. Many young evangelicals in the last two decades have earned their doctoral degrees in mainline academic circles, where they gained a firsthand appreciation for Karl Barth's theological achievement. Many are suspicious of the Enlightenment's fascination with a universally accessible foundation for public discourse, which in evangelicalism often takes the form of evidentialism. Some know historical theology too well to assent to an ahistorical objectivistic propositional view of doctrine. They are more influenced by classic theologians like Athanasius, Augustine, Calvin and Wesley than by moderns such as Carl Henry or Charles Hodge. Like the postliberals, they want to remove Scripture from the control of the academic elite and return it to the church, where it becomes world-creating and identity-forming for the laity.[31] As noted in David Wells's trenchant analyses, they are alarmed by modernity's encroachment on the church and are calling for a recatechetization.[32] Many in this group—Kevin Vanhoozer, David Clark, John Sailhamer and Alister McGrath—are deeply indebted to postliberal thought.[33]

While there exist means to establish a common cause with postliberals, this group has sharply questioned the postliberal agenda. The issue of realism is recurring. Some within this group need to appreciate the postliberal view of doctrine, its recognition of the fallibility of theological constructs, as well as its willingness to learn from other enduring grammars of faith. The continuing conversation between these moderates and postliberals should also focus on identifying evangelical theology's entanglement with foundationalism.

This Book
This book grew out of the 1995 Wheaton Theology Conference, which brought together postliberals and evangelicals. We invited George Lindbeck and George Hunsinger, leaders among postliberals and confessional Christians. George Lindbeck, as noted earlier, is one of the founding fathers of postliberalism (along with the late Hans Frei). George Hunsinger was a student of Frei and has become his major interpreter. The spectrum of evangelical thought represented at this conference made for a wide-ranging and sometimes sharp discussion of the pitfalls and possibilities that exist in postliberal thought for evangelicals. Key issues were raised forthrightly, and many were resolved, establishing a foundation for further understanding and dialogue.

Redactions of some key papers and discussions from the conference appear in this book. In the first section two evangelicals provide broad descriptions and critical reflections of postliberal thought. Then five papers focus on the key recurring central issues—whether evangelicals can be nonfoundationalists (like the postliberals) and whether postliberals are antirealists (as the evangelicals suspect). In the third section the nature of biblical authority and its relation to the church are explored in four essays. Fourth, with the help of postliberal correctives and insights, evangelicals are called to pay closer attention to the doctrine of God and to the inseparable relationship of the cognitive and functional understandings of truth. Fifth, postliberal methodology is applied to the material of theology (the doctrine of the atonement) and to the proclamation of the story. Finally, an edited transcript of the conference's concluding discussion among the four principal speakers demonstrates that profitable discussion between evangelicals and postliberals has begun.

Evangelical Overviews and Critiques

The overviews and evangelical critiques of the postliberals in the first section reflect the diversity and even the fragmentation that exist among evangelicals. While having thoroughly appropriated postliberal insights, Alister McGrath is still intensely critical of Lindbeck's cultural-linguistic theory in two general areas. First, the question of realism looms large. Does the postliberal make ontological claims when confessing the Christian faith? Or is postliberalism a form of antirealism? McGrath argues that a cultural-linguistic theory dispenses with external referents and reduces truth claims to simply "intrasystemic consistency." Second, this produces doctrinal consequences. Are the biblical narrative and the significance of Jesus Christ grounded in anything more than the community process of socialization? That is to say, why is *this* book normative and not some other? The postliberals may be able to answer the question, Who is Jesus? But can they really answer the question "Why Jesus?"

While these core issues reappear in Miroslav Volf's insistence that a cultural-linguistic theory overlooks some indispensable dimensions in religion, he also targets the postliberals' professed attempt to reverse the direction of conformity so that the biblical narrative absorbs the world rather than transforming it. Volf is above all fearful of immunizing the Christian community from an external critique. Are we not shaped in part by the world's political and economic structures? Volf wonders who is really absorbing whom. The heathen provide the spectacles that allow saints to see their texts as spectacles. Truth be told, there is an exchange between the lenses of the text and the lenses of the culture. The "culture" is not a monolith, nor is the Christian ever outside it. Having the gospel absorb the world is not the goal. In our decentralized and pluralistic society we should use the postliberals' insights in nonsystemic, contextual and flexible ways of doing theology.

Realism and Foundationalism

These overviews outline at least two key methodological issues of concern to evangelicals and postliberals. First, are postliberals necessarily antirealists? Jeffrey Hensley answers this recurring question, which began with Henry's encounter. Tackling the controversial passages, including those mentioned by McGrath, Hensley suggests a realist reading of Lindbeck's work. For cultural-linguistic theorists, concepts do not screen external objects but actually provide the bridges to them. They are the means by which we access and perceive reality. Hensley concludes that Lindbeck's theory of truth employs an internal coherence of propositions that as a *whole* correspond to particular states of affairs. But if Lindbeck is misread as an antirealist, Hensley suggests that it is due to his deep commitment to antifoundationalism.

And so we turn to the question of foundationalism. Postliberalism is subject to charges of obscurantism, subjectivism and relativism because postliberals deny that any universally accessible standards for defending Christianity's truthfulness currently exist. Rodney Clapp provocatively exposes evangelicalism's attachment to a form of Enlightenment foundationalism. Employing postliberal insights, Clapp argues that nonfoundationalism can provide resistance to modernity, which has already demonstrated its corrosive work in the evangelical church.

Philip Kenneson tackles the difficult charge that postliberalism is a form of fideistic obscurantism, sectarianism and relativism because it is insulated from any external critique and correction. Creatively outlining a theory of doctrinal change consistent with a cultural-linguistic theory, he answers Volf's key questions. The cultural-linguistic theory does not shut out the world but organizes it and includes a mechanism for responding to criticism. Furthermore, Kenneson questions why believers would not want to claim the superiority of the Christian metanarrative by "outnarrating the competition." To conclude otherwise reflects modernity's assumption that religions are a private choice without any impact on other aspects of life. Rather, by absorbing the world, Christianity shows its comprehensive ability to provide the intelligible framework for all of life.

Finally, David Clark carefully examines the charge that intratextuality eventuates in relativism. This charge is false, he concludes, as long as the postliberal insists on an ultimate truth, even though it may not be currently accessible to all rational beings. Clark demonstrates that classical foundationalism is self-referentially defeating and that evangelicals should reject modernist foundationalism; he prefers instead a "moderate foundationalism" that is sympathetic to Lindbeck's proposal.

The Bible and the Church

The significance of these formal concerns is most evident when we turn to the doctrine of Scripture. While a common focus on the christocentric nature and supreme authority of the biblical narrative links postliberals and evangelicals, Gabriel Fackre explains that their diverse and even conflicting assumptions lead to differences in the understanding of revelation. The postliberals focus on the Spirit's illumination of the community in which the individual believer is socialized to read the "plain sense" of Scripture. Because the community assumes such a dominant place, many evangelicals are suspicious that a postliberal hermeneutic is a road to Rome. But Fackre admonishes postliberals to distinguish inspiration from illumination, giving priority to the former and thereby remembering that the community is accountable to something beyond itself, the Bible, which enables believers to resist the community's distortive socialization. On the other hand, the pietist and experientialist characteristics of evangelicalism emphasize the Spirit's illumination of the believer, tending to individualize the Christian faith, even elevating experience to a criterion displacing Christ's own authority in the creeds and liturgical actions of his church. Fackre suggests that postliberals and evangelicals offer each other a corrective.

Lamenting the postliberal's lack of attention to questions posed by evangelicals on biblical authority, Hunsinger offers a correction. Revisiting the abortive Henry-Frei debate, he shows that Henry's conception of Scripture's truthfulness, unity, authority, factuality and reference is shaped by a prior commitment to modernity's conception of value-neutral and publicly accessible objective truth. It is precisely this subordination of Scripture to modernity or any other external epistemological scheme that Frei resists. Hunsinger brilliantly shows that Frei's conception of Scripture and even of the relation between faith and history accords with the classic emphasis of *sola Scriptura* by the Reformers and their faithful followers, such as the Amsterdam theologians Kuyper and Bavinck. Once the commitment to modernity is stripped away, Hunsinger finds that Frei's understanding of Scripture differs only in degree, not in kind, from an evangelical conception. Evangelicals can maintain their commitment to inerrancy with only an "ad hoc minimalist" commitment to modernity. Hunsinger puts forward John Stott and Alister McGrath as contemporary examples.

Employing postliberal analyses, two evangelicals outline a new paradigm for biblical authority. While carefully respecting the concerns of inerrantists, Jonathan Wilson shows how their prior commitment to a foundationalist epistemology actually frustrates discipleship and elevates the authority of the scholarly elite at the expense of lay believers. Biblical authority, Wilson contends, must be rethought in terms of "practicing the gospel." The first step, then, is not to establish an inerrant text, but to follow the text. Through praxis one understands Scripture not individualistically, but in the church through its communal processes. Here "the church is called to live in such a way that the authority of Scripture is displayed as witness to the gospel of Jesus Christ."[34]

Curtis Freeman advances a similar critique of the evangelical historical-grammatical hermeneutic. Historically this interpretive scheme has accommodated to modernity's individualism and rationalism, weakening the church. In its place Freeman details a strategy for reading the Bible that strengthens the community's faith and practice. A prayerful reading of Scripture, which is christologically focused and practiced, will put Scripture into the hands and feet of the laity, who through saintly models and discernment can resist accommodation to the modern world.

Theology and the Christian Life

Another constant refrain heard at the conference was the postliberal emphasis on the relation of theology to spirituality. It offers a reminder to evangelicals, who have not always done well at keeping together their pietist heart and Reformed mind,[35] while several participants admonished postliberals to keep together the cognitive-propositional and experiential-expressive *with* the cultural-linguistic.

Kurt Richardson identifies the Trinity as a point of convergence for evangelicals and postliberals. While evangelicals have traditionally ignored the importance of this doctrine, Richardson builds on the work of T. F. Torrance to show the essential relationship between the Trinity and the whole of Christian life, from revelation and salvation to worship. Nicea, for instance, is both story and doctrine summarized in a form that inspires worship and proclamation. The Trinity represents what the postliberal is seeking in terms of the grammar of faith and what the evangelical seeks in terms of contact with the reality of God. Both Christian groups would be aided by the emphasis of the other.

Henry Knight shows the fruitfulness of Lindbeck's cultural-linguistic analysis in accounting for Christian spirituality, perhaps providing more precision for some postconservative proposals. Christian affections, as described by Jonathan Edwards and John Wesley, are neither the applications of propositional beliefs nor a generic religious experience. The environment of Scripture, within which the community of disciples lives, forms the Christian character with deep abiding emotions that shape believers to act in certain ways. These affections possess an irreducible particularly; they are not simply culturally relative variations of a more general religious experience. Directed toward specific objects, these affections represent construals of the biblical view of reality.

Picking up Frei's thesis that grounding theology on another foundation distorts the real sense of Scripture, Gregory Clark examines how evangelical worldview philosophy understands conversion. A distinctive evangelical achievement in apologetics, worldview philosophy repudiates fundamentalism's naive dogmatism and obscurantist fideism by arguing for Christianity's rational superiority among the worldview options. But this extratextual move, originating in German idealism, severely distorts Christian faith. Worldview philosophy is committed to a form of spirituality that is different from Christian spirituality. According to the Gospels, Jesus is the center of conversion. This one, whom we worship as the God-man and Truth himself, has brought us out of death and darkness, and we willingly embrace martyrdom for his name. But worldview philosophy displaces the person of Jesus for an outlook on the world; the Christian convert is one who has mastered a theater of worldviews and judged the Christian option as the most consistent and comprehensive, according to limited available information. Is this why the evangelical academy tends to spawn aloofness and skepticism instead of embracing martyrdom?

Putting the Postliberal Model to Work
Postliberals are frequently chided as being too preoccupied with methodological concerns. Clearing one's throat, as Jeffrey Stout notes, can quickly lose an audience. So this conference concentrated as well on developing analyses and showing their possibility and fruitfulness for the evangelical church.

Focusing on the doctrine of the atonement, George Lindbeck shows how postliberalism provides a convincing theological account of its history as well as directives for the contemporary scene. The themes of Christ as victor and victim stand out in the history of the church. Even though both images are biblically based, the social and cultural situation is intertwined with the resulting theories of the atonement. Nevertheless, these theories helped the Bible absorb the world, not the reverse. These divergent understandings of Jesus' central work, constrained by christological and trinitarian guidelines, originate from the same text and help build up the church.

The postliberal hermeneutic acknowledges contextualization, a variety of interpretations and unity at the same time. In the contemporary world, however, the image of Christ as the victim for sinners is fading, and with it the notion that the cross is the means by which our sins are forgiven. The image of Jesus as victorious, the revelation of God's love, the one to be imitated, now dominates. Lindbeck is alarmed at this development. The image of Jesus as victor and example reflects the law, not the gospel, and can only distort Christian vitality. The image of Jesus as victim has nourished a heroic yet selfless love of God and neighbor. Lindbeck calls for theologians to help correct this distortion in the contemporary church by promoting a grammar of faith tied to Jesus as victim.

The Future
Ours is an age of profound cultural change. The old revisionist strategy in theology has degenerated into mere anthropology and succumbed to the political agendas of its proponents. Those unable to confess the normativity of Jesus Christ will have little to offer the church. While the evangelical movement appears to be gaining ground, it is simultaneously suffering an acute identity crisis. Modernity has dissipated much of its confession of Jesus Christ as well. But it is precisely the question "Who is Jesus?" that has momentous consequences for the future of evangelicalism.

Ironically, it is the postliberals, a confessional group from mainline denominational circles, that may provide the most help. They offer a theory for resisting the foreign extrabiblical assumptions of modernity while maintaining confessional identity within the church. The challenge of postliberalism can enable us to refocus attention on the center of Christian belief instead of confusing platitudes for integration or culture for creed. Through the dialogue represented in this volume we can better learn how to help the church remain faithful in the midst of contemporary challenges as it answers Jesus' question, "Who do you say that I am?"

Part II
EVANGELICAL OVERVIEWS & CRITIQUES

2
AN EVANGELICAL EVALUATION OF POSTLIBERALISM

Alister E. McGrath

T he emergence of "postliberalism" is widely regarded as one of the most important developments of Western theology since 1980. The movement originated in the United States and was initially associated with Yale Divinity School, particularly with theologians such as Hans Frei, Paul Holmer, David Kelsey and George Lindbeck.[1] While it is not strictly correct to speak of a "Yale school" of theology, there are nevertheless clear family resemblances between a number of the approaches to theology that emerged from Yale during the late 1970s and early 1980s.[2] Since then, "postliberal" trends have become well established within North American and British academic theology,[3] indicating that it is likely to have a considerable impact on evangelicalism, at least in the next decade, as the latter increases its presence within the academic community. Defining and evaluating the relation between evangelicalism and postliberalism is therefore of major importance.

The distinguishing feature of postliberalism is its rejection of the totalizing projects of modernity, whether they are in the specific form of an Enlightenment-style appeal to universal reason or a liberal appeal to "religion," "culture" or an unmediated religious experience common to all of humanity. Each of these is now considered to be a false universal, a fictitious construction of a totalizing mindset. In the place of such pseudo-universals, postliberalism places religious communities and their traditions, particularly as mediated through narrative.[4] Along these lines, William C. Placher has helpfully identified the following three fundamental features of postliberal thought:[5]

1. the primacy of narrative as an interpretative category for the Bible;
2. the hermeneutical primacy of the world created by the biblical narratives over

the world of human experience;

3. the primacy of language over experience.

It will be demonstrated that this critique of the foundational role of experience represents a decisive move away from the liberal strategy of an earlier generation.

The philosophical roots of this movement are complex. Particular appreciation can be discerned within the movement for the style of approach associated with the philosopher Alasdair MacIntyre, which places an emphasis on the relation between narrative, community and the moral life.[6] In this respect, postliberalism reintroduces a strong emphasis on the *particularity* of the Christian faith, which is a reaction against the strong homogenizing tendencies of liberalism, in its abortive attempt to make theory (that all religions are saying the same thing) and observation (that the religions are different) coincide.

We can now turn to deal with the postliberal critique of liberalism, focusing especially on its rejection of foundational assumptions within theological method and of experientially based theological methodologies.

The Postliberal Critique of Liberal Foundationalism

The emergence of postliberalism may be regarded as a telling indication that the intellectual and cultural credibility of liberalism has been decisively challenged. The notion of "common human experience" is now viewed as little more than an experiential fiction, in much the same way that "universal rationality" is now seen as little more than the idle daydream of reason. The belief in cultural or experiential metanarratives (to borrow from the conceptualities of postmodernism) is acknowledged to be at best flawed, and at worst an invitation to oppression. Ideas such as "religion" and "culture," which an earlier generation of liberal writers happily appealed to as constituting universal foundations of nonparticularist forms of Christianity, are now seen to be fictitious constructs, generally reflecting a specifically Western set of presuppositions. Most significantly, the suggestion that Christian theology concerns the quest for justifiable particularity is no longer deemed "arrogant" or "imperialist."

Liberal critics of postliberalism have argued that it represents a lapse into a "ghetto ethic" or some form of fideism or tribalism, on account of its retreat from universal norms of value and rationality. Yet these same liberal critics seem unable to accept that the Enlightenment is over, and that any notion of a "universal language" or "common human experience" is simply an invention, like Robinson Crusoe's imaginary island (to use Hans-Georg Gadamer's famous analogy). Foundationalism of any kind—whether philosophical or religious—has been widely discredited.[7] Postliberalism has come to terms with the death of the Enlightenment, while liberalism stumbles pathetically and randomly across the intellectual terrain, looking desperately for an absolutely firm foundation in a world which no longer accepts the existence of universals. The birth of postmodernity has been overlooked by liberalism, which seems to prefer living in the past rather than facing up to the harsh new world of today. It is to the credit of postliberal writers that they have faced up to the cultural abandonment of ubiquitous norms and values, even if their liberal critics prefer the cozy nostalgia of the myth of a "universal language" or "public discourse."

As Mary Midgley once commented, the "sad little joke" of universal languages is that nobody seems to speak them.[8] Criticizing postliberalism for its abandonment of a universal discourse is like scolding a child who no longer believes in Santa Claus. The concept may be a reassuring, cozy and useful illusion—but it is an illusion. And, as postmodernism has emphasized, the illusion of universal norms can all too easily become profoundly oppressive, forcing observation to conform to theory and repressing distinctiveness on the part of, for example, a particular religion on account of the prior dogmatic conviction that all are saying the same thing. The reassertion of the discrete nature of Christianity reflects both this reaction against the illusion of universality and a growing awareness of the genuinely singular character of Christian faith. We shall explore the latter point in the following section; our concern now focuses on the critique of liberal foundationalism which undergirds the postliberal enterprise.

Postliberal theologians argue that liberal theology feels an obligation to ground itself in something in the public arena—such as philosophical concepts or "common human experience."[9] Lindbeck describes this concern as a "commitment to the foundational enterprise of uncovering universal principles or structures," whether these turn out to be metaphysical, existential or otherwise.[10] The impulse, which is fundamentally apologetic in intent, is to find a common base for Christian theology and public discourse by a prior analysis of human knowledge, culture or experience. The merit of this critique is probably most evident in the case of Paul Tillich, whose apologetic theology is widely regarded as dictated by extrabiblical and non-Christian concerns and inadequately grounded in the particularities of the Christian tradition.

This attempt to liberate Christian theology from extrabiblical presuppositions will be welcomed by evangelicals,[11] who can certainly ally themselves, at least to some extent, with postliberalism's emphasis on Scripture as the sole normative source of Christian theology and living. Evangelicals and postliberals seem to share the kind of concerns so frequently expressed by Karl Barth regarding the potential enslavement or debasement of Christian thought through a deficient theological method that allows ideas from outside the church to assume a controlling influence within it.

The Postliberal Critique of Experientially Based Theologies
The characteristically liberal idea that human religious experience can act as a foundational resource for Christian theology has obvious attractions. It suggests that Christian theology is concerned with human experience—something which is common to all humanity, rather than the exclusive preserve of a small group. This approach has many merits for those who are embarrassed by the "scandal of particularity." It suggests that all the world religions are basically human responses to

the same religious experience—often referred to as "a core experience of the transcendent." Theology is thus the Christian attempt to reflect upon this common
human experience with the knowledge that the same experience underlies the other
world religions.

This aspect of liberalism also has considerable attractions for Christian apologetics, as the writings of many recent American theologians, especially Paul Tillich and
David Tracy, make clear. Because humans share a common experience, whether
they choose to regard it as "religious" or not, Christian theology can address it. The
problem of agreeing on a common starting point is thus avoided; the starting point
is already provided in human experience. Apologetics can demonstrate that the
Christian gospel makes sense of common human experience. This approach is probably seen at its best in Paul Tillich's collection of sermons titled *The Courage to Be*,
which attracted considerable attention after its publication in 1952. Many observers
believed that Tillich had succeeded in correlating the Christian proclamation with
common human experience.[12]

But there are difficulties here, the most obvious being that there is actually very
little empirical evidence for a common core experience throughout human history
and culture. The idea is easily postulated, but virtually impossible to verify. The
liberal position is best described by George Lindbeck in *The Nature of Doctrine* (1984).
Lindbeck suggests here that theories of doctrine may be divided into three general
types. The cognitive-propositionalist theory stresses cognitive aspects of religion,
emphasizing the manner in which doctrines function as truth claims or informative
propositions. The experiential-expressive theory interprets doctrines as noncognitive symbols of inner human feelings or attitudes. A third possibility, which Lindbeck himself favors, is the cultural-linguistic approach to religion. Lindbeck asso-
ciates this model with a "rule" or "regulative" theory of doctrine. Lindbeck's
explanation and criticism of the second theory is of particular interest to us at this
point.

The experiential-expressive theory, according to Lindbeck, sees all religions as
public, culturally conditioned manifestations and affirmations of prelinguistic forms
of consciousness, attitudes and feelings. In other words, there is some universal
religious experience that Christian theology (in common with other religions) attempts to express in words. The experience comes first, and the theology arrives
later. As Lindbeck argues, the attraction of this approach to doctrine is grounded
in a number of features of late twentieth-century Western thought. For example,
the contemporary preoccupation with interreligious dialogue is considerably assisted
by the suggestion that the various religions are diverse expressions of a common
core experience—an "isolable core of encounter" or an "unmediated awareness of
the transcendent."

The principal objection to this theory is its obvious gross inaccuracy. As Lindbeck
points out, the possibility of religious experience is shaped by religious expectation,
so that "religious experience" is conceptually derivative, if not vacuous. "It is difficult

or impossible to specify its distinctive features, and yet unless this is done, the assertion of commonality becomes logically and empirically vacuous."[13] The assertion that "the various religions are diverse symbolizations of one and the same core experience of the Ultimate"[14] is ultimately an axiom, an unverifiable hypothesis (perhaps even a dogma, in the pejorative sense of the term) because of the difficulty of locating and describing the "core experience" concerned. As Lindbeck correctly points out, this would appear to suggest that there is "at least the logical possibility that a Buddhist and a Christian might have basically the same faith, although expressed very differently."[15] The theory can be credible only if it is possible to isolate a common core experience from religious language and behavior, and demonstrate that the latter two are articulations of or responses to the former.

Therefore, attempts to evaluate this theory are totally frustrated by its inherent resistance to verification or falsification. While conclusive empirical evidence is not available to allow the evaluation of the suggestion that religious language and rites are a response to prior religious experience, the possibility that religious language and rites *create* that experience (for example, through arousing expectation of such experience and indicating in what manner it may arise and what form it might assume) is at least as probable on both the empirical and logical levels.[16] Equally, the suggestion that the experience of individuals is to be placed above or before the communal religion itself seems to invert observable priorities. Schleiermacher, who might be taken as the archetype of such an experientially grounded approach to theology, does not understand "experience" to designate the undifferentiated and idiosyncratic emotions or existential apprehensions of each individual believer; rather, he understands "experience" to be grounded in the memory, witness and celebration of the community of faith.[17] The theological significance of the Christian experience is articulated at the communal, not the individual, level.

The notion of a common core experience which remains constant throughout the diversity of human cultures and the flux of history, while being articulated and expressed in an astonishing variety of manners, remains profoundly unconvincing. Thus Bernard Lonergan wisely concedes that religious experience varies from one culture, class and individual to another,[18] while apparently being reluctant to draw the conclusion his concessions suggest (however tentatively): that it varies from one *religion* to another. While the doctrinal tradition of the church is publicly available for analysis, thereby allowing its allegedly "unchangeable" character to be assessed critically, religious experience remains a subjective, vacuous and nebulous concept, the diachronic continuity and constancy of which necessarily lie beyond verification or—as seems the more probable outcome—falsification.[19]

The main lines of Lindbeck's critique of experiential theories of doctrine are timely and persuasive.[20] For Lindbeck, Christian tradition, and not experience itself, possesses explanatory and revelatory significance. Evangelicalism will readily endorse this aspect of the postliberal program, recognizing its affinity with distinctive elements of the evangelical tradition.

Rediscovering the Distinctiveness of Christianity

There is a growing acceptance within academic theology not simply that Christianity *is* distinct and must be accepted as such, but that any worldview which refuses to acknowledge this distinctiveness must be rejected as seriously at variance with the observable facts. After all, Jesus Christ was not crucified just for reinforcing what everyone already knew! With the end of the Enlightenment and its intellectual satellites, including liberalism and pluralism, the embargo on particularity has been lifted. No longer is the claim that one is saying something *different* seen as irrational. Jews are special: they have a special story and a different set of values. In the same way, Christians are special: they too have a special story and a different set of values.[21] Postliberalism embodies a willingness to respect—indeed, to celebrate—the distinctiveness of the Christian tradition, and sees Christian theology as concerned with the articulation of the distinctive grammar of the Christian faith.

This view is perhaps seen most clearly in the writings of Paul Holmer, most notably in his *Grammar of Faith* (1978). For Holmer, Christianity has a central grammar that regulates the structure of Christian "language games."[22] This language is not invented or imposed by theology; rather, it is already inherent within the biblical paradigms upon which theology is ultimately dependent. The task of theology is thus to discern these intrabiblical rules (such as the manner in which God is worshiped and spoken about), not to impose extrabiblical rules. For Holmer, one of liberalism's most fundamental flaws is its attempts to reinterpret or restate biblical concepts, which inevitably degenerate into the harmonization of Scripture with the spirit of the age. "Continuous redoing of the Scripture to fit the age is only a sophisticated and probably invisible bondage to the age rather than the desire to win the age for God."[23] Theology is grounded on the intrabiblical paradigm, which it is obliged to describe and apply as best it can. To affirm that theology has a *regulatory* authority is not to imply that *it* can regulate Scripture, but to acknowledge that a distinctive pattern of regulation already exists within the biblical material, which theology is to uncover and articulate.

The critical question that arises from this approach, to which we shall return later in this chapter, is whether theology is simply about the grammar of faith, that is to say, the regulation of Christian discourse. To what does this discourse relate? Is there some reality or set of realities outside the biblical text to which the biblical narrative relates? Do theological assertions simply articulate biblical grammar, or are they associated with some objective order, irrespective of whether we recognize this relation or not? As we shall see, one central evangelical anxiety concerning the postliberal approach is that it appears to represent a purely intratextual affair, with little concern for its possible relation to an external objective reality.

One of the most tantalizing aspects of Lindbeck's *Nature of Doctrine* is that he clearly intends it to be a *pretheological* text rather than an exercise in systematic theology. He regards the volume as a framework for the exploration of theological questions and issues, rather than an analysis of those issues directly. This makes the text somewhat difficult for the typical evangelical, who has a specific interest in the outcome of the application of a method. (Evangelicalism judges the reliability of a theological method partly in terms of its consequences.) *The Nature of Doctrine* was published in 1984, allowing ample time for the subsequent application of its approach; however, Lindbeck himself has not yet produced a substantial work which evidences a transition from pretheological inquiry to theological statement.

In what follows, my analysis is therefore necessarily limited to *The Nature of Doctrine* itself, linking analysis of its approach with an attempt to explore what the consequences of its application might be. However, in the part of Lindbeck's pretheological program which includes evaluation of existing approaches, it is particularly appropriate to explain and critique his evaluation of rival approaches. We therefore turn to consider Lindbeck's exposition of the kinds of "cognitive-propositional" approaches to doctrine that are historically associated with evangelicalism.

Lindbeck's Critique of Evangelicalism

In his analysis, Lindbeck identifies three theories of the nature of doctrine. I have already endorsed and explicated Lindbeck's analysis of the approach to doctrine that is characteristic of theological liberalism, particularly in North America, which Lindbeck classifies as "experiential-expressive." Although Lindbeck does not explicitly indicate that he intends to engage evangelicalism, another category he describes would clearly include the movement. This view, designated by Lindbeck as "propositionalist" or "cognitive," treats doctrines as "informative propositions or truth claims about objective realities."[24] This style of approach has a long association with evangelicalism and became especially important in the evangelical renaissance of the 1960s, when theologians such as Carl F. H. Henry reacted against the understanding of revelation associated with neo-orthodoxy by stressing the informative content of divine revelation and its articulation in propositional form. While this approach to Christian doctrine seems to me to be ultimately inadequate, in that it fails to do justice to the full complexity of the biblical notions of revelation, it remains axiomatic for evangelicals that both revelation and doctrine have cognitive aspects. Lindbeck's explicit critique of such methods thus clearly impacts evangelicalism, even if Lindbeck himself does not explicitly make such connections.

Lindbeck argues that the cognitive-propositional position is to be rejected as voluntarist, intellectualist and literalist, even making the suggestion that those who "perceive or experience religion in cognitivist fashion" are those who "combine unusual insecurity with naiveté."[25] A hesitation I have about this criticism concerns its reliability: it appears to be based on a questionable understanding of the cognitive-propositional approach. Lindbeck seems to posit that those inclined toward this position hold that it is possible to definitively, exhaustively and timelessly state the objective truth about God in propositional form.

This cannot be considered an adequate representation of this position in either its classical or postcritical forms. The description fails to register the historical and linguistic sophistication of cognitive approaches to doctrine.[26] For example, Lindbeck's suggestion that the "cognitive-propositional" view of doctrine treats any given doctrine as "eternally true"[27] fails to take account of the evident ability of proponents of this approach to reformulate, amplify or supplement a doctrine in response to changing historical circumstances.[28] Lindbeck attributes an unmerited inflexibility to cognitive systems of doctrine by playing down the notion of "relative adequacy" of doctrinal statements, where "adequacy" can be assessed in terms of both the original historical context of a doctrinal formulation and whatever referent it is alleged to represent.

Most theologians of the medieval period understood dogma as a dynamic concept, a "perception of divine truth, tending towards this truth (perceptio divinae veritatis tendens in ipsam)."[29] It is true that certain medieval writings do indeed suggest that doctrine may be treated as Euclidean theorems: Alan of Lille's Regulae theologiae and Nicholas of Amien's De arte catholicae fidei are excellent examples of this genre dating from the twelfth century,[30] later found in such writings as Morzillus's De naturae philosophiae (1560) and Morinus's Astrologia gallica (1661). Nevertheless, a considerably more nuanced approach to the nature of theological statements is much more characteristic of Christian theology in the patristic and medieval periods.[31] Theology is recognized to be concerned with the clarification of the manner in which affirmations about God are, in the first place, derived, and, in the second place, how they relate to analogous affirmations drawn from the more familiar world of the senses. It is an attempt to achieve conceptual clarity—to avoid confusion by subjecting statements concerning God to close scrutiny. What does the word God stand for? How does the question "Does God exist?" relate to the apparently analogous question "Does Socrates exist?" What reasons might be adduced for suggesting that "God is righteous"? And how does this statement relate to the apparently analogous statement "Socrates is righteous"? Thus Alan of Lille (to note one of the more propositional medieval theologians) is concerned with identifying the ways in which we might be misled by theological affirmations (e.g., by treating them as descriptions of physical objects, or assuming that terms and conceptualities relating to God possess the same meanings as in everyday discourse).[32] Underlying such attempts to achieve clarity of concepts and modes of discourse is the recognition that doctrinal affirmations are to be recognized as perceptions, not total descriptions, pointing beyond themselves toward the greater mystery of God himself.

For such theologians, doctrines are reliable, yet incomplete, descriptions of reality. Their power lies in what they represent, rather than what they are in themselves. The point at which interrogation is appropriate has to do with whether or not such doctrines are adequate (to the strictly limited degree that this is possible) representations of the independent reality to which they allegedly relate. Given that they cannot hope to represent it in its totality, and given the inevitable limitations attending any attempt to express in words something that ultimately lies beyond them, is the particular form of words employed the most reliable form conceivable? The

Nicene controversy is an obvious example of a struggle to articulate insights in this manner. If an experience is to be expressed in words in order to attempt a communal envisioning of this experience, some form of a "cognitive-propositionalist" dimension is inevitable. Yet this would not be reducing the experience to words, but simply an attempt to convey it through words.[33]

This point concerning the verbalizing of experience is valid, whether or not the words used are believed to convey an ontological truth. For example, consider Henry Wadsworth Longfellow's lines from the *Saga of King Olaf:*

I heard a voice that cried,
Balder the beautiful
Is dead, is dead.

These words would not be considered ontologically true. To use Lindbeck's terms, they are intrasystemically true, in that they are consistent within the context of the Nordic Valhalla myth.[34] The lines imply nothing concerning ontological truth or falsity, unless the myth is improperly read as history. Yet C. S. Lewis wrote thus of his reaction to reading Longfellow's lines:

I knew nothing about Balder; but instantly I was uplifted into huge regions of northern sky, I desired with almost sickening intensity something never to be described (except that it is cold, spacious, severe, pale and remote) and then . . . found myself at the very same moment already falling out of that desire and wishing I were back in it.[35]

It would be absurd to suggest that words can adequately capture experience. Ludwig Wittgenstein, who lamented the inability of words to describe or convey the aroma of coffee, has ensured that we are fully aware of this point. Yet is this such a significant matter? Words may not be able to provide a totally comprehensive description of the aroma of coffee; nevertheless, words are good enough to let me know where to find coffee and how to ensure that what I have found is indeed coffee, so that I can then experience its aroma. Cognitive theories of doctrine recognize that words are on the borderlands of experience, intimating and signposting the reality which they cannot capture. To apply pejorative epithets such as "intellectualist" or "literalist" to the cognitive-propositionalist approach is to fail to appreciate the power of words to evoke experience, to point beyond themselves to something inexpressible and to convey an experience that their author wishes to share with his or her readers. It is also, of course, to fail to do justice to the many levels at which cognitive or propositional statements operate.

Theological statements simply do not operate at the same level as mathematical equations. The charge of literalism is vulnerable to the extent that it risks overlooking the richness of nonliteral language (such as metaphor) as a means of articulation and the importance of analogy or "models" as a heuristic stimulus to theological reflection. It is simply a theological truism that no human language can be applied to God univocally. Indeed, it is from the recognition, rather than the denial, of this point that cognitive approaches to doctrine begin.

Lindbeck's criticism of cognitive theories of doctrine has considerable force when directed against neoscholastic understandings of revelation. For example, the view of the neoscholastic writer Hermann Dieckmann that supernatural revelation merely transmits conceptual knowledge by means of propositions is clearly open to serious criticism along the lines suggested by Lindbeck. In this respect, Lindbeck has provided a valuable corrective to deficient cognitive models of doctrine. Nevertheless, not all cognitive theories of doctrine are vulnerable in this way. It is necessary to make a clear distinction between the view that an exhaustive and unambiguous account of God is transmitted conceptually by propositions and the view that there is a genuinely cognitive dimension or element to doctrinal statements. Doctrinal statements need not and should not be treated as *purely* cognitive statements.

The point here is that human words cannot adequately define experience but may nevertheless point toward it, as signposts. Although emphasis on the experiential aspects of doctrine is especially associated with the later Renaissance and the rise of experientially oriented theologies during the Romantic period, hints of such insights are evident in the writings of Augustine of Hippo and his medieval interpreters. Christian doctrine attempts to give shape to the Christian life by laying the foundations for the generation and subsequent interpretation of Christian experience.

Christian theology is obliged to express in words things which by their very nature defy reduction to these words. Nevertheless, there is a fundamental resonance between words and experience. To caricature Christian doctrine as mere wordplay or as an attempt to reduce the mystery of God to propositions is to neglect to appreciate the manner in which words serve us. In order for my experience to be communicated to another person, it demands statement in cognitive forms. That these cognitive forms fail to capture such an experience in its totality is self-evident and hardly a matter for rhetorical exaggeration: it is one of the inevitable consequences of living in history, where one is obligated to communicate in historical forms. Schleiermacher recognized that doctrine expresses an experience constituted by the language of the Christian community, thus pointing to the delicate interplay of cognitive and experiential elements in doctrinal formulations.

Experience and meaning are thus two sides of the same coin, forbidding us to reduce Christianity to bare propositions on the one hand or to inchoate experience on the other. Every experience includes, and is modified by, interpretive elements.[36] As modern theories of scientific observation have made clear, experience is not pretheoretical data but is actually theory-laden, accompanied by interpretive elements.[37] The "brute empiricism" that treats experience purely as raw data that requires interpretation is inadequate: experience is actually "given" within an interpretive framework, however provisional. Theory plays a much more constitutive role in our approach to experience than pure empiricism suggests: theory itself determines, at least to some extent, the experience which that theory is supposed to explain or interpret. As Edmund Husserl's phenomenology stresses, prior knowledge and beliefs play a constitutive role in determining what we observe and experience. It is for this reason that Lindbeck's treatment of cognitive and experiential models of doctrine as antithetical is so profoundly unsatisfactory. The cognitive dimension of Christian doctrine is the framework upon which Christian experience is supported, the channel through which it is conveyed. It is a skeleton that gives strength and shape to the flesh of experience.

Doctrine also provides a conceptual apparatus by which experience may be interpreted and criticized. The preliminary judgments of experience are interpreted within a conceptual framework, ultimately based upon the scriptural narrative and its doctrinal intimations, expressed by doctrine, in order that it may be viewed in a new light. This point has been stressed by Gerhard Ebeling, who notes the need to be able to approach experience itself in such a way that it may be experienced in a new manner.[38] By being viewed in a particular light, experience is correlated with the scriptural narrative and the conceptual framework it engenders, and is allowed to assume a new significance. Doctrine thus opens the way to a new "experience with experience."[39]

As noted earlier, experience itself is an inadequate foundation for theological affirmation. Nevertheless, when interpreted, experience affords central insights into the existential dimension of the Christian faith. The new relevance of the "theology of the cross," as expounded by Jürgen Moltmann and Eberhard Jüngel, points to the need for theology to interpret experience, without being reduced to its categories or bound by its preliminary intimations. Cognitive approaches to theology, such as those affirmed by evangelicalism, retain this vital function of doctrine, seeing it as a net cast over experience in order that it may be more sufficiently grasped and understood.

Lindbeck's Cultural-Linguistic Approach

Lindbeck draws on the writings of the cultural anthropologist Clifford Geertz[40] and Ludwig Wittgenstein[41] in setting up his distinctive approach to the nature of theology. Lindbeck suggests—and the parallel with Wittgenstein here will be clear—that religions may be compared to languages, with religious doctrines functioning as grammatical rules. Religions are cultural frameworks or mediums that engender a vocabulary and precede inner experience.

> A religion can be viewed as a kind of cultural and/or linguistic framework or medium that shapes the entirety of life and thought. . . . It is not primarily an array of beliefs about the true and the good (although it may involve these), or a symbolism expressive of basic attitudes, feelings or sentiments (though these will be generated). Rather, it is similar to an idiom that makes possible the description of realities, the formulation of beliefs, and the experiencing of inner attitudes, feelings and sentiments. Like a culture or language, it is a communal phenomenon that shapes the subjectivities of individuals rather than being primarily a manifestation of those subjectivities. It comprises a vocabulary of discursive and nondiscursive symbols together with a distinctive logic or grammar

in terms of which this vocabulary can be meaningfully deployed.[42]
Just as a language is correlated with a form of life (as Wittgenstein pointed out in relation to "language games"), so a religious tradition is correlated with the form of life it engenders, articulates and reflects.

A fundamental element in this understanding of doctrine and its attending theory of truth is the concept of *intrasystemic consistency*. In part, the cultural-linguistic view is concerned with the rational coherence of systems: doctrines regulate religions, in much the way grammar regulates language. The ideational content of a doctrinal statement is effectively set to one side, in order that its formal function may be emphasized. Lindbeck illustrates this point with a reference to Shakespeare's *Hamlet*: the statement "Denmark is the land where Hamlet lived" makes no claim to ontological truth or falsity, but is simply a statement concerning the internal ordering of the elements of Shakespeare's narrative.[43] Narrative in itself is neither fact nor fiction: it is a vehicle for either or both. Factlike narratives are not necessarily factual.[44] Claims are made regarding the ontological truth or falsity of a statement only if the narrative is considered to be *history*. Thus the Bible may be read as a "vast, loosely-structured non-fictional novel," the canonical narrative that offers an identity description of God. Developing this point, Lindbeck suggests, citing the parable of the prodigal son as an example, that the "rendering of God's character" is not necessarily dependent on the factuality of the scriptural story.

> Meaning is constituted by the uses of a specific language, rather than being distinguishable from it. Thus the proper way to determine what "God" signifies, for example, is by examining how the word operates within a religion and thereby shapes reality and experience rather than by first establishing its propositional or experiential meaning and reinterpreting or reformulating its uses accordingly. It is in this sense that theological description in the cultural-linguistic sense is intrasemiotic or intratextual.[45]

The chief difficulty raised by this approach concerns the origin of the cultural-linguistic tradition regulated by doctrines. Lindbeck seems to assume it is simply "given." It is an axiomatic point of departure. The "language" is just there. Lindbeck notes that languages originate from outside, thus raising the obvious question concerning the origins of the Christian tradition of speaking about God, or articulating human aspiration, in its particular manner, or range of manners. How does the Christian idiom come into being? Throughout his analysis, there seems to be a studied evasion of the central question of revelation—in other words, whether the Christian idiom, articulated in Scripture and hence in the Christian tradition, emerges from accumulated human insight or from the self-disclosure of God in the Christ-event.

Yet Lindbeck's insistence on the primacy of "the objectivities of religion, its language, doctrine, liturgies and modes of action" raises the unanswered question of how these primary data may be accounted for. Where do Christian doctrines come from? How can they be evaluated? To what is the Christian language a response?

What extralinguistic reality is it attempting to describe or depict? Evangelicals find themselves in the position of being able to agree in broad terms with Lindbeck as far as he goes, yet wish that he went much further. For this reason, the most fundamental evangelical critique of postliberalism concerns the inadequacy of its commitment to extralinguistic and extrasystemic realities. We shall explore this point in what follows.

The Evangelical Critique of Postliberalism: Three Questions

On the basis of my analysis so far, we can begin to mount an evangelical critique of postliberalism. Any such critique must be prefaced by a commendation of its many virtues, including

1. an emphasis on the distinctiveness of Christianity, and its studied and principled refusal to follow liberalism's headlong rush into the identification of the truth of the gospel with late twentieth-century liberal American cultural norms;

2. an insistence upon Scripture as the supreme source of Christian ideas and values;

3. a reassertion of the centrality of the figure of Jesus Christ within the life and thought of the Christian church.

Indeed, evangelicalism can learn from postliberalism, especially in the latter's strong sense of community, which stands in sharp contrast to evangelicalism's tendency toward social atomism. Yet given this, three fundamental criticisms must be made, which I shall formulate as questions addressed to three leading postliberal thinkers: Lindbeck, Hauerwas and Frei.

1. What Is Truth?

To what do theological statements refer? In his *Grammar of Faith*, Paul Holmer outlines a regulative theory of theology which has clearly had some influence on Lindbeck's approach. Theology essentially involves the description of intrabiblical rules for speaking about God, Christ and so forth. These rules are not established by theology—they are already given in the biblical material itself.[46] In this sense, theology introduces nothing new to the biblical material but simply delineates the structures which are already present, in much the same way as grammar presents the set of rules governing the use of a language.[47] The grammar is descriptive; it does not establish rules but simply reports back on the rules that are already operational.

Lindbeck believes that theology is concerned with the articulation and exploration of the intrasystemic aspects of Christian faith. Lindbeck here follows the tradition associated with Schleiermacher in adopting an essentially descriptive conception of doctrine. For Schleiermacher, dogmatic theology is "the knowledge of doctrine now current in the church."[48] In essence, theology is an inquiry concerning the adequacy of doctrines to articulate the faith that they express. The theologian is required to consider the "ecclesiastical value" and the "scientific value" of doctrines—in other words, their sufficiency as expressions of religious feeling and their consistency within the context of the theological vocabulary as a whole. Doctrine is descriptive, concerned primarily with intrasystemic cohesion.

Lindbeck thus appears to suggest that the cultural-linguistic approach to doctrine may dispense with the question of whether the Christian idiom has any external referent. Language *functions* within a cultural and linguistic world; it does not necessarily, however, *refer* to anything. Doctrine is concerned with the internal regulation of the Christian idiom, ensuring its consistency. The question of how that idiom relates to the external world is considered to be improper. Lindbeck offers by way of illustration a comparison between an Aristotelian and a non-Aristotelian grammarian. Both would be in agreement that proper sentences have certain components, such as a subject and an object. The Aristotelian would then argue that this sentence somehow "mirrors" reality, whereas the non-Aristotelian would hold that this grammatical affirmation has no necessary ontological implications. In a similar way, Lindbeck argues, the Christian theologian may remain "grammatically orthodox" without making any metaphysical claims, by remaining content with following the rules rather than accepting their ontological implications.[49]

For Lindbeck, doctrine is the language of the Christian community, a self-perpetuating dialect. Indeed, at some points he seems to suggest that viewing theology as the grammar of the Christian language entails the abandonment of any talk about God as an independent reality and any suggestion that it is possible to make truth claims (in an ontological, rather than intrasystemic, sense) about him.[50] Truth is firmly equated with—virtually to the point of being reduced to—internal consistency. Lindbeck thus argues that theology is a "second-order" activity which does not make truth claims, this function being reserved for "first-order" assertions.

> Just as grammar by itself affirms nothing either true or false regarding the world in which language is used, but only about language, so theology and doctrine, to the extent that they are second-order activities, assert nothing either true or false about God and his relation to creatures, but only speak about such assertions.[51]

Yet Lindbeck himself seems to blur the crucial distinction that he introduces between "first-order" and "second-order" assertions. As Bruce Marshall, one of Lindbeck's former students, has pointed out, there are strong parallels between the approaches to truth associated with Thomas Aquinas and Lindbeck.[52] An implicit commitment to views of truth with which evangelicals would find little to disagree underlies Lindbeck's analysis, even though he himself may not explicitly articulate this.

Thus, on the basis of the excerpt above, it would be reasonable to conclude that Lindbeck views theology as a regulator of the way in which Christians speak about God, but does not comment on the truth claims of such statements. Religion is thus the language; theology is just the governing grammar. It makes little sense to ask whether the Greek, Latin and English languages are *true*; however, it does make sense to uncover the rules that superintend their operation in order that they may be understood. Yet it is a simple matter of fact (which Lindbeck seems to concede implicitly, even if he does not draw attention to the fact) that religions do make truth claims, rendering the direct comparison of religion and language deficient in at least this respect. If language is to be adopted as a model for religion, its limitations must be recognized, specifically in this respect.

This apparent evasion of truth claims can be seen in Lindbeck's discussion of the *homoousion*. While illustrating his understanding of the regulative function of doctrines within theology, Lindbeck suggests that the Nicene Creed "does not make first-order truth claims."[53] In other words, the *homoousion* makes no ontological reference, but merely regulates language concerning both Christ and God.[54] This case study is important because it provides one of the few historical, worked examples of Lindbeck's thesis, thus allowing his historical and theological competence to be judged, in however provisional a manner. Lindbeck asserts that Athanasius understands the term *homoousios* to mean "whatever is said of the Father is said of the Son, except that the Son is not the Father," thus demonstrating that Athanasius "thought of it, not as a first-order proposition with ontological reference, but as a second-order rule of speech."[55] Only in the medieval period, Lindbeck suggests, were metaphysical concepts read into this essentially grammatical approach to the *homoousion*. In the patristic period, he argues, the term was understood as a rule of discourse, quite independent of any reference to extralinguistic reality.

Yet Lindbeck appears to overlook the fact that Athanasius bases the regulative function of the *homoousion* on its substantive content. In other words, *given* the ontological relation of Father and Son, the grammatical regulation of language concerning them follows as a matter of course. For Athanasius, it would seem that "the *homoousion*, regulatively construed, rules out ontological *innovation*, not ontological reference."[56] It must be stressed that this is not to say that the patristic christological debates failed to recognize the referential or regulative function of Christian doctrine. Nevertheless, it would seem that Lindbeck has perhaps attributed to the *homoousion* regulative functions that, strictly speaking, were associated with the *communicatio idiomatum*. The grammatical or regulative functions of the *communicatio idiomatum* would seem to be grounded upon the ontological affirmations of the *homoousion*.

With this point in mind, let us return to "Denmark." But which Denmark? Are we talking about the "Denmark" in Shakespeare's *Hamlet*, or the modern nation state of that name? They are not necessarily the same. It may indeed be proper to ensure, in a Lindbeckian manner, that the term *Denmark* is consistently employed within the matrix of Shakespeare's drama. Yet the question inevitably and properly arises: How does this "Denmark" relate to the definite identifiable geographical and political reality called "Denmark," located in the world of human experience? How can we ascertain whether *Hamlet* is fact or fiction? The significance of this question can hardly be denied. How does Shakespeare's Denmark relate to the Denmark of the real world? And how, we must ask as theologians, does the "Jesus" of the Christian idiom relate to Jesus of Nazareth? Has it any identifiable connection with him? Does it *refer* to him or to something else? Can it be shown to have its foundation in him, or is it an independent construction of the human mind?

Lindbeck here appears to illustrate neatly what Rowan Williams identifies as one of the most serious weaknesses of modern theology: the perennial tendency "to be seduced by the prospect of bypassing the question of how it *learns* its own language."[57] The possibility (which Lindbeck seems unwilling and unable to consider) is that the discourse which he identifies Christian doctrine as regulating may be based on a historical misunderstanding; that it may signify nothing other than the accidental forms of historical "givenness," yielding a sociohistorical rootedness that vitiates its wider validity; that it may represent a serious misrepresentation, or even a deliberate falsification, of historical events; and that it may represent a completely spurious interpretation of the significance of Jesus of Nazareth. The Christian idiom cannot simply be taken as a "given": it must be interrogated concerning its historical and theological credentials.

Lindbeck's approach to the Christian idiom appears, at least superficially, to be uncomfortably similar to Rudolf Bultmann's approach to the *kerygma:* both are assumed just to be there, lying beyond challenge or justification. The interrogation that the "New Quest of the Historical Jesus" subjected to Bultmann's kerygmatic Christology must be extended to Lindbeck's understanding of the nature of doctrine. Doctrine, like the *kerygma,* is not something that is just there, demanding that we take it or leave it. Rather, it is something that purports to represent accurately the significance of a historical event, and it is open to challenge regarding its adequacy as an interpretation of that event.[58]

The Reformation and the Enlightenment are obvious historical instances of when doctrines were challenged concerning their historical credentials. Lindbeck, by accident or design, is perhaps somewhat equivocal over whether or not his cultural-linguistic approach to doctrine involves the affirmation or setting aside of epistemological realism and a correspondence theory of truth. Nevertheless, the overall impression gained is that he considers consistency more important than correspondence, raising precisely the questions I have just noted.[59]

At this point evangelicalism makes one of its most serious criticisms of postliberalism. For evangelicals, postliberalism reduces the concept of truth to internal consistency. There can be no doubt that intrasystemic consistency is a quality that is to be admired. However, it is perfectly possible to have an entirely coherent system that has no meaningful relation to the real world. Christianity is not simply about interpreting the narrated identity of Jesus or giving a coherent account of the grammar of faith. It is about recognizing the truth of Jesus Christ as Savior and Lord. It is about the perception of the truth of the gospel, and thereby the perception of the need for Christian theology to give as reliable an account as possible of its identity and significance.

For evangelicalism, theology is grounded upon and evaluated on the basis of the self-revelation of God. This is the ultimate foundation and criterion of Christian theology. The sixteenth-century Reformation frequently figures prominently in evangelical self-reflection on account of its central principle of constantly examining the life and thought of the church in the light of Scripture and undertaking a process of correction as and where appropriate.[60] The Christian language, which is prone to historical development, needs to be periodically corrected in the light of an external criterion.

While acknowledging postliberalism's hesitations over potentially naive approaches to the issue of truth, evangelicalism nevertheless insists that theology must be concerned with the question of telling the truth about God. That truth may take the form of a narrative ("telling the truth") or a doctrinal framework (in which a narrative has been transposed into conceptual forms) or a simple affirmation of the truthfulness and trustworthiness of God. However the concept of truth may be stated, it is firmly understood to be located *outside* the language of Christianity, as well as within it. Christianity aims to provide a systematic, regulated and coherent account of who God is and what God is like—that is to say, that there is an extra-systemic referent which functions as both the foundation and criterion of the Christian language game.[61] Or, to put it another way, evangelicalism is insistent that Christian "truth" must designate both a reality outside the language game and the adequacy of that language game to represent it. In other words, Christian theology must accurately and consistently render the truth of the identity and purposes of God.

For evangelicalism, this theological enterprise is to be undertaken on the basis of Scripture. Postliberalism echoes this emphasis and thus provides us with our cue to move on to explore a second area of the complex interaction between evangelicalism and postliberalism.

2. Why the Bible?

In his highly stimulating *Community of Character*, Stanley Hauerwas stresses the importance of Scripture in shaping the beliefs and values of the Christian community. The Bible makes normative claims on the Christian community, which that community has been happy to accept and reaffirm through the ages.[62] Consequently, the proper sphere for the interpretation of Scripture must be the Christian community itself.[63] The church may therefore expect to find its ideas and values existing in tension with those of secular society, which does not orient itself around the scriptural narrative but recognizes other narratives as authoritative.

Hauerwas presents an important and persuasive account of the manner in which Scripture is used within the church, which is particularly welcome because of the close connection he establishes between the Bible and the church. Yet the critical reader is left with these questions: Why does the Bible possess such authority? Why is it the narrative of Jesus Christ that exercises this controlling authority? Is the authority of Scripture something that has been imposed on the text by a community that is willing to submit itself to this authority but, in principle, would have been prepared to acknowledge additional or alternative authorities? Or is there something inherent in the text itself which establishes such authority, prior to the recognition of this by the community? To ask such questions is to raise the issue of the role of revelation within postliberal theories of theology.[64]

The specific criticism that evangelicalism directs against postliberalism at this point is the following: the prioritization of Scripture is not adequately grounded at the theological level. In effect, the priority of Scripture is defended on grounds that appear to be cultural, historical or contractual. The role of the Qur'an within Islam could be justified on similar grounds. The normative role of Scripture within the Christian community is unquestionably Christian (just as the normative role of the Qur'an within Islam is Islamic); but is it *right*? For the evangelical, truth claims cannot be evaded at this juncture. Scripture has authority not because of what the Christian community has chosen to make of it, but because of what it *is* and what it conveys.

This point can also be seen clearly in Carl Henry's important critique of David Kelsey's *Uses of Scripture in Recent Theology* (1975).[65] Henry notes Kelsey's positive attitude toward Scripture yet confesses himself puzzled by Kelsey's curt dismissal of any attempt to speak of the "authority of Scripture," save in purely functionalist and intrasystemic terms. As Henry points out, the notion of theology as a human response to an objective external norm is precluded by Kelsey's approach, which ultimately leaves the whole idea of "doing theology" caught up in a matrix of an irresolvable epistemological relativism.

Evangelicals have long insisted that the prioritization of Scripture rests in its inspiration, regardless of whether a given community or individual acknowledges it as such.[66] It is not my intention to defend this general evangelical consensus, nor to articulate any of its specific formulations. My concern here is to note a clear tension between this evangelical consensus and the general thrust of the postliberal position, which reflects a deeper and more fundamental tension over the entire doctrine of revelation.

Furthermore, at least in the writings of Holmer and Lindbeck, the postliberal emphasis on Scripture runs the risk of suggesting that Christianity focuses on a text, rather than a person. The maxim of Roland Barthes comes to mind: *il-n'y-a pas de hors-text* (there is nothing outside the text). For evangelicals there is something real that lies beyond the text of Scripture which is nonetheless rendered and mediated by that text:[67] the Christian experience of redemption in Christ. The emphasis on intratextuality tends to obscure the centrality of the person of Jesus Christ in Christian faith (and did so before the texts of the New Testament were ever written down). The historical and theological priority of the person of Jesus Christ over his textual embodiment and interpretation must be acknowledged. Yet postliberalism, at least in the forms associated with Holmer and Lindbeck, risks clouding this point. Its emphasis on Christianity as a language with associated grammatical rules threatens to sever its vital connection with the person of Christ.

Yet "threatens" implies a possibility rather than an actuality. Perhaps postliberalism is wiser in its intuitions than in its ostensive statements. Certainly the writings of Hans Frei demonstrate a genuine commitment to a focus on the person of Jesus Christ. However, as will become clear in the next section, evangelicals will want to express reservations about the particular mode of this focus.

3. Why Jesus Christ?

A further question focuses on the role played by Jesus Christ within a postliberal theological scheme. It is clear that for both Hauerwas and Frei the narrative of Jesus Christ is of central importance to the legitimation of Scripture as a norm for Christian life and thought. But why does this narrative possess such an authority? Frei and Hauerwas, like Lindbeck, perhaps allow us the impression that this is just the way things are. The narrative is "given" and prior to the community, with the result that the historical identity of the community is linked to its founder. In what follows I shall focus on the writings of Hans Frei and attempt to explore the particular role that Jesus Christ plays in his hermeneutical scheme. (I use the term *attempt* deliberately, in that I must confess my verbal defeat by Frei's prose, which is the most opaque I have ever been obliged to wrestle with.)

Frei's position on the relation of meaning and truth in the gospel narratives is notoriously difficult to untangle.[68] In a highly sympathetic analysis, George Hunsinger argues that Frei has succeeded in showing that believers' "knowledge of Christ as present to faith is grounded in their prior knowledge of his identity as depicted in the gospel narratives."[69] A more critical interpreter of Frei would argue that he goes part of the way toward demonstrating the internal consistency of the gospel narrative of Jesus Christ and the connection between this narrative and the community of faith, but that the grounding of this narrative is neither adequately addressed nor explicated. For example, Frei treats the resurrection of Christ as an intrasystemic affirmation of the identity of the self-manifestation of Jesus with the self-manifestation of God, and explicitly excludes reference to an extrasystemic occurrence.[70] Without in any way wishing to minimize the importance of Frei's analysis, it would seem to me that Wolfhart Pannenberg's essay on christological method shows the kind of possibilities that exist for the exploration of the relation of the narrative of Jesus Christ with history.[71]

The problem is that Frei's approach seems to rest on the prioritization of the narrative of Jesus on grounds similar to those outlined by Albrecht Ritschl in 1874. For Ritschl, the priority of Jesus within the community of faith finds its basis primarily at the historical level: Jesus is prior to the community, which bases its ideas and values upon him. Although Ritschl is innocent of Frei's interest in the specific narrative form and literary character of the Synoptic Gospels, the same themes emerge as significant. The Christian ethos is to be understood as the spatiotemporal extension of the ideas and principles represented in the person of Jesus within the community of faith—in other words, the "tradition of Christ propagated in the church [*die in der Kirche fortgepflanzten Überlieferung von Christus*]." This "tradition" is essentially empirical and historical, referring to a general ethical and religious principle first embodied in the historical Jesus. This idea was then taken up and propagated by the community of faith, and has been made available to this day. "Christ comes to act upon the individual believer on the one hand through the historical recollection of him which is possible in the church."[72]

As a consequence, Christ occupies a unique position in regard to all those within the community of faith, expressed in a religious judgment concerning his status. Those who "believe in Christ" (in Ritschl's sense of the phrase) participate in the kingdom of God and are therefore reconciled to God, participating in the same qualitative relationship to God as the founder of their religion. Although Ritschl is severely critical of the Christologies of the Enlightenment, it is very difficult to avoid the conclusion that he regards Christ as an archetypically significant and unsurpassable individual whose significance is primarily to be articulated in terms of his being the founder of the Christian community, thus possessing temporal priority over those who followed after him. Ritschl argues that even though it is conceivable that another individual could arise who is equal in religious and ethical status to Christ, "he would stand in historical dependence upon Christ, and would therefore be distinguishable from him."[73] The concession is significant because it indicates that Christ's uniqueness is understood historically rather than ontologically. He is regarded as a first among equals whose primacy arises through the historical accident of his being the unique founder of the Christian church.

This approach to the significance of Jesus Christ was severely criticized by Emil Brunner.[74] The unique position of Jesus Christ within the community of faith, he argued, was thereby understood to rest upon little more than historical precedence. (This is the concern that even the most sympathetic of evangelical critics would wish to express regarding Hans Frei's approach.) Frei allows us to explicate the significance of the narrative of Christ as "reflection within faith" for the Christian community;[75] it does not, however, allow us to understand the basis of this claim to significance in its original historical context or in the present situation. While the approach does indeed allow us to identify a *Christian* approach to the identity and significance of Jesus Christ, it leaves us with the acutely difficult question of whether this approach is itself justified.

Thus Frei declares that "the New Testament story deals simply and exclusively with the story of Jesus of Nazareth, whether it is fictional or real."[76] While we can immediately concede the positive dimensions of this point, not least its focus on Jesus, the central difficulty becomes clear at once. *Is* the "story" fictional or real? How could one tell that it is not simply "a piece of hyperfiction claiming to be self-warranting fact"?[77] While this question may be dismissed as naive by some theologians, it remains of foundational importance. The central anxiety that eventually led to the crumbling of the Bultmannian approach to Christology was the minimalist christological foundation of the *kerygma*—"*das Dass.*" But what if the *kerygma* got Jesus wrong? The christological implications of this were momentous and demanded exploration as the development of the "New Quest" got under way. As the writings of Ernst Käsemann, Joachim Jeremias and Günther Bornkamm demonstrate,[78] the relation between faith and history, dismissed by Bultmann as an irrelevance, became a central issue of New Testament scholarship and christological reflection.[79] Yet Frei seems to take us back down a discredited Bultmannian route, without any due regard for its perceived weaknesses and subsequent developments.

In view of the importance of this point, we will explore the differences between Bultmann and Gerhard Ebeling on this point.[80] The differences between Bultmann and Ebeling relate directly to their assessment of the theological significance of the historical figure of Jesus of Nazareth. For Bultmann, all that could be, and could be required to be, known about the historical Jesus was the fact that *(das Dass)* he existed. For Ebeling, the person of the historical Jesus is the fundamental basis *(das Grunddatum)* of Christology, and if it could be shown that Christology is a misinterpretation of the significance of the historical Jesus, Christology would be brought to an end. In this, Ebeling may be seen as expressing the concerns that underlie the "New Quest of the Historical Jesus." Ebeling here points to a fundamental deficiency in Bultmann's Christology: its total lack of openness to investigation (perhaps *verification* is too strong a term) in the light of historical scholarship. Might not Christology rest upon a mistake? How can we rest assured that there is a justifiable transition from the preaching *of* Jesus to the preaching *about* Jesus? Ebeling develops criticisms that parallel those made elsewhere by Käsemann,[81] but with a theological, rather than a purely historical, focus. Most importantly for our purposes, Ebeling stresses that even Bultmann's minimal *das Dass* actually requires justification in terms of *das Was* or *das Wie*—that is, in terms of the implicit content of the *kerygma*. This same issue seems to emerge as significant in relation to Frei's attitude toward history.

Evangelicalism has difficulty with any approach, whether originating with Bultmann or with Frei, that apparently weighs history so lightly. It is no accident that evangelicalism places a high emphasis on the importance of New Testament scholarship. It is not merely the internal logic of the New Testament that is regarded as important; rather, it is the demonstration that this logic can be shown to have arisen in response to genuine pressures as a consequence of what is known about the history of Jesus of Nazareth. This does not in any sense make Christology dependent upon an "unknown" historical figure. Rather, it attempts to uncover and explore the correlation between history and theology in the New Testament.[82]

Conclusion

So what is the future relation between evangelicalism and postliberalism? It is clear that the dialogue is still at an early stage. In particular, it should be noted that postliberalism is still perhaps best seen at present as a research program, rather than a definite set of doctrines.[83] However, as Jeffrey Stout (Princeton) once remarked, a preoccupation with method alone is like clearing your throat before a public lecture: you can only do it for a while before your audience loses interest. Sooner or later, postliberalism will have to address a series of doctrinal issues of major importance to evangelicalism. It will be at this juncture that the future relation of the two movements will become clearer. Nevertheless, at least some of the questions that evangelicalism will wish to address to postliberalism are clear; several of them have already been dealt with in the present chapter. The dialogue is clearly going to be both critical and positive, and may well be of considerable importance to both the academy and the church.[84]

3
THEOLOGY, MEANING & POWER

A Conversation with George Lindbeck on Theology & the Nature of Christian Difference

Miroslav Volf

A sense that academic theology has lost its voice is widespread today. Many observers note, as Jeffrey Stout did in *Ethics After Babel*, that theology is unable "to command attention as a distinctive contributor to public discourse in our culture."[1] Equally, if not more, disturbing is the loss of interest in academic theology on the part of the church; as scholars write for scholars and students, the ear of church folk is tuned in elsewhere. Helped by the mass media, popular preachers and a diverse chorus of social critics are dominating the discourse in church and in wider culture. Theologians are on the sidelines. Like the street-corner preachers of yesterday, they find themselves talking to a crowd too hurried to honor them with more than a fleeting glance.

Seeking to redress the inability to get a hearing, theologians have increasingly turned into methodologists. Before addressing the church and the wider culture we think it salutary to talk to ourselves about the conditions of plausibility and intelligibility of our speech. The trouble with this strategy is that the longer you stick with it, the more self-defeating it becomes. Jeffrey Stout has put it starkly: "Preoccupation with method is like clearing your throat: it can go on for only so long before you lose your audience."[2] Though vivid and fitting, the image of clearing the throat is also misleading on two counts. For one, theological method is more analogous to the strategy of an oration than to the clarity of a speaker's voice; learning proper method is more like taking lessons in public speaking than like clearing the throat. Second, method is never just method; "method is message." I do not mean this in the trite sense that the way you communicate also communicates. More profoundly, all major methodological decisions have implications for the whole of the theological edifice and, inversely, all major theological decisions (such as the questions of faith and reason, grace and works, church and society) shape theological method. Like many things in life, reflection on method is good if there is not too much of it.

Since the publication of *The Nature of Doctrine: Religion and Theology in a Postliberal Age* over a decade ago, George A. Lindbeck, a key ecumenical figure, has established himself also as a major authority on "theological throat-clearing," if I may be permitted to return to Stout's somewhat misleading metaphor. As a good theologian and methodologist, Lindbeck is more interested in the act than in the "endless methodological foreplay," to use another of Stout's metaphors. Hence Lindbeck's methodological proposal "to renew . . . the ancient practice of absorbing the universe into the biblical world" is intended both to instruct and to empower theologians to speak authentically to the church and to the culture at large.[3]

After reading *The Nature of Doctrine* I found myself, however, wanting not only to do theology but also to engage Lindbeck about how theology ought to be done. That he has had a similar effect on many others is a testimony to the power of his methodological vision.[4] Though I will be critically examining Lindbeck's proposal, my goal is not so much to clear Lindbeck's throat as my own. To change the metaphor, I am beginning to lay here methodological foundations for a different theological house—partly with his materials and partly with my own.[5]

The major steps I take in my deconstructive-constructive attempt are the following. After agreeing with the substance of Lindbeck's critique of how liberal theology construed the relation between the Christian faith and wider culture, I first note some disturbing ambiguities in his preferred metaphor for expressing this relation, the metaphor of "absorbing the world." Second, I take issue with the correlative metaphor of "inhabiting the scriptural world," pointing out that the religion with which we interpret a given culture is itself always an interpreted religion. Third, I show that the Christian "story" does not only do something to the world but is itself situated in a network of nonsemiotic "relations of force" both at the point of its construction and along the trajectory of its history.

Fourth, I examine the importance both of the cognitive side of religion (the question Lindbeck addresses) and of the relations of power (the question Lindbeck disregards). Fifth, I return to the metaphor of "absorbing the world," suggesting that it is deficient because it tends to immunize the Christian story against the critique from outside because it misleads one to operate with a false dilemma: either absorbing the world or being absorbed by it. Sixth, I argue that Lindbeck's missionary goal to re-Christianize the Western culture is both sociologically and theologically misplaced, because it presupposes that it is a symbolic system that gives unity to Western culture and that the proper place of Christian faith is to be in the center. Finally, I suggest that an important strength of Lindbeck's proposal is that it allows theology to be conceived as a nonsystemic, contextual and flexible intellectual effort.

Absorbing the World

In his short study of the relationship between New Haven (standing for the so-called Yale school) and Grand Rapids (standing for neo-Calvinism), Nicholas Wolterstorff has suggested that there is "no deeper guiding metaphor" in the thought of theologians like George Lindbeck than "reversing the direction of conformation."[6] Instead of translating the biblical message into the conceptualities of the social world we inhabit, as modern theology was prone to do, Lindbeck tells us that Christians should redescribe this world with the help of biblical categories. He has dubbed his proposal "postliberal" or "intratextual theology." In a summary of the proposal that has now become classic, he writes, "Intratextual theology redescribes reality within the scriptural framework rather than translating Scripture into extrascriptural categories. It is the text, so to speak, which absorbs the world, rather than the world the text."[7] Before the dawn of modernity Christians did theology "intratextually"; now at its sunset they should relearn this method, though in a posttraditional and postliberal mode.

Lindbeck's proposal has an edge. It is directed against "liberal" theology, which has elevated conformation to "extrabiblical realities" to a theological program under the guise of "translating" the biblical message. The initial impulse behind liberal theology was, of course, right: to find a way to draw the attention of "cultured despisers" back to "a subject so entirely neglected by them," as Friedrich Schleiermacher puts it in his *Speeches*.[8] To accomplish the task, translation into "contemporary conceptualities" guided by contemporary plausibilities seemed necessary.[9] In Lindbeck's view, however, the good impulse had dubious results. Though translations of the biblical message into nonbiblical idioms may "have made easier the continued commitment to the faith of the would-be believers," the translations tended "to replace Scripture rather than lead to it" and also made Christians "accommodate to the prevailing culture rather than shape it."[10] The time has come to reverse the direction of conformation: Instead of the world absorbing the text, the text needs to absorb the world. Instead of being guided by contemporary plausibilities, we need to be guided by the inner logic of the Christian story.

Though I will argue later that we need more complex ways of relating the "world" and the "text" than the dichotomy between conforming the text to the world (liberal translation) and conforming the world to the text (postliberal absorption) suggests, good reasons speak against the liberal pattern of conformation. In contemporary de-Christianized, pluralistic and rapidly changing Western cultures, only those religious groups that make no apologies about their "difference" will be able to survive and thrive. The strategy of conformation is socially ineffective in the short run (because you cannot shape by parroting) and self-destructive in the long run (because you

conform to what you have not helped shape). A good deal of courage in nonconformity is needed both to preserve the identity of Christian faith and to ensure its
lasting social relevance. Lindbeck is right to insist that "provided a religion stresses
service rather than domination, it is likely to contribute more to the future of
humanity if it preserves its own distinctiveness and integrity than if it yields to the
homogenizing tendencies."[11] I therefore have strong sympathies not only with what
Lindbeck has aptly termed "ecumenical sectarianism" but also with the methodological correlate of such nonsectarian "sectarianism," the critique of "translating" the
biblical message into extrabiblical categories.[12]

Lindbeck's methodological work of art is attractive from afar, if one concentrates
on the contours of the polarity he sets up between "the text absorbing the world"
(redescription) and "the world absorbing the text" (translation). Strange things
happen, however, if one draws near to take a closer look at the polarity. Its sharp
contours blur, and one is no longer sure who is doing the absorbing and who is being
absorbed. Citing as an example Kierkegaard's recasting of the story of Abraham and
Isaac, Rowan Williams rightly asks, "What is going on here? Should we call these
enterprises translations of the world's experience into biblical categories, or the
opposite?"[13] An answer to these questions is not at all clear. Is the realm of risk and
terror beyond morality mapped out by the biblical story or by Kierkegaard's retelling
of it?[14]

Lindbeck could respond that in talking about "the text absorbing the world" and
"the world absorbing the text," he is setting up ideal types that indicate the basic
direction of conformation, rather than fully describing the complex interrelation
between the "text" and the "world"—and could possibly add that it is more fruitful
to concentrate on the general direction of the movement than on the vortexes at
any given location. Yet what is unclear in the examples given is precisely the direction of the movement and its origin, an ambiguity that seriously undermines the
alternative.

To defend Lindbeck, one could suggest that Williams's examples are particularly
inapt. That may or may not be true. The examples Lindbeck himself gives do not
serve his purpose much better, however. We are not surprised to find him pointing
to Augustine's relation to Platonism and Aquinas's relation to Aristotelianism to
demonstrate that "a scriptural world is . . . able to absorb the universe," though even
here we would expect both more awareness that "the universe" did a good deal of
absorbing, too, and more willingness to let the presence of such countermovements
shape the methodological proposal.[15]

But when Lindbeck places Schleiermacher (in his relation to German idealism)
alongside Augustine and Aquinas, we begin to wonder whether the polarity between "the text absorbing the world" and "the world absorbing the text" is not
vacuous. Finally, when we are told that Thomas Huxley was carrying out the scientific enterprise "in an imaginatively biblical world" because he was operating with
the contrast between justification by verification and justification by faith, we are

left perplexed.[16] Has not Lindbeck's program of absorbing the world become yet another form of the criticized "fusion of a self-identical story with the new world within which it is retold," only motivated this time by the nostalgia for a long-lost cultural dominance of Christianity?[17] Is his "ecumenical sectarianism," born out of the insight that religion no longer creates and permeates the very fibers of the social world, just a tactical move calculated to maneuver the church once again onto the center stage of society?

The point I wish to make here is not that Lindbeck is not sectarian enough. If one insists on using the emotionally laden, ambiguous and misleading term *sect* to describe theological positions, Lindbeck is, as I shall argue later, at the same time too sectarian and not sectarian enough. At this point I want only to underline that he is trading on the inherent ambiguity of metaphors, such as redescribing the world, seeing it through scriptural lenses or absorbing it. *Since it is difficult to say who is absorbing whom at any given moment, Lindbeck can programmatically claim to be absorbing extratextual realities into the world of the text while at the same time clandestinely allowing extratextual realities to shape profoundly the textual world he claims to be inhabiting.*

To insist that the world should not absorb the text does not require us to maintain that the text should absorb the world. On the contrary, there are good reasons to abandon this metaphor. A suspicion that this metaphor could be a Christian mirror image of the *world's* absorbing intentions might be one of them. But this is just a suspicion. I want to explore some weighty reasons for avoiding talk about "absorbing the world" by looking at the question of a theologian's location. What is the nature of the world he or she is inhabiting?

Location 1
Lindbeck insists that a theologian should inhabit the "intrascriptural world." How else could she absorb the universe into the world of the text? How else could she see the world with scriptural eyes? Yet Lindbeck himself seems often unable (or unwilling) to follow his own methodological advice. For example, consider one of Lindbeck's substantive theological positions: the extraordinary claim that "there is no damnation—just as there is no salvation—outside the church."[18] Quite apart from whether he is right or wrong on this fundamental theological issue, is this appealing theological position an intratextual or an extratextual one? The issue is not quite clear, but my sense is that whoever placed a bet on extratextuality would more likely be the winner. For Lindbeck at least, the claim that there is no damnation outside the church is a corollary of the claim that there is no salvation outside the church on the grounds of his cultural-linguistic understanding of religion. The ambiguity of the source of some substantive theological claims raises the question of whether or not his methodological proposal to understand Christian faith as a cultural-linguistic system and to do theology intratextually is itself intratextual or extratextual.

Lindbeck himself calls his proposal "a suspiciously secular-looking model of religion."[19] Indeed, all major arguments he adduces for it are extratextual; the examples of Augustine and Aquinas illustrate what Lindbeck wants them to illustrate only because Ludwig Wittgenstein and Clifford Geertz have provided an interpretive grid. Intratextual theology plays on a stage that is erected with a good deal of extratextual material.[20] Lindbeck could respond that we can only rejoice if the heathen give witness to the truths that saints embrace. Yet here the heathen are not simply corroborating what the saints have been told in their holy writings; the heathen are telling the saints how they should approach their holy writings. To use Lindbeck's favorite metaphor, the heathen provide the spectacles that let saints see their texts as spectacles.

In response, Lindbeck could point out that he is engaged in *pretheology* rather than theology. Yet as I suggested earlier, a pretheology is theology, and, inversely, a theology implies a particular pretheology. After all, it was the progenitor of liberal theology, Friedrich Schleiermacher, who wished to distinguish clearly between prolegomena and dogmatics on the grounds that "the preliminary process of defining a science cannot belong to the science itself."[21] On the self-evident grounds that the preliminary process of defining science indeed *defines* science, Karl Barth insisted "that prolegomena to dogmatics are possible only as part of dogmatics itself."[22] If we grant Barth's point, is not something askew when a metatheory (prolegomena), a prescriptive one for that matter, rests on the kinds of theoretical moves that are off-limits in theory (dogmatics)? Should Lindbeck not have applied the proposed method of doing theology to his own methodological efforts?

Let us assume that Lindbeck can succeed in constructing his methodological proposal with intratextual materials. He would not succeed, I think, in putting his methodological proposal into practice. On extrascriptural grounds I would suggest that if he tried consistently to explicate "religion from within" and then from that standpoint attempted to describe "everything as inside, as interpreted by the religion,"[23] he would fail. I will start my argument by examining one aspect of the thought of Clifford Geertz, a thinker to whom Lindbeck's proposal is perhaps most indebted.

Religious symbols, claims Geertz, offer a "perspective," a "mode of seeing," a "framework of meaning," a "world" to live in.[24] Notice, however, how he qualifies this living in the world of religion. He writes:

> But no one, not even a saint, lives in the world religious symbols formulate all the time, and the majority of men live in it only at moments. The everyday world of common-sense objects and practical acts is . . . the paramount reality in human existence—paramount in the sense that it is the world in which we are most solidly rooted.[25]

Instead of simply inhabiting the world of religion, as Lindbeck suggests, in Geertz's view we move "back and forth between" religious and nonreligious worlds.[26] This movement changes a person, and with change in a person there takes place also a change in "the common-sense world, for it is now seen as but the partial form of a wider reality which corrects and completes it."[27] As the transformation of a person suggests, the temporal sequence of habitations is the outward dimension of their inner "spatial" differentiation. A person lives in a complex cultural world and, at the same time, lives in the world of religious symbols. Both worlds live in the individual, and, in a profound sense, he or she *is* these worlds. What one can learn from Geertz is that the world of a Christian is never simply intratextual, but always "intratextual-cum-extratextual" (or, rather, "extratextual-cum-intratextual").

Yet even Geertz is one-sided. It will not do to simply note the movement back and forth between the two worlds, the coexistence of the two in a single person, and the shaping of the commonsense world by the religious world. Talal Asad has argued that Geertz's understanding of the relationship between religious and non-religious worlds is deficient because there is no suggestion anywhere in Geertz "that the religious world (or perspective) is ever affected by the common-sense world."[28] The shaping is unidirectional, from the religious world to the commonsense world. Lindbeck follows Geertz's unidirectional explication of the relationship between the two worlds and, in correspondence with his own strong notion of inhabiting religious symbols, emphasizes the need for religion to absorb the world. We get no sense in Lindbeck that the intratextual and extratextual worlds crisscross and overlap in a believer or a community, or that the religious world is being shaped by the nonreligious world as well as shaping it.

What Lindbeck gains by construing the influence between religious and nonreligious worlds unidirectionally is a strong sense of Christian identity within changing cultures. Yet the gain in religious and theological security comes at the cost of hermeneutical simplicity. We can look at our culture through the lenses of religious texts only *as we look at these texts through the lenses of our culture.* The notion of inhabiting the biblical story is hermeneutically naive because it presupposes that those who are faced with the biblical story can be completely "dislodged" from their extratextual dwelling places and "resettled" into intratextual homes. Neither dislodging nor re-settling can ever quite succeed; we continue to inhabit our cultures even after the encounter with the biblical story.[29]

Hence it is not enough to recognize, as Lindbeck does in a good postliberal fashion, that there is no neutral standpoint, that we are always shaped by traditions of beliefs and practices. An adequate methodological proposal must also take into account *that there is no pure space on which to stand even for the community of faith.* Ecclesial nonneutrality is always already shaped by the culture which the church inhabits, because to inhabit a contemporary culture means, to use Jean-François Lyotard's formulation, not to inhabit a single "grand Narrative" but to live within a complex and mobile "fabric of relations."[30]

Of course, Lindbeck is aware that religion and "experience" (read: nonreligious culturally mediated experience) condition each other.[31] Yet the whole program proceeds as if the religion that does the interpreting is itself not an interpreted religion. If we recognize that the very construction of the inside is shaped by the outside, then a religious person can neither leave the extratextual world and migrate into the intratextual one nor absorb the extratextual world into the intratextual one. *Everything* cannot be inside; *everything* cannot be interpreted by religion. To connect my unease with "inhabiting the text" with my previous unease with "absorbing the world," the metaphor of "absorbing" the extratextual world is problematic because the metaphor of "inhabiting" the intratextual world is inadequate.

It is possible that Lindbeck would grant my last point but add that the metaphors of "inhabiting" and "absorbing" should not be pressed too far. After all, at one juncture in his argument he speaks of "Christianized versions" of various world pictures which are all "far from identical."[32] Moreover, he grants that "readjustments take place in the interpretative scheme" with which we approach these diverse world pictures.[33] The twin claims that the textual world does not completely reconfigure the extratextual world (Christianized world pictures retain their specific identities) and that the extratextual world shapes the textual world (readjustments in the interpretative scheme) amount, however, to an admission that we always inhabit more than the intratextual world and that we never quite absorb the extratextual world. This admission, I believe, must be made part of a methodological proposal.

Two important consequences follow from the notion of "intratextuality-cum-extratextuality." First, we always see the biblical story through the filter of our culture. This does not necessarily entail that we do not see what is there, that we are condemned only to our own not only relative but relativistic perspectives. What it does mean is that what is seen, including the Christian story, is colored by the context of the seer. The second, more felicitous consequence of "intratextuality-cum-extratextuality" is often overlooked. Because we are inescapably inhabitants of both worlds, laying claim to complete inhabitation of the biblical world entails almost as a rule the clandestine attempt to domesticate that world. But awareness of the fact that we can never fully inhabit the biblical world guards the *irreducible externality of the textual world*. Because the textual world reveals God's new world (rather than merely redoubling our world), it always remains partly outside our own cultural and ecclesial setting, a strange word mapping a strange world, while we are inserted in the flux of history, struggling to live in and shape our cultures as we ourselves are shaped both by our religious texts and by our cultures.[34]

Location 2
Let us assume that Lindbeck is persuaded: he is comfortable with the claim that Christians always inhabit more than the intratextual world and is willing to make required adjustments in the program of absorbing the extratextual world. Is the notion of "textuality" on which his methodological proposal rests theologically plausible? Is his description of religion as a "cultural-linguistic system" adequate? For my purposes here, these two questions coalesce in the underlying question of whether or not it is appropriate to speak of Christians inhabiting *texts, semiotic systems or the story*.

The "text" Lindbeck invites us to inhabit stands for "a kind of cultural and/or linguistic framework or medium that shapes the entirety of life and thought."[35] As a cultural-linguistic medium, religion consists both of a language and of its correlative form of life. The language of religion is the "doctrines, cosmic stories or myths, and ethical directives"; the forms of life are "the rituals it practices, the sentiments or experiences it [religious tradition] evokes, the actions it recommends, and the institutional forms it develops."[36] To be a religious person means to inhabit such a cultural-linguistic system; to be a Christian means to interiorize "the language that speaks of Christ" and behavior correlative to such language.[37]

How are "language" and "forms of life" related, however? Lindbeck does not give us a precise answer, but it seems clear, as James J. Buckley has noted, that "the analogy of religions to languages . . . controls the analogy to cultures, ways of living, and forms of life."[38] Following Geertz explicitly, Lindbeck is primarily interested in religion as a "semiotic system," as a "system of meanings embodied in the symbols which make up the religion proper."[39] Such an understanding of religion would correspond to Geertz's notion of culture as "the framework of beliefs, expressive symbols, and values," or "the fabric of meaning" in terms of which "human beings interpret their experience and guide their action."[40] To be a religious person is to inhabit a particular semiotic system; to be Christian is to inhabit a semiotic system called "Christ's story" (which entails not only accepting certain stories, doctrines, and ethical directives but also exhibiting certain ways of living).

If we accept a Geertzian interpretation of Lindbeck—and he himself has summarized his position in thoroughly Geertzian terms—a significant contrast emerges between how Lindbeck and how the New Testament (and the Christian tradition) speak of the location of Christians.[41] There we read, of course, nothing of inhabiting a "cultural-linguistic system" or "texts." Much more prosaically, we are told that Christians live, on the one hand, "in Corinth" or "in Rome" and, on the other hand, in some mysterious way also "in God" or "in Christ." They inhabit both "Corinth" and "God," "Rome" and "Christ," at one and the same time. It is not that the New Testament is ignorant of the relationship between Christians and the language of faith. But the relationship is exactly inverse of the one Lindbeck postulates between Christians and the Christian "story": the "word of Christ" is supposed to "dwell in [them] richly" (Col 3:16), not they in the word of Christ; they, "the holy and faithful brothers [and sisters]," dwell in that peculiar double habitation described with the unusual phrase "in Christ at Colossae" (Col 1:2).

Someone could object that my argument is naively biblicistic. Lindbeck, the objection could continue, is saying the same, just one step removed and in a more contemporary philosophical and anthropological jargon. To inhabit the Christian cultural-linguistic system *is* a way of living in Corinth and in God. Yet behind the difference in language lies a difference in perspective. Consider the obvious: Both "Corinth" and "God," both "Rome" and "Christ" are more than cultural-linguistic systems, more than symbols and corresponding patterns of behavior. "Rome" is also a political power and economy; "Corinth" is also drives and desires. Talal Asad rightly underscored that "the social life is not simply a matter of systems of meaning (whether conventional or intentional), even if it is true that communication between human beings is necessarily present in every domain of social activity—that social life is not identical with communication, although communication is necessary to it."[42] To live in Rome or Corinth means to be inserted into the nexus of political and economic interests and powers, to struggle with drives and desires that form one's personality structure.

Consider also God, whom the New Testament tells us Christians "inhabit." According to Christian tradition, God undergirds both "semiotic systems" (even those that are necessary to access God!) and the multiple relations of power in which semiotic systems are always involved. God's relation to us and ours to God are therefore always more than the model of "language and signs" can express. To say that one inhabits "a semiotic system" and that one inhabits "Corinth" and "God" at one and the same time is to say two different things (even if cognitively both "Corinth" and "God" are accessible to us only through a system of signs).

What the talk about inhabiting a cultural-linguistic system tends to hide from us (and what the talk about inhabiting "Corinth" and "God" implies) is that Christians are always shaped by more than just the Christian cultural-linguistic system. As citizens of "Corinth" we are shaped by structures of our political and economic life and by the structure of our personalities. Though the system of signs which our culture represents shapes these, they are partly independent factors, shaping both who we are and how we practice our faith. As those who dwell in God, we are touched by God not simply through the language and behavioral patterns we learn but at the depths of our souls. God is there "touching" us before we inhabit the Christian cultural-linguistic system, and God continues embracing us if we choose to move out of it. What all of this amounts to is that at different levels we need to talk about structures, forces and experiences when we talk about Christian faith in the world, not just about "cultural-linguistic systems" and their influence on how we see the world and behave in it.

The same forces that shape us as Christians shape also our cultural-linguistic system. One way to get at my point here is to ask an innocent (but I believe profound) question: If I am supposed to be located in a Christian "cultural-linguistic system," where is that "system" itself located? Like some blimp fashioned out of a canvas of religious intersignifications, Lindbeck's cultural-linguistic system seems to float in midair: we get into it and we see the whole reality anew from within it, and we behave differently because we are in it.[43] "Cultural-linguistic system" is connected to the rest of the social reality, but only, so to speak, at the back end of it, rarely at its front end. Lindbeck explores what the cultural-linguistic system does *to the world* (and occasionally what *people as agents do* with the semiotic system to the world), but *not what the world does to "the semiotic system."*[44] The movement is all in one direction: the cultural-linguistic system does something to the larger social reality, lets us see it from a different perspective, lets us behave in it differently. What remains unexamined are questions such as, What does it take for the semiotic system to emerge, to be kept alive, to do things we see it do? What keeps the blimp of religious intersignifications and their corresponding behavioral patterns in the air?

If in the previous section ("Location 1") I pushed Lindbeck to take more seriously the hermeneutical tradition, here I want to push him not to disregard some important Marxian and poststructuralist insights. Though I believe that Michel Foucault slights the "domain of signifying structures" and elevates unduly the "relations of force," he is right in warning against reducing the relations of power to relations of meaning.[45] "Semiology" may indeed be a way of avoiding the violent character of social conflict "by reducing it to the calm Platonic form of language and dialogue," as he suggests.[46] If we grant that Foucault's distinction between the relations of force and the signifying structures is significant, we need to ask, What is the interplay of semiotic elements and nonsemiotic forces involved in the construction and enduring power of the Christian semiotic system both at its emergence and in the course of its history?[47] I see no reason why Lindbeck could not incorporate this crucial poststructuralist insight into his proposal, provided he gives more attention to "experience" than he, constrained by his largely legitimate polemic against the misplaced liberal appeal to experience, actually does.

Construction
Consider, first, the emergence of the Christian semiotic system.[48] Allow me to begin with a stark (but I hope noncontroversial) thesis: God did not send us a "semiotic system" so that we might see the world and behave in it differently, but became flesh and suffered on a cross in order to redeem and transform the world. The place where the Christian "semiotic system" emerges is *the history of God with the world*, a history that is more than a network of discursive and nondiscursive intersignifications.

Notice the interplay of semiotic elements and nonsemiotic forces in that history. We read about the angel's annunciation and about the "power of the Most High overshadowing" Mary, about the pain of birth and about wise men paying homage, about flight from the terror of massacre and the instruction to return from Egypt, about the proclamation of John the Baptist and the waters closing in on Jesus while the heavens burst open, about Jesus' proclamation and healing touch, about his praying in the night and walking on the streets, about his being caught between the common people, religious leaders and Roman occupying forces, about his swinging the whip at the money-changers and being whipped by the soldiers, about his wearing a crown of thorns and being mocked as the King of the Jews, about nails cutting into his flesh and a his cry of despair addressed to an absent God, about his last breath and his surge of new life from deep within the hewn rock—and all this is framed in fleshly descent from Abraham and a rich memory of God's people on the one hand, and by intersecting economic and political forces and interests on the other.

The point I wish to make should be clear: the history of Jesus Christ is *more than* a complex "web of significance."[49] Even though the history is accessible to us only with the help of a system of intersignifications, this history itself is always much more than this system of intersignifications. If to disregard the semiotic dimension of culture is to pound culture into the ground of diffuse "experiences" and physical causalities (so much so that we cannot distinguish between a "twitch" and a "wink"), then to disregard the nonsemiotic dimension of culture is to suspend culture in the thin air of meanings.

The history of Jesus Christ is about how symbolic fields intersect with relations of force, how the systems of signification that come from Jesus Christ influence the systems of significations and the fields of forces around him, how his own nondiscursive and nonsemiotic behavior shapes the field of multiple forces and influences the webs of significations of the culture in which he lived. The point of the history of Jesus Christ is precisely the impact of his system of meanings and his unique power on the systems of signification and the fields of powers; his history has no other point but that. It cannot be translated into anything else, and it cannot be replaced by anything else, not even by the "story" of that history.

Postliberals have rightly warned against translating the story of Jesus Christ into ethical and doctrinal principles or paradigmatic religious experiences. Hence their stress on the untranslatable narrative of Jesus Christ. I think we need to be equally careful not to drain the blood from the flesh of Jesus Christ by replacing the earth-bound history of his semiotic and nonsemiotic relations—relations appropriate to the Word that has become flesh—to his people and his God with an inhabitable semiotic system. In objecting against the liberal tendency to denarrativize Jesus Christ and abstract him into a replaceable principle or experience, postliberals should take heed not to docetize Jesus Christ and evaporate him into an irreplaceable chain of religious intersignifications.

My point here is not that narrative is inappropriate as a medium of expressing Christian faith. To the contrary, because Christian faith is not a philosophy resting on a principle, but a religion involving a drama (God's complex history with the world he has created), *narrative is the most basic way to talk about Christian faith*. But we should resist inserting our narrative discourse into a model of Christian faith as a semiotic system.

Consider, second, the history of the Christian semiotic system. Just as it is not free-floating at the front end, at the point of its emergence, so also is it not free-floating in the middle, along the trajectory of its life through history. Talal Asad has objected that Geertz's semiotic understanding of culture and religion disregards the issue of power. We need to inquire, he argues, into the sense "in which power constructs religious ideology, establishes the preconditions for distinctive kinds of religious personality, authorizes specifiable religious practices and utterances, produces religiously defined knowledge."[50]

Geertz did not inquire into the relation of power to religion, power being not simply the force that legitimate or illegitimate political or ecclesial authority exercises upon people but the whole realm of nonsemiotic forces into which a religious semiotic system is embedded. My sense is that Lindbeck has not addressed this question adequately either.

What is the place of "power" in the survival and embracing of the Christian faith? Traditionally, theologians have always added the Spirit of God to the Word and the witness of the Christian church. And they were right. The power of the Christian semiotic system is the power of the third person of the Trinity, a semiotically mediated power that is more than the power created by the semiotic impact of the system of symbols and practices.

The power of the Spirit having been granted (and I see no reason that Lindbeck would not grant it), the crucial theological question is, *How* does the Spirit work? To point back to the Christian semiotic system with its corresponding practices would constitute only part of the answer, though an extremely important part. The fuller answer consists of *the interplay between semiotic and nonsemiotic dimensions in the life of the Christian church.* Think of the stories at bedside and the radiance of a face reflecting the love of Christ, words of admonition and the silent holding of the hand of a person in pain, eating and drinking the bread and wine, worship of the one true God, holiness and failure, manipulation and sword, the blood of the martyrs, the lives of the saints, hypocrisy and lust for power among church dignitaries and the rest of us, and economic interests and political machinations. My point is that in addition to semiotic dimensions there are important nonsemiotic ("experiential," if you wish) dimensions in the transmission of Christian faith.

The difficulty with nonsemiotic dimensions is, of course, that as soon as we begin to think and talk about them, they enter the chains of significations and cease to be nonsemiotic. So it seems impossible to get at the nondiscursive, nonsemiotic domains. Yet it seems, for example, beyond doubt that a person becomes a human being not only by learning her mother's language but also by feeling her mother's touch and hearing the sound of her voice. Similarly we become Christians not simply by learning the language of faith but also by being "touched" by other Christians and ultimately by God on a nonsemiotic level. The Christian semiotic system lives in the lives of the people of God through the interplay of nonsemiotic dimensions of church life (which are meaningless without the semiotic) and semiotic dimensions of church life (which are powerless without the nonsemiotic).

The Christian semiotic system can survive and have an impact on people because right in the midst of the intersecting cultural systems of significations and relations of forces the Holy Spirit has created flesh-and-blood people connected by a semiotic system as well as by nonsemiotic relations back to that one person who proclaimed in words and power that "the kingdom of God [has come] near" (Mk 1:15). The Christian cultural-linguistic system "lives" because people who inhabit their own cultures are drawn in multiple ways, through relations of signification and relations of power, to follow (right where they are) the One who was crucified and resurrected for their salvation.[51]

This is what salvation means: not that we get into the Christian cultural-linguistic system (by learning the language of faith and the corresponding behavior), but that the word and the power of Jesus Christ dwell in us by the Spirit and are thereby inserted into the multiple signifying and nonsignifying relations that the world we inhabit represents.

Truth

Lindbeck contrasts his own postliberal and postcritical cultural-linguistic account of religion with a traditional precritical "cognitivist" account on the one hand and a liberal critical "experiential-expressive" one on the other. One way of reading the previous section is to see it as an attempt to retrieve the experiential dimension of Christian faith, which got swept away by the force of Lindbeck's legitimate critique of the liberal experiential-expressive model. In the present section I want to examine briefly some ambiguities of his critique of the cognitivist account of religion. As "a comprehensive scheme or story used to structure all dimensions of existence," religion is, claims Lindbeck, "not primarily a set of propositions to be believed, but is rather the medium in which one moves, a set of skills that one employs in living one's life."[52] The trick in interpreting a sentence like this is to know what "not primarily" means. How secondary is the propositions-to-be-believed side of religion?

The question is not easy to answer. Lindbeck does claim that in the case of some religions, such as Christianity, truth is "of the utmost importance."[53] Yet we are never told what work the propositional side of religion does; it seems idle. When he compares religions, for instance, the focus is not on truth claims but on the power of religion to conform people "to the ultimate reality and goodness that lies at the heart of things."[54] Since a given religion defines the ultimate reality and goodness, religions end up being tested in terms of their capability to make good on their own promises. What matters is the performative side of religion. A religious utterance "acquires the propositional truth of ontological correspondence only insofar as it is a performance, an act or deed, which helps create that correspondence."[55]

Important in Lindbeck's stress on performance is the insight that religious language aims at correspondence not only of the mind but of the whole human being to the reality of God. What is deeply troubling, however, is the small word *only*: religious utterance "acquires the propositional truth of ontological correspondence *only* insofar as it is a performance," he claims.[56] This seems to imply that propositionally or ontologically true claims (such as "Christ is Lord") are *propositionally false* when they do not produce or are not accompanied by corresponding performance.[57] Conversely, propositionally vacuous claims (such as "God is good," according to Lindbeck) are *propositionally true* if through them we commit ourselves "to thinking and acting as if God were good."[58] Lindbeck seems to consider religious sentences primarily connected with other religious sentences, and all of them together (and singly) are true not because they are adequate to reality but because and insofar as they make reality adequate to them. If I see correctly, this would be the epistemological side of religion as a free-floating semiotic system that seeks to absorb the world.

Bruce Marshall has argued that such an interpretation of Lindbeck (shared by many other interpreters) rests on a misunderstanding: adequate performance does not make a statement ontologically true, but provides the conditions "under which one can state a sentence which is a true proposition."[59] Lindbeck has endorsed Marshall's interpretation.[60] Though I have some reasons to remain obstinate, it would be foolish from my perspective not to grant that Marshall and Lindbeck are right on Lindbeck.[61] For if they are, then one can speak of the ontological truth of religious utterances apart from the concrete performance of what they affirm, and then the cognitive aspect of religion is no longer idle (which is what I think one ought to assert).

Whatever the proper interpretation of Lindbeck is, it would seem curious to downplay the propositional side of religion. Phenomenologically, at the level of the self-perception of religious actors, propositionality seems built into the very fiber of religious belief. Geertz, at any rate, maintained that religion constructs meaning under two conditions: it must affirm something, and what it affirms must have "an appearance of objectivity."[62] "What any particular religion affirms about the fundamental nature of reality may be obscure, shallow, or, all too often, perverse; but it must . . . affirm something."[63] And what it affirms must be portrayed not "as subjective human preferences but as the imposed conditions for life implicit in a world with a particular structure."[64] This is to say that the "meaning" acceptable to religious actors cannot be seen by them as constructed out of arbitrary signs, but (at least in part) out of true propositions. Of course, to generate meaning and to exert social influence, a religion needs to be more than just a set of propositions believed to be true, but propositions *are* essential to these functions of religion.

It could be that I am mistaken about "religion." Perhaps (but just perhaps) in some postcritical age, religious semiotic systems will flourish, we will know that they are not true in the ordinary sense of the word, and we will still let them shape our lives because they project a world we would like to inhabit. But in such an age, should we be content with adding our own Christian religious cultural-linguistic system to many others? I think not. Earlier my argument was that the purpose of the Christian story is not to make us inhabit that story. Instead, the story witnesses to the re-creation of the world that God has brought about through Jesus Christ's entrance into the networks of significations and of powers, proclaiming and enacting the kingdom of God when he was crucified, resurrected and seated at the right hand of God.

The *primary truth* of the Christian story consists in adequately pointing to the "performance" of Jesus Christ and the Spirit of God—not in eliciting our performance, though that is what this story aims for. If *God* and *God's grace* are the proper objects of religion and theology (rather than religion and theology being just efficacious talk about the talk about God), then religion and theology must be propositional at their core.[65] It is possible that Lindbeck would not disagree, though I wish he were more cheerful about emphasizing the propositional content of religious language.

Power

Whether religious language is true because it corresponds to who God is and to the history of Jesus Christ or because it creates this correspondence, it is essential for theologians not to be simply interested in the propositional side of religious language. As Lindbeck rightly underlines (following in part J. L. Austin's philosophy of language), religious language is meant to *do* something. This brings us again to the question of power—that nonsemiotic something that undeniably shapes our individual and social behavior.

In his complex analysis of truth and power, Michel Foucault insists on a reciprocal relation between the two (though tending to dissolve truth into a product of power). On the one hand, each society develops a "regime of truth" by means of its own network of power relations and power techniques; on the other hand, "truth" also induces "effects of power."[66] Through mechanisms of power a society creates and "conveys its knowledge" as well as "ensures its survival under the mask of knowledge."[67] Power produces truth; truth exerts power. Lindbeck, I suspect, would be comfortable with the idea of truth exerting power, for he insists that the true story creates correspondence with the divine reality. But how about the other side of the relation? I think it is incumbent on theologians to think about the way power is involved in the creation and maintenance of "truth."

If we clearly distinguish between what is "true" and what is "made to function as true"—a distinction Foucault does not seem overly eager to embrace—the idea that *knowledge never functions outside power* seems theologically very significant. In Foucault's thought, this idea is closely related to the claim that power is not simply localized here or there or possessed by this or that person (say, a sovereign). Instead, power is " 'always already there,' and one is never 'outside' it."[68] Power is "coextensive with the social body; there are no spaces of primal liberty between meshes of its network."[69] On this account of power, an individual is not so much an originator of power as an "effect of power" and an "element in its articulation."[70] As a consequence, one possesses knowledge or even truth always *within* multiple relations of power.

It would not be difficult to show how such an account (though modified) of power and knowledge could be defended on theological grounds. Assuming that it can, I wish here only to draw attention to the consequences of such a view concerning the interrelation of power and knowledge for the understanding of Christian faith and the task of theology. Consider first Talal Asad's exploration of what it takes to attain religious faith. If we want to understand this process, he argues, we must examine not only "sacred performance," as Geertz suggested, but also "the entire range of available disciplinary activities, of institutional forms of knowledge and practice, within which dispositions are formed and sustained and through which the possibilities of attaining the truth are marked out—as Augustine clearly saw."[71] In other words, "the different kinds of practice and discourse [i.e., different from religious semiotic systems] are intrinsic to the field in which religious representations (like any representation) acquire their identity and their truthfulness."[72] This statement can be read as Foucault adapted and applied by an anthropologist to the question of religious belief.

As theologians we could be tempted to dismiss Asad and Foucault's contention and seek refuge in the reaffirmation either of the cognitive power of our "sets of beliefs" (if we are traditionalists) or of the semiotic power of our system of intersignifications (if we are postliberals). However, to do so would be a serious mistake, the fact that it is frequently made notwithstanding. Though the question of power is almost absent from the writings of theologians, in the Bible it figures prominently. We need to pay careful attention to the biblical discourse of power and explore what kind of power Christians should exercise. The answer, I suggest, is neither "worldly power" nor "no power," but *"the power of the crucified Christ."*

Consider the interrelation between wisdom and power as Paul addresses the "foolishness" and the "weakness" of the cross in 1 Corinthians 1—2. The "rulers of this age" (2:8), the "strong" (1:27), do not understand the cross; it is foolishness and weakness to them. But to those who are "called" by God (1:24), the "message of the cross" (1:18)—or rather "Christ crucified" himself (1:23)—is both the power and the wisdom of God. The nature of the Christian church and its proclamation, Paul argues, must correspond to the life of the One who is proclaimed. The crucified Christ must be proclaimed "in weakness and fear, and with much trembling" (2:3), not with "wise and persuasive words, but with a demonstration of the Spirit's power" (2:4), so that the faith of the hearers "might rest not on [human] wisdom, but on God's power" (2:5).

Notice that the crucified Christ is not a messiah without power; he is a messiah with a new kind of power—the power of "the weak," which puts to shame "the strong," the power of "the things that are not" which "nullify the things that are" (1:27-28). Theology as reflection on the word of the cross must be embodied in the community of the cross *whose particular kind of weakness is a new kind of power inserted into the network of the powers of the world.* That new network of power does not create Christian truth and cannot therefore be a substitute for it. Instead, it sustains the truth, not so much by providing plausibility structures, as Peter Berger would argue, as by providing a space within networks of power in which the truth about Christ, which is always a truth about power, can be lived out; the new network of power sustains truth by providing livability structures.[73] The new network of power, which Christian community should be, sets the truth free to exercise its own specific kind of power.

The power of weakness and the power of the truth together, however, are no guarantee of success. Jesus Christ, the true king witnessing in powerlessness to the truth (Jn 18:29-37), was crucified; Paul managed to convert only those who were "called" (1 Cor 1:24).

Directions of Conformation

The strength of Lindbeck's postliberal proposal over against its liberal counterparts lies in his desire to reverse the direction of conformation in the relation between Christian faith and the wider culture: rather than translating the biblical message into the conceptualities of the wider culture guided by the plausibilities of that culture, Christians ought to inhabit the biblical story and from there seek to absorb the world.

Given Lindbeck's primary audience, the liberal theological establishment, one can see how the mutually reinforcing metaphors of "reversal of conformation" and of "absorption" would be attractive to him. The trouble with them is that they tend to immunize the Christian story against critique from outside, even making it difficult for Christians to learn anything important from their compatriots.

Would it not be both arrogant and foolish of churches to interpret their social environments only from their own perspective, not paying attention to how these social environments interpret themselves or how they interpret the beliefs and practices of the churches? Yet how can communities of faith take seriously into account extratextual perspectives if those communities should never conform to extratextual realities but always absorb them? Wolterstorff, who endorses the metaphor "reversal of conformation," asks rightly: "But is the relation of the Church theologian to the non-theological disciplines exclusively that of melting down gold taken from the Egyptians? Isn't some of the statuary of the Egyptians quite OK as it is? Does it all reek of idolatry? Isn't there something for the Church theologian to learn from the non-theological disciplines?"[74] Should churches have not learned from the sciences that the earth is not flat, and instead nested themselves cozily into the world of the biblical texts in blissful ignorance? The same question should be asked about the place of women in society and the church, and other important issues.

Lindbeck would not deny the need of Christians to learn from outsiders. He wants a postcritical, rather than a precritical, reading of the Bible. Moreover, he explicitly states that religious change and innovation must be understood "as resulting from the interactions of a cultural-linguistic system with changing situations." A religious interpretive scheme, continues Lindbeck, "develops anomalies in its application in new contexts," and when this happens the scheme needs to be changed.[75] Yet we are not told how such change in the Christian cultural-linguistic system, triggered by the outside culture, accords with the unidirectional notion of absorbing the world out of a space mapped by that cultural-linguistic system itself.

I have argued that it is better to think of Christians inhabiting "Corinth" and "God," of being "in Rome" and "in Christ," at one and the same time; "the story," on the other hand, remains always external. What could the reversal of the direction of conformation mean from such a perspective? The reversal takes place not in that we inhabit the texts in order to absorb the world, but in that we let the story, lived out in the communities of believers, shape our culturally situated selves (our communal thinking and our communal practices) so that we in turn, as inhabitants of our cultures, can embody "Christian difference" and insert it wherever needed and whenever possible. The goal here is not to situate symbolically the extratextual realities within the Christian semiotic system, but to insert the Christian difference into the extratextual realities by practicing that fine and methodologically nonspecifiable art of accepting, transforming, subverting or replacing from within various aspects of the cultures we inhabit.

Part of the problem with the metaphors of "reversing the direction of conformation" and "absorbing the world" is that they suggest a general way of relating to the culture as a whole: you either absorb it or are absorbed by it; you either conform it to yourself or conform yourself to it. For two reasons such a general approach to the wider culture will not do. First, since you are never outside the wider culture, that culture is part and parcel of who you are. Second, the wider culture is not a monolithic whole but a differentiated network of beliefs and practices. On the grounds that culture is not monolithic, John Howard Yoder has rightly refused to set up a new typology of Christ and culture after his devastating critique of Niebuhr's classic *Christ and Culture*.[76] He explicitly rejects "the kind of total formal answer around which the entire Niebuhr treatment is oriented, namely, the call for a global classification of all of culture in one category."[77]

Once you accept that "culture" is not "monolithic" (as Yoder underlines) and that being a Christian is a way of inhabiting a culture (as I would add), then you must reject the Niebuhrian assumption that "culture" as "a whole must be responded to somehow as a monolith, either affirming it all, rejecting it all, synthesizing with it all, or paradoxing it all," or as Lindbeck would put it, absorbing it all.[78] *There is no single correct way to relate to a given culture as a whole, or even to its dominant thrust; there are only numerous ways of accepting, transforming or replacing various aspects of a given culture from within.*

Center and System

If I am reading Lindbeck correctly, what drives his project at least in part is the desire to retrieve the unity of Western culture lost in the wake of progressive de-Christianization. Though he is aware that under the conditions of postmodernity the church might be more likely to live in the catacombs than to reign from the throne, he maintains that the mission of the church in the postmodern world is to supply the wider culture with "the conceptual and imaginative vocabularies, as well as grammar and syntax, with which we construe reality."[79] The language of Christian faith must become again "the tongue," the medium of the larger cultural conversation about the great issues of the day.[80] In his hand, outstretched to the culture, Lindbeck holds the scriptural world, and he is issuing an invitation to come inhabit it. He senses that "a new Christian culture" is more likely to "emerge in Africa, Asia, or the Islands of the Sea" and that the Western church of the future might "lead an increasingly ghettoized existence in shrinking enclaves and unfriendly societies."[81] Yet his missionary program remains the same: re-Christianize the de-Christianized Western culture.

If I am reading contemporary societies correctly, the re-Christianization of the culture (which Lindbeck rightly distinguishes from the re-Christianization of society) will not succeed, not because the world is worse than it used to be but because it is structured in such a way that it must reject all hands that want to help it the way Lindbeck seemingly does. Whereas in traditional societies there was a symbolic center that held them together and through which influence on the whole could be exercised, in contemporary societies this is no longer the case. What sociologists call the functional differentiation of society—the fact that various subsystems specialize in performing particular functions, such as economic, educational or communication activity—implies (relative) self-sufficiency and self-perpetuation of those social subsystems. And self-perpetuation means resistance of the subsystems to the values brought to it from the outside.[82]

It is not easy to know what the social role of Christian faith can be under these conditions. One of the major challenges for theology today is to rethink Christian social responsibility in a functionally differentiated world. What is certain, however, is that re-Christianization will not work for the simple reason that Christian faith cannot locate itself at the center in order to exercise from there an integrative function; a social center no longer exists. Should the impossibility of re-Christianization of the Western culture trouble Christians? It can be persuasively argued that the center is not the place where Christian faith should be anyway: it was born on the margins to serve the whole humanity. The Messiah of the world was crucified outside the gate; the resurrected Lord, with all authority on heaven and earth, appeared to a few, charging them with a mission. Social marginality is not to be bemoaned but celebrated—not as a ghetto protected from the rest of the culture by a tall wall of private communal language and practices, but as a place from which the church can, speaking its own proper language, address public issues and, holding fast to its own proper practices, initiate authentic transformations in its social environment.

Closely related to the functional differentiation of contemporary societies is their insuppressible cultural plurality, reinforced by rapid social change. As a consequence we inescapably inhabit a multicultural and multilingual world. It would be a mistake in such a situation to seek to retrieve the language of faith as some kind of universal metalanguage, unifying all other languages we speak, a Christian version of the universal Esperanto of modernity or a post-Christian version of a premodern cultural Christianity. Robert Bellah suggested that instead we need to become "genuinely multilingual, speaking the language of science and psychology where they are appropriate, but also speaking the language of the Bible and of citizenship unashamedly and well."[83] How these overlapping "languages" should relate can never be stated in advance of an actual encounter between them; that a meaningful conversation can take place between the various "languages" without the medium of a metalanguage is something that can be doubted only by those who make it their business to find reasons why it should be impossible to do what most of us find no difficulty in doing.

A theology appropriate to multilingual people living in functionally differentiated and culturally pluralistic societies should be conceived primarily as a nonsystemic and critical intellectual endeavor. In a time of "increasing interdependence, cultural diversity and historical change," Stephen Toulmin argues that the intellectual task before natural and social scientists is "not to build new, more comprehensive systems of theory with universal and timeless relevance, but to limit the scope of even the best-framed theories, and fight the intellectual reductionism that became entrenched during the ascendancy of rationalism."[84] We should "pay less attention to *stability* and *system*, more attention to *function* and *adaptability*."[85] The same, I would argue, holds true of theology. The more systemically rigorous and timeless our theologies are, the less useful they will be in the diverse situations of our fast-changing cultures (which by no means entails the claim that the *least* systemically rigorous theology, a haphazard conglomeration of theological assertions, will be the most useful).

Does theology so conceived forfeit its universal claim? To the contrary: it is *because* "Jesus Christ is the same yesterday and today and forever" (Heb 13:8), it is *because* Christian faith is for all times and all places, that our theologies need to be nonsystemic, contextual and flexible. Lindbeck's cultural-linguistic theology (along with other narrative theologies) is an important contribution to the search for such a nonsystemic, contextual and flexible way of doing theology.

Conclusion: Theology Between Pain and Delight of God

Jürgen Moltmann, who has offered his public both beautiful and complex theological melodies, reserving most of his throat-clearing to the privacy of his study, started his keynote address at the American Academy of Religion in Chicago (1994) with the following words: "It is simple, but true to say that theology has only one, single problem: *God*. We are theologians for the sake of God. God is our dignity. God is our agony. God is our hope." But who is this God? he asked. Both the subject of God's own existence and a passionate lover of the world, he answered. And then, turning from the vision of God to the character of theology, Moltmann continued,

> For me theology springs from a *divine passion*: that is the open wound of God in one's own life and in the tormented men, women, and children of this world. But for me theology also springs from God's *love for life*, the love for life which we experience in the presence of the life-giving Spirit, and which enables us to move beyond our resignation, and begin to love life here and now. These are also Christ's two experiences of God, and because of that they are the foundation of Christian theology too: God's delight and God's pain.

Because God's delight and God's pain are not circumscribed by the walls of ecclesial communities and universities, theology can neither just feed the pious souls in the church nor just delight the inquisitive minds in the academy. Beyond the church, beyond the academy, the horizon of theology is the world as the place of the coming reign of God. For the sake of the future of the world, that object of God's pain and God's delight, theology must be a public endeavor, Moltmann insisted, "a public theology for the public gospel."

The purpose of my critical conversation with Lindbeck was to rethink public theology in a post-Christian and postindustrial context. I argued that Christians and their theologies are always situated in a given culture; we understand Christian faith as we do because we see it with spectacles tinted by our culture ("Location 1"). At the same time I insisted that the truth Christians are called to proclaim and theologians to guard is a public truth, addressed to all and accessible in principle to all ("Truth"). I argued that Christians and their theologies are always situated in a given field of personal and social forces—drives, desires and interests, struggles for goods and for power ("Location 2").

At the same time I insisted that Christian faith does not entail renunciation of relations of power, but insertion of a different set of relations of power—the power that is set free when people walk in the footsteps of the crucified Messiah—into the larger field of forces ("Power"). I argued that nonconformity must be Christian if extinction is not to be the Christian fate. At the same time I insisted that the only adequate way of being nonconformist is to reject the notion that there is a single correct formal answer as to how to relate to a given culture as a whole ("Directions of Conformation"). Finally I argued that theology in a post-Christian and postindustrial context should celebrate the social space it is forced to inhabit (the margins) and shed all traces of nostalgia for the life in the center. It is from the margins, in the form of a nonsystemic, contextual and flexible critical reflection, that Christian theology should exercise its role of addressing public issues in the light of the coming universal reign of God.

Here then is a vision of a public theology for a public gospel: looking through the spectacles of its own culture, it sees the city whose builder and architect is God. Situated in multiple relations of power, it advocates the weakness of the Crucified as a new form of power; dwelling on the margins, it seeks to bring the reign of the triune God to bear on all domains of life. The vision, however, needs to be embodied in the people whose hearts throb with the pain and delight of God. If not, it will remain nothing more than fading ink on a sheet of paper, sound waves disappearing in space.[86]

Part III
REALISM & FOUNDATIONALISM

4

ARE POSTLIBERALS NECESSARILY ANTIREALISTS?

Reexamining the Metaphysics of Lindbeck's Postliberal Theology

Jeffrey Hensley

At first glance, the historical and social differences between evangelicalism and postliberalism appear too great to sustain any hope for the formation of a constructive partnership between these two theological movements. Their diverse historical developments (evangelicalism's growth out of fundamentalism compared with postliberalism's evolution out of mainline Protestant liberalism) coupled with their disparate social contexts (evangelicalism's predominantly low-church, sectarian setting in contrast to postliberalism's high-church, mainline milieu) complicate if not eliminate the possibilities for mutually beneficial theological cooperation.

Yet the prospects for such a theological partnership might not be as bleak as the social and historical contexts of evangelicalism and postliberalism seem to indicate. For example, evangelicals and postliberals formally share a desire to recover premodern conceptions of theology and methods of biblical interpretation, despite their significant material differences over how those premodern methods should be understood and implemented in contemporary theological practice. Thus, perhaps issues concerning theological method—and, specifically, the philosophical assumptions built into methodological reflections—provide the best point of departure for comparing and contrasting evangelical and postliberal orientations to Christian theology, and ultimately for assessing the potential for developing a cooperative theological partnership.

When one examines issues and orientations in theological method, philosophical commitments naturally become the central focus, for all theologies, despite their respective views on the use of philosophy in theology, operate with implicit and often explicit philosophical assumptions (e.g., concerning the nature of reality, the good, and knowledge). But which of the wide array of philosophical commitments operative in evangelical and postliberal theology are most instructive for our purposes? In this essay, I propose to focus on the underlying *metaphysical* commitments of evangelical and postliberal theology, for it is generally assumed that their respective metaphysical viewpoints are quite evident and explicit. Hence, they presumably provide an excellent, noncontroversial basis upon which to compare the theological methods of these two historically and socially diverse theological movements.

On the one hand, evangelicals are *metaphysical realists* who believe that reality exists "out there," independent of their minds or cognitive activity. Though we have mental and linguistic representations of the world in the form of beliefs, experiences and theories, there is a world "out there," so the realist claims, that is totally independent of these representations. For example, facts about reality such as the elliptical orbit of the planets around the sun, the atomic makeup of nitrogen, the amount of coffee in my mug and the metaphysical nature of God are "true," independent of human representations or conceptions of these phenomena. In short, realists claim that such objects "exist" whether or not we have a concept or cognitive grasp of them.[1]

On the other hand, postliberals, it is widely argued, are *metaphysical antirealists* who deny that reality exists independently of human minds. They argue that what we take to exist "out there" is, in fact, dependent upon our conceptual schemes or systems of representations. More specifically, our concepts, according to the antirealist, "cut up the world" or "construct reality" to the degree to which reality is relative to our conceptual construction. Consequently, reality is not mind independent, as the realist maintains, but its existence is dependent upon human cognition. In short, then, the differences seem quite clear between the methodological assumptions of evangelicals and postliberals: they hold contradictory metaphysical viewpoints! And thus, in light of their conflicting views on the nature and existence of reality, there would appear to be little hope for establishing a cooperative theological partnership between the movements.

But are these metaphysical differences as apparent as many interpreters have supposed? And if they are not, then does there yet exist some chance for theological collaboration between evangelicals and postliberals? Clearly, most if not all contemporary evangelical theologians are, implicitly or explicitly, metaphysical realists; however, I argue, not all postliberal theologians are necessarily metaphysical antirealists. In fact, I claim that while many commentators (evangelicals and nonevangelicals alike) have interpreted postliberal theology as antirealist in its metaphysical orientation, this is an unfortunate and crucial *misreading* of the postliberal project. Specifically, I contend that postliberal theology, especially as it has been articulated by George Lindbeck, is not committed to an antirealist metaphysics. In fact, I maintain that Lindbeck, in his seminal work, *The Nature of Doctrine*, is metaphysically neutral with respect to the realism-antirealism debate.[2]

This neutrality, therefore, indicates that there are no methodological constraints built into postliberalism that would prevent it from being oriented around a realist metaphysics. Furthermore, if Lindbeck's postliberalism is, in principle, compatible with metaphysical realism, then there exists more hope for the formation of a mutually beneficial theological partnership between evangelicalism and postliberalism than may have initially appeared.

The Antirealist Reading of Lindbeck's Postliberal Project
In order to defend an interpretation of Lindbeck's postliberal project as compatible with metaphysical realism, I must first examine the prevailing antirealist interpretation of his work if I am to criticize it as a misreading of his methodological assumptions. Not surprisingly, this antirealist reading of Lindbeck is the primary focus of criticism leveled by most evangelical theologians against his theology. The strong realist tendencies of evangelical theology seem to clash directly with the supposed antirealism that they find within Lindbeck's theological method, and, specifically, within his account of the nature of religious doctrine and truth.

For example, Donald Bloesch, a noted contemporary evangelical theologian, has recently argued that Lindbeck's concept of the nature and tasks of theology is inherently antirealist. Postliberal theologians like Lindbeck, Bloesch contends, conceive of theology "as primarily descriptive rather than ontologically normative" and thus focus, for instance, on "the analysis of the text [of Scripture] as narrative rather than on the text as the bearer of intrinsic, quasi-metaphysical meaning."[3] Bloesch further claims that Scripture for Lindbeck becomes "a *mosaic* that redesigns reality" and thus "conjures up a vision of the world that does not necessarily comport with objective or historical reality. It creates a picture of a followable world" rather than refers to the actual, objective world.[4]

Over against Lindbeck's conception of theology, Bloesch argues that theologians "do not simply tell stories but present truth claims." Christian theologians must venture beyond interpreting Scripture intratextually, for from a metaphysical realist perspective, "church language 'is adequate to a revealed reality that does more than witness to a particular intrasystematic viewpoint.' "[5] In summary, Bloesch argues that with the rise of postliberal theology,

> the emphasis has shifted from exploring the metaphysical implications of the faith to investigating the story of a people on pilgrimage. While reflecting certain biblical concerns, this development is nonetheless fraught with peril. Theology can ill afford to ignore the issue of truth, for it is truth that gives narrative its

significance. . . . The divine incursion into history sets the stage for an excursus in ontology. Theology is certainly more than a generalized description of the faith of the community: it entails a metaphysical probing of how this community is grounded in reality.[6]

Thus Bloesch argues that Lindbeck's *descriptive*, intratextual theology, since it has forsaken metaphysical realism, has lost all grounds for a normative, *prescriptive* critique of either Christianity itself or of the wider reality to which it refers.

Other evangelical interpreters of Lindbeck have also described his theology in antirealist terms. The evangelical philosopher Thomas Morris, for example, criticizes Lindbeck's "move toward theological anti-realism" with respect to his concept of doctrine. Morris notes that for Lindbeck doctrines are not "first order truth claims about reality. They are instead, in Lindbeck's view, grammatical *rules*. Or so he argues." Morris goes on to question Lindbeck's notion of "the time-conditioned *relativity* of all doctrines" and argues that if doctrines are merely true in relation to an operative linguistic framework, then they lose any reference to reality and become "[mere] functions of socially constructed world-views."[7]

Like Morris, Alister McGrath notes that in *The Nature of Doctrine*, Lindbeck "seems to suggest that conceiving theology as the grammar of the Christian language entails the abandonment of any talk about God as an independent reality and any suggestion that it is possible to make truth claims (in an ontological . . . sense) concerning him." This "abandonment," according to McGrath, is the result of Lindbeck's "persistent Wittgensteinian reserve concerning the external referent of doctrinal statements, and a perceptible hesitation over the claims of epistemological realism."[8]

Thus, in summary, Bloesch, Morris and McGrath emphasize the antirealist aspects of Lindbeck's descriptivist theological method and particularly stress his supposed antirealist view of Christian doctrine and truth.[9]

Understanding Metaphysical Antirealism

Before we can assess these antirealist readings of Lindbeck's theology, we must first understand the meaning of the antirealist position itself; second, we must clearly distinguish the ways in which interpreters of Lindbeck see his theology as committed to antirealism.

So, first, what is the antirealist thesis? In answering this question, we must distinguish between two senses of metaphysical antirealism—namely, antirealism with respect to truth, or what I will call *alethic antirealism*, and antirealism with respect to concepts, or *conceptual antirealism*.[10] We will return shortly to alethic antirealism, but first let us examine what it means to be a conceptual antirealist.

Conceptual antirealists claim that concepts are the instruments we use to cut up the world into the objects of our experience. Apart from such conceptual cuts, so antirealists argue, there "are" no objects of our experience. In other words, the worlds of our experience are not ready-made, but are constructed by the application of our concepts to our experience. As Hilary Putnam, an influential antirealist philosopher, puts it, "Objects do not exist independently of conceptual schemes. [Rather] *we* cut up the world into objects when we introduce one or another scheme of description."[11]

But what does it mean to say that "we cut up the world" by using concepts? Is this a species of metaphysical idealism whereby the existence of objective, mind-independent and even material entities is denied? I think not, for the following reason: the conceptual antirealist has no problem asserting the *existence* of physical objects. As Putnam remarks, "Do *fields* 'exist' as physically real things? Yes, fields really exist; relative to one scheme for describing and explaining physical phenomena."[12] Thus Putnam emphatically affirms the existence of material objects like fields, tables and chairs, and, therefore, clearly distinguishes his conceptual antirealism from metaphysical idealism.[13] In fact, Putnam further claims that metaphysical idealism is "disastrous" since it "denies precisely the common man's kind of realism, his realism about tables and chairs"—a realism, ironically, that Putnam believes his conceptual antirealism preserves.[14]

Thus it appears that the conceptual antirealist must be arguing for what Alvin Plantinga calls "creative anti-realism," or the thesis that "there would be nothing at all if it weren't for the creative structuring activity of persons."[15] The condition for the possibility of the existence of anything at all, according to this reading of conceptual antirealism, is that there be persons who are using conceptual schemes. *We* cut up the world through *our* concepts. Thus for the "world" to be the world of objects, *we* must be active in conceptualizing it.

But when conceptual antirealists assert that concepts cut up and structure the world, do they mean that "objects do not exist independently of conceptual schemes"? Nicholas Wolterstorff persuasively argues that conceptual antirealists are *not* creative antirealists in Plantinga's sense of the term, for this would commit conceptual antirealists to an absurd view of the history of the universe.[16] If conceptual antirealism is best thought of as creative antirealism, as Plantinga argues, and thus if conceptual antirealists claim that there would be nothing at all if there were no human thinkers, then how can conceptual antirealists account for the existence of such objects as stars and planets and such life forms as dinosaurs prior to the existence of any human cognizer? In other words, it seems that the creative antirealist is committed to the claim that there were no stars, planets or dinosaurs before there were human beings. But this clearly contradicts a commonly held belief concerning the history of the universe—namely, that humans came into existence much later than stars, planets or dinosaurs. Thus, in an attempt to give the most charitable interpretation of antirealism possible, Wolterstorff argues that creative antirealism cannot be what the conceptual antirealist has in mind.[17]

So, again, what is conceptual antirealism? I have suggested that conceptual antirealism is not a species of idealism and thus clearly does not deny the existence of some ordinary category of entities like material objects. Moreover, Wolterstorff rightly argues that conceptual antirealism is not a form of creative antirealism and, subsequently, does not claim that the literal existence of everything (both mental and physical objects) is dependent upon the occurrence of human conceptualizing. So what is conceptual antirealism?

At the heart of the conceptual antirealist thesis is the notion that the concept of "existence" must be understood as relative to our conceptual schemes.[18] For example, in an important passage Putnam clearly states this core claim of antirealism: "We don't have notions of the 'existence' of things or of the 'truth' of statements that are independent of the versions we construct and the procedures and practices that give sense to talk of 'existence' and 'truth' within those versions."[19] Thus when the conceptual antirealist argues that concepts cut up the world, the existence of material objects is not denied, nor is all existence claimed to be dependent on cognitive activity. Rather, it is asserted that the existence of kinds of entities, entities of those kinds and their interrelation are all relative to our human conceptual schemes or the ways in which we represent our experience. Humans are active in constructing their conceptual schemes, so, by inference, they are active in cutting up the world in the process of understanding the world through their various conceptual frameworks.[20]

Thus, briefly, *alethic antirealism*, or antirealism with respect to truth, can be construed as claiming that truth is likewise relative to human conceptual schemes. We cannot as humans crawl out of our conceptual skins, as it were, but are always construing the world relative to the ways in which we represent it. What we take to be true (or false for that matter) will never be concept-free but will always depend on conceptual interpretations of our experience.[21] To put it another way, truth is radically *epistemic*, and thus we should think of truth as a relationship among sentences or beliefs themselves, rather than in the realist sense as a relationship of sentences or beliefs to something external to the mind, such as a mind-independent world. If truth is relative to human conceptual schemes, then, according to alethic antirealism, for a sentence to be true means merely that humans have warrant to believe it. As Richard Rorty, another prominent antirealist thinker, succinctly puts it, truth is "shaped rather than found."[22]

Given this thumbnail sketch of metaphysical antirealism in its two predominant senses, let us now turn to the antirealist reading of Lindbeck's theology and classify these interpretations under our notions of conceptual and alethic antirealism. Bloesch and McGrath clearly read Lindbeck as a conceptual antirealist. But Lindbeck's descriptive theological method only describes the conceptual scheme or framework of the Christian community, and thus Lindbeck does not claim that his conceptual scheme refers to any reality independent of that conceptual scheme.

Moreover, Morris and McGrath interpret Lindbeck as an alethic antirealist. On this reading Lindbeck's claim that doctrines do not make first-order truth claims but function rather like rules that guide and direct Christian discourse amounts to the contention that doctrines are relative to particular conceptual schemes, particular theological frameworks or ways of conceiving of the central realities of the Christian faith. As grammatical rules, they are relative to the linguistic framework in which they are articulated and govern. Their "truth-value," if they even have a truth-value, is relative to other doctrines within the Christian conceptual scheme or language game, and thus is not "found," to use Rorty's term, in relation to a mind-independent world or state of affairs.

Assessing the Antirealist Reading of Lindbeck's Postliberal Theology

So is there any basis for this antirealist interpretation of Lindbeck's theology? Consider the following three quotations from Lindbeck's influential text *The Nature of Doctrine*.

> For those who are steeped in them, no world is more real than the ones they create. A scriptural world is thus able to absorb the universe. It supplies the interpretive framework within which believers seek to live their lives and understand reality.[23]

> The first-order truth claims of a religion change insofar as these arise from the . . . shifting worlds that human beings inhabit. What is taken to be reality is in large part socially constructed and consequently alters in the course of time. [For example,] the universe of the ancient Near East was very different from that of Greek philosophy, and both are dissimilar from the modern cosmos. Inevitably, the Christianized versions of these various world pictures are far from identical.[24]

> Just as grammar by itself affirms nothing either true or false regarding the world in which language is used, but only about language, so theology and doctrine, to the extent that they are second-order activities, assert nothing either true or false about God and his relation to creatures, but only speak about such assertions.[25]

Clearly, these passages complicate a reading of Lindbeck's postliberal project (which is in principle compatible with metaphysical realism), but I do not think that it is rendered impossible. In an attempt to demonstrate Lindbeck's openness to metaphysical realism, I will give an interpretation of these passages in light of other texts from *The Nature of Doctrine* that, I believe, make plausible a realist reading of Lindbeck's overall theology.

In the first passage, Lindbeck refers to the ability of Scripture to "absorb the universe." Scripture has the capacity, according to Lindbeck, to provide us with a rough, nonsystematic narrative framework through which we understand all reality. Theology conceived of *intra*textually does not look for *extra*textual or *extra*scriptural frameworks through which to describe reality but "absorbs" these frameworks for the purpose of understanding the world from the perspective of biblical narratives. In other words, theology is "the scholarly activity of second-order reflection on the data of religion"; thus it is by nature a descriptive enterprise that seeks to uncover the underlying grammar of Christian discourse.[26] Scripture, and especially the realistic narratives within Scripture, generate the grammar or conceptual framework of Christianity.[27] Hence, Scripture provides theology with its own distinctive vision of the world. As Lindbeck states, "Intratextual theology redescribes reality within the scriptural framework rather than translating Scripture into extrascriptural categories. It is the text, so to speak, which absorbs the world, rather than the world the text."[28]

Based on this passage and the first problematic passage quoted above, it is clear that Lindbeck is in no way a creative antirealist. There is a world that the text absorbs, and likewise, there is a text that absorbs the world. The narrative of the text does not *create* the world, nor does the reality of the world, as it were, *create* the text, but they instead derive their existence apart from each other. Lindbeck's point is that if theology is understood intratextually, then the biblical narratives *shape* the way Christians view the extrascriptural world. Christians should see the world, as it were, through the "lenses" of their Christian identity as rendered by Scripture.[29]

So if Lindbeck is not asserting creative antirealism, is he nevertheless guilty of conceptual antirealism? In other words, is the *existence* of the extrascriptural world as kinds and particulars relative to the intratextual framework of Scripture? While the passage quoted first appears to some interpreters to suggest that Lindbeck is committed to a form of conceptual antirealism, I believe that one need not read him in this manner. Rather, for Lindbeck, meaning—not existence—is conceptually relative. The concepts and categories of Scripture and "the narrative framework rendered by Scripture" absorb the world in the sense that biblical idioms and concepts should pervade the way we think about extrascriptural realities. Kinds and particulars exist but lack meaning apart from scriptural categories. "Scripture creates its own domain of meaning," Lindbeck contends, "and [therefore] the task of interpretation is to extend this over the whole of reality."[30]

Thus when Lindbeck states that "no world is more real than the ones [humans] create," we must understand that he is speaking rather loosely and thereby asserts no particular metaphysical stance by way of this statement. He is simply pointing out that the frameworks through which we view the world deeply influence the way in which we understand its nature and existence. And when he asserts that we cannot get out of our "conceptual skins" when we view the world, he is not arguing that the world's existence and nature are relative to our conceptual skins. While the world metaphysically exists as kinds and particulars independently of our frameworks for understanding the world, these frameworks nevertheless deeply influence the way we view this world of entities and their kinds. In short, Lindbeck is arguing that Christians should view the world intratextually as absorbed by the conceptual framework of Christian Scripture.

Lindbeck further develops his perspective on the relationship between the world and conceptual frameworks by articulating his now famous "cultural-linguistic" account of religion. He summarizes his view when he states,

A religion can be viewed as a kind of cultural and/or linguistic framework or medium that shapes the entirety of life and thought. . . . It is not primarily an array of beliefs about the true and the good (though it may involve these), or a symbolism expressive of basic attitudes, feelings, or sentiments (though these will be generated). Rather, it is similar to an idiom that makes possible the description of realities, the formation of beliefs, and the experiencing of inner attitudes, feelings, and sentiments.[31]

As an *idiom*, religion provides religious believers with a language and set of concepts that are necessary for making sense of the world. In fact, the reasonableness and longevity of religions, Lindbeck argues, are largely a function of what he calls their "assimilative power" or their "ability to provide an intelligible interpretation in [their] own terms of the varied situations and realities adherents [of a religion] encounter."[32] Here again, for Lindbeck the existence of the world as kinds of entities and entities of those kinds is not relative to this idiom; rather, they are illuminated by it.

So what does Lindbeck mean when he states in our second problematic passage that "what is taken to be reality is in large part socially constructed and consequently alters in the course of time"?[33] Here, it seems to me, is where Lindbeck comes the closest to asserting an antirealist position. But note carefully his language: he claims that what is *taken to be reality* is socially constructed, not reality or the world itself. In other words, Lindbeck holds that what we as humans take to be the nature of reality, its characteristics and values, are essentially cut up by the concepts that we embrace in our given conceptual frameworks. Once again, he is careful not to assert that the *existence* of reality itself as kinds and particulars is dependent upon or relative to our conceptual cutting.[34] Rather, people throughout history have thought of the world in different ways given their perspectives on the world (since they have operated with various conceptual schemes). This conceptual mediation of reality is necessary for them to describe the world in ways meaningful to their overall conceptual frameworks, but this in no way means that the *existence* of reality and the *nature* of things are relative to their changing conceptual frameworks.[35]

Perhaps, one might argue, Lindbeck is merely pointing out that there is no concept-free experience of the world. There is no "God's-eye point of view" on reality, since perception is necessarily "concept- or theory-laden." Doesn't this amount to a conceptual antirealist position? I posit that it does not. In fact, I argue that a denial of the possibility of a concept-free, God's-eye point of view is compatible with metaphysical realism.

From a realist viewpoint, our concepts are neither *screens* between us and the world of kinds and particulars nor *instruments* in the making of those kinds and particulars, as the antirealist contends. Rather, for the realist, concepts function as *bridges* between us and the world.[36] Like bridges, concepts connect two independently existing objects and are necessary for getting from one object to another—from one side of the bridge, as it were, to the other. Thus according to some accounts of realism, objects possess properties, and we grasp these properties through our concepts; we get to the objects *by way of* our concepts. Subsequently, we find that our conceptual schemes make sense of those properties and that our conceptual schemes themselves make sense or, in Lindbeck's words, have "assimilative power," when the very properties that objects possess are the properties that we grasp and believe to be exemplified in them. Thus if concepts are the grasping of properties, and objects have natures or properties independent of our conceptual grasping of them, as the realist claims, then the realist can agree with full consistency that perception is concept- or theory-laden and yet hold that we perceive mind-independent entities through the senses.

Consequently, when Lindbeck asserts that all experience of reality is concept-laden, he is not necessarily denying realism or asserting conceptual antirealism. He is instead simply noting that we as human cognizers necessarily use concepts to describe and understand our experience. Concepts *bridge* rather than *screen* our idioms for understanding reality with reality itself.

If my reading of Lindbeck up to this point is correct, and he in fact is not a conceptual antirealist, might his theology still be characterized as antirealist with respect to truth? More specifically, if Christian theology, in asserting various doctrines, lays out the rules for how Christians should talk and behave, then isn't it the case that the truth of those doctrines is in some sense dependent upon the Christian conceptual scheme? In other words, isn't Lindbeck committed to the claim that the truth of doctrine does not depend upon some reference or correspondence to a state of affairs that is independent of that conceptual scheme?

In our third passage, Lindbeck appears to many of his interpreters to be making just such an alethic antirealist claim. Theology and doctrine, in Lindbeck's words, "assert nothing either true or false about God and his relation to creatures, but only speak about such assertions."[37] But note Lindbeck's careful wording of this passage. Theology and doctrine, he claims, *to the extent that they are second-order activities*, have no truth-value. Here Lindbeck is making a claim about theological utterances functioning *as doctrines*, as second-order statements or rules that govern Christian discourse, and not about theological statements functioning *as first-order assertions*, as, for example, in cases of catechetical or doxological utterances.[38]

For example, when the statement "Jesus Christ is fully human and fully divine" functions as a first-order statement uttered in the context of worship, it makes a truth claim concerning the nature of the person Jesus of Nazareth. But as a second-order statement uttered in an academic lecture on Christology, it states a rule about the limits of christological discourse. According to Lindbeck, the latter use of the statement as doctrine does not make a truth claim per se, but rather governs or regulates what truth claims are appropriate for Christians. Yet "to say that doctrines are rules," Lindbeck cautiously notes, "is not to deny that they involve propositions, . . . for a doctrinal sentence may also function symbolically or as a first-order proposition."[39]

Subsequently, Lindbeck's analysis gets complicated by the frequent simultaneous use of the same sentence as both a first-order truth claim and a second-order rule for forming appropriate Christian discourse. And this necessary complication of his account of doctrine, I think, leads many to misunderstand his position. Yet his distinction between the two uses of theological statements is crucial, for only if such a distinction is made can doctrinal statements continue to have validity when conceptual categories undergo fundamental change.[40]

So, contrary to Morris's interpretation, Lindbeck maintains that doctrines, when they function as first-order statements, have a truth-value.[41] But are their truth-values relative to the Christian conceptual scheme? And if they are, isn't Lindbeck nonetheless an alethic antirealist? Here I can only sketch what I take to be Lindbeck's position.[42]

Lindbeck seems to deny that correspondence to reality is a *sufficient* condition for truth, but he does not deny that it may in fact be a *necessary* condition for an overall account of truth.[43] Rather, truth is best understood as fixed by a combination of an internal coherence of the statement under consideration with other statements within the discourse—what Lindbeck calls "intrasystematic truth"—and a correspondence of the entire collection of statements (the entire discourse) with reality, or what he calls "ontological truth."[44] Thus theological statements that meet these two criteria can be "categorically true" because they contain "adequate categories [that] can be made to apply to what is taken to be real."[45] And thus truth is partially established with reference to reality "out there," but on Lindbeck's account, this correspondence to reality is a necessary but not sufficient condition for fixing truth. Correspondence, he argues, involves the entire conceptual framework and practice of the religion corresponding in some measure "to the ultimate reality and goodness that lies at the heart of things," but one need not specify how that correspondence takes place in order to be justified in claiming it.[46]

If Lindbeck holds that truth is fixed (albeit partially) by correspondence to reality, then he is clearly not asserting a purely epistemic or antirealist account of truth. While Lindbeck does insist upon an internal-coherence criterion for truth, he does not maintain that truth is fixed *solely* by the coherence of statements within a given conceptual framework; "intrasystematic truth is a necessary but not sufficient condition for ontological truth."[47] Truth, according to Lindbeck, also requires correspondence to reality and thus, ultimately, is a relation between statements and the reality to which they refer. Consequently, while Lindbeck does not hold either a pure coherence or a correspondence theory of truth, it appears that nonetheless he maintains a realist or nonepistemic account of truth, whereby truth is thought of as an internal coherence of propositions which as a whole relate to particular states of affairs.

Conclusion

In the discussion above, I have argued that the common reading of Lindbeck as a conceptual and alethic antirealist is unwarranted when the whole of his theological project is considered. Alternatively, I have claimed that Lindbeck is metaphysically neutral concerning this question, or at least nonmetaphysical in the development of his cultural-linguistic account of religion and theology. Why then has Lindbeck been repeatedly read (and, as I argue, misread) as committed to various forms of antireal-ism? Why, in other words, do many interpreters find it difficult to read Lindbeck as being methodologically open to metaphysical realism? In closing, let me suggest one reason that this is the case. I suspect that it is due in part to Lindbeck's deep commitment to epistemological antifoundationalism.[48]

Characteristic of many modern thinkers is a staunch commitment to the enterprise of epistemological foundationalism—trying to find certain, indubitable grounds for belief which will in turn provide a foundation for all knowledge. Descartes, for example, thought that through systemic doubt he could determine which beliefs, out of the entire array of beliefs that he held, were indubitable and thus certain. Only the certain beliefs that he could not conceivably call into question could count as knowledge (or *scientia*, as he called it), and thus only those beliefs could provide a secure foundation on which to build the house of knowledge.[49]

And as in the case of Descartes, characteristic of most modern epistemological foundationalists is an equally staunch commitment to some form of metaphysical realism. In fact, this correlation of foundationalism and realism became so tightly joined in modernity that when philosophers and theologians started questioning foundationalism as an adequate account of the justification of belief, many consciously or unconsciously submitted metaphysical realism to the same critique.[50]

Thus today many so-called postmodern thinkers, who have rejected modern forms of foundationalism, also reject metaphysical realism.[51] So, for better or worse, realism has been lumped together with foundationalism and antirealism with anti-foundationalism. Hence it is difficult for postmodern interpreters to recognize meta-physical realism when it is coupled with epistemological antifoundationalism or the rejection of the modern, foundationalist quest for certain grounds for knowledge.[52] Consequently, when an antifoundationalist thinker like Lindbeck articulates his po-sition, interpreters naturally read him as a metaphysical antirealist.

I have interpreted Lindbeck as an antifoundationalist thinker who is in principle open to metaphysical realism.[53] Evangelicals are clearly metaphysical realists, and an ever increasing number are epistemological antifoundationalists. If evangelical theol-ogy continues to move in the realist, antifoundationalist direction, then at least at the level of some basic, underlying methodological commitments, there is great potential for an evangelical-postliberal cooperative theological partnership. As is the case with all theological movements, time will tell if such a partnership can or will develop, but I think that the possibilities are great indeed.[54]

5
HOW FIRM
A FOUNDATION

Can Evangelicals
Be Nonfoundationalists?

Rodney Clapp

Once when I was in college, an evangelistic group visited our dormitory. A pair of incognito evangelists appeared at my door, bearing clipboards and announcing that they were doing a survey. No polltakers ever showed up in the country town of my origins, so it seemed to be an opportunity for validation as a real citizen of the modern world—one who has not merely voted, but has responded to a scientific survey. I flung the door open and gratefully awaited my anointing. But then the first question was "If you died tonight, how certain are you, in percentage points, that you would go to heaven?" As I soon found out, the only answer acceptable was "100 percent." Zero to 99 percent made no difference—anything other than absolute, unqualified, mathematically certifiable certainty betrayed a soul adrift. My "85 percent" response, calculated to combine confidence with becoming humility, elicited not a declaration of fellowship but a full-scale evangelistic presentation.

How could I have known? I was just a little Methodist boy, saved enough to refuse beer drinking my entire freshman year, but who grew up in a rural part of Oklahoma once known as "No Man's Land" and strained to pass basic algebra. Years later, settled in the evangelical subculture in Wheaton, Illinois, I learned that this particular evangelistic strategy and its opening question came from D. James Kennedy and his Evangelism Explosion. I learned yet later to put a name to the epistemology framing that question and its ideal reply: foundationalism.

And today, nearly two decades after that encounter in my dormitory room, I want

to suggest that evangelicals are better off disavowing foundationalism, and argue
that one of the better reasons for abandoning it is that the abandonment will enable
us to be more devout Christians and less devout liberals.

Foundationalism by the Numbers

By "foundationalism" I mean what has been called "the pervasive Western philosophical doctrine that in a rational noetic structure every non-basic belief must
ultimately be accepted on the basis of a-cultural and universally compelling beliefs
or realities, themselves in need of no support."[1] Foundationalism is that theory of
knowledge usually chased back to Descartes.

René Descartes was a man living in chaotic times. The Reformation, which oc-
curred nearly a century before his prime, was putting to bloom not only the flowers
of truth but also the toxic weeds of dissension. Luther had insisted on the power
of all Christians to discern right and wrong on matters of faith. Calvin had looked
to the absolute certainty of inner persuasion. There came to pass in consequence
a crisis of authority—or should we say of authorities? There were in fact now more
authorities than before, and potentially innumerably more authorities, since each
individual conscience theoretically constituted its own separate pope. The result, as
Jeffrey Stout writes, was that "for over a hundred years, beginning roughly at the
end of the last session of the Council of Trent and continuing throughout most of
the seventeenth century, Europe found itself embroiled in religious wars."[2] This was
the playing field of history onto which Descartes stepped.

Descartes was not alone in his anxiety about the violent disagreement surround-
ing him. Nor, I should add, was the worry solely over religious chaos. As the historian Lorraine Daston observes:

> Seventeenth-century science was a battlefield where rivals and factions stopped
> at nothing to scientifically discredit and personally abuse (the two were seldom
> distinguished) one another. [To name only stars of the first magnitude,] Galileo
> relished blistering polemics and was a master of the *ad hominem* pamphlet title, and
> Newton crushed his adversaries by fair means and foul. . . . Newton nearly drove
> Robert Hooke out of the Royal Society over a priority dispute concerning the
> inverse square law of attraction; he not only stacked the Royal Society committee
> to which Leibniz had appealed for an impartial settlement of the priority dispute
> over the invention of calculus—he wrote its report, thus embittering relation-
> ships between British and Continental mathematicians for nearly a century. It
> comes as no surprise that the 1699 regulations of the Paris Academy of Sciences
> had to explicitly forbid its members to use "terms of contempt or bitterness
> against one another, both in their speech and writings."[3]

Thus situated, it is not hard to imagine how Descartes and others yearned for less
partisanship and a more widely shared method for arriving at certainty. The problems at hand seemed clear: time changes everything, including beliefs. And ideas or
identities based in localities—whether cities, cantons or states—are a veritable recipe

for interminable fighting. But no longer were philosophers, scientists and politicians answerable to the church. Furthermore, the church was no longer a unified, consolidated authority, the generally accepted conduit of truth eternal, truth from beyond time and place, for all times and places. Thus Descartes sought a secular, or nonecclesial, foundation of knowledge that rested on grounds beyond time and place. This turned out to be his famous *cogito ergo sum*. This knowledge was at once indubitable and universally self-evident, unbeholden to any concrete and disputatious set of religious convictions. From this sure foundation one might reliably deduce the truth on any number of otherwise controvertible matters, across the range of human endeavor. Without recourse to the now-discredited church, a singular and compelling authority was thereby regained. The wars—scientific and religious, figurative and literal—could cease.

With such aims, it's hardly a wonder that Descartes modeled his epistemology on mathematics. Stephen Toulmin has pointed out that the comprehensive term *logic* is confusing because it can be modeled on the rationalities of several different fields: his own preference of jurisprudence, as well as psychology, sociology, technology or mathematics. Descartes, tapping into a deep, age-old well, chose the latter. As Toulmin puts it, the "history of philosophy [is] bound up with the history of mathematics." Plato directed a school of geometers and saw geometrical proof as the ideal of all sciences. In a similar frame of mind, Descartes invented a branch of mathematics known as "Cartesian Geometry" and was attracted, Toulmin says, "by the idea of establishing in a quasi-geometrical manner all the fundamental truths of natural science and theology." Surely Descartes, Leibniz and others gravitated toward mathematical logic in large part because pure mathematics is "possibly the only intellectual activity whose problems and solutions are 'above time' " and heedless of place.[4]

Thus "foundationalism" as I am now using the term is characterized by mathematical certainty, individualism and acontextualism:[5] its truths aim to be indubitable and precise, along the lines of the geometric or scientific proof, and they are supposedly available to rationally able, well-intended individuals quite apart from any particular tradition or social context.

As my college encounter with the evangelists indicates, foundationalism as such has long been attractive to North American evangelicals. George Marsden's *Fundamentalism and American Culture* abounds with examples of how evangelical intellectuals assumed foundationalism as they popularized the Common Sense Realism of Thomas Reid. On this account the Princeton theologians Hodge, Alexander and Warfield taught that "any sane and unbiased person of common sense could and must perceive the same things" and that "basic truths are much the same for all persons in all times and places."[6]

Protestant liberal foundationalism was based on experience, beginning with Schleiermacher's putatively universal feeling of absolute dependence. But the evangelicals, of course, turned to Scripture as the universally and individually accessible foundation, which implies that it stands as such apart from the church. So Charles Hodge could declare, "The Bible is a plain book. It is intelligible by the people. And they have the right and are bound to read and interpret it for themselves; so that their faith may rest on the testimony of the Scriptures, and not that of the Church."[7] In true and crowning foundationalist fashion, Hodge saw theology as concerned with the "facts and the principles" of this perspicuous Bible in just the way natural science is concerned with the "facts and laws of nature."[8]

However, foundationalism was in dire philosophical straits well before Hodge's time. In our time even those who hold to it do so with qualifications that, I would argue, effectively put them in a different world from that of the Princetonians, let alone Descartes.[9] Historically, foundationalism eroded because that singular, universal, supposedly nonparticular foundation could never for long or everywhere be agreed on. Soon enough Descartes's *cogito* crumbled. Hume championed the affections, Kant exalted innate reason, and these were only the first in what have now become myriad trains of positions (including evangelical biblical inerrancy) that are not all gauged to run on the same tracks. The problem, as Toulmin describes it, involves the eventual recognition that

> the exercise of rational judgement is itself an activity carried out in a particular context and essentially dependent on it: the arguments we encounter are set out at a given time and in a given situation, and when we come to assess them they have to be judged against this background. So the practical critic of arguments, as of morals, is in no position to adopt the mathematician's Olympian posture.[10]

Because foundationalism followed the mathematical model of rationality, Toulmin argues, it failed to see logical categories as contextual or "field-dependent." It sought instead "field-invariant standards of validity, necessity and possibility."[11] By doing so, it hoped to make foundationalist logical necessity a necessity stronger than any religious, historical, social or even physical necessity. All these other "necessities," after all, were particular and local on one scale or another, and as such clearly open to contention. But one large difficulty soon became apparent. Foundationalism's abstracted, idealized and impractically rigorous epistemological standards invalidated the undeniably field-dependent work and conclusions not just of theologians and scientific quacks but also of astronomers, archaeologists, historians, ethicists and psychologists—not to mention car mechanics, bricklayers, plumbers, farmers and others whose skill and knowledge undergird the conduct of our daily lives.

Evangelicals and the Foundationalist Habit

Foundationalism, in short, demands a kind and degree of certainty and decontextualization that is simply not available to most, if any, substantial human endeavors. Even mathematics, if it is to be material and applicable, cannot escape context. For example, it is not true that in all times and places 7 plus 9 equals 16. Computer programmers can correctly tell us that 7 plus 9 equals 10—in a base 16 system.[12]

The importance of taking context into account is being recognized more and more broadly. Accordingly, I am not sure which, if any, contemporary evangelical thinker would, if pressed, hold to the virginal, innocent foundationalism of the seventeenth century, or even to the initiated (but married and chaste) foundationalism of late nineteenth-century Princeton. But many evangelicals still hold to the mood and rhetoric of foundationalism.

Consider the work of Ronald Nash. Professor Nash admits that "the degree of influence or control that a particular belief has within any given noetic structure will be person-relative." He has read his Plantinga and argues that noetic structures contain a number of significant beliefs presupposed "without support from other beliefs or arguments or evidence." He affirms that different presuppositions will lead to different conclusions, that "one's axioms determine one's theorems." He can on occasion use W. V. O. Quine's web metaphor, employed by the holist Quine in explicit opposition to foundationalism. He even speaks about conversion from one worldview to another in terms that would warm the cockles of the holist's heart, insisting that conversion occurs gradually, over time, in response to several cumulative causes. Then somehow a gestalt clicks, and, "quite unexpectedly, these [converts] 'saw' things they had overlooked before; or they suddenly 'saw' things fit together in a pattern so that there was meaning where none had been discernible before."[13]

But as Nash develops his epistemology, he seems the philosophical equivalent of someone trying to quit smoking.[14] He appears convinced that the foundationalist habit will lead to no good, but he must sneak a drag here and there. Then, before the chapter ends, the nicotine kicks in and, forget it, Nash will remain a foundationalist, if only in moderation. Pretty soon he's reenlisted Descartes's "innate ideas" and is dropping confident allusions to the "dispositions" Thomas Reid says were endowed to all by the Creator.[15] By now we are past the point of a smoke after dinner and back on the way to a pack a day. Human beings are assumed to be *sometimes* capable of "approaching sense-information in an impersonal and detached way." And sense-information is itself somehow separable from interpretation of it.[16]

At last Nash withdraws to the parlor with the confirmed foundationalist (and smoker) C. S. Lewis. He quotes Lewis to the effect that there is for all persons in all times and places a singular and innate sense of fairness. So, says Lewis, when two people quarrel, one seldom says,

> To hell with your standard. Nearly always he tries to make out that what he has been doing does not really go against the standard, or that there is some special excuse. . . . It looks, in fact, very much as if both parties had in mind some kind of Law or Rule of fair play or decent behaviour or morality or whatever you call it, about which they really agreed.[17]

This, I allow, may have freighted cogency in Lewis's forties and fifties England. But today our society is sufficiently pluralistic and candid that it is exactly different standards that seem to be at work. Thus the pro-choicer's "decent behaviour" is the pro-lifer's "murder"; the Muslim fundamentalist's "fair play" is Salman Rushdie's unconscionable censorship; and the homosexual's "morality" is Jimmy Swaggart's "sodomy."[18]

Professor Nash does not mention such objections, which seem glaring to me. But by now he has regained his smoker's cough and is reevaluating the habit. He concludes by resorting to mostly holist strategies for judging between worldviews: "Honest inquirers say to themselves, *Here is what I know about the inner and outer worlds. Now which touchstone proposition, which world-view, does the best job of making sense out of all this?*"[19]

He allows, "Once one leaves the arena of purely formal reasoning for the world of blood, sweat, and tears, one is required to abandon logical certainty for probability." A nonfoundationalist could nuance and live with either of these statements. But Nash remains enough of a foundationalist that he still wants certainty, even if it can now only be "moral" or "psychological" certainty.[20]

Similarly, the evangelical statesman Kenneth Kantzer commends evangelicalism as the truth because "it fosters a sense of life on a higher plane of human existence than is provided by other alternatives" and offers a "more coherent, fully elaborated world and life view by contrast with any presented by its contemporary rivals."[21] Unless I grossly misread George Lindbeck, William Placher, Stanley Hauerwas, John Howard Yoder, James McClendon, Nancey Murphy and other nonfoundationalist theologians, this is quite similar to the sort of argument they want to make for Christianity. Dr. Kantzer says Christianity "fosters" a higher "sense of life," and I take it that such fostering acknowledges the importance of specifically Christian practices for Christian formation, as do all the nonfoundationalist theologians just cited. James McClendon and Nancey Murphy, like Dr. Kantzer, also explicitly appeal to coherence.[22] And if Dr. Kantzer sees Christianity opening the way to life on "a higher plane of human existence," Stanley Hauerwas, in his unbuttoned theological style, can declare that God has entrusted the church with "the best damn story in the world."[23]

Of course, there are important differences between Kenneth Kantzer's apologetic and the "unapologetic" apologetic of the nonfoundationalists.[24] It is crucial that Dr. Kantzer couch his apologetic in abstracted, highly conceptualized rhetoric that conceals any point of view. The nonfoundationalist theologians also confess Christianity as uniquely and finally true, but they are profoundly aware that this truth, like any truth, must be confessed or professed. That is, it can be lived, believed and put forth only from a specific perspective or point of view. As George Lindbeck writes,

> The issue is not whether there are universal norms of reasonableness, but whether these can be formulated in some neutral, framework-independent language. Increasing awareness of how standards of rationality vary from field to field and age to age makes the discovery of such a language more and more unlikely and the possibility of foundational disciplines doubtful.[25]

Thus Lindbeck and other nonfoundationalists recognize the assertion of Christianity's unique and final truth as an argument far from settled. It is necessarily an assertion open to profound, honest, multifaceted and ongoing disagreement. But, perhaps misled by his own quasi-foundationalist language, Dr. Kantzer retreats to the fortress of certainty built by the likes of Gordon Clark and Cornelius Van Til. Therefore, he sympathetically summarizes Clark's presuppositionalism accordingly:

> The regenerate believer can show a higher degree of internal consistency or coherence of the data on the basis of his Christian theistic supposition than is possible with all alternatives which are necessarily inconsistent at their foundation. In this way Clark presents the unbeliever with a challenge either to speak rationally and in a Christian-like manner or to be silent in irrational unbelief.[26]

How Foundationalists Really Argue

Again, Clark, Nash, Kantzer and other conservative evangelicals seem to work with many nonfoundationalist tools.[27] They admit, for instance, that their base beliefs are presuppositions, not universally shared predispositions. But they persist in presenting their conclusions in foundationalist rhetoric, with the foundationalist attitudes of aperspectivalism and absolute certainty. In fact, I suspect that all the real work in their thinking and writing is done with nonfoundationalist tools.

What happens when they encounter actual, serious disagreement? Of course it takes no one anywhere to simply declare to the Muslim interlocutor, "Your way of life is inconsistent and irrational at its foundation. Get objective and start talking like a Christian or shut up." Instead, Professor Nash or Kantzer would respectfully initiate the painstaking process of examining and comparing Islamic and Christian presuppositions. They might argue from history, philosophy, theology, psychology—or even the experiences of missionary friends. They might attempt to locate the nub of their Muslim interlocutor's objection to Christianity and respond to it. They might try to learn what it is about Islam that fascinates and compels the Muslim, then seek to show that Christianity is more fascinating and compelling on analogous grounds. In the give-and-take, they would no doubt allow their Muslim friend some points, and admit some difficulties with the Christian case. And since Drs. Nash and Kantzer certainly are admirable and compassionate men, concerned to win others to the truth, they would welcome the opportunity to continue the conversation, not insisting that the Muslim either convert on the spot or fall silent.

Let me try to drive home this point by locating the disagreement closer to home, within evangelicalism itself. What happens when two evangelical, confessedly foundationalist parties disagree? Take the issue of gender egalitarianism. You will have no trouble locating evangelical feminists and evangelical antifeminists, each convinced that they are objectively, foundationally right and that the others are objectively, foundationally wrong. Since they are all (at least in their own eyes) evangelical, they spend a great deal of time arguing about what the Bible "really says" about the role of women. Thus the argument comes down to who is reading the Bible correctly. How is this to be decided? Again, in actual practice it is not going to be substanially decided in any foundationalist, objectivist sense. That is, one side is not suddenly going to fall down and say, "Silly us. We had our prejudices, our pet ideas, our traditions and personal histories. Now we've decided to set those aside and be objective. We know that all along you've been beyond traditions and prejudices. And we congratulate you on being right."

What actually happens is exemplified by the description of their own hermeneutics provided by the evangelical antifeminists John Piper and Wayne Grudem. Like professors Nash and Kantzer, Piper and Grudem cannot let go of foundationalist rhetoric, but even in this language their recommendations of hermeneutical practice betray a fundamentally holistic, perspectival method. So they pose for themselves the objectivistically couched question "How do you know that your interpretation of Scripture is not more influenced by your background and culture than by what the authors of Scripture actually intended?" But initially they respond not by insisting on their absolute and incontrovertible objectivity, based on a foundationalist certainty from beyond time and place. Instead, they admit their own fallibility and susceptibility to "the forces of culture, tradition, and personal inclination, as well as the deceitful darts of the devil." They suggest that they probably do not have the final or perfect interpretation of Scripture on women's roles, and they pledge openness to correction. Then they admit that it will take no one anywhere to simply impugn the other side's motives and lack of objectivity. "It is clear from the literature that we all have our suspicions."

Finally they list five "facts" that undergird their confidence in their convictions:
1) We regularly search our motives and seek to empty ourselves of all that would tarnish true perceptions of reality. 2) We pray that God would give us humility, teachability, wisdom, insight, fairness, and honesty. 3) We make every effort to submit our minds to the unbending and unchanging grammatical and historical reality of the Biblical texts in Greek and Hebrew, using the best methods of study available to get as close as possible to the intentions of the Biblical writers. 4) We test our conclusions by the history of exegesis to reveal any chronological snobbery or cultural myopia. 5) We test our conclusions in the real world of contemporary ministry and look for resonance from mature and godly people. In humble confidence that we are handling the Scriptures with care, we lay our vision before the public for all to see and debate in the public forum.[28]

It seems clear that on many counts that what these very conservative evangelicals appeal to runs against the substance of foundationalism. Rather than being an individualistic epistemology, their epistemology develops its conclusions within the tradition of biblical exegesis and submits its conclusions to the public for all to see and debate. It cannot pretend to be beyond history and in fact hopes to be checked and corrected by history. It does not disallow ongoing, difficult, contestable judgment; in fact, it implicitly demands such. There is, for instance, regular prayer and searching of motives. There is also the imperative of testing conclusions in light of the discernment of "mature and godly people." Yet not only may "mature and godly people" differ among themselves, it is an ongoing event of judgment to determine who are and what makes "mature and godly people," to say nothing of the "best methods" of biblical study.

The False Dichotomy: "Objectivism" Versus "Relativism"

What then? Are we all practically, if not rhetorically, rank relativists? It is only the lingering power of the foundationalist schema that makes us believe we must choose between the polar opposites of timeless and placeless objectivity and sheer, arbitrary and solipsistic relativism. As Alasdair MacIntyre has painstakingly shown, and as Piper and Grudem's hermeneutical method demonstrates, traditioned inquiry is constrained by many powerful checks and must always answer to the world around it, however that world is perceived. Foundationalism, modeling its logic on mathematics and striving for an analogous kind of precision and certainty, led philosophers, theologians and others to regard anything less as bogus knowledge. But the goal was set too high, or, to say it better, was of the wrong sort. Allow for different logics and you immediately achieve possibilities other than absolute objectivism and rank relativism.[29]

To put the matter metaphorically, it is as if foundationalists are on the playground of knowledge and insisting that everyone frolic only on the slippery slide. They believe that only there can knowledge be safely found. Foundationalists fear that, freed from the slide alone, some relativistic children may tire of any restrictions and wander into the street. But I think foundationalists need to admit that there is no such thing as safely and absolutely secured knowledge. Knowledge is particular and perspectival, and as such is always contestable. And it is after all not entirely safe living atop the slide, which is why those who do so are obsessed with slippery slopes. Dismounting it, we are at least freed to accurately assess danger in all its varieties. And we are freed to admit that danger is inescapable in a finite (and fallen) world.

In short, if evangelicals can be coaxed down from the slippery slide, they can admit to themselves that they, like other practicing holists, rationally examine any worldview in regard to consistency, coherence and the adequacy of beliefs to experience.[30] But of course those still half-on the foundationalist slide, sneaking a few more puffs of the objectivist weed, will now protest: "How do I choose between competing worldviews?" The question itself betrays residual foundationalist hopes of achieving some Archimedean point beyond time and space from which the pristine individual can detachedly lord over all "reality" and exercise imperial choice—but I will not dwell on that. I instead refer again to Alasdair MacIntyre's work.[31]

MacIntyre insists that all inquiry is tradition-constituted and tradition-dependent. Translation of concepts from one tradition to another is always difficult and sometimes impossible. But we can, and in fact often do, learn the language of another tradition as a "second first language." Then we can sometimes show that a rival tradition has key problems it cannot answer. Our tradition may not have these key problems and is in that regard a stronger tradition. Better yet, it may have resources to solve the other tradition's key problems, and thereby show itself to be the superior tradition.

Of course, the opposite may also happen. In the real world the Christian does not always win—and perhaps most often no one "wins," at least not in the full-scale sense of converting another to one's own faith. But in any event nothing is gained by resorting to the foundationalist mood and rhetoric. In fact, foundationalist rhetoric actually makes conversation and conversion more difficult, since it inclines us toward believing that those who disagree are necessarily benighted or ill-intentioned. And who of us tries to listen harder to someone who regards us as stupid or immoral?

Lest we forget, the Christian confession is that we all see through a glass darkly and it is only on the last day that every knee shall bow and every tongue confess Jesus as Lord. We do better, I think, to come down from the foundationalist slide, recover an eschatologically informed epistemology and place that epistemology firmly in the bed of ecclesiology. It is the community called "church" that teaches people the language and culture that enables them to know Jesus as Lord. And it is the church in the fullness of its life—not primarily its arguments—that draws others to consider the Christian faith.

It is not foundationalism, but in fact the commonly occupied ground of testimony and witness, that allows us to commend and defend the faith to others. So when asked by the non-Christian to provide reasons for the hope within us, we appeal to the (quite contextual) considerations that produced our own judgments. As vividly and persuasively as possible, we show the relevance of our analyses to our interlocutor's experience. And finally we try to point out the desirability of the change we propose (ultimately confession of Jesus Christ as Lord and baptism into his body) in relation to our interlocutor's own (quite contextual) interests and projects. By drawing others into Christian friendship, telling Christian stories and sharing Christian worship, we may alter the way others interpret their experience and introduce a new set of desires into their desires.[32]

Foundationalism and Liberalism

Such, at least, are Christian evangelism, mission and apologetics as I understand them.[33] It is of course altogether possible, according to the terms of my own argument, that with all this and more I will fail to coax any conservative evangelicals down from the slippery slide of foundationalism. But I have one more appeal.

I have learned, primarily from my postliberal brothers and sisters, that foundationalism and liberalism are of a single species. Now I do not mean liberalism in the unfortunately shallow political sense in which it is used in the United States. "Indeed," as George Parkin Grant writes, "what is meant in the U. S. by 'conservative' is generally a species of modern 'liberal.' 'Conservatives' want to hold onto consequences of the earlier tradition of our liberalism which more modern 'liberals' are willing to scrap in the interest of the new and the progressive."[34]

That earlier and deeper liberalism, a liberalism that too easily engulfs us all, is the liberalism of Kant, Locke, Rousseau, Mill and other beacons of the Enlightenment. This is the liberalism that told us we must escape the particularities of history and tradition, substitute state neutrality for the pursuit of any substantive common good, and allow individuals in "public" to choose autonomously, answering only to the principles of a supposedly universal and innate reason.[35] As MacIntyre writes, "It is of the first importance to remember that the project of founding a form of social order in which individuals could emancipate themselves from the contingency and particularity of tradition . . . was and is not only, *and not principally*, a project of philosophers. It was and is the project of modern liberal, individualist society."[36]

In short, it is primarily the liberal project that has privatized faith, obsessed us with the nation-state and led us to neglect the church, and made us defer speaking about the God of Israel and Jesus Christ as our firm foundation until we have first proven ourselves in the supposedly more basic terms of foundationalist, universal reason. I have argued that in the pluralized, postmodern world in which we now live, few if any careful thinkers actually rely on foundationalist reasoning. I am now arguing that it is also time to leave foundationalist rhetoric because it is, in the beginning and the end, liberal rhetoric.[37]

If we quit foundationalist rhetoric we can claim the specifics of the Christian tradition and forthrightly speak the name of Christ in any public forum. We can admit that our argument is contestable, as are the arguments of Marxists, Hindus, free-market capitalists and every other party, then speak unapologetically as Christians.

If we quit foundationalist rhetoric we can more easily perceive and draw attention to liberalism itself as a tradition. Otherwise liberalism is free to hegemonically normalize all it encounters while pretending it has no norms. If I may be so bold as to paraphrase Stanley Fish, foundationalist liberals create a situation in which they can say, "We're for fairness and you're for biased judgment; we're for merit and you're for special interests; we're for objectivity and you're playing politics; we want religion everyone can affirm and you want the Jewish tribal faith of Christianity."[38] Admitting foundationalism for what it is—part and parcel of a particular tradition— we are free to challenge head-on objectivity and other liberal prejudices.

Finally, and most important, if we quit foundationalist rhetoric we can leave off the inevitably violent ways of liberalism and live true to Christ's nonviolent, nonhegemonic persuasion.[39] The God revealed in Jesus Christ is the God who created a free world, and when that free world wrecked itself, he entered into the suffering, confusion and ambiguity of that world to woo it back. True to the character and ways of such a God, Jesus "has always admitted that if we entrust our life to him and his cause, we will never be proven right until beyond the end of this story and cannot count on being positively reinforced along all of the way."[40] We are not liberals who have come to tell people what they always already really knew. We are evangelicals. We confess that Israel and the church are not characters in a greater story called "the world," but instead that the world is a character in God's story, a character that does not even know its true name apart from Israel and the church. We are not liberals come to make the gospel intelligible to the world, but are evangelicals come to help the world see why it cannot be intelligible without the gospel.[41]

Nonfoundationalist *Because* Evangelical

In short, I am saying that we should be nonfoundationalists exactly because we are evangelicals. And, as John Howard Yoder writes,

For a practice to qualify as "evangelical" . . . means first of all that it communicates *news*. It says something particular that would not be known and could not be believed were it not said. Second, it must mean functionally that this "news" is attested as *good; as shalom*. It must be public, not esoteric, but the way for it to be public is not an a priori logical move that subtracts the particular. It is an a posteriori political practice that tells the world something it did not know and could not believe before. It tells the world what is the world's own calling and destiny, not by announcing either a utopian or a realistic goal to be imposed on the whole society, but by pioneering a paradigmatic demonstration of both the power and the practices that define the shape of restored humanity. The confessing people of God is the new world on its way. . . . [And] the credibility of that which is both "good" and "news" consists precisely in its vulnerability, its refusability.[42]

Just so, I think. And so might evangelicals move from decontextualized propositions to traditioned, storied truths; from absolute certainty to humble confidence; from mathematical purity to the rich if less predictable world of relational trust; from detached objectivist epistemology to engaged participative epistemology; from control of the data to respect of the other in all its created variety; from individualist knowing to communal knowing; and from once-for-all rational justification to the ongoing pilgrimage of testimony.[43]

6

THE ALLEGED INCORRIGIBILITY OF POSTLIBERAL THEOLOGY

Or, What Babe Ruth & George Lindbeck Have in Common

Philip D. Kenneson

I f you have seen *The Babe*, the 1992 film about Babe Ruth that stars John Goodman in the title role, you will likely remember two of its central scenes. The film opens with the seven-year-old Ruth being delivered by his father to St. Mary's Industrial School for Boys, where his future caretakers are informed that his parents can no longer control him. The priests, who quickly get a firsthand taste of Ruth's unruliness, list the young Ruth on the school's register as "incorrigible."

This charge—that Ruth is incapable of being reformed—is repeated later in the film during an argument Ruth has with his wife, Helen, on the team train. Helen admits that she used to wonder why Ruth's parents abandoned him, but that now she understands all too clearly. When she hurls the charge of "incorrigibility" at Ruth, it seems that all his tragic past passes before his eyes. The result? Ruth flies into a rage and begins overturning tables and whatever else is at hand. By this time in the film one has seen enough evidence of Ruth's unruly behavior to know that the charge of incorrigibility is not without basis, though most viewers will also wonder to what degree this was a self-fulfilling prophecy.

One might argue that postliberal theology is still in its childhood. And those of you who have been following its career since its birth are likely to be aware that it too has been orphaned by some critics for its alleged incorrigibility. Such charges have often been leveled against the proposals of George Lindbeck, who in many ways remains the most articulate advocate of postliberal theology. To my knowledge, no one has yet charged that Lindbeck is *himself* incorrigible; nevertheless, plenty of people believe that his view of the Christian faith and theology ought to be abandoned for just this reason. Indeed, those who make this charge rarely stop the accusations there. Postliberalism's view of the Christian faith is downright dangerous, we are told, because its incorrigibility, its exemption from "external" critique and correction, leads to such vices as sectarianism, fideism, relativism, tribalism, obscurantism and religious totalitarianism. In what follows I will examine both the basis for this charge and the presuppositions that underwrite the charge, as well as question the latter's adequacy. Along the way I offer the outlines of a constructive proposal for conceptualizing critique and change within a postliberal framework. It is my hope that evangelicals might find such a proposal consonant with many of their own convictions and sympathies.[1]

An Overview of Postliberal Theology
Before examining the charge and its underlying assumptions, let me sketch enough of the pertinent tenets of postliberal theology to make plain the logic of such a charge.

First, postliberalism suggests that the Christian faith is best understood as a cultural-linguistic system. As such, the Christian faith provides an idiom for "construing reality, expressing experience, and ordering life."[2] By viewing the Christian faith as an idiom, "a comprehensive scheme or story used to structure all dimensions of existence," postliberalism insists that Christianity is not *primarily* either a set of propositions to be believed or a set of inner experiences to be expressed. Rather, the Christian faith is viewed as "the medium in which one moves, a set of skills that one employs in living one's life."[3] One of the most important implications of viewing Christianity through this model is that it suggests that becoming a Christian is more like learning a language than it is assenting to a set of propositions or having some kind of religious experience.

Second, postliberalism insists that at the heart of this cultural-linguistic system are the canonical texts of Scripture. As Lindbeck writes: "For those who are steeped in them, no world is more real than the ones they create. A scriptural world is thus able to absorb the universe. It supplies the interpretive framework within which believers seek to live their lives and understand reality."[4] Postliberalism does not encourage believers to "find their stories in the Bible, but rather that they make the story of the Bible *their* story. . . . Intratextual theology redescribes reality within the scriptural framework rather than translating Scripture into extrascriptural categories. It is the text, so to speak, which absorbs the world, rather than the world the text."[5]

Third, if postliberals see the Christian faith as a cultural-linguistic system, they see Christian doctrine *primarily* as the "grammar" governing communities of practice. As such, doctrine functions as second-order language which governs, among other things, the church's first-order language (such as its language in worship). So, for example, the doctrine of the Trinity is first of all a guide to the worshiping community about how to address the God it worships. By suggesting that doctrine serves a primarily regulative function as the grammar of the Christian community, postliberals helpfully remind us of the crucial but subordinate role that doctrine plays in communities of faith. Just as grammar books do not themselves create communities of language users, so church doctrines do not create communities of faith. Anyone who has tried to learn a foreign language knows that the best way to learn one is to be immersed in a community of competent language users. When that is not possible, we do what we believe to be the next best thing: we attempt to acquire the language by learning its constitutive parts, including its formal grammar.

The parallel is important. The best way to "learn" the Christian faith is to become immersed within a community of competent practitioners who have themselves internalized the grammar of the faith, even if they can articulate little formal doctrine. If that is not possible, then one might do what is arguably the next best thing: study Christian doctrine or Christian "grammar," if you will, to get an idea of how Christian discourse and practice are connected.

The Charges and Their Basis

Perhaps this very brief sketch is enough to suggest where the charge of incorrigibility gets its foothold. Some of the most powerful insights of the postliberal scheme stem from its suggestion that we should think of religions as languages and doctrine as their grammars. Yet it is precisely at this point that postliberalism's critics become worried, if not agitated. And the reason is not hard to see.

Once you adopt language and grammar as master tropes, how do you conceptualize critique? Normally, we don't think it appropriate to criticize an entire language by comparing it to another. For example, most of us wouldn't presume to criticize French because it doesn't carve up the world the way German does; they're simply different languages. In a similar way, grammars appear to be incorrigible from anything outside the system. One wouldn't try to correct French grammar by trying to make it conform to German grammar; they're simply different grammars whose intelligibility is internal to their respective systems.

This is precisely what bothers the critics of postliberalism. So-called religious ways of construing the world are placed alongside other ways of construing it, such as the "scientific." The implication, of course, seems to be that these are just *different* ways of looking at the world, with no way to adjudicate disagreements between them. The result, according to the critics, is that each view becomes self-enclosed and self-justifying, with no possibility of critique from anything outside them. The

Christian faith becomes, in a word, "incorrigible." The critics believe not only that such a move is devastating but also that it leads to other egregious excesses. Listen to a few representative salvos from two of postliberalism's critics. Mark Corner writes:

> By emphasizing the cultural-linguistic approach to religious statements to a point where he can say: "The question is: 'What *is* Christianity?' and not 'Is Christianity *true?*'," Lindbeck effectively rules out of court the sort of critique of the Christian religion which seeks to expose the inadequacy of its truth claims.[6]
>
> [Lindbeck] appears to provide a recipe for the churches to lock themselves into an Orthodox time warp, forever immersed in a totalitarianism of tradition.[7]

James Gustafson writes:

> The incommensurability of scientific and religious language means that the same person and communities will have two very different ways of construing the reality of life in the world side by side. From this perspective of the division of languages one has no bearing upon the other. Theology and the morality of the Christian community necessarily become what I have called sectarian. . . . It is difficult to see how one can make any critique of the tradition, internal or external. . . . Doctrine becomes ideology. It isolates theology from any correction by other modes of construing reality.[8]

And finally, with reference to postliberalism's emphasis on narrative and intratextuality, Gustafson writes:

> If [theology] simply adopts a text, even the Bible, without addressing what justifies the text as worthy of interpretation, the interpretation is open to sectarianism. Hermeneutics can become a method for purely descriptive theology, making a fideism. The Bible can become the *only* text for the life of the Church, and the question of its authority and limits of authority for theology can be bypassed. . . . My point again is this: the acceptance of a text, even the Bible, as that which is to be interpreted, can constrict the task of theology so that it avoids critical interaction with other "texts," that is, other ways of interpreting how things really and ultimately are. . . . Fidelity to the narratives becomes virtually self-justifying in the sectarian temptation and both theology and ethics become incorrigible by anything outside of the community itself.[9]

These are obviously serious charges that need to be examined closely. Most evangelicals would want to proceed cautiously in their courtship of postliberalism if they became convinced that these charges were true. Indeed, if the critics are right, if postliberalism really does fail to "provide a critical religious vision of reality that can aggressively interact with other ways of construing the world,"[10] then I suspect many evangelicals would want to call the whole thing off.

Before examining the presuppositions that underwrite the charge of incorrigibility, let me suggest that the charge contains within it two separate and seemingly quite different accusations. First, there is the charge that postliberal theology construes the Christian faith in a way that insulates it from *any* external criticism.

We might call this kind of incorrigibility the impulse to isolationism. Here the Christian faith is incorrigible because it is *sealed off* from other forms of discourse. Second, there is the charge that postliberal theology so privileges the Christian narrative that all other narratives and explanatory schemes are subordinated to it. We might call this kind of incorrigibility the impulse to imperialism.[11] Here the Christian faith is incorrigible because its story is considered *superior* to other narratives. Although these two charges are clearly related, it may be helpful to distinguish them as we proceed to examine the presuppositions underlying them.

Incorrigibility Due to Isolationism
Critics charge that cultural-linguistic communities or interpretive communities appear to be isolated from each other in hermetically sealed spheres, incapable of talking to each other or of learning from anything outside the scope of their own assumptions. As a result, they appear inherently conservative and resistant to change. In fact, one might think that such communities are so isolated (at least conceptually, if not in actuality) that they would be incapable both of attending to criticism and of enacting change.[12]

Let's examine several of the presuppositions that underlie this charge. The first is that the modern fragmentation of life into autonomous spheres—such as the religious, moral, political, economic, medical—each with its own discourse and inner logic, is normative. When the Christian faith presumes to speak about something that ostensibly belongs to another sphere, it must take into account that sphere's discourse and practice. To refuse to do so is to lapse into sectarianism by insulating the Christian faith from "legitimate" critiques that those disciplines might render. Listen to the following powerful argument by Gustafson:

> The sociological assumption [which underwrites postliberal theology and ethics] . . . breaks on the rocks of the fact that Christians do (and ought to) participate in their professions, their political communities and other aspects of the social order. Their moral lives are not confined to some Christian community; they take place where choices have to be made that are not only moral but economic, political, medical and so forth. If the test of the morality of Christians becomes its conformity to some version of the imitation of Christ, or some fidelity to the meaning of the Biblical narratives, either Christians are put into positions of intense inner conflict or they must withdraw from participation in any structures which would presumably compromise their fidelity to Jesus. . . . Even descriptively the sociological assumption of this is false. Christians, whether they choose to or not, are members of, and make choices in, other social communities.[13]

This leads us to the second presupposition: that because most of us live in more than one of these communities, we must reject incommensurability as a possibility or consign ourselves to living lives of frustration as we move in and out of disparate discourses and practices that seem to share no common frame of reference. Faced with such a choice, the critics of postliberalism insist that there simply *must* be some

reasonable way to adjudicate these competing claims on our lives. Listen to Gustafson again:

> Sectarians might admit that the Christian community does not live in a cultural
> ghetto, but go on to propose that there are double, triple, or quadruple truths
> which are incommensurable with each other. Christians live in separable com-
> munities each with its own language. This seems to me to create problems of
> moral and intellectual integrity for Christians; they would have to interpret and
> explain the same events in different ways as they left the doors of the Church
> and went home to read the newspapers, the scientific journals, or watch televi-
> sion.[14]

A brief analysis of these two presuppositions should begin with an admission: Gustafson is correct to point out the dangers of "community" language here. There
certainly are ways in which the language of community can be used which too easily
give the impression that the boundaries separating communities are clear and fixed.
Nevertheless, I continue to believe that Gustafson is overly optimistic about com-
mensurability. Indeed, I can see no reason why the Christian community is in worse
shape than anyone else on this score. If narratives and their concomitant practices,
along with our loyalty to them, define the contours of communities, then Gustafson
is right: we all likely find ourselves in multiple communities. But surely Christians
are not the only ones who find themselves trying to negotiate their participation in
competing narratives and practices (and therefore communities). Take, for example,
the issue of human action and responsibility. How should we conceive the relationship between the narratives that shape our legal system and those that are being
told more frequently in scientific journals? Do we have any idea what it would be
like to live in a society where people were no longer considered responsible for their
actions? Do we have the nerve to *desire* such a society if "science" tells us this is the
way things *really* are?

   The problem is that Gustafson seems to beg the question of what the relationship
between these multiple commitments and narratives ought to be. He simply assumes, as a child of modernity, that these autonomous spheres ought to remain
autonomous, except that the Christian community ought to be open to correction
from other disciplines when it deals with matters that are the province of one of
these other autonomous spheres. Thus, if Christian discourse is cut off from other
discourses it is not completely the fault of Christians seeking to insulate their discourse from criticism, for there is much about modernity itself that encourages this
kind of isolation. Moreover, Gustafson's talk of correction seems to assume that
competing discourses share enough in common for "correction" to take place. But
it is not at all clear that such commonalities are always in place. Yet perhaps this
is not the kind of correction Gustafson has in mind. Perhaps what he really wants
is for Christian discourse to be corrected by ostensibly more authoritative discourses. To see this more clearly, one need only ask Gustafson whether he is willing
for politics, economics, medicine and morality to be "corrected" by Christian theol-

ogy, or whether this corrective process is only a one-way street. (But more of this later.)

Third, and finally, the charge of incorrigibility as isolationism assumes that the language of "internal" and "external" is not problematic. Indeed, at times the critics write as if the distinction between internal and external were almost empirical. Over and over again they insist that the Christian faith must remain open to "external" criticism. But the language of external and internal is quite slippery. As Stanley Fish has helpfully pointed out, the danger is in thinking that "the distinction between outside and inside is empirical and absolute, whereas in fact it is an interpretive distinction between realms that are interdependent rather than discrete."[15] There is always the possibility that what is external will become internal, but when it does, it will always be the result of a redrawing of the lines from the inside.

For example, when the early Jewish followers of Jesus were confronted with the mission to the Gentiles, they were willing to redraw the boundaries at least partly because they were capable of conceptualizing this change *from the inside*. Thus, when the Council of Jerusalem met, as recorded in Acts 15, it dealt with the Gentile question as if it were the scribe to whom Jesus alludes: the Council brings out of its treasure what is old and what is new (Mt 13:52). The inclusion of the Gentiles is obviously new, but continuity with the old is maintained both by arguing for this change on the basis of Scripture (Amos 9:11-12) and by insisting that the Gentiles respect those prohibitions that were enjoined even of non-Israelite strangers (cf. Lev 17:8-9, 12, 14-15; 18:16-18).[16] This seems to confirm Fish's point that

> when the community is persuaded (by arguments that rely on assumptions not at the moment being challenged) that its project requires the taking into account of what had hitherto been considered beside the point or essential only to someone else's point—the boundaries of outside/inside will have been redrawn, and redrawn from the inside.[17]

It seems to me that much of the use of the Old Testament in the New could be profitably understood in such terms.

A Response: Change in the Christian Community

What critics of postliberalism seem to overlook is that the Christian faith, like all frameworks, includes a mechanism for responding to criticism and making judgments about change. So a full-fledged cultural-linguistic model is not as monolithic and self-confirming as its critics suppose; rather, it is an instrument for organizing experience in a way that does not preclude but makes intelligible its own transformation. This is especially true, it seems to me, when part of the grammar of the Christian faith *itself* is that the church is always being reformed (*ecclesia semper reformanda*). It is for these reasons that I think Fish is right when he insists that an interpretive community "is an engine of change because its assumptions are not a mechanism for shutting out the world [as the critics of postliberalism seem to assume] but for organizing it, for seeing phenomena as already related to the interests and goals that make the community what it is."[18]

Said another way, some critics of postliberalism seem to confuse the impetus for change with the substantive reasons given for making a change. The issue isn't whether the Christian community is open to critique and change so much as it is how it conceptualizes that change. Consider a basketball analogy. Several years ago college basketball instituted a three-point line. The *impetus* for making this change was the desire to make the game more exciting, especially for television audiences. But if this had been the only *reason* given, then something would have been wrong. It would have been viewed by many as altering the game from the outside. But this basketball change could be and was discussed on basketball terms (rather than on television rating terms). For example, in the past the rules have favored centers, and so the game has been dominated by the inside play of taller players. But the three-point line was promoted on terms of bringing the guards back into play. In other words, what was being initiated was not a new game but a new style of playing the same game. This is one kind of change that attempts to change with integrity, with some sense of what it is about. This way of conceptualizing change seems completely consistent with the proposals of Lindbeck and other postliberals.

But the kind of critique and subsequent change that Gustafson and other critics of postliberalism seem to have in mind is of a quite different sort. If you will pardon another sports analogy, what the critics of postliberalism seem to have in mind is more like the institution of the designated hitter in baseball. Here you have a change that came about for many of the same reasons that the three-point line was instituted: the desire for more offense, which sells better to national television audiences. But what happened in baseball seems to have been of a different order. By instituting the designated hitter, the grammar, if you will, of what it meant to be a baseball player in the American League was significantly altered. No longer did each player in the starting lineup need to be competent at both offense and defense. Now each team was allowed two specialists: the pitcher who specializes in defense, and the designated hitter who specializes in offense.

Now on the surface, both basketball and baseball have "changed" in the past few years. Both have responded to "outside" pressure, and both have changed in ways that have affected the manner in which the games are played. Yet I am suggesting that despite these similarities, these two changes are of a different order, because one change seems capable of being conceptualized internally while the other does not. I readily admit that this is a matter of judgment, since the boundaries between internal and external are always contestable. No doubt someone who views a national television audience as integral to the game of baseball could argue that the designated hitter rule can be explained in terms internal to the game. But even so, my point remains the same: most of us think it important that changes be explained primarily in terms internal to the system with which we are operating, regardless of the original impetus for the change.[19]

My reason for belaboring the point is this: Gustafson and other critics of postliberalism imply that there are contradictory and competing cultural voices that the church simply must listen to and be corrected by. If in so doing significant aspects of the Christian tradition must be left behind, so be it. In short, those who charge postliberalism with being incorrigible assume that certain languages or discourses are necessarily privileged; they simply must be attended to on their own terms and adjustments to the Christian faith made accordingly.[20] Gustafson gives the following example of what he has in mind:

> Several years ago I was asked to meet with a denominational group that was writing a statement on "Death and Dying." The first part of the statement was on "Biblical background and basis." I noted that the section ignored a Biblical view that death was caused by the sin of Adam and Eve. I was told that it was not clear from the Bible whether that death was physical, or whether it was spiritual. I cited historic theologians, including Luther, who thought it *was* physical. Then I was told that the whole notion would have to be demythologized in the light of modern knowledge. I suggested that this group had two alternatives: either to say honestly that it no longer believed the tradition or try to demythologize the tradition so the laity could understand why they engage in such work. My point is this: In modern culture few persons with average education any longer *believe* that biological death is caused by the sins of Adam and Eve, including few who write theology or participate in the Church. A persuasive alternative way of explaining why we die exists. Neither theologians nor people in the churches can avoid it. The tradition, on this point, simply has to be revised because Christian theology and Christian churches are informed by the culture of which they are parts.[21]

It seems to me that Gustafson failed to offer a third option: the group could have discussed whether it thought the tradition's view of death was central enough to the grammar of the Christian faith to warrant insisting that Christians recover that insight, despite what they might think about the status of persuasive "alternatives." Indeed, I suspect that it is because both Scripture and tradition are themselves ambiguous on this issue that we find ourselves open to being persuaded by some other "more authoritative" discourse.

But if we take an example of a doctrine that is widely considered to be central to the grammar of the Christian faith, we discover more clearly what couldn't happen. Try to imagine the following: the church becomes convinced by "external" experts that the church has been wrong all these years about Jesus Christ: that he was a human being, like all human beings, but no more, and the church should henceforth stop worshiping him. There just isn't any way to envision how that could happen, any more than one can envision that the rules of basketball could be changed in such a way that we would have twenty people playing at a time, using something resembling a hockey puck, and the point being to see how many people you could knock unconscious. This might be a fine game, and one that you would want to commend, but few people would feel good about calling it basketball.

What the postliberals are saying that is most helpful, I believe, is similar. Doctrine is a kind of grammar that shows you the limits of what you must affirm about the Christian faith in order to feel relatively confident that you are still speaking about the Christian faith and not Islam, New Age or the contemporary self-help movement.

The critics of postliberalism speak as if these sectarians retreat or withdraw to their enclaves, ignoring to their detriment the external world that would force them to correct or adjust their views of the world and God. But this way of pitting external and internal is misleading. The external world never forces itself upon us in this way. Those who have studied the history and philosophy of science know that even in science the physical world never forces itself upon us, demanding that we interpret it in a certain way, in the manner in which Gustafson and others seem to assume. In fact, what Gustafson calls alternative or competing ways of viewing God and the world are not "external" to the church at all; rather, they show up in the church's narrative in all kinds of ways: as interesting, or enriching, or deficient, or misleading, or dangerous ways of knowing about and being in the world. In other words, they are not so much "external" as they are located within the overarching metanarrative that the church tells about God's relationship with the world and God's people. What, after all, could be external to that?

Incorrigibility Due to Imperialism
This brings us to the second aspect of incorrigibility, to which I have already alluded: the impulse to imperialism. Here we have all those who cringe when Lindbeck, Frei and company speak of *absorbing* the universe into the world of the Bible. The image which haunts them is no doubt something akin to those hideous amoebalike creatures that inhabit late-night television and that absorb everything in sight. How can the Christian faith be anything *but* incorrigible if it is absorbing everything in the universe, including its critics?

Here I will be brief, for I wish to examine only one of the presuppositions that underlie this charge: that Christian narratives ought to be made less imperialistic by being subordinated to or embedded within other more fundamental master narratives. To my knowledge no one has stated this presupposition quite so bluntly, but it seems to me to inform much of the criticism of postliberalism (and indeed, much of American life).

My hunch is that everyone employs some form of master narrative, some overarching metanarrative within which other narratives are embedded. In a culture of hyperindividualism such as ours, this will often take the form of a personal narrative; individuals will locate all other narratives with respect to their own. Ironically, even those who suggest that metanarratives are dangerous and thus to be avoided are themselves offering a kind of metanarrative: a metanarrative that attempts to ensure that different and competing narratives remain different and competing narratives. There is, of course, nothing wrong with such a suggestion, but we ought to be honest enough to admit the ways in which it continues to function as a kind of metanarrative.

A Response: What Is Your Metanarrative?

Simply put, the question seems not to be *whether* you will employ a metanarrative to make sense of the world, but which one you will employ. Critics of postliberalism seem to presuppose that there is some more fundamental and determinative narrative which is external to the Christian community and by which the Christian community's imperialistic impulses are to be tempered. But why should Christians grant certain "external" narratives a privileged position, when in fact such narratives are internal to a quite different way of viewing and living in the world? Doesn't this amount to subordinating the church's narrative to some more fundamental narrative, such as that of liberal democracy? It is interesting that Gustafson himself recognizes this danger. He writes:

> The continuing issues are those of authority. . . [such as] what weight the evidences and theories of the sciences are to carry in the reformulation of theological ideas. At what point are there beliefs and concepts the cost of whose abandonment would be the loss of identity and integrity of Christian theology itself? What degree of reformulation runs the risk of tipping the balance from a presumption in *favor* of the Christian tradition to a presumption *against* it?[22]

One of the marks of modernity is that it has tipped this balance. As heirs of this tradition, we are encouraged to believe that Christian discourse and practice are best understood and explained by recourse to other more fundamental discourses and practices, such as those of the social sciences. But many Christians are beginning to question the wisdom of this, and perhaps evangelicals, who have a penchant for "integration," should listen carefully to these cautionary voices. For example, John Milbank has mounted an impressive critique against the notion that Christian theology must adjust itself to the knowledge offered to us by the social sciences. To subordinate the narratives and practices that shape the Christian faith to a different set of narratives and practices thought to offer more secure knowledge amounts to nothing less than a denial of the central claims that Christian theology has always made. Milbank writes:

> A gigantic claim to be able to read, criticize, say what is going on in other human societies, is absolutely integral to the Christian Church, which itself claims to exhibit the exemplary form of human community. For theology to surrender this claim, to allow that other discourses—"the social sciences"—carry out yet more fundamental readings, would therefore amount to a denial of theological truth. The *logic* of Christianity involves the claim that the "interruption" of history by Christ and his bride, the Church, is the most fundamental of events, interpreting all other events. And it is *most especially* a social event, able to interpret other social formations, because it compares them with its own new social practice.[23]

Or as he says in a different context:

Theology purports to give an ultimate narrative, to provide some ultimate depth of description, because the situation of oneself within such a continuing narrative is what it means to belong to the Church, to be a Christian. However, the claim is made by faith, not a reason which seeks foundations.[24]

The Christian community is a community of faith. This does not, however, mean that the Christian community's claims are made apart from the giving of reasons. Lindbeck helpfully suggests that the reasonableness of Christianity (like any religion) "is largely a function of its assimilative powers, of its ability to provide an intelligible interpretation in its own terms of the varied situations and realities adherents encounter."[25]

But even if the Christian faith is reasonable in this sense, it hardly warrants granting Christian discourse and practice a privileged position. On what grounds could we possibly grant it the kind of imperialistic status that the postliberals seem to claim for it? Or asked another way, why should this narrative be the master narrative? Rodney Clapp has already suggested why there is no satisfactory answer to this question if we are looking for the kind of certainty that foundationalist epistemologies would encourage us to seek. Even so, this does not mean that there are no reasons for thinking one narrative "better" than another. Lindbeck argues that it is impossible to decide between major alternative interpretations or traditions on the basis of reason alone, though it is possible to subject theological proposals to "rational testing procedures not wholly unlike those which apply to general scientific theories or paradigms (for which, unlike hypotheses, there are no crucial experiments)."[26] This means that the Christian faith, like other faiths, is not susceptible to "decisive disproof." Our selecting one over another has less to do with proving or disproving certain details of a tradition and more to do with the ability of those traditions to offer a comprehensive and intelligible framework. This is why John Milbank has suggested that if one can speak of the superiority of the Christian faith to other ways of construing and living within the world, it will hinge on the Christian faith's ability to, if you will, "out-narrate" the competition.[27]

This suggests that one way of viewing the challenge that postliberalism presents to American theology is to see it in terms of two competing metanarratives. Liberal democracy is, among other things, a set of institutions and practices that make sense only within a narrative framework. For example, part of this story is that human life can be divided into separate spheres that operate according to their own inner logic and principles. So we have economics, politics, religion, law, medicine, education, etc. The only overarching principles that apply across the board to all these areas are the mythic elements of this story: that people should be allowed to pursue their own understanding of happiness unimpeded unless that pursuit brings about demonstrable harm to other people and their similar pursuit. Within this liberal democratic epic, "religion" is that compartment of human life which is most private. Because human beings cannot agree about issues in this arena (or even agree about criteria for judging disagreements), human beings are left to choose their religious preferences with as little interference from the nation-state as possible. This neutrality with regard to religion is one of the touchstones of this epic. However, by embedding "religion" within this larger narrative, liberal democracy, it turns out, is anything but neutral toward religion. Indeed, what it will least tolerate is real difference—that is, not merely a difference about which principles should govern any given compartment, but about the whole liberal democratic epic.

This seems to be part of what is so irritating about those who are routinely labeled sectarians: they simply refuse to play by the liberal democratic rules. These Christians believe that all other narratives are best understood as subordinate to and embedded within the narrative of God's ongoing relationship with the world through Israel, Jesus of Nazareth and the church. But this violates the spirit of the liberal democratic epic, which insists that multiple stories are always better and that no single story should be taken too seriously. Indeed, those who take any one story too seriously are considered to be at best close-minded and narrow and at worst fanatics and sectarians. The exception to this rule about not taking any one story too seriously, of course, are those who take very seriously the liberal democratic story that no story should be taken too seriously. But instead of considering themselves fanatics or sectarians for elevating this epic to the status of master narrative, they flatter themselves by considering themselves open-minded. Why are Christians so willing to let the metanarrative of liberal democracy provide the overarching framework for all other narratives, including the Christian narrative?

But doesn't replacing the metanarrative of liberal democracy with some form of the Christian narrative still amount to a dangerous form of imperialism, even if we think such imperialism justified? Perhaps, but before we could decide, we would need to find an example of a nonimperialistic metanarrative that would give the charge of imperialism intelligibility. Frankly, I'm not sure I know where to look. But as Richard Middleton and Brian Walsh have argued, there are substantive reasons for thinking that the Christian metanarrative has internal resources that may aid it in resisting those forms of ideological and totalizing discourse that are most dangerous.[28] I leave you to explore and evaluate their arguments.

Several years ago, Jeffrey Stout defined "postmodern" or "postliberal" theology as "the quest, initiated in recent years by the most interesting American followers of Karl Barth, to get beyond all forms of modernism in theology; either a *cul de sac* or the harbinger of a new theological age (too soon to tell)."[29]

As you can probably tell, I'm hopeful that it is the latter. But if evangelicals are to embrace postliberalism, they will need to be willing to think hard about their understandings of truth, apologetics, conversion, Scripture and the church. It is odd if not ironic that contemporary evangelical views of each of these seem closer to the liberal view than to the postliberal one.

I'm pleased that many of these issues are addressed within this volume. Rigorous conversations need to take place. My modest aim has been to keep these necessary conversations from being prematurely foreclosed by those who would hastily dismiss postliberalism for its alleged incorrigibility. There may be serious problems with postliberalism, but I do not think that they lie in this direction.

Many people in the United States have become disillusioned with theology in the same way Americans became disillusioned with baseball after the Black Sox scandal of 1919. Those of you who know history know that one man almost single-handedly rescued baseball from oblivion. Some people, including myself, believe that postliberal theology has extraordinary promise, particularly for evangelicals who insist that Scripture remain central to any theological framework. It is of course too early to tell what the future of postliberal theology will be in this country, but perhaps we will see the day in which postliberalism's contribution to the revitalization of American evangelical theology is regarded by many to be as significant as the Babe's redemption of our great American pastime.[30]

7
RELATIVISM, FIDEISM
& THE PROMISE
OF POSTLIBERALISM

David K. Clark

Since the 1962 publication of Thomas Kuhn's ambiguous but provocative *Structures of Scientific Revolutions*,[1] Western academics have increasingly adopted a critical stance toward the received epistemological tradition even in the sciences. At one time knowledge, both in the human sciences and the natural sciences, was deemed quite objective. Then scholars gradually limited objective knowledge to the natural sciences, coming to view the humanities (including theology, philosophy and history) and the soft sciences as socially conditioned. Today this historicism has permeated even the hard sciences. A few academics even seem willing to embrace "the absolute *equivalence* . . . of all possible world-pictures."[2]

In this context, we want to explore the encounter of evangelicals with narrativism and postliberalism. As part of the dialogue between these two perspectives, we should examine whether or not postliberalism succumbs to relativism and gets mired in a strong form of fideism.[3]

What Postliberalism Emphasizes

Postliberalism is one mode of narrative theology. Narrative theology is a network of views that give "categorical preference for story over explanation as a vehicle of understanding."[4] Narrativists in theology will value theology rooted more directly in the concrete biblical story and the specifics of Christian history over against philosophized theology that traffics in abstract conceptions. Despite general agreement on the value of concrete narrative, however, narrativists use *narrative* in quite varied ways. Sorting them out has become, says one writer, a cottage industry.[5]

The varieties of narrative approaches are not easy to catalog.[6] But it is common to distinguish two poles of narrative theology. Converging toward one pole are those who stress that Christian thought must engage the categories of the modern world. They are ready to interpret the Christian metanarrative by using the critical techniques long favored by liberals. Fearing isolation in the academy, they want theology to draw connections with the rest of what the modern world accepts as true. These "impure" narrativists like Paul Ricoeur, David Tracy and Sallie McFague are "revisionist, hermeneutical, Gadamerian-inspired correlationists." Gathering at the other pole are those from Yale, who stress the uniqueness of Christian life and thought in contrast to the categories of modernism. They want to elucidate the Christian metanarrative on its own terms. Fearing distortion at the hands of modernism, they want theology to declare its independence from Enlightenment-inspired modernist thinking. These "pure" narrativists like Hans Frei (the movement's elder statesman), George Lindbeck (who coined the word *postliberal*), Stanley Hauerwas, David Kelsey, Ronald Thiemann and William Placher are "antifoundational, cultural-linguistic, Wittgensteinian-inspired descriptivists."[7] If the ethos of the impurists is Tillichian, the purists are Barthian in spirit.

Postliberalism is most closely associated with the purist pole of narrativism. Lindbeck's *The Nature of Doctrine* represents a prominent expression.[8] This book develops a view of theology and doctrine to explain certain features of ecumenical experience. Lindbeck proposes that *doctrines* are second-order normative statements *about* the beliefs and behaviors of a religious community. They are not themselves first-order statements of theological content. Two other viewpoints—the *propositional-cognitivist* (doctrines describe external spiritual realities) and the *experiential-expressivist* (doctrines describe inward spiritual experiences)—give doctrines a first-order describing function. But Lindbeck suggests that doctrines have primarily a second-order function. The proper role of doctrines is to regulate the first-order statements much as rules of grammar regulate our use of language without adding any specific cognitive content to our speech.

A major advantage of this view of doctrine is its ability to make sense of ecumenical discussions. How can two groups (say, Lutherans and Catholics) begin by saying that they disagree, then come to agreement through ecumenical dialogue, and yet claim that doctrine does not evolve? The key is that obedience to an unchanging doctrinal rule means different things in different circumstances; the same general doctrinal rule may require different first-order formulations in different situations. If a theological expression is superseded, what has changed is not the doctrinal rule but the circumstances. Thus earlier expressions are permanently valid for their time, but new expressions are appropriate for new times.[9]

What Evangelicals Can Learn from Postliberalism

Postliberalism does offer promise for dialogue with evangelical thinking. Let me mention three areas. The first is the autonomy of Christian theology. Postliberalism focuses on the internal logic of the Christian worldview—this is intratextuality. It emphasizes that Christian theology is right to live up to its own rules.[10] In other words, theology belongs to the church, not to the academy with its own principles and values. Academic freedom, for example, is a value of the academic guild that emerges from the individualism and anticlericalism of the Enlightenment period. In theology, however, it is not appropriate to give this value the unquestioned status that it enjoys in the secular academy.

Postliberalism is right to throw off the hegemony of Enlightenment and modernist thinking, which are committed to classical foundationalism in epistemology and to liberal experiential-expressivism in theology. On the one hand, classical foundationalism is self-referentially incoherent. On the other, the Schleiermachian mode of theology is flawed at several levels. It posits as the common core of all religions a sui generis religious experience. It suggests that different religions simply interpret this common experience in conformity with their different conceptual traditions. The step from this view of religious experience to a pluralistic assessment of religions is a short one. Evangelicals can rightly join postliberalism in adopting a skeptical stance toward the experiential-expressive view of theology—too many evangelicals have yet to digest the news that modernist epistemology is defunct.

A second advantage is theocentricity. In disowning Roman Catholicism, the Reformers rightly repudiated an anthropocentric soteriology in which salvation depends partly on human merit. Traditional Calvinism uses the notion of God's sovereignty to safeguard the theocentricity of theology from encroachment by anthropocentrism. To give God absolute prominence, Calvinism highlights sovereignty and then defines it in a compatibilist fashion.[11] Some are troubled, however, because in protecting the ultimacy of God for theology in this way, Calvinism appears to make God directly responsible even for evil events.[12]

A theologian who highlights the theocentricity of Christian theology over against the anthropocentricity of liberalism and some forms of Arminianism is Karl Barth. In my view, Barth's theocentric emphasis preserves the centrality of God for Christian thinking. Yet Barth does not use a compatibilism of divine action and human action as his strategy for preserving God's freedom. Barth shows, in other words, that even if we do not speak of God's controlling our actions in a compatibilist way, we can still affirm with the Reformers the centrality, ultimacy and supremacy of God for Christian theology and living.[13] Similarly, the spirit of postliberalism rightly seeks to bring every thought captive to Christ (2 Cor 10:5). The postliberal way to say this is to affirm that Christians should fit the world into the biblical narrative rather than the other way around.[14] Evangelicals can entirely agree with the idea that the biblical narrative plays a critical and central role in shaping a Christian worldview.[15]

A third benefit of narrativism is that it highlights the complex ways in which Christians formulate and use theology. Postliberalism rightly emphasizes that we can express theology in many ways. These ways include both historical narrative and didactic/propositional discussion. Some scholars, overly influenced by the neo-orthodox, overstate their *distaste* for propositions, as if the word has a foul odor to it. Yet this gratuitous denigrating of propositions is an overcorrection that is essentially on the right track: it overreacts against an evangelical subculture that thinks *theology* means only discursive argument and abstract, philosophical discussion while *biblical theology* refers primarily to Paul's epistles. How much evangelical preaching uses Pauline texts, and how much addresses the Old Testament and the Gospels?

The point of theology, of course, is spiritual life, not propositions. This is obvious, but not always practiced. Christians could benefit from retrieving the ancient Augustinian sense that theology is wisdom *(sapientia)*, not first and foremost academic knowledge *(scientia)*.[16] Getting this right preserves a balanced relation between theological statements and faith. Clearly, the point of theology is spiritual life—one's very life with God—not just talk about that life. Of course, theological reflection will require cognitively meaningful propositions.[17] But evangelicals should agree that theology, whether in narrative or propositional genre, is important because it enables us to find the right relation to God, to obey his will and to be conformed to the image of his Son.[18]

Conceptual Relativism and Incommensurability

The benefits that could accrue to evangelical theology from dialogue with postliberalism are significant. Like any theology, evangelical theology must resolve the perennial tension between the *uniqueness* of its thought by comparison to other human modes of thought and the *connection* of its thought to those other forms of thinking. How can Christian thinking be true to itself and yet true also to all human thinking (since, as is often claimed, all truth is God's)? In classical terms, this is a facet of the problem of faith and reason.

Liberal thinking of the experiential-expressivist sort seems to evangelicals to have capitulated to foreign modes of thought. Liberalism's views of God and Scripture, sin and salvation, leave much to be desired. Liberalism is, at root, an anthropocentric perspective. Sensing Barth's wisdom on this point, some evangelicals have embraced the spirit (if not all the details) of his thought.

Yet Barth leaves many evangelicals with a nagging sense of theological angst. They see his thought as too self-contained and subjectivist. They think that in creating a theology that is true to its own principles, Barth succumbed to a strong form of fideism. Many evangelicals, like some others, feel similar apprehensions about postliberalism. They believe that in emphasizing the autonomy of Christian thinking, postliberalism errs as Barth did in overrelativizing the faith. This leads to the commonly posed questions: Does postliberalism entail a form of relativism? Does it sustain itself fideistically? Does it fall prey to the standard objections to relativism?[19]

The form of relativism in view in most criticisms is conceptual relativism. This is not simply the claim that individual propositions are imprisoned by the speaker's time and place. This form of skepticism has a long heritage. More specifically, conceptual relativism makes all propositions relative to larger conceptual schemes, explanatory paradigms or intellectual frameworks. The claim is that *within* these webs of belief, reasoning and warranting are possible. The choice *between* these webs of belief, however, is not rational or objective. (More modest claims that interparadigm choices are less than absolutely certain or not decidable on completely neutral grounds are not at issue here.) Conceptual relativism is the strong claim that rules out rational interparadigm choices.

The notion of incommensurability captures this sense of the independence of conceptual grids. Two incommensurate paradigms are not calibrated on the same system. They have no common denominator, no common scale. They are like IBM and Macintosh back in the good old days before IBMs and Macs could read each other's mail. If two paradigms are incommensurate, then, in Kuhn's words, the "competition between paradigms is not the sort of battle that can be resolved by proofs."[20]

The difficulty with this claim, as with many statements of incommensurability, is that it is ambiguous. In some instances, those who appeal to incommensurability imply that the independence of conceptual grids is total and complete. According to this stricter version of the incommensurability thesis, Kuhn means that rational judgment is entirely useless in judging the relative merits of different paradigms. It seems clear that any Christian theologian who defends incommensurability in this strict form succumbs to a strong version of fideism. A series of weaker versions of the incommensurability thesis, however, claim only that religious debates are not straightforwardly decidable on rational grounds.[21] Forms of incommensurability at the softer end of the continuum do not entail fideism. Part of the difficulty here is that defenders use the same evidence (e.g., the observation that facts are never entirely theory-neutral) to support positions at various points on the continuum from strict to soft incommensurability.

There are good reasons to reject strong forms of conceptual relativism (and the strict incommensurability thesis). The literature raises two standard objections (although other criticisms are possible). The first is Donald Davidson's: the very notion of distinct, internally coherent but mutually incommensurable conceptual schemes is incoherent.[22] If two conceptual schemes are both about the real world, they will have some connection. If they have no connection at all, they could hardly be about the same object.[23]

The second is that relativism is self-referentially incoherent or commits the self-exempting fallacy.[24] Criticizing a position because it is self-defeating is a move known to all beginning students in philosophy. It simply involves turning a position's basic pronouncements back on itself. Suppose someone says something like

   p: Propositions, theories and systems of thought are relative to some historical,
   social or cultural context, and therefore are only true for some persons, not for
   all persons.

We are right to ask whether p itself is true only for the speaker or is true only in relation to the speaker's particular context.

Demonstrating that some person or position really advocates conceptual relativism is no easy task. Conceptual relativism is strongly counterintuitive. In any bold
formulation, its obvious self-referential problems come immediately to the fore. For
this reason, those who dabble with strong forms of relativism often moderate their
stronger claims in other contexts. Richard Rorty is an instructive example. He often
sounds as though he believes that all systems of thought we use to live in the world
are entirely incommensurate—self-contained and hermetically sealed. Yet at other
times he writes as though we can transcend this conceptual relativism. I sympathize
with Bernard Williams:

> Sometimes [Rorty] seems quite knowing about the status of his own thoughts.
> . . . At other times, he seems to forget altogether about one requirement of self-
> consciousness, and like the old philosophies he is attempting to escape, naively
> treats his own discourse as standing quite outside the general philosophical sit-
> uation he is describing.[25]

It does appear that the self-referential incoherence criticism undermines conceptual
relativism (and the strict incommensurability thesis). When someone affirms conceptual relativism, he says that all beliefs are relative to their respective paradigms.
Yet he purportedly offers his own statement, the one describing conceptual relativism, as a belief that is not relative to any one paradigm, but true of all paradigms—
that is, of all human thinking (or at least he seems prima facie to be doing so). If
he says he is not making a claim that applies to all human thinking, we are right
to inquire just what it is the statement does refer to. If, on the other hand, he makes
statements that are true of all paradigms in order to defend conceptual relativism
and then, on that basis, criticizes his opponents' views because they err in claiming
universality, he certainly must bear the burden of proof to explain how his own
statement escapes his own criticism.[26]

Postliberalism and the Charge of Relativism and Fideism

Evangelicals interested in dialogue with postliberalism will want to know whether
postliberalism must buy into conceptual relativism and sustain itself in a fideist
manner. Lindbeck recognizes these twin questions. In evaluating whether postliberalism will "help make religions more intelligible and credible," he writes that the
question can be formulated in two parts:

> First, intratextuality seems wholly relativistic: it turns religions, so one can argue,
> into self-enclosed and incommensurable intellectual ghettoes. Associated with
> this, in the second place, is the fideistic dilemma: it appears that choice between
> religions is purely arbitrary, a matter of blind faith.[27]

Shortly thereafter, he says, "If intratextuality implies relativism and fideism, the cost
for most religious traditions is much too high."[28] Must postliberalism entail relativism and fideism?

Perhaps critics think that postliberal thinking is relativistic and fideistic because

Lindbeck suggests that languages are incommensurate. In discussing large-scale theories, he writes, for example, that "the case for or against a comprehensive theory can only be suggestive rather than demonstrative. . . . Theoretical frameworks shape perceptions of problems and their possible solutions in such a way that each framework is in itself irrefutable."[29] To support this general viewpoint, Lindbeck notes that observations are theory-laden, that no neutral perspectives for adjudicating large-scale theories exist and that such theories are not open to "decisive confirmation or disconfirmation" even in the sciences.[30]

Such statements are sprinkled throughout the writings of some postliberal thinkers. Yet several reasons suggest that postliberalism is speaking too strongly here and need not adopt conceptual relativism. First, a cultural-linguistic understanding of religion posits that one role of religious language is to shape the character of people in a community. Evangelicals should have little to quarrel with here. Do not the parables of Jesus perform this function? But there is an important difference between saying that shaping the character of a community of people is *one thing* language does and saying that it is the *only thing* language does. Surely commitment to the former does not entail agreement with the latter. Lindbeck does not and need not argue that language *only* forms our character.[31]

Second, the distinction between second-order and first-order language supports this. Claiming that second-order language (doctrine) regulates a community's discourse (in its role as church teaching) entails neither that first-order language fails to describe the world nor that Christians are without rational resources to make rational judgments about statements that purportedly describe the world. The grammatical rule "Subjects and verbs must agree in number" does not tell us about the world, but about language. But the first-order language which the second-order grammatical rule describes could still speak about a real world. If first-order language does connect to a real world, then we can bring to bear various kinds of tests to help decide the degree to which some first-order statements are more adequate and others are less adequate in their descriptions.

Third, in some statements of narrative theology, the authority of Scripture is determined by community assent. When a community recognizes a sacred work, that work then gains for that community an authoritative status (the status of revelation, for instance). But certain postliberal themes militate against this approach. As Ronald Thiemann argues, postliberalism stresses God's initiative in the divine-human encounter. Thus a postliberal theologian could hardly argue that the practices of a community or the community recognition of some narrative is the decisive issue in *establishing* the truth of that narrative. Of course, a community must recognize a narrative as true; nothing in orthodoxy precludes this. The narrative's being true would have no value if that truth were not acknowledged and lived out. But human recognition does not make a narrative true—this tack grounds a narrative anthropocentrically. Postliberals would not want to say that the *fruitfulness* of religious claims in shaping a community is what *makes* the religious claims true. They could agree, however, that their being true is what makes them fruitful.[32]

A discussion between Hans Frei and Carl Henry is very revealing on this point. In an evaluation of narrative theology, Henry questions whether postliberalism sees theology as cognitive. He wonders whether narrative implies that "historical actuality should be considered unnecessary to the interpretation of any narrative literature." He suggests that narrative's "flight from history to the perspectival . . . enjoins no universal truth-claims."[33] Frei responds by acknowledging somewhat reluctantly,

> Of course I believe in the "historical reality" of Christ's death and resurrection, if those are the categories which we employ. . . . If I am asked to use the language of factuality, then I would say, yes, in those terms, I have to speak of an empty tomb. In those terms I have to speak of the literal resurrection. But I think those terms are not privileged, theory neutral, trans-cultural, an ingredient in the structure of the human mind and of reality always and everywhere for me, as I think they are for Dr. Henry.[34]

For Henry, theology must be true to a real state of affairs; it must do more than shape community. Frei seems to agree. But the two differ in emphasis and on whether to adopt the modernist view that knowledge is objective, certain and neutral. But Frei's hesitation about Henry's modernism does not entail that Frei's theology is a fideistically grounded, socially constructed community narrative that lacks all contact with real states of affairs.

In interpreting postliberalism, my inclination is to place any strong relativist and fideist statements made by postliberals in the context of moderating qualifications. I find William Placher's summary to be right to the point:

> Christian theologians ought to avoid letting philosophers or anyone else set their agendas or the rules for their activity. . . . Postliberal theologians have brought this into clear theological focus. Sometimes, however, that emphasis risks sounding like radical relativism—like the claim that Christian doctrines express merely the rules for talking within the Christian community. Other communities, other rules—and no ontological claims, one way or the other.
>
> Going that far is a mistake.[35]

Going that far *is* a mistake. I doubt postliberals want to do so.

Epistemic Foundationalism

This discussion raises a number of issues. Among them is postliberalism's opposition to foundationalism. One commentator describes it as an "antifoundational, cultural-linguistic, Wittgensteinian-inspired" movement.[36] Some evangelicals have adopted an antifoundationalist position as well. In my view, the discussion on this matter needs some clarification. Much confusion reigns on this point because *foundationalism* can describe so many different positions. Fundamentally, our problem is that *foundationalism* is used in the literature for two different classes of views. One of these is a broader class of epistemologies which assert that some individual propositions are known directly, not by inference from other propositions. We may call this *epistemic foundationalism.* The other is a narrower class of religious epistemologies which hold that some universal source of knowledge or set of evaluative principles stands at the basis of theological knowledge. We may term this *modernist foundationalism.*

Epistemic foundationalism says that the structure of thought is like a building. A building's foundation supports the rest of the building. Similarly, a class of basic beliefs undergirds a thought structure. Foundationalism is a *class* of theories about knowledge or warrant which says that I know some things directly and other things indirectly.[37] Those things grounded directly in experience are basic beliefs. I know, for instance, that my lips feel dry, not on the basis of some argument, but directly. However, I infer that the 1979 Chevy truck I just bought will get about fifteen miles per gallon because I read in *Consumer Reports* that other 1979 Chevy trucks get that mileage. The indirectness makes it a nonbasic knowledge. I know basic beliefs without inferring them from other beliefs, but I know nonbasic beliefs by inferring them from more basic beliefs. Any theory of epistemology that distinguishes basic and nonbasic beliefs is a form of foundationalism.

Now assume that *transfer of warrant* refers to the belief-inducing quality that is passed from a basic belief to a nonbasic one. If I see rain coming down and hitting my windshield, I can infer that the umbrellaless hitchhiker standing on the side of the road is getting wet. My knowledge that it is raining is grounded directly in my perceptual experience, and so this is a basic belief. As I zip past the hitchhiker two lanes away, perhaps I am unable to see directly whether he is dripping. Yet by inferring from the basic belief (along with certain other background beliefs), I will legitimately form a nonbasic belief that the man is soaking wet. In this way, I form a nonbasic belief because I possess a basic belief in a certain context—the basic belief transfers warrant to the nonbasic belief. Furthermore, foundationalism implies that basic beliefs give reason to believe nonbasic ones, but not the other way around. More generally, if belief x is the basis for believing y, and y is the basis for believing z, then y does not support x, and z supports neither x nor y. The transfer of warrant goes only in one direction.

Many different subtypes of epistemic foundationalism are possible. These differ mainly on the kind of beliefs they allow in the foundation. The most commonly discussed version of foundationalism is *classical foundationalism.* Classical foundationalism is distinguished by its very strict rules about what counts as a basic belief. In its modernist form, classical foundationalism asserts something like

   q: Basic beliefs must either be *self-evident* or *incorrigible.*[38]

Enlightenment philosophers hoped to achieve pure objectivity, indubitable premises, strict deductivism and absolutely certain conclusions using self-evident and incorrigible foundational beliefs.

An important theme in the movement called Reformed epistemology is its critique of classical foundationalism. The main argument points out that q is neither self-evident nor incorrigible. Nor can we easily infer q from premises that are self-evident or incorrigible. So q sets up criteria for justification that q fails. Thus the position is self-defeating. Its problem is that in trying to ensure that no error creeps into our structures of thought, classical foundationalism creates very high standards of knowledge. These standards are so high that it cannot meet them itself.

This leads to the related argument: classical foundationalism eliminates many other things that we normally and legitimately know. As we observe how people actually do come to know the world, we find their knowing processes much more open and flexible than classical foundationalism allows.[39] Thus Reformed epistemology appraises classical foundationalism as fatally flawed, and finds that many allies agree.[40]

Unlike classical foundationalism, however, broader or more modest forms of epistemic foundationalism which have been emerging since about 1975 allow for many more beliefs to count as properly basic or legitimately foundational. Broad foundationalism does not limit the range of foundational beliefs so severely as classical foundationalism does. Alvin Plantinga's claims that belief in God is properly basic represents the strategy of a broader foundationalism. Belief in God cannot be properly basic according to classical foundationalism. But classical foundationalism is itself mortally wounded. So one cannot show that Christians are in error to consider God's existence as a properly basic belief simply by assuming classical foundationalism.

Plantinga's position illustrates a modest form of foundationalism.[41] This view differs from classical foundationalism in important ways. Robert Audi suggests three: modest foundationalism "(a) takes the justification of foundational beliefs to be at least typically defeasible, (b) is not *deductivist* . . . and (c) allows a significant role for coherence."[42] The first point means that modest foundationalism counts as basic beliefs some beliefs that, in another context, could be defeated by other considerations; that is, upon further inspection or at the discovery of new information, they might turn out to be false. The second point allows for the use of varying patterns of inductive inference and argument by analogy. These other patterns include, as the third point indicates, the principle of coherence.

Coherentism
The alternative to epistemic foundationalism is the class of views called coherentism. Coherentism assumes that the coherence test for truth is not just *necessary* for knowledge (as proponents of modest foundationalism will agree) but also *sufficient* for truth. The test for truth involves the internal logic of propositions—their connection to each other. There is no distinction between basic and nonbasic beliefs. Thus if, in one context, belief x grounds one's believing y, and y grounds z, then, in another context, belief z supports one's believing y, and y supports x. In other words, the transfer of warrant (the passing of belief-inducing quality from one belief to an-

other) can go in either direction equally. In coherentism, no permanent foundation of the noetic building supports the whole structure.

Coherentism suffers several severe problems. For one thing, it is difficult to explain just what *coherence* means. Consider:

r: The Garden Club of New Brighton, Minnesota, will hold a bake sale on July 4.

s: Perth is the capital of Australia.

Are r and s coherent? Well, they do not contradict each other. But neither do they directly relate to each other, so surely r and s confer no warrant on each other. Further, s is false. We know that because it contradicts

t: Canberra is the capital of Australia.

So t (combined with some background beliefs) helps us decide whether s is true. But how do we know t? Not solely by inferring its truth from its coherence with other propositions. Perhaps we know t because historical research turns up evidence of the legislative action that declared Canberra the capital. But knowledge of that point requires experience of the proper sort.

This brings up a related issue: How does coherentist epistemology incorporate human experience (including perception)? Without experience, two entirely different patterns of thought could both be coherent yet give very different pictures of the world. How could a coherentist tell a psychotic that he is wrong for holding to an internally coherent picture of the world that includes the belief "I am Jesus Christ"? This is the *isolation problem,* and it is a difficulty faced by conceptual relativism. Foundationalists solve the problem by saying that the coherent psychotic is wrong not because he is guilty of incoherence but because his world picture does not picture the world. His picture is not true to experience, has no explanatory power and cannot account for the world. Any coherentist who says that the principle of coherence alone leads us to knowledge will struggle mightily to decide on rational grounds which of several internally coherent perspectives is the better explanation of our experience of the world.[43]

If coherentism cannot distinguish among several equally coherent worldviews, then the denial of epistemic foundationalism does lead to conceptual relativism (knowledge claims are relative to whichever coherent worldview one adopts) and to fideism (worldviews and the knowledge they produce are not chosen rationally, but in some other way, perhaps by an exercise of will). Evangelicalism, which claims, for better or worse, that God has acted decisively in history to reveal truth about the world, should eschew relativism and fideism. While recognizing fully the noetic effects of sin and the fallibility of human knowledge due to our historical location, evangelical theologians should not capitulate to the view that worldviews are linguistic ghettos inhabited by isolated communities. God's revelation is for all peoples. If antifoundationalism of a particular kind leads to conceptual relativism, and conceptual relativism undercuts the universal character of the gospel, then evangelicals should reject that antifoundationalism.

Modernist Foundationalism

Much is written about postmodernism. Postmodern scholars of all sorts agree in denying foundationalism. When postmodernists reject foundationalism in the theological arena, however, they often have in mind something other than epistemic foundationalism. Postmodernism is, among other things, a movement greatly concerned with resisting any restrictions on individualism and freedom (and in this sense, perhaps, it really is a radical modernism). One liberating strategy for throwing off the oppression of the past involves undermining "totalizing discourses," the worldviews and philosophies of the past: "Postmodernism tends to claim an abandonment of all metanarratives which could legitimate foundations for truth. And more than this, it claims that we neither need them, nor are they any longer desirable."[44]

While discussing the "shattering of foundations," Carl Raschke blames the current impasse in theology on a so-called Roman habit of mind. The Romans wanted to build an eternal city, and so they created a tradition based on a structure of authority. Catholicism vested the office of Peter with this authority. Protestants retained the " 'Roman' habit of mind," but simply changed the locus of authority to Scripture. Protestants are Pauline, not Petrine. Like Roman imperialism, Catholicism and Protestantism, modernity is "fundamentalist" in seeking foundations for thought. "The infirmity of modernity," Raschke says, "stems from its very preoccupation with securing foundations for reflection and action."[45]

What is the foundationalism that postmodernists resist? It is typically not the epistemic foundationalism we just discussed. Rather, it is *modernist foundationalism*. Modernist foundationalism is "the idea that knowledge is the reflection of truth and that we can discover a stable foundation for it in God, History or Reason."[46] As Lindbeck describes it, one instance of modernist foundationalism is "the liberal commitment to the foundational enterprise of uncovering universal principles or structures—if not metaphysical, then existential, phenomenological, or hermeneutical." From this commitment grows the "apologetic approach that seeks to discover a foundational scheme within which religions can be evaluated, and that makes it possible to translate traditional meanings into currently intelligible terms."[47]

How do epistemic foundationalism and modernist foundationalism differ? The former speaks of *individual beliefs* as foundational; individual convictions (including simple beliefs like "I ate Cheerios this morning") are properly basic—meaning they are grounded in experience and not warranted solely by their coherence with other beliefs. The latter, modernist foundationalism, speaks of a *holistic substructure* of logic, language and method as the absolutely certain and universally accessible grounds of all rationality and knowledge.

While we may speculate on the motivations of some postmodernists for rejecting universal modes of reason, Lindbeck makes his intentions clear. His main agenda is rebutting the liberal, experiential-expressivist plan to translate religions in general (and Christianity in particular) into the conceptual framework of modernity. The liberals seek in this way to take a message that seems foreign to the contemporary person and translate it into modern categories. But postliberalism says that we must gain fluency in Christianity's own native language. "Religions, like languages, can be understood only in their own terms, not by transposing them into an alien speech," says Lindbeck.[48]

I have already argued that postliberalism's insistence on Christian theology speaking its own language is a point of strength, an insight evangelicals should heed. Yet some will fear that any insistence on the particularity of Christian thinking and speaking leads precisely to the twin positions of relativism and strong fideism. They claim that without the foundation that modernist liberalism seeks, theology will find itself imprisoned in its own linguistic jail cell. But Lindbeck, for one, rejects this inference. Antifoundationalism does not lead to irrationalism, he tells us. Intratextuality is not the death of apologetics (although it would require that apologetics be more ad hoc and contextually sensitive).[49] The choice between frameworks is not left to chance, he claims. In religion, as in science, differing viewpoints are subject to testing and to argument.[50]

Should evangelical theologians follow postliberalism and commit themselves to antifoundationalism? A distinction is necessary here.

u: There is an ultimate perspective, a final paradigm of meaning, a definitive conceptual scheme that the various forms of human reasoning (in all their cultural, linguistic plurality) approximate to greater or lesser degrees.

v: There is an ultimate perspective, a final paradigm of meaning, a definitive conceptual scheme which is identifiable and definable by all humans in a neutral, certain and conceptual "pure" manner.

The second option, *v*, is especially troublesome. Modernist foundationalism longs for something of this sort. On the contrary, Lindbeck explicitly denies *v*, and evangelical theologians should too. Only Omniscience could know in the way described by *v*. Here is where modernism, starting with Descartes, went wrong.

What about the first proposition? Should evangelicals defend *u*? I say yes. Surely the Omniscient One's perspective represents a final paradigm of meaning, a definitive conceptual scheme. If *u* were false, then language would lock us into cultural ghettos. But we are not confined in this way. Religious people can debate their views, testing them against other perspectives to see which, if any, explains the world effectively. These debates will meander. The testing is not always conclusive. But that is because we are epistemically handicapped. We cannot know God's mind perfectly, and so we trudge along, doing our best to understand the world and ourselves and God. Yet these efforts to understand others' perspectives need not end in complete frustration. With lots of effort and goodwill, people do come to understand each other. At least we can say that the hope that cross-paradigm conversation will yield understanding (and perhaps even areas of agreement) presumes something like *u*.[51]

Perhaps surprisingly to some, Lindbeck says the same thing. "Antifoundationalism . . . is not to be equated with irrationalism. The issue is not whether there are universal norms of reasonableness, but whether these can be formulated in some neutral, framework-independent language."[52] The implication here is that there are universal norms of reasonableness. One of Lindbeck's points, apparently, is that we cannot frame these by following the sort of universal, once-for-all method that Enlightenment-inspired modernists hoped to use.[53] Evangelical theologians can certainly agree with this.

Conclusions

This leaves us with twin claims about the foundations the modernists hoped to find. First, some sort of final reasonableness does hold sway in this universe. Second, only God understands that reasonableness fully, since finite human knowers always operate under significant epistemic handicaps. How should Christian theologians communicate these twin claims? In a previous era, when the Enlightenment vision held our culture captive, honest Christians stressed that the human grasp of universal reasonableness will always be limited. We used phrases like "noetic effects of sin."

In our postmodern era, we face a different environment. The different situation calls for different emphases. Now that relativism is axiomatic, faithful Christians should stress that although our knowledge of these matters is surely limited, the universe possesses a determinate structure and our grasp of truth should conform to that structure. In a day when everyone from prestigious philosophers to New Age-ish movie stars assumes relativism in religion, evangelical theologians should recognize that affirming antifoundationalism without proper qualification entails risks. In rebutting strong (and therefore self-refuting) forms of foundationalism, we should not overstate the case by hitching our intellectual wagons to strong (and therefore self-refuting) forms of postmodern relativism. Indeed, when we must stress the limits of human knowing, retrieving our Christian ways of making that point seems less likely to mislead than does borrowing the insights of postmodernism.

Much contemporary discussion of these issues suffers from semantical problems. That we cannot achieve certainty and absoluteness means that *classical* foundationalism (a form of epistemic foundationalism) and *modernist* foundationalism are false. So, *properly qualified*, antifoundationalism is true. But modest foundationalism (represented by Robert Audi and expressed by something like proposition *u*) is another matter. Modest foundationalism is preferable to the alternatives. Therefore, I believe that opposing foundationalism *without giving nuanced qualification* as to the form of foundationalism one is rejecting will mislead all but unusually careful and honest readers. Conversely, defending foundationalism in the way I have spelled out—and this also requires equally nuanced qualification—is one leg of a culturally sensitive apologetic for Christian truth that evangelical theologians may rightly offer to a pervasively relativistic culture.

Part IV
THE BIBLE
& THE CHURCH

8
NARRATIVE
Evangelical, Postliberal, Ecumenical

Gabriel Fackre

Billy Graham sings it, and George Lindbeck talks about it. Ronald Thiemann chants it, and Carl Henry expatiates upon it.

Billy: "We've a story to tell to the nations. . . . For the darkness shall turn to dawning, and the dawning to noonday bright."

George: The Bible is "a canonically and narrationally unified and internally glossed (that is, self-referential and self-interpreting) whole centered on Jesus Christ, and telling the story of the dealings of the Triune God with his people and his world in ways which are typologically . . . applicable to the present."[1]

Ronald (and the Lutheran eucharistic prayer): "Holy God, mighty Lord, gracious Father: Endless is your mercy and eternal your reign. You have filled all creation with light and life. . . . Through Abraham you promised to bless all nations. You rescued Israel your chosen people. Through prophets you renewed your promises; and at the end of all ages, you sent your Son."[2]

Carl: "The unity of the Bible . . . is found in the message and meaning of the book, namely that the living sovereign God stands at the beginning of the universe . . . the Creator and Governor, and at the end as final Judge; that he made mankind in his likeness . . . that human revolt precipitated disastrous consequences . . . that the divine promise of deliverance disclosed in the course of Hebrew redemptive history to the prophets finds its fulfillment in Jesus of Nazareth; that the incarnation, crucifixion and resurrection of the logos of God marks the beginning of the new and final age."[3]

All of these cases above deal with the community's "web of belief." Through it the church, as Dean Thiemann says, "remembers the story of God's saving acts, trusts in God's continued faithfulness to his promises, and hopes for his final return in power."[4] The biblical story celebrated in song and sacramental liturgy takes form as well in the sequence of the classical loci of Christian teaching, the "common places" of Christian doctrine: Trinity, cosmology, anthropology, Israelology, Christology, ecclesiology, soteriology and eschatology with their prolegomena on revelation, authority and interpretation.

The web/narrative/loci constitute a vantage point from which to investigate both the convergences and the divergences of evangelicalism and postliberalism. More specifically, the matter at hand is the narrative of *revelation*. The commanding question in the conversation between evangelicals and postliberals has to do with the *knowledge of God*. Situating the conversation against the backdrop of this comprehensive revelatory tale helps to make clear what each point of view contributes to the church's witness today and also where questions must be posed to each by the other. In the language of the current Lutheran-Reformed dialogue, the narrative context provides the occasion for "mutual affirmation and admonition."[5]

We should mention in passing that the centrality (and even the existence) of this overarching biblical story has its critics, even from friendly quarters. So Walter Brueggemann in *Texts Under Negotiation*, challenging the coherent narrative he finds Ronald Thiemann and Hans Frei arguing for, declares that

> to take this one-line drama as the core of biblical faith is excessively systematic and is imposed upon the Bible out of a scholastic grid by those who have never read the Bible closely. . . . [Further] as the Bible does not consist in a single, large drama, but in many small, disordered dramas, . . . we [must] give folk freedom and permit [them] to attend to the minor unincorporated dramas of our own life, which are not to be run over roughshod.[6]

This criticism has something to do, of course, with the long-standing debate between the particularities of the biblical scholar's work and the universalities associated with the theologian's vocation. But the dismissal of the Bible's "large drama" illustrates a problem posed to both evangelicals and postliberals: how to relate, but not capitulate, to cultural premises. Today's postmodern advocates, calling our attention to particularities and disjunctions, can sensitize us to Scripture's angularities and surprises. But to make postmodernity a censor of the Great Story that both Scripture and tradition have told is to enter the familiar land of Babylonian captivity.

The Revelation Story

Let me first give a quick account of the "comprehensive story" as it bears on the subject of revelation. I'll attempt an ecumenical reading of it, using the revelatory imagery of Scripture. More attention will be given to those chapters where issues between evangelicals and postliberals arise.

Prologue. The doctrine of revelation, narratively considered, rises from the inner being of the triune God, the immanent Trinity. God as the Life Together of three coinherent Persons is also the "Light Together" of the Father, Son and Holy Spirit—a triune Knowing-in-Unity as well as a triune Being-in-Unity. God is, in the inner transparencies of the triune Society, self-communicating. The will to disclosure of the economic Trinity, therefore, is grounded in the revelatory internal relations of the immanent Trinity. Or to put it in the figures of Scripture, "God is light; in him there is no darkness at all" (1 Jn 1:5).

Chapter 1: Creation. The world is brought into existence for partnership—to be with God and one another, and to know God and one another. Creatures are intended for a life together, and also a "light together," reflecting who God is (Gen 1:28-31; 2:18-25).

Yet the knowledge willed for us is not a "God's-eye" view, but is hedged about with creaturely restraints: "You must not eat from the tree of the knowledge of good and evil" (Gen 2:17). Divine wisdom is for God alone.

Chapter 2: The Fall. But we listen too readily to the tempter: "Eat . . . you will be like God" (Gen 3:5). We reject our creaturely station, bent as we are on knowing as God alone has a right to know. Thus our stumble and fall, with its broken image of God, and our descent into an epistemological night.

Chapter 3: Covenant—Part 1. "I have set my rainbow in the clouds, and it will be the sign of the covenant between me and the earth" (Gen 9:13). The covenant with Noah is the divine promise not to abandon a rebel creation. So out of the darkness a "rainbow sign" appears—enough light shed over the world to show it the way to go, enough power for a fallen world to discern the rudimentary laws of life together, and enough light to see the dignity of the creature with the human face and hear the command to honor the covenant given to all of us Noachides: Do not shed "the blood of a human . . . for in his own image God made humankind" (Gen 9:6 NRSV).

Covenant—Part 2. There is a specificity as well as a generality of promise given by the long-suffering God: "You only have I chosen of all the families of the earth" (Amos 3:2). Biblical imagery of light moves from a rainbow to a pillar of fire and a chosen people. Israel is claimed for the stewardship of life and light together—in the faith of Abraham and Sarah, in liberation from Egyptian bondage, in decalogic law, in the wisdom of sages, in prophetic pointings to *shalom*, in messianic hopes—focal light and power to discern the original vision shadowed by the Fall.

Chapter 4: Jesus Christ. "The people living in darkness have seen a great light; on those living in the land of the shadow of death a light has dawned" (Mt 4:16). For Christian eyes the horizon lights up, the shadows of sin and finitude recede, and there is given "the light of the knowledge of the glory of God in the face of Christ" (2 Cor 4:6). The chapter on which the narrative of revelation turns is the deed of God done and the disclosure made in Jesus the Jew. In the person and work of Christ is revealed who God is, who we are, where we are going and what we are to be and do.

Chapter 5: Church. But how will this Word made flesh now make its way in the world?

Suddenly a sound like the blowing of a violent wind came from heaven. . . . They saw what seemed to be tongues of fire that separated and came to rest on each of them. . . . "We hear them declaring the wonders of God in our own tongues!" (Acts 2:2-3, 11)

So the blazing Sun of God who ascended to the heavens now descends as pentecostal tongues of fire. The Holy Spirit comes upon the apostles, opening their eyes to see and their tongues to tell of "the wonders of God." Here in the inaugural homilies of Peter is given an account of the beginning of the drama in God's primal purposes, its focal act in Israel and its defining moment in Jesus Christ. So the apostolic testimony that soon comes to be part of the church's biblical charter, a special noetic gift given within the body of Christ to seers of the divine Light by the power of the Holy Spirit—the "inspiration" of Scripture.

The pentecostal power of discernment does not end with the apostolic canon, for "ever-new light and truth shall break from God's holy Word."[7] "Illumination" is the gift given to the Christian community that enables it to read aright the story told in its normative Scripture. "To read aright" means to see its meaning at each new point in the still-unfolding story of God and grow in understanding by the grace of its "ever-new light."

To read aright also means to give attention to the wisdom of the whole body, and thus to the catholicity of its judgments: "The eye cannot say to the hand, 'I don't need you!' " (1 Cor 12:21). The wisdom of the body—from yesterday's ecumenical creeds to today's conversation among its many body parts (Roman Catholic, Lutheran, Reformed, evangelical and postliberal) in ecumenical form—is integral to continuing illumination.

While both inspiration *and* illumination are part of the church chapter of the story, the distinction is critical. The apostolic community, which was inextricable from the defining deed of God in Christ, gave us the authoritative witness to the center by the grace of inspiration. The postapostolic community—the church from then to the present time—is given illumination for reading that Scripture. One of the signs of this distinction, and the priorities within, is the canonical process itself, wherein the church lifts above itself the biblical canon, thereby declaring its accountability to Scripture. Included in that Spirit-enlightened judgment is the validation of Hebrew Scripture as "prophetic" Old Testament trajectory toward the apostolic New Testament.

Chapter 6: Salvation. Light is healing as well as illuminating, saving as well as searching. Light convicts, convinces and converts. The light of Christ shines on the "single one."[8] There is a personal transforming Word, one by one, for you and for me at this pass of Thermopylae. As the triune Persons are distinguishable as well as inseparable, so life and light are for believing persons. The God who counts the hairs of the head and marks the sparrow's fall speaks the saving Word *pro me*. Revelation, therefore, is the eye of faith opened by the light of the Holy Spirit and the heart strangely warmed by the power of the Holy Spirit, *testimonium internum Spiritus sancti*.

Chapter 7: Consummation. "When perfection comes, the imperfect disappears" (1 Cor 13:10). For our eyes the earthly disclosures, as Paul says, are signs only "dimly" seen. Even the boldest tongues telling the best of tales will cease, and all our presumed "knowledge" will come to an end. So the modesty appropriate to the divine mystery, revealed now only "in part," for the fullness of light and power await the "face to face" of the not yet.

There are many places that the evangelical-postliberal conversation can be taken up along the horizon of this revelatory drama. I chose several that illustrate the ecumenical formula of mutual affirmation and admonition—points in the story that suggest two mutual affirmations, and two mutual admonitions.

Mutual Affirmations

Jesus Christ. Alister McGrath entitles a section of his chapter on evangelical distinctives in his recent *Evangelicalism and the Future of Christianity* "The Majesty of Jesus Christ."

> For evangelicalism, Jesus Christ is of central importance. He is the focal point of Scripture. He alone is raised from the dead. He alone possesses the unique distinction of being at one and the same time "true God and true man." Through his atoning death alone can we have access to God.[9]

Christology, understood as both the person and work of Christ, takes center stage here. And with it comes its epistemological import, for McGrath is making the claim for the centrality of the noetic as well as the soteric concepts of Christ as "truth" and Christ as "way and life."[10] As Scripture confesses, "Full and true knowledge of God is to be found only in him. . . . 'No one has ever seen God, but God the One and Only, who is at the Father's side, has made him known' (Jn 1:17-18)."[11]

Evangelical piety makes this epistemological point, its hymnody providing us with an interpretive clue. When the story is told in the gospel song, it regularly goes to the central chapter. Thus Catherine Hankey's "I love to tell the story of unseen things above, of Jesus and his glory, of Jesus and his love." Or Jemima Luke's "I think when I read that sweet story of old, when Jesus was here among men, how he called little children as lambs to his fold." Or Fanny Crosby: "Tell me the story of Jesus, write on my heart every word."

Now we turn to the parallels in postliberalism. In much postliberal writing "narrative" refers consistently, indeed primarily, to the Jesus narrative—the "centrality of the story of Jesus." As Hans Frei puts it:

> Christian tradition tends to derive the meaning of . . . sacraments, the place of the "law" in Christian life, the disposition of love . . . directly from (or refer them directly to) its sacred story, the life, teachings, death and resurrection of Jesus the Messiah. This narrative thus has a unifying force and a prescriptive character in both the New Testament and the Christian community.[12]

This identity, of course, is found, as Frei says, in the narratives of the New Testament that give us the "identity of Jesus Christ," that "render his character."[13] Thus

Ronald Thiemann, to whom we looked for the liturgical evidence of the macronarrative, develops his point in detail by exegeting Matthew's narratives.[14]

Both evangelicals and postliberals, therefore, turn first and foremost to the revelatory hinge of God's history, the christological chapter of the biblical story and its "stories of Jesus." Here is a place for mutual affirmation.

Scripture. The *biblical* story is another convergence in the revelatory tale. Scripture is the source of our knowledge of the center, Jesus Christ. So we return to McGrath's evangelical distinctives, and thus "the supreme authority of Scripture." "Scripture is, for evangelicals, the central legitimating resource of Christian faith and theology, the clearest window through which the face of Christ may be seen."[15] Here McGrath is articulating the formal principle of both classical Protestantism and its heir, evangelicalism. To put it in the language of narrative, Scripture is the *source* of the substance as well as the center, the source of the story as well as its central character, Jesus Christ.

But why is that so? Common to all branches of evangelicalism is the doctrine of biblical inspiration. One of the works of the Holy Spirit is the inspiration of the canonical writings. *How* that inspiration takes place (words? ideas? authors? communities?) is a disputed question among evangelicals. What is not in dispute is that the privileged place of the Bible is warranted by the noetic work of the Spirit.[16] In the framework of the narrative of revelation we earlier traced, evangelicals have a pentecostal chapter, part 1, that undergirds their assertion of biblical primacy.

What of postliberalism and the Bible? Mutual affirmation is in order on the *what* of the matter, the acceptance of the formal principle of biblical authority. Scripture is the *source* of the story—the macronarrative—and its central chapter, Jesus Christ. Postliberal refrains about "absorbing the world" into the biblical world, or redescribing the world in biblical idiom, are ways of asserting the primacy of Scripture. In an interesting essay on the loss of biblical literacy, George Lindbeck concludes, "God has promised to be with his people as judge and savior both in the catacombs and on the throne, and for either of these destinies believers need a mastery of their native tongue. . . . Relearning the language of Zion is imperative whatever the cultural future of the church."[17] Scripture is the source of the "language of Zion," without which the church loses its identity.

Mutual Admonitions

Scripture and community. Having noted the mutual affirmations, we turn to the mutual admonitions. What is the warrant for biblical authority in postliberalism? Why do we go where we go for the Jesus stories and the macronarrative? In postliberal writing, it is difficult to find anything comparable to the evangelical assertion of the inspiration of Scripture. Why then is Scripture a trustworthy account of the Jesus story and the "comprehensive story" in which it is lodged?

Bruce Marshall, on various occasions, has helped to sort out ambiguities in postliberal arguments. He did so on the status of propositions in a cultural-linguistic view of doctrine, as acknowledged by George Lindbeck.[18] And I find him helpful on this question as he discusses the "plain sense" of Scripture, drawing on the commentary of Kathryn Tanner:

> By "plain sense" I mean, borrowing Kathryn Tanner's definition, "what a participant in the community automatically or naturally takes a text to be saying on its face insofar as he or she has been socialized in a community's conventions for reading the text as Scripture." It is chiefly by appeal to the plain sense of Scripture that the Christian community tests and reforms its own current web of belief and practice. And since the identification of the plain sense of Scripture is itself part of the community's current web of belief and practice, the normative plain sense funds a significant distinction between text and interpretation. The community's on-going engagement with the text in which its categories are "paradigmatically encoded" may require revisions of the way the community identifies the plain sense of that text. . . . What the community tests by appeal to the plain sense is not only its own faithfulness to its textually encoded identity, but the *truth* of its own discourse, and by extension of any discourse it may encounter. That is what it means to say that the plain sense has justificatory primacy.[19]

That is a mouthful. I take it to mean, first, that the Bible in its "plain sense" is both normative for the beliefs of the community and ontologically referential ("revelatory") regarding those beliefs. Amen.

But there is a second premise here, one very different from that of evangelicalism. "Plain sense," of course, is common to both evangelicals and postliberals, heirs of the normative *sensus literalis* of the Reformation. But "plain sense" for postliberals is discernible only "insofar as he or she has been socialized in a community's conventions for reading the text as Scripture." Indeed, the community's engagement with Scripture over time and place "may require revisions of the way the community identifies the plain sense." *The community* enters here in a very big way. The answer given to the question at hand—"Why is Scripture authoritative?"—appears to shift to "How is Scripture authoritative?" The answer is: according to socialization in the community's conventions, which are subject to revision with continuing community engagement. But there is a "why?" implicit in this "how?"—a doctrine of revelation implicit in the theory of communal interpretation. What is referred to earlier in this essay as ecclesial "illumination" in the narrative of revelation functions as the grounds for investing the community with the normative role of discerning the plain sense of Scripture. The key to the story told in Scripture's plain sense is in the hands of the community by the Holy Spirit's gift of illumination.

The role assigned to the community in the interpretation of Scripture, I believe, is an advance over the individualism that too often reigns in the Protestant tradition. Evangelicalism is particularly vulnerable to this temptation, as I will shortly argue. But evangelical instincts, at this point, are a right challenge to postliberal premises, if I have fairly identified them. Namely, the community is accountable to something beyond itself. In Karl Barth's words, "The Bible must always be over against the interpreting Church. This is the reason for exegesis. The Bible must be free, that is, sovereign, over against the Church."[20]

The reason evangelicals give for the priority of Scripture over the continuing Christian community lies in the doctrine of inspiration, and with it the distinction between inspiration and illumination. In our narrative of revelation, both appear in the chapter on "Church," but a basic distinction is made between the work of the Spirit in the normative apostolic (and prophetic) witness found in the church's charter and the successive Christian community of interpretation. Here an evangelical admonition to postliberalism is in order.

Many related questions circle around this exchange. First, the postliberal (influenced here by cultural-linguistic anthropologies and postmodern premises) asks, How can texts be read other than communally? The answer has something to do with a counterquestion: Why should, on your own accounting, secular postulates determine how we read Scripture? Based on another chapter of the revelation story, can't the Word speak *against* the community, and empower one to resist socialization into the community's conventions by the "internal testimony of the Holy Spirit"? Doesn't the sovereignty of the Word testified to in Scripture free us from the constraints of a theory of the social construction of reality?

Second, how close does a communal view of plain sense bring us to what the Reformation resisted so mightily? What of Karl Barth's warning, "Without the Bible over against the Church, then we are in the Roman Catholic camp"?[21] Is there an *evangelical* catholicity that honors the role of the universal Christian community, its historic doctrine and even a pastoral teaching office, but holds each of these determinedly accountable to a christologically read Scripture and thus is neither awed nor tempted by the claims of Rome?

Third, is it possible to take into account a communal understanding of the plain sense but include other senses of Scripture? What if exegesis worked toward a *commonsense* meaning of a text in a communal sense but also welcomed to the interpretive process a *critical sense* (historical-critical and literary-critical) based, I would argue, on a doctrine of common grace and a chapter on the covenant with Noah? And what if all of these were held accountable to a *canonical sense* (Brevard Childs)? Finally, what if we moved from ascertainable biblical meaning to a *contextual sense* (both social and personal)? I have argued for these four exegetical moves as a modification of the fourfold sense of Scripture in the second volume of my systematics.[22]

Scripture and personal experience. We turn next to postliberal admonitions for evangelicals. They have to do with the subjective underside of evangelical hermeneutics, the "internal testimony of the Holy Spirit," which serves evangelicals so well in listening for the Word *pro me.* Surely this saving Word that initially convicts the evangelical soul of its sin and converts it to the divine mercy, and ever and again convinces it of the personal messages to it in biblical texts, is part of the revelation story, the soteric chapter. Indeed, there are echoes of this in the *pro me* aspect of postliberalism, especially its Lutheran expressions.[23]

Yet the importance of subjectivity in evangelicalism can seduce the movement into giving it epistemic pride of place. The sharpest challenges to this evangelical temptation (rather, tendency) come from evangelicals themselves. Thus David Wells's critique of the fast-growing evangelical megachurches and allied media, parachurch and educational ventures. Mirroring the self-absorbed, therapeutic culture around them, evangelicals

> proceeded to seek assurance of faith not in terms of the objective truthfulness of the biblical teaching but in terms of the efficacy of its subjective experience. . . . Testifying to having experienced Christ personally is peculiarly seductive in the modern context, because it opens up to view an *inner experience* that responds to the hunger of the "other-directed" individual but often sacrifices its objective truth value in doing so.[24]

A case could be made that this inordinate subjectivity is indeed reflected in the "story" refrains in evangelical gospel songs, that more often than not the word alludes to personal story instead of to either the Jesus story or the comprehensive biblical story. Thus Fanny Crosby's "Blessed Assurance" with its line "This is *my* story, this is *my* song," James Rowe's "His Grace Is Satisfying *Me*," with "the story telling, the praises swelling, for grace is satisfying *me*," and much more—"wounded for *me*," "he lifted *me*," "Jesus loves even *me*."

In the narrative of revelation the "inner experience" of the believer is critical, for it personally *attests* to the truth of a gospel that is established on other grounds (Israel's election, Christ's incarnation, biblical inspiration, ecclesial illumination). The Spirit's gift of individual illumination takes what is "true for all" and "true for us" by those warrants and makes it "true for me." Inner experience attests, but it does not *test*, Christian truth. When experience occupies that latter place of authority, it displaces the professed evangelical primacy of a christologically read Scripture.[25]

An important corrective to evangelical experientialism is the postliberal accent on communal norms in doctrine, the web of Christian belief and their sacramental and liturgical habitat. A believer "socialized" into the language and culture of the historic Christian community, and ever and again reminded of its doctrinal constraints, will be less apt to allow personal experience to become the arbiter of Christian faith. Such a calling to communal account would be something of a replay of the Mercersburg theology's critique of the nineteenth-century evangelical "anxious bench," with Nevin and Schaff's invitation to catechism, creed, liturgy and sacrament. This Mercersburg "evangelical catholicity" should be known better by evangelicals, for it would make possible an appreciation of the postliberal program and also provide a Reformation alternative to the road to Rome or Constantinople for those who have discovered the subjectivist temptations of their own evangelical tradition.

Conclusion
Surely there is other business to be attended to between evangelicals and postliberals. On admonitions, evangelicals will continue to ask postliberals about ontolog-

ical referents, historical and transcendent, as Mark I. Wallace does:

Is theological discourse something more than a *witness* which instantiates certain grammatical rules (Lindbeck), something more than a literary *interpretation* of biblical stories (Frei)? Does not theology also make *assertions* that refer *extra nos* to realities that exist independently of this grammar and these stories?[26]

In our macronarrative framework, the question is, Has ecclesial illumination absorbed even the ontological world "out there"?

And postliberals will have their own questions for evangelicals on the subject of absorption. Has the chapter on biblical inspiration absorbed the chapter on the Incarnation? That is, where evangelicals are wed to the hermeneutics of inerrancy, has the epistemic Word, Scripture, been given a status that belongs alone to the epistemic Word, Jesus Christ? Indeed, Scripture has been accorded an epistemological perfection in its human underside that is not even granted to the humanity of Christ, who "grew in wisdom" as well as in stature, not having always and everywhere the human knowledge attributed by some evangelicals to the biblical autographs.

And those committed to what we have called the ecumenical narrative may ask both postliberals and evangelicals if they have business to do with chapter three, part 1 (the covenant with Noah). Evangelicals do have a doctrine of common grace and general revelation that grounds their interest in apologetics. Is it taken up clearly in the Great Story to be told to the nations—a story that moves from darkness through storm and rainbow to the dawning? (The rainbow that gives enough light for human inquiry to see a little way ahead has its implications for the broken use of reason in biblical inquiry.[27])

And do postliberals have an epistemological warrant for the ad hoc apologetics they deploy? When expressing willingness to absorb eclectically whatever might be learned from the philosophy of Aristotle or the cultural anthropology of Geertz, they might take a leaf from Judaism's recognition of the Noachides and thus see the modest epistemological warrants for their practice in the Noah chapter of the metanarrative.

I conclude with a very practical postscript. Admonitions aside, the mutual affirmations—about a common overarching narrative, the common assertion of the centrality of Christ, the common commitment to the primacy of Scripture—are of such commanding importance that evangelicals and postliberals should find themselves as comrades in the church struggle of our day. That struggle is marked by the same issue that brought the Barmen Declaration to be: the issue of revelation. It is no accident that neoconfessing movements are appearing in various denominations that take as their rallying cry Barmen's words:

Jesus Christ, as he is attested for us in Holy Scripture, is the one Word of God which we have to hear and which we have to trust and obey in life and in death. We reject the false doctrine, as though the Church could and would have to acknowledge apart from and beside this one Word of God, still other events and powers, figures and truths as God's revelation.

Here, explicitly, is the centrality of Christ and the authority of Scripture, and implicitly the gospel story.

Let the admonitional conversation go forward between evangelicals and postliberals. But let us do our talking with full awareness of the common struggle we have against those "other events, powers, figures and truths [that claim to be] . . . God's revelation."

9

WHAT CAN EVANGELICALS & POSTLIBERALS LEARN FROM EACH OTHER?

The Carl Henry-Hans Frei Exchange Reconsidered

George Hunsinger

A ll human truth," writes Hans Küng, "stands in the shadow of error. All error contains at least a grain of truth. What a true statement says is true; what it fails to say may also be true. What a false statement says is false; what it means but does not say may be true."[1] This reminder that claims to truth—especially in the midst of controversy—are always fraught with complexities, pitfalls and ambiguities seems salutary for the enterprise I am about to undertake. For what I hope to do, even if only in the form of a thought-experiment, is to suggest that evangelicals and postliberals might actually have something to learn from each other.

No enterprise such as mine can hope to succeed, however, if it does not at least try to remain sensitive not only to matters of straightforward truth and falsity but also to those gray areas that include grains of truth, omissions of truth and inadequate formulations of truth, assuming of course, as I think we must, that truth in theology, however fragmentarily, can be approximated even at all. Hans Küng continues,

It is a simplified view of the truth to suppose that every sentence in its verbal formulation must be either true or false. On the contrary, any sentence can be true *and* false, according to its purpose, its context, its underlying meaning. It is much harder to discover what is meant by it than what it says. A sincere, fearless and critical ecumenical theology, the only kind which can be constructive, must give up throwing dogmas at the other side. Theology today must be actively concerned to try and see the truth in what it supposes to be the errors of the other side, and to see the possibility of error in what it itself believes. In this way we would reach the situation which it is essential that we reach: the abandonment of supposed error and a meeting in common Christian truth.[2]

My hope is that the following discussion will reflect something of what Küng means by "sincere, fearless and critical ecumenical theology" and that it will thereby contribute to the possibility of "a meeting in common Christian truth" between evangelicals and postliberals today.

A Preview of Coming Attractions

The centerpiece of my discussion will be an exchange that took place between two figures whose credentials seem impeccable: Carl F. H. Henry for the evangelicals and Hans W. Frei for the postliberals. In November 1985 Carl Henry gave a series of three lectures at Yale. One of them offered his critique of what he called "narrative theology," with particular reference, among others, to Hans Frei. Frei himself responded to that lecture, and both contributions later appeared in *Trinity Journal*. In *Types of Christian Theology* Frei returned to Henry's views, placing them in the unlikely company of David Tracy and other modern theologians. Theologians of this type, Frei argued, approach specifically Christian doctrines and beliefs in a way that seems overly determined by general philosophical considerations.

Among the issues that emerged from the Henry-Frei exchange, the most stubborn seem to involve the place of Holy Scripture within the Christian knowledge of God. Henry asks Frei very pointedly not only about the unity, authority and inspiration of Scripture individually but also about the extent to which these three need to be grounded in a logically prior doctrine of scriptural inerrancy. Above all, Henry seems concerned throughout about the overly disjunctive relationship, as he sees it, between biblical narrative and historical factuality in Frei's theological proposal.

Frei, however, frames the issues between Henry and himself rather differently. He thinks that they disagree primarily about the "sufficiency" of Scripture as opposed to matters of unity, authority or inspiration. This disagreement seems connected to a further difference about just exactly what the subject matter or the "factual" referent of Scripture is. Finally, Frei responds to Henry's question about factuality by posing a counterquestion about differing habits of mind and frameworks of understanding. Whereas Henry presents himself as an exponent of historic Christian orthodoxy, Frei wonders whether some of Henry's central contentions do not actually reflect modes of thought that are heavily conditioned by modernity in significant and unfortunate ways. One of Frei's deepest worries is that evangelicals and liberals, however much they may see themselves as archenemies, have more in common in their thinking about Scripture than anything that sets them apart, so that they end up being "siblings under the skin."[3]

In trying to discern what evangelicals and postliberals might learn from each other about Holy Scripture, I will try to uncover various points where concessions might be made from each side. I will look especially for concessions that can be made without compromising the basic convictions that seem definitive of either position. I will therefore be looking for areas of possible convergence rather than for areas of complete or outright agreement.

In this thought-experiment I will grant Frei's point that Henry seems bound by an excessive commitment to modernity. I will go on to argue, however, that other and very different formulations of Henry's concerns have standing within the evangelical community, formulations that uphold a strong doctrine of "inerrancy" without Henry's modernist excesses. In particular I will suggest that the views of Abraham Kuyper and Herman Bavinck offer a greater possibility for fruitful evangelical dialogue with postliberalism than the tendency represented by Carl Henry. (And in order not to make things too easy for myself, I will not follow the interpretation of Kuyper and Bavinck advanced by Jack Rogers and Donald McKim,[4] but instead that by Richard B. Gaffin Jr. of Westminster Theological Seminary, who subjects the Rogers-McKim interpretation to a full-fledged revision and critique.[5])

Once the encumbrances of excessive modernity are shed and left behind, the real theological issues can emerge with greater clarity, and the differences between evangelicalism and postliberalism—though still strong—begin to look more like a matter of degree than a matter of kind.

In the other prong of my thought-experiment, I will grant Henry's point that in general the account of scriptural unity, authority and inspiration among the postliberals is, to say the least, fairly thin and unsatisfying so far. This thinness symptomizes the heavily "formal" character of postliberal theology, at least in the versions of it emanating from Yale. Evangelicalism, after all, is a historic stream of theological reflection that reaches back as far as the Reformation or post-Reformation period.[6] However promising it may be, postliberalism by contrast is little more than a current of recent provenance. Postliberals would do well, I will argue, to pay careful attention to the historic doctrinal concerns of the evangelicals, however much it may be felt that reformulations are in order. Focusing above all on the historic evangelical plea for an adequately biblical understanding of the saving death of Christ, I will nominate the work of John R. W. Stott and Alister McGrath as representing the kind of proposals from which postliberals would have much to learn.

Henry's Appraisal of Narrative Theology

In the course of his critical survey, Henry acknowledges several points of agreement with narrative theology. Although they are not strongly emphasized, they should not be overlooked. The appreciative comments that Henry makes all seem to focus on what might be called the integrity of Scripture. He observes that narrative theologians tend to work with the received scriptural text, taken as it stands. Theologians like Frei, he writes, emphasize "that the entire book is important to the meaning, and not just preferred sections as in non-Evangelical criticism."[7]

This acceptance of the received text carries a number of implications. As Henry rightly notes, it means that he and Frei hold significant affirmations in common—namely, that Scripture is a harmonious unity, that historical criticism has not invalidated the relevance of Scripture, that the biblical world is the real world which illuminates all else and that Jesus is the indispensable Savior.[8] It also means that Scripture can function as Scripture "apart from the question whether we can demonstrate the historical factuality of events to which it refers. The authority of the biblical text is independent of confirmation or disconfirmation by historical critics."[9]

Despite this impressive range of common affirmation, Henry proceeds to subject the work of various narrative theologians to severe and vigorous criticism. In what follows I will summarize the concerns that he sets forth under several headings that are similar to, but not identical with, those that he uses himself, and I will concentrate only on those points that seem to pertain directly to Frei. Henry sees himself as differing from Frei on four main questions: the unity of Scripture, the authority of Scripture, the factuality of Scripture and the truth of Scripture.

Although discussed only briefly, the unity of Scripture seems to me to be a point on which Frei is questioned for good reason. Is the category of narrative, Henry asks, really sufficient to account for the unity of the Bible, whether in terms of form or of content?[10] "Not all of Scripture," he continues, "falls into the narrative genre."[11] Because so much of the Bible is not narrative, the narrative category cannot account for the Bible's unity. The point is as telling as it is obvious, for the thinness of the narrative account of scriptural unity seems to suggest a larger problem in postliberal theology as a whole. As Gabriel Fackre has pointed out, "Most proponents of narrative theology are more concerned with method than with theological content."[12] Not much is said about doctrinal substance, and doctrine itself is in danger of dwindling into a set of rules with no more than a regulatory function. Based on such considerations, Henry concludes rather severely that "Frei diverts attention from revelation."[13] I will return to this criticism at the end of the essay.

A second question that Henry has for Frei pertains to the authority of Scripture. Among the many and diverse points that arise here, I will mention only one, though it seems to be at the heart of Henry's concerns—namely, a perceived drift toward subjectivism in matters of biblical authority. Henry repeatedly accuses narrative theologians of failing to arrive at a consensus among themselves in their interpretation of Scripture.[14] The lack of hermeneutical consensus in narrative theology indicates that it has "no objective criterion for distinguishing truth from error and fact from fiction." This is "the unresolved dilemma facing narrative theology." Its method cannot eliminate "divergent and contradictory theological claims"[15]—although I suspect that when they are together *en famille*, evangelicals may not be wholly innocent of divergent and contradictory theological claims. If I am not mistaken, it has been difficult even to find a definition of the term *evangelical* around which a consensus can be built.[16] But what seems to disturb Henry is a certain absence of objective criteria.

If I do not misinterpret him, Henry seems to hold that if Scripture is really authoritative, then we should be able to arrive at consensus in biblical interpretation by means of objective criteria. Beyond a certain point this seems an odd thing to say. If we take the Nicene-Constantinopolitan Creed and the Chalcedonian Definition as established criteria for the church's interpretation of Holy Scripture—as I think postliberal theologians like Hans Frei and George Lindbeck are prepared to do—then I don't see how these standards qua standards could ever be said to conform to Henry's canons of "objectivity" in the nonperspectival or value-neutral sense that seems so important to him.[17]

There are two points here. First, as is notorious, even these standards will not eliminate all significant theological diversity and contradiction; second, the standards themselves are articles of faith. Could it be that Henry's concerns about an arbitrary subjectivism, while not entirely without merit, are somehow driven by canons of objectivism so stringent that in this life, fallen and finite as we poor creatures are, none of us can ever really meet them? Note that Henry does not shrink from asking in criticism of Fackre as a narrative theologian: "But is his epistemology immune to critical miscarriage and to perversion of tradition?"[18] This is an interesting question. Is Henry's epistemology immune to critical miscarriage and to perversion of tradition? Is anyone's? Here we confront for the first time the counterquestion about a certain peculiar frame of mind that Frei will pose to good effect in his published response.[19]

A third question has to do with factuality in the biblical narratives. This is undoubtedly the issue in Frei's work that worries Henry most deeply. Although revelation "is conveyed in and through Scripture," Frei also holds that realistic narrative "has a loose and unsure connection with historical actuality."[20] This establishes an unhappy "disjunction" between the literary witness of scriptural narrative and the redemptive events it depicts. Positing such a disjunction, laments Henry, has "distortive consequences" in theology as well as being epistemologically "destructive" of the "orthodox heritage."[21] By contrast, writes Henry, "evangelical orthodoxy routinely affirms" the full "historical factuality" of the biblical narratives along with their "objective inspiration and inerrancy."[22]

Henry rightly sees that for Frei the central question is a question of genre. The Gospels are allegedly misconstrued if they are taken as reliable historical reports whose meaning is to be found in historical events. He also rightly sees that for Frei "the narrative content is not necessarily historical."[23] As Henry does not tire of insisting, however, the relevant question that still remains is whether the events of the historylike narratives—whether miraculous in their depiction or not—"are in fact historical."[24] Again, Henry is correct in perceiving that for Frei the scriptural narration is "realistic" whether or not the depicted action is factual, and that the depicted action functions to render a character in a story. In this sense the narrative form constitutes, not just illustrates, the meaning of the narrative. The meaning is thus located inside, not outside, the text.[25]

Beyond a certain point, however, Henry unfortunately fails to grasp what Frei is claiming. Henry asks, Wouldn't Frei have to say that faith retained its full validity and saving power "even if historical investigation were to discredit the empty tomb and Jesus' bodily resurrection?"[26] "It is difficult," the critique continues, "to find a categorical statement that if Christ's body disintegrated in the tomb Christian faith would be impaired. . . . Narrative hermeneutics embraces uncertainty over historicity."[27] Frei's approach is so open to fictional elements in the narratives that it "clouds the foundations of a stable faith. . . . It is incumbent on those who claim that narrative story and history are not compatible to clarify which historical specifics are nonnegotiable."[28] Despite referring to Frei's book *The Identity of Jesus Christ*, Henry does not seem to have read it carefully enough to discover just how Frei has answered these very questions.

Since an account of those answers is better postponed until a later section of this essay, it will be fruitful here to pursue an important theme in Henry's own constructive proposal. This theme concerns how faith in the biblical testimony is related to the question of verifying or disconfirming the events depicted by biblical narratives. This theme is not so much a question of "faith and history" as of "faith and historiography" or of "faith and modern historical investigation." At first glance what Henry has to say on this theme seems fairly straightforward. He states repeatedly that faith is independent of historiography. "The Evangelical belief in the divine redemptive acts does not depend on verification by historical criticism but rests on scriptural attestation."[29] Or again he states: "The biblical redemptive acts are not established as historical only if historical method confirms them, nor discredited if it does not do so, for empirical investigation is always incomplete and its verdicts subject to revision."[30] Henry even acknowledges that "questions about the supernatural fall outside the method's competence."[31] Were there no more to Henry's position than this, he and Frei, as it turns out, would not widely disagree.

Elsewhere in the same essay, on the other hand, Henry seems to become strangely equivocal. What are we to make, for example, of the following assertion? "Unless the historical data are assimilated not only to faith but also to the very history historians probe, the narrative exerts no claim to historical factuality."[32] This seems to be a claim (again quoting Henry) that "the factual implications of the text" cannot be upheld "independently of historical criticism."[33] Factual implications must apparently be validated by historical criticism. Faith, says Henry in the same vein, cannot focus merely on the narratives "independently of all historical concerns." If "faith" is split off from "reason" and "history," "that would in principle encourage skepticism and cloud historical referents in obscurity."[34] Most surprising of all, despite what we heard about supernatural matters falling outside the competence of historical-critical method, we are told almost in the same breath that a skillful use of this method "would uncover an objective transcendent revelation, even if confined to historical events or acts."[35]

The principle of charity dictates that one should try to construct a plausible account that would reconcile these apparently contradictory statements. Since my knowledge of Carl Henry's writings is not extensive, the best I can do is to offer the following hypothesis. I suspect that Henry's overall position might plausibly be described as one of "systematic consubstantiation." If so, this position will separate him not only from postliberals like Frei but (as I hope to show) also from evangelicals like Kuyper and Bavinck.

"Systematic consubstantiation" between faith and historiography would mean something like the following. Although faith is independent of historiography, it makes systematic use of it in two ways. First, it makes a negative case that events depicted by biblical narratives (for example, Christ's resurrection) have not in fact been disconfirmed by historical-critical method. Second, so far as possible, it makes a positive case (by means of that method) for the historical factuality of those events.[36] Such a position seems to be what Henry means when he writes that evangelicals "lean on inspired Scripture *more than* on historical research for assurance of past salvific events."[37] Faith, according to this statement, seems to substantiate itself and to find assurance not only through Word and Spirit but also through historical research. It seems to require a reliance on historical-critical method as well as on Scripture itself, though not in the same way or to the same degree. However, if faith were to forgo a systematic reliance on historical-critical method as a secondary means of verification and certainty, then the consequences as Henry understands them would be dire indeed. For in that case not only would skepticism be encouraged, but the foundations of a stable faith would remain clouded in obscurity. Here is another point to which we will return.

Henry's questions to Frei about the unity, authority and factuality of Scripture are finally sealed by a question about the truth of Scripture. Once again we confront a very large topic that can be treated only very briefly. In any case, Henry is clearly concerned about what he calls "objective truth," which seems to be defined as truth that can be known in a value-neutral way apart from any self-involving perspectives or presuppositions.[38] This kind of truth—namely, disinterested cognitive truth about objective realities—is what Henry seems to have in mind when he suggests that Scripture has two primary functions: first, it conveys "propositional truths about God and his purposes," and second, it gives us "the meaning of divine redemptive acts."[39] If I understand Henry correctly, it seems that the propositional truths conveyed by Scripture demand our intellectual assent, whereas the meaning of the divine redemptive acts as mediated exclusively by Scripture demands not only our assent but also our personal commitment. More succinctly, whereas the truth demands our assent, the meaning demands our commitment.

When Henry reads Frei, what he finds missing is a concern for this kind of objective truth. What he finds instead is simply a set of ungrounded assertions, however commendable some of them may be. "It takes more than strenuous assertion," he states pointedly, "to establish historical factuality and objective truth. . . . Really to turn the flank of destructive criticism requires an articulate view of revelation and reason and of revelation and history, and a public test of truth."[40] The significance of Henry's drive to defeat modern skepticism on its own terrain—"really to turn the flank," as he says, "of destructive criticism"—can scarcely, it seems, be overestimated. Modern skepticism will not be defeated merely by strenuous assertion. A whole array of conceptual weaponry and armor will be required, none of which can be found in Frei's depleted arsenal. To defend the factuality of biblical narrative against the onslaught of modernity, one needs to wield a public test of truth. To fortify the meaning of the facts attested, one throws up a towering theory of revelation. And to safeguard the truth of biblical assertions, one rolls out the ultimate weapon: a doctrine of inerrancy.

Theologians such as Frei are wrong, Henry urges, to "reduce biblical historicity and inerrancy to second-order questions."[41] It is to Henry's insistence on the centrality of inerrancy that we must turn, however briefly. Although I wish to make only a small observation, it will prove to be important when we come to Kuyper and Bavinck. "Evangelical theology," writes Henry, "roots the authority of Scripture in its divine inspiration and holds that the Bible is inerrant because it is divinely inspired."[42] Only the doctrine of inerrancy, he continues, can finally "protect the identity and centrality of Christ" as well as "the authority and inspiration of the Bible."[43]

Note the logical order and relation of these ideas. The authority of Scripture is seen as grounded in its divine inspiration, and this inspiration is then seen as the source of inerrancy in all matters of factuality and truth. Whereas inspiration is the source of inerrancy, inerrancy is the ultimate ground of truth. The doctrine of inerrancy thus emerges from Henry's account with a peculiar logical status and conceptual force. Logically, it is the final ground (though not the source) of biblical truth. Functionally, it serves to make that truth objective, certain and secure.

Frei's Response to Henry's Appraisal

In responding to Henry's critique, Hans Frei opens with his famous plea for a "generous orthodoxy." He states: "My own vision of what might be propitious for our day, split as we are, not so much into denominations as into schools of thought, is that we need a kind of generous orthodoxy which would have in it an element of liberalism—a voice like the *Christian Century*—and an element of evangelicalism—the voice of *Christianity Today*."[44] With characteristic modesty he continues, "I don't know if there is a voice between those two, as a matter of fact. If there is, I would like to pursue it."[45]

Frei's opening remark signals that he wants to reframe the entire discussion. Although he approaches both liberalism and evangelicalism with critical sympathy, he will accept neither on its own terms. Only a new framework of understanding, he suggests—one that overlaps both liberalism and evangelicalism, while transcending the limits of each—will show the way forward. Henry's critique gives Frei the opportunity to say something about the possibilities and limitations of evangelical theology, at least as Henry represents it.

Henry's concern about the unity of Scripture elicits no more from Frei than a small concession: "Not all of Scripture is narrative, obviously," he admits.[46] In an early and programmatic essay, Frei had indicated how Scripture's unity might be set forth:

> For a beginning, let's start with the synoptic gospels, or at least one of them, because their peculiar structure as narratives, or at least as partial narratives, makes some hermeneutical moves possible which we don't have available elsewhere in the New Testament. And having started there, I would propose to go on to say, let's see how much more of the New Testament can be coordinated by means of this series of hermeneutical moves.[47]

Although Frei clearly believed that more was necessary than narrative analysis, he unfortunately never got around to making those larger hermeneutical moves. As I have already suggested, this kind of deficit seems to typify the Yale variants of postliberal theology to this day.

Frei goes on to make a remark in passing that, for all its simplicity, seems to cut to the heart of his disagreements with Henry. Frei states,

> The Bible has a very *particular* story to tell. That doesn't mean all the elements in the Bible are narrative. It only means, so far as I can see, that something like John 1:14—"And the word was made flesh and dwelt among us, full of grace and truth"—is something that we don't understand except as a sequence enacted in the life, death and resurrection of Jesus. The Christian tradition by and large took verses like that to be the center of its story.[48]

This statement implies that Frei departs from Henry's conception of meaning and truth. He does not share the view that cognitive truth is necessarily propositional in form. Remember that for Henry propositions demanding our assent are the only way (or only proper way) that truth is conveyed. As he insists in an essay called "Is the Bible Literally True?" both the metaphors and the stories of Scripture need to be restated in propositional form; otherwise, Henry argues, they cannot really be understood.[49]

For Frei, however, the stories are not secondary in significance to doctrines. Although Frei thinks that doctrines are indeed conceptual redescriptions of the biblical narratives, it is the narratives themselves that have the priority in conveying meaning and truth. Whereas Henry seems to think the narratives are finally about the doctrines, for Frei it is just the reverse. Although doctrines indeed arise from the narratives and point back to them, it is the narratives that properly convey biblical truth. We don't understand doctrinal statements, Frei argues, except by understanding the stories. A doctrinal statement like "The Word became flesh" is something that we don't understand except through the biblical accounts of Jesus' life, death and resurrection. A statement like "The Word became flesh" is not a logically prior or independent proposition; it is the center of the gospel *story*.

There are clearly several issues here. Unlike Henry, Frei does not think that cognitive truth is *necessarily* propositional in form, or, more precisely, that propositions are the only *proper* form of cognitive truth. Nor does he think that cognitive truth is the only *kind* of truth, or even the primary kind of truth, that the Bible conveys to us—though he certainly agrees with Henry that biblical truth is not noncognitive. Rather, Frei thinks that biblical truth is primarily narrative in form and that this form of truth demands more than just our cognition. In particular, though the doctrines and the stories are inseparable, Frei thinks that in the end the doctrines are understood through the stories rather than holding, with Henry, that the stories are finally understood through doctrinal propositions. On such matters as these, I will argue, Kuyper and Bavinck represent a form of evangelicalism that seems closer to Frei than is possible for someone like Henry, because Henry has committed himself more heavily than they have to certain rationalist forms of modernism.

Along with arguing for the primacy of biblical narrative, Frei also argues for the sufficiency of Scripture. Remember that Henry took a position on this matter that was ambiguous or at least complex. Although in principle he did not wish to challenge the idea that Scripture functions independently of modern historical criticism, in practice he insisted that the two must be systematically correlated. What Frei denies is precisely the necessity of systematic correlation. Whereas Henry stands for something like "systematic consubstantiation," Frei pleas by contrast for something like "ad hoc minimalism." That is, for Frei faith and historiography are related in a way that is not systematic but ad hoc; and the ad hoc use that faith makes of historiography is not maximal, as Henry proposes, but minimal. Faith needs no more from modern historical criticism, Frei urges, than two very minimal assurances: first, that Christ's resurrection has not been historically disconfirmed,[50] and second, "that a man, Jesus of Nazareth, who proclaimed the Kingdom of God's nearness, did exist and was finally executed."[51] This much and more Henry could have learned about Frei's position from a careful reading of *The Identity of Jesus Christ*.

Frei presents a complex set of reasons for this stance of "ad hoc minimalism."[52] Although they cannot all be pursued here, some of them form the background to what he says in response to Henry about the sufficiency of Scripture. Three points in particular are worthy of note. The first has to do with the actual state of the evidence. Frei thinks the existing historical evidence is so sparse and so indeterminate that it can be given a plausible shape by any number of mutually conflicting positions, ranging all the way from extreme skepticism at one end to measured credence at the other.[53] The indeterminate state of the evidence alone would be enough to rule out any such strong reliance on it as Henry requires. In any case, what little relevant evidence exists is not enough to disconfirm faith in Christ's resurrection, yet it is enough to confirm a certain historical minimum about his life, teaching and death, and that is basically all that faith needs to know from the use of historical-critical method.[54]

Second, whereas the possibility of disconfirmation raises one set of issues, that of confirmation raises quite another, so that the two ought not to be run together and confused. Whereas in principle the resurrection of Jesus could be disconfirmed by historical evidence (though in fact it is not), in the nature of the case his resurrection could not possibly be confirmed by that means. "Actual belief in the resurrection is a matter of faith," writes Frei, "and not of arguments from possibility or evidence."[55] Confronted by the claim that Jesus Christ rose from the dead, historical-critical method simply reaches its categorical limit. In the nature of the case, Jesus Christ can be known for who he is only through our response of faith to his own self-witness as the risen Savior, by means of Word and Spirit.

"Concerning Jesus Christ and him alone," argues Frei, "factual affirmation is completely one with faith and trust of the heart, with love of him, and love of the neighbors for whom he gave himself completely."[56] Note that the response as Frei describes it is not simply one of assent, but one that involves trust and love. Since the truth of the gospel is fundamentally a Person rather than a proposition, our proper grasp of this truth always involves us somehow as whole persons.

Unlike Henry, Frei thinks that we properly grasp the truth of the gospel not just with our heads but also with our hearts and our hands. Although the term *God* as used by the language of faith is "in some sense referential," Frei writes, "it is also true in some sense other than a referential one."[57] In other words, the truth of the gospel requires more than just cognitive confirmation, because the category of truth has performative as well as cognitive and referential aspects. The truth is not just something to be known but also something to be done.

Furthermore, these two aspects of truth—the cognitive and the performative—are so deeply interrelated in practice that this interrelation defies all attempts at strict or systematic conceptualization. Hence the word *God* as used by faith, says Frei, "is true by being true to the way it works in one's life, and by holding the world, including the political, economic and social world, to account by the gauge of its truthfulness."[58] In short, "the word 'God' is used both descriptively and cognitively, but also obediently or trustingly, and it is very difficult to make one a function of the other. . . . You have both uses together."[59] As will become clear in a moment, Frei's conception of truth means that in his low-key epistemology the objective and the subjective, the factual and the meaningful, the cognitive and the performative cannot be so neatly separated and detached from each other as they are in Henry's discourse.

Third, Frei understands the genre of the Gospel narratives differently from Henry. He sees them not primarily as reports about historical facts but rather as depictions of a particular Person. By means of these stories Jesus is depicted as the unique and indispensable Savior. The stories seem more like a realistic though mysterious portrait than they do like a historical report. The values governing the construction of this portrait are not necessarily the same as those that would govern a work of modern history. Although some aspects of the narratives are surely factual in the modern sense, other aspects may well be depictions of the risen Savior in the lineaments of the earthly Jesus. That is, at certain points and to varying degrees, the narratives may actually depict the earthly Jesus in a way that conflates him with the risen Christ, or that superimposes the risen Christ on the earthly Jesus. And yet they may function quite aptly to portray his identity as the narrative intends to convey it. The validity of the narrative portrayal does not necessarily depend on factuality as narrowly conceived. For the chief "fact" that the narratives wish to convey is precisely that the earthly Jesus and the risen Christ are one and the same.[60]

This understanding of how faith is related to history provides the background for what Frei says to Henry about the sufficiency of Scripture. We refer to Jesus Christ by means of the gospel story, writes Frei, and "the text is sufficient for our reference."[61] Beyond the minimal use of historical method, faith does not need the kind of systematic external validation that Henry so zealously demands. "It is enough," writes Frei, "to have the reference to Christ crucified and risen."[62] To suppose otherwise is not so much to set about refuting skepticism on its own terms—which would in any case be an inordinately ambitious project—as it is to verge toward a kind of practical atheism. Systematic human efforts at independent validation, however well intended, can all too easily overshadow our reliance on the promises and faithfulness of God. Frei's minimalism, I would suggest, is really an epistemological adaptation of "justification by faith alone apart from works of the law." Ad hoc miminalism seems to honor the Reformation principle of *sola scriptura*—of the sufficiency of Scripture—in a way that systematic consubstantiation does not.

The question of validation is a function of the question of reference, and reference in the biblical narratives is a complex matter. "I would say," Frei remarks, "that we refer in a double sense. There is often a historical reference and often there is textual reference; that is, the text is witness to the Word of God, whether it is historical or not."[63] Either way, says Frei, the mode of reference is analogical, not (as Henry would have it) literal or univocal.[64] For Frei the sufficiency of Scripture in matters of reference means being bound to the basic patterns of scriptural usage and depiction, not to the literal details. "We start from the text: that is the language pattern," he writes, "the meaning-and-reference pattern, to which we are bound, and which is sufficient for us."[65] The linguistic patterns of the narratives are what identify Jesus Christ, Frei seems to be saying, and these patterns are sufficient because they stand in a good enough or analogical relation to what is factually the case.

What is factually the case, however, is also complex. The dual referentiality of the narratives pertains to the twofold factuality of Jesus Christ. In other words, the narratives are so constructed that they refer not only to Jesus in his earthly life (whether we can verify that factuality by modern methods or not) but also and at the same time to the risen Jesus Christ who lives to all eternity, and who attests himself to us through those narratives here and now. Faith in Jesus Christ involves a confidence that the Gospel narratives are sufficient for us in the arresting, complex and subtle ways that they depict and refer to Jesus Christ in this twofold sense. By contrast, a faith that anxiously seeks to prop itself up by means of systematic and external validation, and to invalidate its opponents by defeating them, seems in danger of ceasing to be faith.

From Frei's point of view, Carl Henry consistently makes a series of category mistakes—mistakes about reference, factuality, genre and truth—mainly because he is excessively committed to the canons of modernity. "I am looking for a way," writes Frei, "that looks for a relation between Christian theology and philosophy that disagrees with a view of certainty and knowledge which Evangelicals and liberals hold in common."[66] Evangelicals and liberals, each according to their own kind, subscribe to modernist views of how we obtain certainty and knowledge in a way that ends up either distorting or denying the gospel. "Unlike Dr. Henry," writes Frei, "I think 'reference'—to say nothing of 'truth'—in Christian usage is not a simple, single or philosophically univocal category."[67] Nor does he think that the concept of "fact" is theory-neutral.[68] Such terms "are not privileged, theory-neutral, trans-cultural"; they are not "ingredient in the structure of the human mind and of reality always and everywhere."[69] They are modern terms that depend on modern ways of thinking. While they need not be banned from Christian theology, they ought not to be used systematically.

The alternative to using modern epistemological categories systematically is simply to use them "eclectically and provisionally,"[70] always striving to grant primacy to the witness of the gospel itself. Theories that are logically independent of the gospel ought not to be used as frames of mind that end up distorting its intrinsic mysteries and certainties. When modernist versions of formal certainty and clarity are leavened by a more modest view that allows for an ineffaceable degree of sub-jectivity, commitment, cultural-historical location and other forms of self-involve-ment in all our cognitive judgments, then fact and meaning, cognition and perform-ance, mystery and clarity, humility and certainty need no longer be so radically divorced from one another as they are by the epistemological excesses of modernity. It should then be possible to see with postliberals like George Lindbeck and Hans Frei that we never have truth—least of all theological truth—except under a depic-tion. "The truth to which we refer," writes Frei, "we cannot state apart from the biblical language which we employ to do so. And belief in the divine authority of Scripture is for me simply that we do not need more."[71]

Beyond Excessive Modernity: The Promise of Old Amsterdam

At this point my remarks become much more conjecture than analysis. Although I do not know the writings of Abraham Kuyper (1837-1920) and Herman Bavinck (1854-1921) very well, the impression I receive from reading those who do is that these two theologians have not committed themselves as heavily as Carl Henry has to the canons of modernity. Although they hold a high view of scriptural inerrancy, they do not seem as encumbered as Henry does by excessive epistemological anxieties about skepticism, factuality, reference, certainty and objectivity, even when they also express concern about such matters. In general, their conceptions of scriptural unity, factuality and truth seem less distorted by the systematic use of theories that are logically independent of the gospel. Above all, their conceptions of inerrancy seem to have a different logical status, and to play a different conceptual role in their theologies, from what we find in the case of someone like Henry. The likes of Kuyper and Bavinck therefore emerge as more fruitful dialogue partners, it seems to me, than the likes of Henry for any future discussion between evangelicals and postliberals. I can do no more here, however, than to sketch hastily some themes that might be of interest in such a discussion.

One such theme is the unity of Scripture. When Kuyper discusses this question, he highlights two matters that seem to differentiate him from evangelicals like Henry, while also placing him at the same time within hailing distance of postliberals like Frei or Lindbeck. The first is that the unity of Scripture is the presupposition of a faithful reading of Scripture, not a logical inference independent of faith. Since the contents of Scripture are obviously diverse, faith cannot arrive at Scripture's unity unless it takes that unity as the starting point. Kuyper writes, "He who, in the case of Scripture, thus begins with the multiplicity of the human factor, and tries in this way to reach out after its unity will never find it, simply because he began with its denial in principle."[72] Or again he states, "And however much it is your duty to study that multiplicity and particularity in the Scripture (both materially and formally), yet from that multiplicity you must ever come back to the view of the unity of the conception, if there is, indeed, to be such a thing for you as Holy Scripture."[73] One notes with interest Kuyper's view that Scripture's unity does not efface its real diversity as well as his emphasis on the priority of faith as a necessary condition for perceiving that unity. Kuyper shows no anxiety that he has somehow lapsed into a fatal form of subjectivism.

Nor does he try to present Scripture's unity, as Henry does, as a "logical system of shared beliefs"[74] or as a comprehensive "rational unity."[75] Instead Kuyper stresses that "Christ is the whole of Scripture, and Scripture brings the *esse* of the Christ to our consciousness."[76] He also cautions against restricting the Logos to words, even though the Logos is now embodied for us in Scripture.[77] He almost seems to be following George Lindbeck when the latter recommends reading Scripture "as a Christ centered narrationally and typologically unified whole in conformity to a Trinitarian rule of faith."[78] By contrast, when Henry writes of scriptural unity, he does not (to my surprise) concentrate on a Christ-centered reading.[79] Rather, he comes close to postulating a dichotomy between propositional content and personal encounter with Christ (as though they somehow failed to form a unity).[80] Finally, he elevates cognitive propositionalism over the person of Christ in his account of Scripture's "logically interconnected content."[81] I suspect that Kuyper would have had little sympathy with such moves.

Even more interesting, however, is the view taken by Kuyper and Bavinck when they come to the question of Scripture's factuality. For both theologians, according to Richard Gaffin, "the biblical records are impressionistic; that is, they are not marked by notarial precision or blue-print, architectural exactness."[82] Nevertheless, neither theologian thought that "this impressionistic quality" in any way detracted from the certainty of biblical truth.[83] The truth of Scripture, they held, is appropriate to its unique divine authorship.[84] As the ultimate author of Scripture, God is more like an artist than a photographer.[85] "It is not even [Scripture's] purpose," wrote Bavinck, "to provide us with an historical account according to the standard of reliability which is demanded in other areas of knowledge."[86] The historical narratives of Scripture, he also stated, "are not history in our sense but prophecy."[87] They do not intend to convey "historical, chronological geographical data . . . in themselves"; rather, what they intend to attest is "the truth poured out on us in Christ."[88]

The doctrine of inerrancy advanced by Kuyper and Bavinck is in accord with their understanding of Scripture's "impressionistic" quality of factuality and truth. Although, as Gaffin demonstrates, inerrancy for them extended to all matters, including historical data, nonetheless they finally understood inerrancy "in an impressionistic, nontechnical sense."[89] They both felt, writes Gaffin, that "pushing infallibility into the limelight is intellectualism" of the kind "that began with the rationalists."[90] Kuyper even went so far as to remark that "if Satan has brought us to the point where we are arguing about the infallibility of Scripture, then we are already out from under the authority of Scripture."[91] Infallibility for Kuyper and Bavinck, it seems, is not the kind of intellectualistic doctrine that it is for someone like Henry. It does not function as the linchpin of objectivity, certainty and truth. It seems more nearly to be a nontechnical term for the reliability and sufficiency of Scripture.

With these views of scriptural unity, factuality and truth, Kuyper and Bavinck arguably stand midway on a continuum that begins with someone like Calvin at one end and that stretches to figures like Frei and Lindbeck at the other. Like any careful reader of the Gospels, Calvin was aware that the writers of the narratives were not overly concerned about strict factual accuracy. "It is well known," he wrote, "that the Evangelists were not scrupulous in their time sequences, not even keeping to the details of the words and actions [of Jesus]."[92] What they were really interested in, Calvin tells us, were not the details so much as the patterns by which the identity and significance of Jesus Christ could be disclosed to us. "The Evangelists had no intention of so putting their narrative together as always to keep to an exact order of events," he wrote, "but to bring the whole pattern together to produce a kind of mirror or screen image of those features most useful for the understanding of Christ."[93]

Kuyper and Bavinck go at least one step further by devising conceptions of factuality, inerrancy and truth that would seem to conform to the kinds of interests and practices that Calvin noticed in the Gospel writers. In this connection postliberal theologians like Frei and Lindbeck could then be seen as going at least one step further still. For although they see a greater discrepancy between biblical narrative and historical fact than did their predecessors, they retain a high sense of biblical authority about what they think really matters—namely, the literary patterns of the texts by which Jesus Christ's identity and significance as the risen Savior are really disclosed to us.

What I wish to suggest, therefore, about what evangelicals might learn from postliberals is simply this. Although on these matters they may not wish to go as far as theologians like Frei and Lindbeck, they should at least be prepared to go as far as theologians like Calvin, Kuyper and Bavinck. Freed from the encumbrances of excessive modernity, the real conversation could begin.[94]

Beyond Postliberalism: The Promise of Evangelical Theology

Carl Henry, it will be recalled, accused Hans Frei of diverting attention from revelation; and Gabriel Fackre observed (more justly) that theologians like Frei and Lindbeck seem more concerned with method than with theological content. As my thought-experiment now moves into its final phase, I am prepared to grant that postliberal theology, at least in the versions from Yale, has run up a considerable deficit in producing works of doctrinal substance. In this light, the promise of evangelical theology, at the very least, is that it has never allowed itself to focus on questions of method, so dear to academic theologians, at the expense of the kind of real theological work that the church needs in order to fulfill its task of faithfully proclaiming the gospel.

More important, evangelical theology, it seems to me, has always had an admirable sense of priorities. Within the field of Christian doctrine per se, it has consistently been the standard-bearer of the Reformation in so far as it has stood—often in a lonely and exposed position—for "Christ alone," "grace alone" and "faith alone" in all matters pertaining to salvation.

Although evangelicalism has not always been so strong in upholding other traditional loci such as the doctrine of the Trinity (although the chapter on this theme in Alister McGrath's new book *Christian Theology: An Introduction* makes my observation obsolete[95]), evangelicalism has historically been of inestimable value right down to the present day for its uncompromising insistence on the saving death of Christ as the very heart of the gospel. The cross of Christ, writes John R. W. Stott, "lies at the center of the historic, biblical faith, and the fact that this is not always everywhere acknowledged is in itself a sufficient justification for preserving a distinctive Evangelical testimony."[96] Stott continues, "Evangelical Christians believe that in and through Christ crucified God substituted himself for us, and bore our sins, dying the death we deserved to die, in order that we might be restored to his favor and adopted into his family."[97] Stott is also commendable for his attempt to set forth not only what I was earlier calling the "cognitive" aspects of this doctrine but its "performative" aspects, or practical implications, as well.[98]

In conclusion, let me suggest not only that postliberals would indeed have much to learn from evangelicals in these matters but also that evangelicals seem to have run up a deficit directly opposite to that of their postliberal counterparts: they are more concerned about content than about theological method. If I may, let me put it like this. Although evangelicals have consistently produced an impressive number of distinguished biblical scholars over the years, especially in the field of New Testament studies (and have also produced a distinguished crop of philosophers and of historians of Christianity in North America), they have not done nearly so well in producing truly distinguished theologians, and this shortfall may have something to do with their failure to attend sufficiently to questions of theological method.[99]

It is not surprising, therefore, that when George Lindbeck proposes to widen the scope of postliberalism beyond what we know from Yale, the theologians, undeniably distinguished, to whom he is drawn are Karl Barth and Hans Urs von Balthasar. Lindbeck observes,

> Here are twentieth century theologians whose use of the Bible is more nearly classical than anything in several centuries and who yet are distinctively modern (e.g., they do not reject historical criticism). Both are wary of translating the Bible into alien conceptualities; both seek, rather, to redescribe the world or worlds in which they live in biblical terms; both treat Scripture as a narrationally (or, for von Balthasar, "dramatically") and typologically unified whole; and in both the reader is referred back to the biblical text itself by exegetical work which is an integral part of the theological program. In short, these two theologians inhabit the same universe of theological discourse as the fathers, medievals, and Reformers to a greater degree than do most modern theologians.[100]

Most interesting is the conclusion that Lindbeck then draws: "Discussions between them are possible—perhaps even decidable—by reference to the text because they approach Scripture in basically similar ways."[101] If I am not wholly mistaken about the continuum that seems to run from the likes of Calvin through the likes of Kuyper and Bavinck to the likes of Frei and Lindbeck,[102] then it would not seem amiss to suggest that a similar possibility exists also for evangelicals and postliberals today.

10
TOWARD A NEW EVANGELICAL PARADIGM OF BIBLICAL AUTHORITY

Jonathan R. Wilson

I n the midst of many competing accounts of how to know an evangelical when you meet one—Marsden versus Dayton versus Johnston versus Bloesch, and so on—one of the common themes is a commitment by evangelicals to biblical authority. This commitment may be formulated in many different ways. One of the most common distinctions in past years was the debate among various accounts of inerrancy, and between inerrantists and infallibilists. As I will note, this debate has been rather inactive in recent years. Over that time, many new challenges to biblical authority have arisen. So in this essay I will propose a new account of biblical authority for evangelicals that draws on new resources to meet new challenges.

By so doing I hope to plant some new seeds for theological growth in a field that has lain dormant. I do not expect my proposal to become dominant, but I do hope to make use of some recent developments to promote a fertile discussion of biblical authority among evangelicals. In particular, I will draw on the *possibilities* of postliberal theology as a resource for my account.

Two convictions motivate my work. First, I am convinced that evangelicals have a particular commitment to biblical authority and can contribute much to any discussion of it. (I remember one of my professors in my doctoral program at Duke telling me that the great hope for the future of theology is in fundamentalists, because, he said, "they still care about the Bible.") Second, I am convinced that the evangelical account of biblical authority must be revisited by every generation—new questions, new challenges and new insights continually arise. If evangelicals do not keep that discussion lively and current, our commitment to biblical authority may wither due to neglect.

Recent History

Let me begin with a brief, impressionistic history of the doctrine of biblical authority among evangelicals. The past three decades witnessed an incredible focus of theological energy on the doctrine of Scripture by evangelicals. These thirty years coincide with my own development as a theologian. How well I remember my last two years as a student at Free Will Baptist Bible College. For Raymond Coffey, Daryl Ellis and me, two questions occupied our energies: "Can the resurrection of Jesus be proven?" and "Is the Bible inerrant?" Great excitement accompanied every new discovery of an argument for inerrancy. Clark Pinnock, John Warwick Montgomery, the Ligonier Conference, *God's Inerrant Word* and, later, B. B. Warfield, Carl Henry and others became our theological mentors.[1] I am a theologian today in large part because of the passion generated by those friendships and our debates.

When Clark Pinnock joined the faculty of Regent College, I went there as a student to sit under his teaching. During those years *Battle for the Bible* ignited theological controversy.[2] I remember Clark's struggles in the midst of the debate, a public forum on the issue at Regent that packed the largest classroom until it overflowed, and my asking a question at that forum that provoked a strong reprimand from Ian Rennie (who would probably do the same if he were here today). This was also the time when Robert Gundry, now my senior colleague at Westmont, provoked considerable debate within the Evangelical Theological Society with his commentary on Matthew.[3] I still have in my files a prepublication copy of his "Theological Postscript" to the commentary with a handwritten note at the top that reads "pirated by stealth—CHP." What exciting times—to be part of such theological ferment. Out of that ferment arose the Rogers-McKim proposal and responses to it, as well as the International Council on Biblical Inerrancy (ICBI) and its massive anthologies.[4]

Disquieting Notes

But in the midst of the ferment, there were some disquieting notes. For me, the first was raised by F. Leroy Forlines, my first and great professor of theology at the Free Will Baptist Bible College. Professor Forlines, a staunch inerrantist, kept asking me what kind of proven error in Scripture would change the way I lived. He also kept insisting that theology was for the whole person, not just the mind. Discussions of inerrancy appeared to neglect this, he argued, because they seemed never to move theology beyond Scripture as a source of information.[5]

The second disquieting note was the observation by a Regent professor (I do not remember which one) that inerrancy did not seem to produce works by evangelicals in other areas of doctrine. Since then evangelicals have been immensely productive theologically, but at the time the observation produced some agitation. Moreover, this later theological productivity seems to have little to do with the affirmation of inerrancy. For me, this observation is reinforced by the experience of the participants in the ICBI when they tried to move on from inerrancy to the question of biblical manhood and womanhood. Suddenly those who had agreed on a rather detailed statement of biblical inerrancy came to different conclusions regarding other biblical teachings. Perhaps inerrancy is not, and never was, the theological panacea I was seeking.

The third disquieting note was the discovery that my non-Christian friends to whom I witnessed were rather uninterested in my views on inerrancy. As I presented to them my hard-won insights on inerrancy, their eyes would glaze over. This attitude has been neatly captured recently by John Stott. With his typical cultural sensitivity and evangelical faithfulness, Stott has observed that "in the contemporary world, people are more interested in whether Christianity is relevant than in whether it is true."[6]

Finally, I have been unsettled more recently by the relative absence of the discussion of biblical authority among evangelicals. Since the conclusion of the ICBI, there has been little discussion of their work or of other accounts of biblical authority. This seems to be caused more by exhaustion than by agreement. What we need, perhaps, is a happy medium, where discussions of biblical authority are neither neglected nor consumers of most of the theological energy of evangelicals.

So some troubling aspects arise—not arguments *against* inerrancy, but some questions that caused further reflection. Is it possible, then, to formulate a new paradigm of biblical authority that takes into account this disquiet, remains faithful to the evangelical tradition and yet revitalizes a discussion of biblical authority? I think that it is possible, and I think that the most fertile source for that new paradigm is the "postliberalism" of Lindbeck and others.

The Postliberal Contribution

In *The Nature of Doctrine*, George Lindbeck argues in typical typological Yale fashion for a new understanding of religion and doctrine.[7] Drawing in large part on the cultural anthropology of Clifford Geertz, Lindbeck argues for the superiority of a cultural-linguistic understanding of religion over what he designates as experiential-expressivist and cognitive-propositionalist understandings. Drawing on the philosophy of Wittgenstein, Lindbeck argues for a "rule theory" of doctrine.[8] Lindbeck elaborates his proposal and argues for it in a variety of ways. Although he does not directly address the issue of biblical authority and inerrancy, his proposal offers some directions for a new paradigm of biblical authority.

By drawing on Lindbeck's proposal and extending it, I will develop a new evangelical paradigm of biblical authority rooted in practicing the gospel, living in community and interpreting the world.[9] As I develop this new evangelical paradigm of biblical authority, I can think of at least three questions that should arise. Is this new paradigm a betrayal of the evangelical tradition? Is it simply a restatement of infallibility? Is it irrelevant to the concerns addressed by inerrancy? The answers are no, no and no. I elaborate on these answers throughout my constructive account.

Against Foundationalism
In order to develop my account of practicing the gospel, I must first attend to some developments in the realm of epistemology which are reflected in Lindbeck's proposal. The trajectory of his proposal moves us away from the context of modernity, though some argue that he has not gone far enough with these developments. In the context of modernity, we seek to base our knowledge on a certain foundation. In philosophy, this sure foundation is universal reason or sensory data. Once this foundation is established, by use of the proper method we can erect a superstructure of knowledge. Thus epistemology becomes "the first philosophy."[10]

In most evangelical accounts of biblical authority, inerrancy serves as our sure and certain foundation. The inerrancy of Scripture is proven by demonstrating its accuracy in matters of history, science, geography, culture and the like. Once this foundation is established, by the proper methods of interpretation we can build a theological superstructure that accurately reflects the teaching of Scripture. This conviction helps explain the enormous theological energy devoted to inerrancy: a sure and certain foundation must be laid before the structure can be built. This conviction is also reflected in many evangelical doctrinal statements. For example, at Westmont College our Articles of Faith begin not with confession of belief in the triune God but with confession of belief in the inerrancy of Scripture. On more than one occasion, I have heard a Westmont faculty member say that our Articles of Faith begin with this confession because once you have the inerrancy of Scripture, the rest of our faith follows ineluctably. Clearly, these characteristics of evangelical theology reflect a foundationalist epistemology.

One other note may be added to help us understand the way foundationalism works in theology. In the context of foundationalist epistemology, theological error results either from having the wrong foundation or from using the wrong method to build upon that foundation. Thus evangelicals view theological error as the result of the rejection of inerrancy or as the result of the wrong method of biblical interpretation.

Now let me say clearly that within the context of the foundationalist epistemology of modernity and its challenges to biblical faith, avowal of the inerrancy of Scripture is precisely the proper response. As appeals to reason and sensory data were used by a foundationalist epistemology to challenge the truth of the gospel, theologians were right to counter with the doctrine of inerrancy. As many have noted, inerrancy is a defensive position, a response to attacks. Those who responded to those attacks used the weapons at hand in that cultural context. That is, they rightly used the resources of foundationalist epistemology.

Today, however, we have other challenges and other resources available to pursue another line of defense and response by questioning the assumptions of modernity and its foundationalist epistemology. (Since the primary focus of this paper is not epistemology, what follows is a rough-and-ready sketch of this new possibility.) Quine's *Web of Belief* calls into question the picture of epistemology that forces us to be foundationalist or antifoundationalist.[11] He asks us to think of our knowledge as a web of belief. More radically still, Rorty's *Philosophy and the Mirror of Nature* introduced a philosophical program that rejects modernist epistemology and metaphysical realism.[12] (By the way, I accept the first part of Rorty's program and reject the second.) Among other things, Rorty's argument exposes the historicist nature of our knowledge.

As a result of these developments, some have noted ironically how "modern" evangelical theology has been, even as it sought to stand against modernity. This judgment, I believe, is correct, but I do not believe it is a reason for rejecting our heritage. Some have done just that by questioning whether or not our theological forebears should have been more aware of how much modernity was determining the evangelical response. Inerrancy, they say, is a faulty doctrine determined by wrong assumptions. I disagree. I am enough of a historicist to believe that we must respond to the particular circumstances in which we find ourselves and "make do" with the resources at hand. Indeed, one of the main reasons I am writing this paper is that I believe that the circumstances have changed and other resources are at hand.

Thus the inerrantists were right to meet the challenges they faced in the manner they did. But the circumstances and challenges have changed so that inerrancy no longer serves the purpose of faithfully asserting biblical authority. To use a slightly prejudicial historical example, the Maginot Line was a brilliant tactical strategy in World War I, but useless in the face of Hitler's Blitzkrieg. Likewise, inerrancy is a brilliant response to foundationalist attacks on the gospel, but unless we respond to new challenges, we will find ourselves defenseless and overrun, unable to assert the truth of the gospel that we have inherited.

However, even as I reject foundationalism, I want to recognize that our faith has a "foundation." As Paul says, the church is "built on the foundation of the apostles and prophets, with Christ Jesus himself as the chief cornerstone" (Eph 2:20). But this foundation is far from foundationalism. Foundationalism looks for a foundation separate from any particular convictions that a Christian might have. In other words, a foundationalist epistemology seeks to ground knowledge in truths that anyone can accept. Thus an inerrantist who applies a foundationalist epistemology might say, "Set aside any convictions about Jesus Christ, God and salvation through the cross of Jesus Christ. I will show you that the Bible is true through historical, geographical and scientific study that everyone agrees on. Now, if the Bible is true on these matters, you should also accept what it says about God, Jesus Christ and salvation."

This approach may be effective at certain times and places, but it is no longer where the main challenges to biblical authority occur. Nor is a foundationalist epistemology what Paul appeals to when he refers to the apostles, prophets and Christ

Jesus. Paul's appeal is already situated within particular Christian convictions. So we need to give an account of biblical authority that does not depend upon a foundationalist epistemology.[13]

In response to biblical assertions and critiques of foundationalism, some have located biblical authority in an appeal to the Word and the Spirit.[14] In its appeal to the Spirit, this approach resists foundationalist epistemology. Indeed, in the way that Word and Spirit are intertwined, it is closer to Quine's "web of belief" than to foundationalism. What is usually underdeveloped in this account is the role of the community.

In this context we need to draw on Lindbeck's proposal of a cultural-linguistic approach to religion. In this understanding "religion" is shaped and transmitted by a particular community—in the case of Christianity, the church. In addition, the religion of the community is conveyed by the linguistic practices of the community. Here Lindbeck applies to religion Wittgenstein's dictum that meaning is use. In other words, in contrast to modernity—where the meaning of language is found in its reference—in the postliberalism of Lindbeck, the meaning of religious language is found in the ways the community uses the language. This is a much richer account of religious language, since it allows for such practices as confession, praise and thanksgiving, as well as assertion.

Practicing the Gospel
Together, a cultural *and* linguistic understanding of religion turns our attention to the practices of the church and produces an account of biblical authority different from the account that would be given by an inerrantist. In this cultural-linguistic account, biblical authority is rooted in what Nicholas Lash calls "performing the Scriptures."[15] In his article, Lash argues that the proper interpretation of Scripture is not found in a biblical commentary or a theological text, but in Christian discipleship. Developing his argument with analogies from drama and music, Lash argues that interpretive performance is the proper activity in response to these "texts" and to the text of Scripture.

Before offering some nuances to my position, I want to push the arguments of Lindbeck and Lash further, to argue that in the contemporary cultural context, the "first philosophy" is no longer epistemology but (theological) ethics. A number of arguments may be made for this notion of ethics. Emmanuel Levinas, the source of the notion of ethics as first philosophy, is an obvious source, as are some arguments from Rorty's "Priority of Democracy to Philosophy."[16] But even more important for theology are arguments that may be made from Scripture. Jesus' words in John 8:31-41 indicate the importance of "doing," as do many of his other statements. The letter of James likewise calls us to doing. Even in 2 Timothy 3:16, inerrancy is an inference drawn from the verse. The verse itself describes the importance of Scripture for living, not knowing.

While inerrantists certainly cannot be accused of neglecting doing, in that whole debate doing was an inference from knowing; that is, ethics followed from episte-mology. With recent developments, we now have the cultural and intellectual re-sources to articulate clearly and forcefully the biblical emphasis on doing the word. This is admittedly a potentially radical shift that needs further exploration, but it is one we must explore for the sake of the gospel.

Here we enter a tangle of issues that will never become entirely clear. Certainly, doing is a kind of knowing and knowing is a kind of doing. Moreover, in order to do what Jesus calls us to do, we have to know what he calls us to do. In the face of these rather intractable complications we may note that a foundationalist ap-proach to biblical authority often has the (unintended?) effect of postponing obe-dience until we are certain of the truth of Scripture. Moreover, it often leads evan-gelical scholarship into a quest to say why the Bible is authoritative rather than saying what God, through an authoritative Bible, calls us to do. Reasserting the importance, perhaps even the priority, of doing recovers the biblical call to disciple-ship. After all, the disciples did not learn that Jesus was the Messiah and then decide to follow him. Rather, they realized his messiahship by following him.

Those who know the theological tradition may at this point have several objec-tions. Some objections will be resolved only through dialogue. Others may stop dialogue before it begins. Let me address two dialogue stoppers. First, some may think that this approach simply reenthrones experience as authority and thus leads us into a new "liberalism." Lindbeck's original account disarms this objection by clearly distinguishing the role of experience in an experiential-expressivist approach from the role of experience in a cultural-linguistic approach.[17] In the former, Scrip-ture is interpreted by our (authoritative) experience. In the latter, our experience is interpreted by Scripture through the Spirit-led community. Therefore, my appro-priation of Lindbeck's proposal does not elevate experience. Rather, it recognizes the proper role of experience and disciplines it by Scripture.[18]

A second objection to my proposal may be raised by some who think that this is only a restatement of the old "infallibilist" position that Scripture is our infallible rule (only) of faith and practice. However, that infallibilist claim was still made within the context of epistemology as the first philosophy—that is, it was a "limited iner-rancy" position that was still concerned with what we could know from Scripture with certainty. It accepted the presuppositions of modernity and narrowed the Christian claim to knowledge. The claim that ethics is the first philosophy differs from this infallibilist position by denying the epistemological priority granted by modernity.

This move to ethics as first philosophy is what I have called in theology "practicing the gospel." In this view the first step toward biblical authority is not establishing an inerrant text which we then follow; rather, the first step is following the text. In this approach, there is still a place for the avowal of inerrancy, but it now follows from doing rather than vice versa. As Lash has pointed out, there is also still a role for "the expert"—scholars of the biblical languages, text critics, exegetes, historians and theologians—though these roles are no longer, in the technical sense, "foundational."

Finally, this move also responds to the disquiet I noted earlier. Forlines's concern for the whole person is met by the emphasis on living, not just knowing. The experience of the ICBI in attempting to move from the foundation of inerrancy to questions of practice arguably displays the need to displace epistemology as the first philosophy. Stott's concern for the relevance of the gospel is met by the call to live the gospel before the watching world. What, we may ask, would be the result for biblical authority if the world observed Christians practicing the gospel to which Scripture bears witness? Should we not explore this possibility together?

Living in Community
In addition to practicing the gospel, Lindbeck's proposal directs our attention to living in community.[19] Drawing on Geertz, Wittgenstein and others, Lindbeck argues that linguistic practices take place within what we may call "interpretive communities."

We may get at this notion by briefly considering the layout of most contemporary biblical commentaries. These commentaries are usually structured to address at least two interpretive communities. Some sections of the commentary reflect the interpretive interests of the academy—of other biblical scholars. These sections follow conventions, arguments and concerns that only biblical scholars understand and care about. Other sections, variously labeled "Exposition," "Application" and the like, reflect the interpretive interests of the community of believers.

This conflict of interpretive interests raises many questions that we cannot pursue here.[20] My purposes in describing it is to help us understand how biblical authority may be stated differently in different interpretive communities. For my purposes, we must recognize that the assertion of the inerrancy of Scripture may often (not always) play into the interpretive interests of a community at odds with the community of disciples. Is inerrancy the first thing that we, as disciples of Jesus Christ, want to say about the authority of Scripture?

This emphasis on the community of interpretation accords well with Scripture and opens up the process of biblical interpretation in ways that are wonderfully described by John Howard Yoder.[21] In "The Hermeneutics of Peoplehood," Yoder uses the doctrine of spiritual gifts to show how a community of disciples practices moral reasoning. Although he applies it specifically to "practical moral reasoning," his description fits all processes of faithful interpretation. Yoder describes the contributions to interpretation of biblical scholars and historians (agents of memory), prophets (agents of direction), administrators (agents of due process), philosophers (agents of linguistic self-consciousness) and others. Together, and guided by the Holy Spirit who gives these gifts, the community discerns the authority of Scripture in their circumstances. One can argue that this is precisely the picture of biblical authority reflected in the account of the Jerusalem Council in Acts 15 and in the accounts of the later Ecumenical Councils.

In the context of foundationalist epistemology, inerrancy works against this communal process. Instead, it tends to foster a process of interpretation that Lash labels "the relay method."[22] Here the biblical expert determines the inerrant foundation and applies an interpretive method that yields "what the text meant." This product is passed to the theologian-ethicist, who then determines "what the text means." This product is in turn passed on to the "laity" for their consumption.

In the new paradigm that I am seeking to develop, biblical authority is centered in the community of disciples, not in the work of the expert. Before the watching world, the church is called to live in such a way that the authority of Scripture is displayed as a witness to the gospel of Jesus Christ. Again, there is a place for inerrancy in this paradigm, but it is no longer the province of the expert, nor is it foundational. Instead, it is part of the web of belief.

Many concerns and objections may be raised in response to this emphasis on community. Let me address two of them. First, in response to the arguments of literary critics like Stanley Fish, some may object that this emphasis on interpretive communities may dissolve the text. That may or may not be the case with Fish (I think that it is a misunderstanding of Fish's argument produced by his extreme rhetorical style); it should not be the case for Christians. For Christians, the text of Scripture is the indispensable and authoritative means by which God forms the community of the redeemed. It is, in Donald Bloesch's words, "sacramental."[23]

A second objection raises the specter of relativism. If biblical authority and interpretation is dependent on the community, then how do we confront other interpretive communities or malformed Christian communities?[24] We may begin the process of disarming this objection by noting that foundationalist epistemologies and other formulations of biblical authority have not been terribly successful in avoiding or dissolving conflict. Of course, the more basic concern of this objection is that all conversation among various communities will cease.

We Christians have a particular contribution to make here. Since we believe that the God who has redeemed us and called us together is the Creator and Redeemer of all humanity and that we have been commissioned to make disciples of Jesus Christ among all nations, we must also believe that God will enable us to carry out that commission. We are unfaithful to this calling when we downplay the conflict of communities; there is a Prince of Darkness against whom we do battle. But we are unfaithful to the gospel when we engage these conflicts as the world does and with the weapons of the world. Rather, we are called and equipped by the gospel to be peacemakers. As we recognize the line between the community of the faithful and other communities that runs even through our own lives, we may be enabled to display more faithfully the authority of Scripture and the work of redemption through Scripture that is the good news of Jesus Christ.

Interpreting the World

The third element of my proposed paradigm, interpreting the world, reinterprets Lindbeck's claim that "intratextual theology redescribes reality within the scriptural framework rather than translating Scripture into extrascriptural categories. It is the text, so to speak, which absorbs the world, rather than the world the text."[25] Lindbeck's move here reflects the analyses and proposals of Hans Frei.[26] For Frei and Lindbeck, theology should not seek to interpret or translate Scripture into categories, concepts or convictions found outside the Bible. Rather, the flow should be just the reverse. It is not that "believers find their stories in the Bible, but rather that they make the story of the Bible their story. The cross is not to be viewed as a figurative representation of suffering nor the messianic kingdom as a symbol for hope in the future; rather, suffering should be cruciform, and hopes for the future messianic."[27]

But note that inerrancy leads us to do just what Lindbeck argues we should not do. Inerrancy seeks to demonstrate the authority of the Bible by showing how it meets the demands for accuracy and precision pressed upon theology by the world. In other words, in spite of our conservatism and desire to be faithful to the gospel, we end up interpreting the Bible for the world.

Following Lindbeck and others, I want to argue that the proper way to practice the authority of Scripture is through a theology that interprets the world according to Scripture. In my account, I want to go beyond Lindbeck's, which focuses too much on the text. It is not the text that absorbs the world, but the practices of the community formed by the Holy Spirit through the text that "absorb the world." In order to enforce this difference, I speak of "interpreting the world."

An account of the community's practice of interpreting the world incorporates a number of my previous points. Through Scripture, God incorporates us into the work of redemption in Jesus Christ. Redemption gathers us into the people of God and a particular form of life that simply is participation in the reality of redemption. As a result, we are formed by a cultural-linguistic "world" and taught a view of reality. Our way of life and our language, then, interpret the world according to the gospel.

So, for example, when Christians see nonviolence as the appropriate way to live in a world created by God in peace, marked by Christ's forgiveness through death and determined by the resurrection of Christ, then our way of life interprets the world according to that reality.[28] Likewise, when Christians through Christ confess their sinfulness, ask for forgiveness and receive assurance of that forgiveness, we interpret the world and ourselves as fallen from God and redeemed by God. As we live our lives in these and other ways, we are learning to live in the world established and revealed in Jesus Christ. As we learn to live in this world, we are interpreting the world for ourselves and others.

These acts of interpretation are themselves particular kinds of truth claims for which the community must be prepared to argue. How the argument will go cannot be specified ahead of time (thus the concept of "ad hoc apologetics"), but we cannot be content merely to say, "Well, that's the way we see things—too bad for you if you don't. So there." As I noted earlier, our convictions—the world established and revealed in the gospel—lead us to seek to persuade all of the truth of the gospel. As Julian Hartt warns us, we cannot be content merely to tell and retell the story. We must also be prepared to say and show how we are to live according to the story.[29]

Conclusion

In Scripture we have God's witness to the reality of the kingdom: God and humanity reconciled through Jesus Christ. Through Scripture the faithful are gathered into the community of the redeemed and commissioned to witness to the gospel so that others may enter the kingdom. That kingdom, as Julian Hartt has taught me to say, is an everlasting actuality; it is at work even today and until the end of the age. In order to be faithful to that gospel and commission, we must be continually enabled by the Holy Spirit to discern the threats to and possibilities for the gospel in our present circumstances. We are living through changes that are altering our circumstances significantly from those to which the doctrine of inerrancy responded. The new paradigm of biblical authority that I am developing here is an attempt at evangelical faithfulness. I look forward to companions along the way who will correct, instruct and encourage.

11
TOWARD A *SENSUS FIDELIUM* FOR AN EVANGELICAL CHURCH

Postconservatives & Postliberals on Reading Scripture

Curtis W. Freeman

I have a confession to make. I am a postconservative, postliberal, evangelical catholic. This seems to be a very odd beginning for a discussion about the possibility of a consensus reading of Scripture. Indeed, what can these juxtaposed terms mean? Had I admitted to being a fundamentalist, a liberal, a dispensationalist or a liberationist, it would have been clearer who I am. But a postconservative, postliberal, evangelical catholic? Perhaps this odd conflation of trendy labels is an oblique gesture toward the common postmodern practice of the political reading of texts. In the interest of easing the minds of the faithful (and at the risk of disappointing the radical) I am not about to propose that the adoption of deconstructive literary theory will add to the *sensus fidelium* (the sense of the faithful) in a way that historical-critical exegesis has failed to do.

What I want to suggest is that such a confession *is* an important way to begin thinking about how to read Scripture. It will (once you understand the terminology) identify who I am by providing a narrative context within which to situate the subsequent claims I will make. And I hope my confession also suggests something of a direction whereby evangelicals and postliberals might chart a new course through the dark waters of biblical interpretation.

On Taking "the Story" Seriously

My own particular confession is that of a Southern Baptist, although I am not always pleased with what that designation implies. I join James McClendon in describing myself as a "little *b*" baptist, seeking to find kinship in the broader believers' church tradition of the Radical Reformation.[1] But despite my misgivings, it would be disingenuous to deny the debt I owe to the simple biblicism which is the heritage of this evangelical tradition.[2]

During the course of my graduate studies, however, I underwent what can only be described as a second conversion. I began as a conservative, and I became a liberal. By this I mean I rejected the naive hermeneutical assumption that "the Bible says what it means and means what it says" in favor of the historical-critical studies of the Bible and the liberal assumptions of modernity.[3] As a postconservative liberal, I attempted to practice the basic two-step hermeneutic that separates the historical-critical discipline of discovering "what it (the biblical text) meant" from the theological task of proclaiming "what it means."[4]

This dichotomy between *meant* and *means*, however, became increasingly problematic as I attempted to proclaim the gospel each Sunday. How does one make the transition from the historical meaning to the theological message? Could I honestly preach from one of the great servant songs of deutero-Isaiah without suggesting that these find their fulfillment in Jesus of Nazareth? And if I proposed a christological interpretation, was I maintaining the integrity of historical-critical exegesis?[5] This second conversion loosed the chains of naiveté, but it also produced a schizophrenia between the conclusions of history and the affirmations of faith.

It was also during the course of these studies that I began to read the books of Ludwig Wittgenstein, Alasdair MacIntyre, Stanley Hauerwas, Hans Frei, James McClendon and George Lindbeck. Each of them challenged the assumptions of modernity and suggested that there is an alternative to the hermeneutics of liberalism. Lindbeck puts the matter quite clearly:

> The issue which concerns us is the extent to which the Bible can be profitably read in our day as a canonically and narrationally unified and internally glossed (that is, self-referential and self-interpreting) whole centered on Jesus Christ, and telling the story of the dealings of the Triune God with his people and his world in ways which are typologically (though not, so at least the Reformers would say, allegorically) applicable to the present.[6]

Thus did I come to abandon liberalism and embrace the postliberal way of reading Scripture "as a Christ-centered narrationally and typologically unified whole in conformity to a trinitarian rule of faith."[7] One might describe this as a third conversion.

This explains how I came to understand myself as postliberal and postconservative, but what about being a catholic? As I began searching for a dissertation topic, it was suggested that I might read St. Augustine's *City of God* as a narration of the Christian story.[8] I discovered that this strategy of reading the Bible, which I thought was *new*, was in fact a *very old* way of reading.[9] It was the universal (or catholic) way of reading for centuries. I felt as foolish as G. K. Chesterton, who likened his embrace of Christian orthodoxy to "an English yachtsman [who] slightly miscalculated his course and discovered England." As Chesterton reflected, "I tried to be some ten minutes in advance of the truth. And I found that I was eighteen hundred years behind it."[10]

This *new* way of reading shares something in common with the *pesher* method of the rabbinic *Tannaim*, the eschatological use of Scripture by the apostles, the allegorical readings of ancient Alexandrian Christians, the figural exegesis of the Latin Fathers, the fourfold sense of the medieval church, the *lectio divina* of Benedictine monasticism and the *devotio moderna* which became expressed in the simple biblicism of the baptist vision. That *something* which is shared by all these methods is the conviction that the Scriptures maintain a narrative unity only when they are read within a believing community who live out the story. I recognized that reading the Scriptures faithfully so that they are illumined by Christian convictions requires understanding oneself as a member of the whole church, diachronically (that is, through time) and synchronically (that is, at the present time).

Ironically, one of the few matters on which liberal critics and conservative interpreters have agreed in modern times is that this sort of spiritual exegesis is a bad idea. For conservatives the Scriptures are rightly read by the grammatical-historical methods of the Reformers, and for liberals the meaning of the biblical text can only be recovered by historical-critical exegesis. But both liberals and conservatives agree that spiritual exegesis, whether typology or allegory or anagogy, imposes alien meanings on the Scriptures and should be eliminated.[11]

How is it that conservatives and liberals joined together to eclipse the spiritual reading of the Bible? My answer is that these two forces are really two stages in the same trajectory of the eclipse: stage one (the Protestant Reformation) and stage two (the Enlightenment).[12] Both of these, in different ways, have failed because they separate the historical meaning of the biblical text from the spiritual message of the living Christ.

I have reached the conclusion that the failure of the historical and grammatical hegemony calls for a *new* evangelical way of reading the Bible that is postconservative, postliberal and catholic.[13] Having heard of the journey that led me to this end, perhaps you now possess a better understanding of my opening confession. But the point of this story is more than just background information for the thesis I wish to defend. It is also a reminder that each of us has a story to tell, and, most important, that *God* has a story to tell. When our lives are situated within this universal community, we begin to understand that the church is more than simply the people who tell the gospel story. The church *is* the story.[14]

This is the narrative unity to the Bible. Reading Scripture in this new way requires more than the mastery of historical principles and ancient languages. It demands an account of our life together in communion with Christ within the community of Christ. Only then may we open the Bible, not as disembodied minds seeking knowledge, but as embodied selves with histories searching for the story of our lives.

On Taking Modernity Seriously (but Not Too Seriously)

For fifteen hundred years Western Christendom was held together by a single magisterial authority through which the Scriptures were to be rightly read. Martin Luther's nailing of his ninety-five theses to the door of the Wittenberg church in 1517 was dramatic evidence of the fragmentation of the grand catholic synthesis. Soon Europe was divided between Catholic and Protestant states. The ensuing struggle for authority led to a horrific period of religious wars. In the eighteenth century there was an attempt to forge a new synthesis that would reestablish a single authoritative viewpoint based on autonomous reason and sound argument, unlike the shattered synthesis, which had been built upon revelation and tradition. This bold new project known as the Enlightenment marked the culmination of modernity's intellectual vision.

The Enlightenment project was not without monumental achievements in philosophy, science and history. Indeed, the historical-critical method and liberal theology are children of the Enlightenment, but ironically they are no more so than modern fundamentalism and evangelical theology. Nevertheless, one of the few matters about which there is consensus in contemporary academia is that the Enlightenment project has proven to be a failure.[15] The hegemony of reason, like the reign of ecclesial authority, has lost its power to persuade. Thus, we postmoderns live "round the decay of that colossal wreck."[16]

Postliberals contend that the collapse of the Enlightenment foundations calls into question the theology of Protestant liberalism, which was built on the assumptions of modernity. Thomas Oden puts the matter quite forcefully:

> In the past two hundred years, many liberals have sold out under the influence of modernity. What unites such diverse thinkers as Rudolf Bultmann, Paul Tillich, Charles Hartshorne, Mary Daly, and Karl Rahner? Accommodation to modernity. This underlying motif unites the seemingly vast differences between many forms of existential theology, process theology, liberation theology, and demythologization—all are searching for some more compatible adjustment to modernity.[17]

When it comes to the reading of Scripture, postliberalism has called for a reassessment of the underlying assumptions of the historical-critical method and for the subordination of biblical criticism to the narrative unity of the Bible. The individual trained in historical and linguistic skills with the goal of recovering the objective meaning of the text apart from its theological message has been replaced as the hermeneutical arbiter by the ecclesial community that exercises the classical strategy of reading the Bible. The use of typological and figural devices supplies a canonical unity insofar as the story is told within the social and linguistic context of a community that possesses a distinctive set of beliefs and practices—namely, the church. Thus postliberals have taken up this *old* method of reading the Bible with a *new* turn.

George Lindbeck calls this new way of using the old method *intratextuality*. "Intra-textual theology," Lindbeck explains, "redescribes reality within the scriptural framework rather than translating Scripture into extrascriptural categories."[18] In this new sense, the interpretive community does not situate the Christian narrative within the world (i.e., extratextuality); rather, they situate the world within "the strange new world of the Bible" (that is, intratextuality).[19] The intratextual strategy provides a way for Christians to read Scripture in a postmodern era whereby even the results of modern critical scholarship may be assimilated into the postliberal research method.[20] By affirming this old method in a new way, Lindbeck hopes on the one hand to maintain a narrative unity in the biblical canon by centering on the story of Jesus Christ. On the other hand, he attempts to avoid the historicist crit-icisms of premodernity by translating the story of the world into the biblical nar-rative, rather than vice versa.[21]

How seriously do postliberals take modernity? Some might raise a concern that they have not taken modernity seriously enough but rather beg important historical questions. Others might argue that the intratextual telling of the Christian story which includes modernity, albeit in an intratextually renarrated version, still defines postliberalism too much in terms of modernity.[22] As Karl Barth (who is claimed as a forerunner of postliberalism) deliberated over a response to the anthropocentric theology of Ludwig Feuerbach, he suggested that "anyone who is not able to laugh in [Feuerbach's] face . . . will never get at him."[23] Postliberals suggest that it is the whole Enlightenment project, not just Feuerbach, at which we must be able to laugh. It might be said, then, that postliberals do take modernity seriously but only serious-ly enough to get the joke.

If Protestant liberalism is an outgrowth of modernity, Protestant fundamentalism as a religious movement in North America is also unintelligible apart from moder-nity. The five "fundamentals" (a verbally inspired and inerrant Bible, the virgin birth, a substitutionary atonement, a bodily risen Lord and an imminent second coming) reveal more about nineteenth-century liberal theology than about the his-toric orthodoxy of the church. But the modernity of fundamentalism runs deeper than its reaction to liberalism. When it came to reading the Bible, fundamentalists were just as committed to the notions of objective historical evidence and autono-mous individualism as were liberals. How did fundamentalists come to embrace individualism and rationalism?

Beginning in the nineteenth century with the camp meeting revivals, American Protestantism underwent a theological shift. Conversion, which historically had been understood as a slow and painful process, became dramatically shortened. In the institution of revivalism, sinners could get saved between the second and third verse of the invitation hymn. An even more significant change than the immediacy of conversion was the radical individualism of the "salvation experience." No longer was there a need for the church to guide and interpret the process of conversion. It became an unmediated and unassailable experience of the individual believer.[24]

The religion of revivalism thus endowed American evangelicalism with the confidence of individual experience, but whence the evangelical rationality?

Charles Blanchard, who was president of Wheaton College from 1877 to 1925, wonderfully illustrates the fundamentalist commitment to objective rationality. Blanchard argued that the historical veracity of Scripture was evident to anyone through the use of common sense. Unbelief, he continued, did not originate "with the common man" but rather with false teachers in the church, and he suggested that "the critics of our time have been usually men who have poisoned their nervous systems and injured their minds by the use of narcotic and other poisons."[25] For Blanchard, the meaning of the Bible was self-evident to anyone—at least to anyone who was not a moron or a dopehead.

Few fundamentalists and fewer evangelicals today would agree with Blanchard's crusade against biblical scholars and educated ministers, but the difference between Blanchard and modern evangelicals is less a quarrel over hermeneutical theory than a disagreement about the application and practice of it.[26] Blanchard clearly represents the conservative Protestant heritage of confidence in commonsense reasoning when it comes to the question of how to read Scripture, especially in the *sensus fidelium* of fundamentalism. That is, "the Bible says what it means and means what it says."[27]

To the extent that evangelicals have inherited this tradition shaped by revivalistic individualism and commonsense rationality, they (no less than liberals) believe that the Bible can be read by rational individuals apart from a community of spiritual transformation. And to the extent that evangelicals have not recognized revivalistic individualism and commonsense rationality as simply modernity in another incarnation, they have not been able to laugh. Yet it is precisely for the reason that evangelicals have taken the joke of modernity too seriously that there needs to be a shift toward a postconservative hermeneutic. The analogue for such a move is postliberal theology.

One way of describing the problem is to recognize that liberals and conservatives are two sides of a continuum. Liberals will not believe anything that cannot be proven to be historical, and conservatives assert the historicity of everything that they believe.[28] Hans Frei noticed this liberal-conservative affinity when he placed liberal David Tracy and evangelical Carl Henry together in the same type of theology because of their insistence that "theology must have a foundation that is articulated in terms of basic philosophical principles."[29] Postliberals have attempted to step out of the liberal-conservative continuum by recovering a more classical sense of Scripture as a historylike narrative (not a historiographically accessible text) and by rediscovering the cultural-linguistic practice of biblical interpretation.[30] It remains an open question whether evangelicals can escape their fundamentalist past without simply moving along the continuum toward liberalism by endorsing the use of historical-critical exegesis.[31] If evangelicals wish to join postliberals in a new paradigm for reading Scripture, it will require no less than stepping outside the liberal-conservative continuum to explore a new hermeneutic.[32]

Regulating Spiritual Exegesis

How might postliberals and postconservatives begin to read the Scriptures in this *new* way so that it might enhance the practice of Bible study, not just for the scholars in the academy but among the faithful within the church? This is the question of the *sensus fidelium*. One of the bold claims of modernity was that the practice of the historical-critical and grammatical-historical methods would forestall abusive allegory with its esoteric senses of Scripture and render the Bible understandable to scholars and nonscholars alike. That these modern methodologies have failed to enhance the *sensus fidelium* is surely evident. The historical study of the Bible has become more than ever the province of a scholarly guild, as it is difficult for laypeople to practice such technical skills.

But the question still remains: Can the disciplined exercise of spiritual exegesis be regulated so that it avoids the more bizarre expressions against which the Protestant Reformers and modern critics reacted? I will attempt to answer this question by sketching out four rules for a spiritual strategy of reading, following Lindbeck's suggestion that such a practice should conform to a trinitarian rule of faith, adhere to a Christ-centered narrative and cohere to the cultural-linguistic practices of the community.

On the *Paraclesis* of the Spirit

James McClendon has suggested a hermeneutical motto for the practice of spiritual exegesis: *"We* are Jesus' followers; the commands are addressed directly to *us."*[33] For McClendon this insight grows out of the Pentecost sermon in which Simon Peter declares *"this"* (that is, the event of Pentecost) *"is that"* (that is, the prophecy of Joel). One does well to ask how Peter (or the primitive church) made such a connection between their world and the biblical narrative. Was it purely the work of the human imagination, or was it perhaps the *paraclesis* of the Holy Spirit?[34]

The community of disciples, who had been instructed by Jesus in his earthly ministry, arrived at the radical understanding that they had become the eschatological community that was guided by the risen Lord through the presence of the Spirit. They discovered that their lives and their world were displayed in the biblical narrative. If McClendon is correct, Christians today may understand themselves as both the primitive and end-times people of God to whom the Spirit speaks in Scripture.

But to say that the Bible is a spiritual book leads one to ask the question of how it may be read spiritually. Abraham Heschel speaks to this matter with great wisdom:

> The divine quality of the Bible is not on display, it is not apparent to an inane, fatuous mind; just as the divine in the universe is not obvious to the debaucher. When we turn to the Bible with an empty spirit, moved by intellectual vanity, striving to show our superiority to the text; or as barren souls who go sight-

seeing to the words of the prophets, we discover the shells but miss the core. It is easier to enjoy beauty than to sense the holy. To be able to encounter the spirit within the words, we must learn to crave for an affinity with the pathos of God. To sense the presence of God in the Bible, one must learn *to be present to God in the Bible.*[35]

Modern biblical critics engage the Bible with a set of assumptions that limit the scope of meaning to the facts that can be derived by the historical and linguistic skills of the readers. Such a scientific strategy of reading regards the Bible as a text to be objectified and studied. But the spiritual posture suggested by Heschel holds the reverse to be the case. It is the readers who are the object as the God who is present in the Bible speaks through the Spirit. This spiritual strategy of reading underlies Karl Barth's claim that readers are invited to enter the "strange *new* world of the Bible," not to study the strange *old* world of the ancient Near East. By entering the biblical world, readers encounter the word of revelation *for us (pro nobis).*[36] This new narrative world, in which readers participate, exists as a counterworld to the secular interpretations of modernity.

In his classic study of medieval spirituality *The Love of Learning and the Desire for God,* Jean Leclercq contrasts the monastic and scholastic schools. Scholastic education was *exterior;* monastic learning was *interior.* The scholastic curriculum was *liberal;* the monastic study was *liturgical.* The operative method of the scholastics was *quaestio* (questioning); the definitive practice of the monastics was *oratio* (praying). The aim of the scholastics was *scientia* (knowledge); the goal of the monastics was *sapientia* (wisdom). The process of scholastic education was *rational;* the mode of monastic formation was *contemplative.*[37]

That the monastic and scholastic milieus were very different from one another is true, but, as Leclercq observes, each was also interrelated and indebted to the other.[38] It was, however, scholastic education that became the model for the training of medieval clerics. Moreover, it was this tradition that most deeply shaped the schooling of the Protestant Reformation, and it was from the scholastic tradition that the great European universities developed which gave voice to the Enlightenment project of modernity.

The dominance of the scholastic tradition of education from medieval to modern times is a partial explanation for how the spiritual reading of monastic Christianity became eclipsed in modernity, and it also clarifies the claim that liberal and conservative exegesis are simply variant extensions of the modern perspective.

What was the spiritual strategy of reading in the monastic schools which was eclipsed? It is often called the *lectio divina.* The Cistercian Arnoul of Boheriss describes the monastic discipline of *lectio* in this way: "When he reads, let him seek for savor, not science. The Holy Scripture is the well of Jacob from which the waters are drawn which will be poured out later in prayer. Thus there will be no need to go to the oratory to begin to pray; but in reading itself, means will be found for prayer and contemplation."[39]

The *lectio divina* is essentially a prayerful reading of Scripture. The practice of the *lectio divina* has two major movements. The first is *lectio* (reading), in which the biblical text is read, usually aloud. As one recites, the question is asked, "Lord, what are you saying to me?" The second is *oratio* (praying), in which the words of the text are personalized and addressed back to God. Within each movement the prayerful reader pauses for *silencio* (silence), *meditatio* (meditation) and *contemplatio* (contemplation).[40]

To the casual observer, the practice of spiritual interpretation by monastic readers may appear esoteric and arbitrary. For example, in sermon 85 of the Canticles, Bernard of Clairvaux reflects on the verse "By night on my bed I sought him whom my soul loveth" (Song 3:1 KJV).[41] The exposition begins with the affirmation that it is a great good to seek God, which is echoed by the psalmist (Ps 105:4), but Bernard wonders how the wandering soul can seek God if it depends entirely on the will of the seeker. For as the apostle Paul says, "To will is present with me; but how to perform that which is good I find not" (Rom 7:18 KJV). The psalmist who is conscious of his wandering and prays, "Seek your servant" (Ps 119:176), desires nothing else than to be sought. So also the bride who rises and goes out into the streets of the city seeking her beloved (Song 3:2) describes the soul that seeks God only insofar as it is clearly understood that it is able to seek because it was first sought. Thus the soul that seeks the good of loving God does so by virtue of the prevenient grace that arouses the desire in the first place.

One will search in vain for grammatical or historical connections between the text of the Canticles and Bernard's sermon on it. He moves circuitously from the Canticles to Psalms to Romans and back to the Canticles. Biblical critics might argue that Bernard has not read the Canticles at all but rather has simply given an account of the church's doctrine of grace. Yet his reading is connected to the text in that Bernard as the reader is a member of a spiritual community that shares a common set of assumptions about what kind of text this is and how it may be read. The shared life of community provides him with the hermeneutical clues to see that *this* is *that*.

It is not that, for Bernard, the literal sense of the text is unimportant, although purely historical questions were uninteresting to him. Spiritual reading was interesting precisely because it linked the determinative biblical story that was displayed in the liturgical life of the church with the devotional life of prayerful readers. And because they thought of Scripture like a fountain, each new reading produced new meanings as the Spirit spoke forth in fresh ways.

Recovering spiritual exegesis at the very least requires a willingness to practice reading under the discipline of the church's preaching, which calls readers to prayer. The petition of a prayerful reading is *veni creator Spiritus* (Come, O come, thou Spirit of life). By inviting every Christian to become a prayerful reader of the Bible, the *sensus fidelium* would surely be enhanced. Such an account of Bible reading dislodges the scholarly critic as the final arbiter of meaning and restores the interpretive activity of the spiritual community as the connecting link between text and reader.[42]

But it follows that there will be as many meanings as there are readers. The resulting proliferation of interpretations is a cause for concern for many modern readers. One is led to ask, "With all these meanings how can I discern the ones that are good readings?" Is there not a very real danger that a heterodox cacophony will triumph over an orthodox symphony, and thus the *sensus fidelium* would be undermined rather than enhanced? Consequently, there is a need to think further about how competing spiritual readings are to be regulated, and so I turn to a second rule.

On the *Anamnesis* of the Lord
The first rule disciplines the practice of reading the Bible by suggesting that readers begin with an openness to the *paraclesis* of the Holy Spirit. The second rule instructs readers to proceed in the *anamnesis* of the Lord. How can reading be a way of remembering Jesus, and how can such a memory regulate the practice of reading? The classic hermeneutic that Lindbeck and the postliberals have attempted to reclaim is a strategy of reading Scripture "as a Christ-centered narrationally and typologically unified whole."[43] Remembering Jesus is thus the key to envisioning this center and unity in the Bible. But how is Jesus to be remembered?

The central (but not the only) act of remembrance is the Communion meal, which the church has been instructed to continue performing as a memorial until the Lord returns (1 Cor 11:23-26). The Zwinglian tradition has long emphasized that the Lord's Supper was instituted for the church to remember Jesus. More recently, Joachim Jeremias has argued that the Eucharist was established for God to be reminded of the Messiah.[44]

But this remembrance is not merely a matter of psychological or theological recollection about Jesus. It is a performative action through which the story of Jesus is memorialized. The Lord's Supper (along with baptism) is a "remembering sign" in which the church repeatably enacts the gospel story, and through the repeat performances of this sign the church learns how to read Scripture as an evangelical story.[45]

The enactment of the Eucharist declares that this story is about Jesus Christ, and in each performance the community of the baptized is invited to join their destiny to his as he makes their story his story. As Nicholas Lash has written,

> Christian practice, as interpretative action, consists in the *performance* of texts which are construed as "rendering," bearing witness to, one whose words and deeds, discourse and suffering, "rendered" the truth of God in human history. The performance of the [Scriptures] enacts the conviction that these texts are most appropriately read as the story of Jesus, the story of everyone else, and the story of God.[46]

Thus the liturgical performance of Scripture is not fully complete until the story is enacted by the baptized community that imitates Christ. But without the liturgical enactment of the remembering signs, readers would not know what kind of text the Bible is or how it may be read.

It is important to note that the primitive church celebrated the Eucharist and proclaimed the gospel long before there was a New Testament. Their interpretation of the Hebrew Scriptures was different from Judaism's, because this eucharistic remembrance enabled them to read the story of Israel as a Christian narrative that finds its unity in Jesus as the Christ of God. This christological center determined the content of the developing New Testament canon as it took shape in the second century, and it continued to guide the church's understanding of how both testaments of the Christian Scriptures were to be read faithfully.

The christological center of the Old Testament is beautifully illustrated in Dietrich Bonhoeffer's reading of the Psalms, first expressed in a lecture called "Christ in the Psalms" (1935-1936), later in *Life Together* under a section entitled "The Secret of the Psalter" (1938) and finally in the brief work *The Prayer Book of the Bible: An Introduction to the Psalms* (1939).[47] Bonhoeffer calls attention to the place of the Psalms in the primitive church. The Psalms are alluded to in Ephesians 5:19 ("Speak to one another with psalms") and Colossians 3:16 ("Let the word of Christ dwell in you richly as you . . . sing psalms"). The Psalter, Bonhoeffer observes, occupies a unique place in Scripture as a message of God's Word and as a model of human prayer. But how can it be both at once? Bonhoeffer's answer is Jesus Christ. The careful reader of the Psalms of innocence recognizes that "Someone else is praying, not we; that the One who is here protesting his innocence, who is invoking God's judgment, who has come to such infinite depths of suffering, is none other than Jesus Christ himself. He it is who is praying here, and not only here but in the whole Psalter."[48]

The Psalter is truly the prayer book of Jesus Christ. As the congregation prays the Psalms, Jesus Christ prays in his congregation, and as Jesus Christ joins in the prayers of his people, he is their intercessor before the Father. In this way, Bonhoeffer says, "we understand how the Psalter can be prayer to God and yet God's own Word . . . [because] Jesus Christ prays through the Psalter in his congregation."[49]

The christological rule not only opens up Scripture, it also limits the range of interpretations. The limiting use is plainly displayed in the conflict between Roger Williams and the New England Puritans.[50] Williams came to embrace separatist theology and fled Old England to escape the purge of Puritans instigated by Archbishop Laud. In New England Williams hoped to find a freedom of worship in the new experiment of church and state, but his hopes were unrealized as he soon found himself at odds with the authorities in Plymouth, Salem and Boston. The problem for Williams was that the churches of New England were yet unseparated from the English church and thus were corrupt. He was forced to flee Massachusetts in the winter of 1636 under the banishment of the Puritan magistrates, and he eventually settled in Rhode Island.

The Puritan cleric John Cotton attempted to justify the punishment of Williams based on a typological reading of the Old Testament. The Puritan church, Cotton argued, was the typological fulfillment of Israel. This reading produced a theology of a unified church and state which approved the use of magisterial authority to discipline "heretics and schismatics" like Williams. Yet Williams recognized the danger of a violent state's using coercive power to protect an impure church. Against Cotton's exegesis Williams argued that the authority given to the magistrate under the Old Testament has been superseded under the New Testament.

But the *coup de grace* of Williams's argument was the insight that all the types of the Old Testament, especially those of kingdom and priesthood, were fulfilled in Jesus, who lived humbly among humanity, was rejected by the powers of the world and chose death by crucifixion at the hands of the earthly authorities. McClendon summarizes the force of Williams's insight:

> Therefore no claim to found [a] Puritan or any other government on the precedent of Israel as depicted in the Old Testament was valid; all its typological force had been fulfilled in Jesus Christ. *From Jesus onward*, government interference in anyone's faith, be that faith false or true, constituted disobedience to Jesus himself; if undertaken for supposed biblical reasons, it was self-refuted.[51]

The recovery of spiritual exegesis requires an openness to the Holy Spirit through the communal discipline of prayer (rule number one), but it also demands that the performance of Scripture be coherent with the enacted convictions and social practices of the community that remembers Jesus (rule number two). As Lindbeck has written, when the crusader cries out "Christ is Lord" to authorize cutting off the head of the infidel, it is a false utterance because "it contradicts the Christian understanding of Lordship as embodying . . . suffering servanthood."[52] Similarly, readings of Scripture that do not cohere with the communal practices of remembering Jesus are no less false than the authoritative claims of the angry parent who announces to the child, "I the court pronounce you guilty of not cleaning up your room!" or the frustrated wife who declares to her husband, "In the name of the Constitution of the United States I command you to do the dishes!" Truthful interpretations, like truthful confessions, require a communal practice to sustain them.

Williams's understanding of the christological rule provides a necessary critique of abusive typology. Unfortunately, he was not confident that any true church could exist to embody the authority of the gospel until the Lord's return. It is worth thinking about how such a community might practice the discipline of the spiritual reading of the Bible under the guidance of the liturgical enactments of remembrance. But before sketching out an ecclesial pattern of discernment, it is important to describe another kind of performative enactment that regulates the reading of Scripture.

On the *Mimesis* of the Saints

The remembrance of the Lord in liturgical performance is not complete until the story is enacted by the community of the baptized, but communal enactment at its best is guided by imitating the exemplary performances of the saints. The practice of reading Scripture is then further guided by the *mimesis* of the saints. As the apostle

Paul invited the Corinthians, "Follow my example, as I follow the example of Christ" (1 Cor 11:1). Who are the saints, and how does one imitate them? Richard Kieckhefer offers three definitions of sainthood. At the most basic level of understanding a saint is "a person who is leading or has led a life of heroic virtue" (i.e., exemplification). A second definition denotes "a person who has gone to heaven" (i.e., beatification). A third and more formal meaning describes "a person who by virtue of the church's judgment that he or she is in heaven" is the legitimate object of devotion (i.e., canonization).[53]

The magisterial Catholic theology permits the veneration of saints because they are close to God by virtue of their beatification and accessible to humankind by means of their supererogation. Although Protestants dispensed with a formal theology of sainthood, an informal practice of hagiography survived the Reformation. The lives of some were so exemplary that they became transcending images for whole communities: Luther and Calvin among the Reformed, Wesley for the Methodists, Bunyan with the Baptists, Moody to the evangelicals. The deaths of others were of such faithfulness that their stories were told as sources of strength: *Memoires* of Simon Goulart with French Protestants, *Foxe's Book of Martyrs* for English Puritans, *The Martyrs' Mirror* among Dutch Mennonites. These traditions name saints whose examples illumine the lives of others. Frederick Buechner describes them as the handkerchiefs that God drops in a continuing flirtation with the world.[54]

But the exceptional virtue of the saints is not always obvious. As Anne Tyler suggests in her book *Saint Maybe*, holiness is often hidden from view. Ian Bedloe, the hero of Tyler's novel, blames himself for the "accidental" death of his older brother and drops out of college to raise his brother's three orphaned children. Nurtured by the good people in the Church of the Second Chance, Ian becomes attuned to the logic of faith that is not understood by others. When he explains his plan to his parents, they react with disbelief:

"Ian, have you fallen into the hands of some *sect?*" his father asked.

"No, I haven't," Ian said. "I have merely discovered a church that makes sense to me, the same as Dober Street Presbyterian makes sense to you and Mom."

"Dober Street didn't ask us to abandon our educations," his mother told him. "Of course we have nothing against religion; we raised all of you children to be Christians. But *our* church never asked us to abandon our entire way of life."

"Well, maybe it should have," Ian said.[55]

Not even the children whom he takes in seem to grasp the depth of his sacrifice. With a tone of derisive irony, the youngest, Daphne, rails against her uncle: "You think I'm some ninny who wants to do right but keeps goofing. But what you don't see is, I goof on purpose. I'm not like you: King Careful. Mr. Look-Both-Ways. Saint Maybe."[56]

But Saint Maybe is exactly who he is. It is a discovery that the others make in retrospect. They recognize only too late that his life was the fount of goodness that sustained them. Tyler rightly observes that neither ecclesial nor familial beatification is all there is to the making of saints. Canonized or not, they enrich us by their presence. Ian Bedloe is an ordinary person who does extraordinary things. He acts with quiet grace yet exceptional virtue, and he *is* a saint precisely because he *does not know* he is one.

Saint Maybe is a wonderfully crafted narrative, but it invites us to think about sainthood as far too private an affair. What is important is that the reader recognize Ian Bedloe as a saint, even if the characters do not. Moreover, if the reader cannot identify with Tyler's hero, there are always other novels from which to choose a story that better suits one's private notions of sainthood. Perhaps this is not so much a criticism of Tyler as it is an indication of the powerful role that novels have filled in the modern quest of individual self-identity. But when the imitation of the saints is guided by preference, the richness of the communion of saints is lost.

Naming the saints is a communal affair in the Christian traditions. Sanctification is the work of God, but canonization (even informally) is the work of the church.[57] *Remembering the saints* is also communal practice. Inasmuch as the *communio sanctorum* is mediated by the worship and memory of the church, there is a resistance to the kind of privatization encouraged by modern novels. In Christian hagiography we confront the fact that the stories that narrate the possibilities of life in Christ are not of our own making or choosing. *Celebrating the saints* is a communal matter by virtue of their commonality with all of God's children. Because the saints are the people of God collectively, they are so individually. Thus to tell the stories of the saints well displays the holy life as a shared life.[58]

Robert Wilken suggests that "by observing the lives of holy men and women and imitating their deeds we become virtuous." He adds that "before we become doers we must first become spectators."[59] I want to suggest further that the extent to which Christians become good Bible readers is correlative with the habits they acquire by being careful saint watchers. But one still may ask, why imitate the saints? Why is it not enough simply to remember Jesus? Karl Rahner provides an answer that can be embraced by all Christians:

> Herein lies the special task which the canonized Saints have to fulfill for the Church. They are the initiators and the creative models of the holiness which happens to be right for, and is the task of, their particular age. They create a new style; they prove that a certain form of life and activity is a really genuine possibility; they show experimentally that one can be a Christian even in "this" way; they make such a type of person believable as a Christian type.[60]

The lives of the saints visibly and palpably re-present the life of Christ, and therein others observe the way of life displayed in these stories as a real alternative to the secular interpretations that define modern existence. The biblical warrant for the imitation of the saints as the imitation of Christ is powerfully reinforced in Paul's letter to the Philippians. After urging them to imitate the Crucified One (Phil 2:5-11) they are enjoined to imitate the apostle (Phil 3:7-17). So also, without the saints contemporary Christians simply could not begin to imagine what it might mean to follow Jesus faithfully, but because the saints are truthful representations of Jesus their exemplary performances can be imitated.

When Augustine came to Milan as a teacher of rhetoric, he was attracted to the eloquent preaching of Ambrose, not to hear *what* he said but *how* he said it. As Augustine listened, he says that he began to love "that man of God . . . because he was kindly disposed towards me."[61] As Augustine's affection for Ambrose grew, he continued to listen and (more important) to observe. The Manichees had trained Augustine to read the Old Testament literally, which rendered much of its content morally and religiously offensive. This way of reading according to the letter "killed," but from his saint-watching Augustine discovered another way of reading the Bible according to the Spirit that "gave life" (see 2 Cor 3:6). The deadening effect that Augustine knew all too well was sufficient cause to abandon the Manichees, and the biblical promise of life that (he hoped) would cure the sickness of his soul was reason enough to return to the church.[62] But the spiritual life promised in Scripture became intelligible to Augustine because he first saw the healing word of the gospel embodied in Ambrose and was drawn to imitate him.

Stanley Hauerwas calls attention to the concluding chapter of Athanasius's *On the Incarnation of the Word of God*, in which he appeals to the regulative function of the saints for the reading of the Bible. Athanasius writes,

> But for the searching of the Scriptures and true knowledge of them, an honourable life is needed, and a pure soul, and that virtue which is according to Christ; so that the intellect guiding its path by it, may be able to attain what it desires, and to comprehend it, in so far as it is accessible to human nature to learn concerning the Word of God. For without a pure mind and a modelling of the life after the saints, a man could not possibly comprehend the words of the saints. . . . He that would comprehend the mind of those who speak of God must needs begin by washing and cleansing his soul, by his manner of living, and approach the saints themselves by imitating their works; so that, associated with them in the conduct of a common life, he may understand also what has been revealed to them by God.[63]

That Augustine's saint-watching guided his reading of Scripture in the way described by Athanasius is surely so, as he soon discovered other saints to imitate— Simplicianus, Victorinus, Ponticianus, Anthony, and his mother Monica. Their lives were faithful performances of Scripture, and their stories were invitations to be changed into the likeness of Christ. But for Augustine, imitating the saints began in earnest when, by the grace of God, he "put on the Lord Jesus Christ" (Rom 13:14)[64] and by baptism was initiated into the community of those who had already begun the journey of transformation.[65] So would the *sensus fidelium* of the contemporary evangelical church be enhanced and regulated by a more deliberative habit of imitating the saints.

On the *Diacrisis* of the Community

In his book *Unleashing the Scripture*, Stanley Hauerwas begins by asserting that "no task is more important than for the Church to take the Bible out of the hands of individual Christians in North America." He recommends that Scripture not be given to children but rather that parents should be instructed that their sons and daughters "are possessed by habits far too corrupt for them to be encouraged to read the Bible on their own."[66]

Placing the Bible in the hands of the people is indeed a dangerous act, as the Duke of Newcastle under King Charles II of England recognized when he wrote, "The Bible in English under every weaver's and chambermaid's arm hath done us [royalists] much hurt."[67] Indeed it did. It may be the case that the seventeenth-century Englishman knew more about the Bible than most twentieth-century Americans and that they were more spiritual readers as a result of the residual Christian culture that shaped their character toward the gospel, whereas the post-Christian society in which we live trains us to operate under secular assumptions. But putting the Bible in the hands of the people is no less political an act now than then, and putting the Bible in the hands of the people is precisely what is at issue in the *sensus fidelium.*

This is not to say that the Bible should be placed indiscriminately into the hands of laypeople. After all, this essay has described how a postconservative-postliberal strategy of reading might proceed under the discipline of a spiritual community that remembers Jesus and imitates the saints. But one still might ask, What is to prevent spiritual readings of Scripture from resulting in the perverse experiments of Jonestown or New Mount Carmel? At least the historical-critical method can rule such bizarre interpretations to be badly mistaken, and any exegetical theory that cannot do the same would seem to be severely deficient.

One might counter such a charge by pointing out that the historical-critical method did not rule out the idolatry of National Socialism in pre-World War II Germany, nor have commonsense readings of Scripture been a prophylaxis against the fomenting civil religion among right-wing evangelicals in America, nor did a simple biblicism prevent Baptists in the southern United States from endorsing slavery on biblical grounds, nor (might I add) did the practice of spiritual exegesis prevent Bernard of Clairvaux from the folly of preaching the Second Crusade. Perhaps the lesson of these bad examples is that the truthfulness of a performance based on any method is only as faithful as the community that sustains the discipline of reading. Consequently, I will attempt to delineate an ecclesial process of discernment that further regulates and disciplines the spiritual strategy of reading.

John Howard Yoder has proposed a model growing out of the Radical Reformation that he calls "the hermeneutics of peoplehood." He notes that as the Protestant Reformation developed in Germany and Switzerland, Zwingli and Luther struggled with the issue of opening the interpretive process to the whole congregation so that "every prophetic voice is heard and every witness evaluated."[68] Zwingli called this congregational process of biblical interpretation "the rule of Paul" (1 Cor 14:26-29). Yet Luther witnessed the dangerous tendencies of an undisciplined practice of such openness in the Zwickau prophets and the peasant revolt of the 1520s.

The Reformers' worst fears were realized in 1534, when rebellion broke out at Münster, renamed the New Jerusalem, where radical Anabaptists gathered to await the second coming of Christ. The revolutionaries insisted that everything must conform to Scripture—that is, everything except the command against taking up the sword. The end was tragic. The city was recaptured by the opposing Catholic army, and the Anabaptist leaders were executed. Mainline Protestants identified the debacle of Münster with the open congregational process of biblical interpretation. In the generation after Münster, however, the community of baptists that followed the teachings of Menno Simons gave witness to the peaceable practice of "the hermeneutics of peoplehood."

By interrelating elements of the radical Protestant witness with the biblical warrants, Yoder attempts to display a normative account of this communal hermeneutic. The description is organized around four agents of the conversation. First, there are *agents of direction*, or prophets, who explore the direction of the Spirit of God to guide God's people through the means of human discourse. Second, there are *agents of memory*, or scribes, who prayerfully and critically study the biblical text and (I would add) the communal tradition. Although Yoder does not mention it as a function, these agents of memory must surely bear witness to the catholicity of the tradition and remind forgetful readers that there is more than "the New Testament and the now."[69] Third, there are *agents of linguistic self-consciousness*, or teachers, who articulate a coherent account of biblical interpretation within the community. Fourth, there are *agents of order*, or elders, who moderate this lively conversation so that every voice is heard and the health of the community is not endangered.[70] All four agents must be present, and to the extent that they are absent or diminished the process is always in danger of distortion.

It is conceivable that such a hermeneutical process still does not rule out the possibility of another Jonestown or New Mount Carmel. This is regrettably true. Other communities might well justify bizarre interpretations just as a lunatic may claim to be Jesus Christ. Chesterton wisely observed that although these kinds of theories explain "a large number of things," they do not explain things "in a large way."[71] Such a suggestion may mean that a community displays things "in a large way" when it is able to maintain the peaceable expression of a multitude of witnesses. In short, the hermeneutics of peoplehood is ultimately about how to carry on conversation within the church catholic.

There is certainly more that needs to be said about such an account of communal discernment and whether the *sensus fidelium* will be both enriched and regulated in concert with the discipline of spiritual formation, the practice of remembering Jesus and the habit of imitating the saints. But perhaps, as Yoder concludes (and I concur), "the only way to see how this will work will be to see how it will work."[72] My assumption is that evangelicals and postliberals have taken the first step in that experiment, and my hope is that the resulting performances will be faithful renderings of the gospel.

Part V
THEOLOGY &
THE CHRISTIAN LIFE

12

THE CONTEMPORARY RENEWAL OF TRINITARIAN THEOLOGY

Possibilities of Convergence in the Doctrine of God

Kurt Anders Richardson

Modern theology has been typified by doctrinal minimalism. For Protestants the roots of this go back to interconfessional conflict and the encounter with modern science. Evangelicals were minimalist in the interest of spiritual awakening and common cause with all like-minded. Liberals, however, were minimalist in the interest of a public theology that could embrace as many nominal Christians as possible—indeed, perhaps the whole society. The difference between the two minimalisms by the turn of our century proved to be so substantive as to divide the denominations into separate camps. Liberal theology by this time was moving beyond its own minimalism to a reductionism that could not accommodate or be accommodated by evangelical minimums. Evangelicals had placed their theological emphasis on the uniqueness of Christ's atoning work and on the reality of revelation in Scripture. They remained theological minimalists, separating from their parent denominations, and founded a great many denominations and institutions.

Evangelicals and Postliberals

To this day, evangelicals are theological realists. In other words, they believe that the teachings of Scripture correspond in some sense to the way things really were and are. Evangelicals are certainly not the only segment of the church (or better, the *oecumene*) to hold this view, but in North America they certainly constitute a very large portion of Protestants.[1] There is, however, a growing awareness that the theological minimalism of the evangelicals has left them nearly incapable of coping with the long-term tasks of the church—maintaining the best of Christian tradition and applying its truth claims to the present situation.

The theological disorientation within this large coalition of American Christianity is discussed in some detail in a recent article by Noll, Plantinga and Wells.[2] These authors appeal to their evangelical ranks to rejuvenate theological writing according to the "grand tradition" of Christian theology. Alister McGrath's *Evangelicalism and the Future of Christianity*[3] is a detailed enunciation of just the kind of program evangelical theologians might pursue. After surveying the many issues competently covered by McGrath, I am reminded of the statement by the Jesuit theologian Avery Dulles in his *The Craft of Theology*[4] about the Eastern Orthodox and evangelicals:

> Hitherto the principal participants in ecumenism have been the more liberal churches, those with the least demanding doctrinal and liturgical heritage. Churches with firm doctrinal standards and stable traditions were considered at best dubiously ecumenical. In an ecumenism of mutual enrichment, such as I am here recommending, the priorities are reversed. The churches that have held most steadfastly to the deposit of biblical and patristic faith, and those that have best resisted the allurements of modernity, may have most to offer to an age that is surfeited with the lax and the ephemeral. The time is ripe to welcome the more traditional and conservative churches into the dialogue. For the Catholic Church it may not prove easy to reach a consensus with either the Orthodox or the conservative evangelicals, but these churches and communities may have more to offer than some others because they have dared to be different.[5]

Of course there remains the question as to how different "successful" evangelicals are willing to be. At the same time, the Orthodox and evangelicals are here said to be the more suitable ecumenical partners. Indeed, this idea has already been acted upon by a number of leading evangelicals.[6] But just exactly what it means for evangelicals to enter into ecumenical dialogue is yet to be determined. This is where the postliberals may very well enter the scene, as they bring with them this dialogical experience as well as a commitment to the realities of revelation in Christ.

Postliberals are those theologians within the mainline Protestant denominations whose yearnings find a voice in the late Albert Outler, who lamented in 1985 that after "three decades of unabated disorder" it was time for a new age in theology.[7] Writing in view of the works of George Lindbeck, Brevard Childs and Hans Frei, Outler pointed to "a postliberal hermeneutics . . . to reposition Holy Scripture as a unique linguistic medium of God's self-communication to the human family." This repositioning, he declared, should take place through a process of "consent" to the truth of the text and "participation" in the real work of God in our time.[8] But this postliberal move is much older than Outler, for it stretches back to Barth.

Hans Frei, in the posthumously published and highly differentiated book *Types of*

Christian Theology,[9] offers one type of postliberal position. Along with his deft presentation of five "types" of theology, his appendix on the Busch biography of Karl Barth is particularly valuable. In it Frei reminds us of the liberal crisis and the corresponding postliberal movement by Barth. This led the latter to the great themes of Trinity and predestination, which have been and are so often neglected. Frei writes,

> Barth was about the business of conceptual description: He took the classical themes of communal Christian language molded by the Bible, tradition and constant usage in worship, practice, instruction and controversy, and he restated or redescribed them, rather than evolving arguments on their behalf. It was of the utmost importance to him that this communal language, especially its biblical *fons et origo*, which . . . he saw as indirectly one with the Word of God, had an integrity of its own: It was irreducible.[10]

Frei points out how Barth resurrected theological discourse, which was 250 years in abatement, in order to confirm that Christian theology was all about the irreducible norm of its revealed truth in Christ. It would be left to one of the editors of Frei's book, George Hunsinger, not to write a summary of Barth's massive *Church Dogmatics* but to provide the necessary *How to Read Karl Barth*.[11]

A Place of Convergence: The Trinity

Here at the end of the century, a whole new project of recovery of doctrinal substance and its authority is required. Minimalism, criticism, reductionism and their effects on doctrine have not sufficiently nurtured the church, no matter the type of Protestantism—evangelical or postliberal. Clearly, the realism concerning revelation and atonement on the part of the evangelicals is a large measure of what has given them staying power and numbers. Postliberals want to go beyond critical reductionism to the renewal of catechesis in Bible and doctrinal study. Some do so merely against the radicalism that liberal theology evolved into, but others because they truly believe that a real word from God has been given to humankind in the man Jesus Christ. My contention, following Thomas F. Torrance, is that the doctrine of the Trinity is the evangelical doctrine that will supply the foundation for renewal and convergence of believers.

Evangelicals have never taken issue with the doctrine of the Trinity, and neither did the Reformers. I say this even though some evangelicals have wondered aloud if a doctrine not explicitly taught in Scripture should be considered essential for Christian faith. But none have disputed the eternal reality of Father, Son and Spirit revealed in the life of Jesus and the early church. Once we recognize that the life and teaching of Jesus make a real relationship between himself and the Father and the Holy Spirit explicit, the doctrine of the Trinity is quite unavoidable. Indeed, this doctrine was held in common by all the Christian churches—Reformed, Free, Catholic and Orthodox. A book edited by Mark Heim, *Faith to Creed*, reminds us that the churches of the ancient East could subscribe in various ways to the *Niceanum*.[12]

Today, with the extreme state of biblical and doctrinal illiteracy among the faithful, the sense of theological superficiality and the religious confusion of the pluralistic context, the doctrine of the Trinity is becoming the one that defines Christian identity and whose truth will function more comprehensively than once thought.

Probably the greatest stimulus to the renewal of trinitarian theology in the twentieth century has been Karl Barth.[13] But is Barth for evangelicals? It is curious that after Barth was left behind by many liberals in the 1960s, he was and is cautiously read and his thought employed by a growing number of evangelicals who have moved beyond the reductionistic fundamentalism of their forebears. We must realize that certain highly pejorative readings of Barth predisposed evangelicals to dismiss him. Still, because of Barth's view of biblical inspiration and the ornate architecture of his theological discourse, he likely will remain a somewhat obscure theologian for evangelicals.

My appeal here is to Torrance. There are many reasons for this, one of which is his signal leadership in ecumenical progress in interchurch and theological relations. His Scottish tradition in theology displays a form of theological discourse congenial to American Protestants. But there is perhaps a much more profound reason for commending him: Torrance's formation as a theologian and many of his writings precede both the postliberal and current generation of evangelical theologians. Although retired from the University of Edinburgh since 1978, Torrance hardly ceased his labors; indeed, it may be argued that his greatest contributions theologically and practically have unfolded since then. Unflagging in propounding classic Christian orthodoxy, Torrance is recognized internationally as one of our contemporary premier theologians.

Torrance and, more recently, the likes of Colin Gunton[14] are theological bridgebuilders between evangelicals and the best of Barth, and can act as models for the renewal of trinitarian theology for both evangelicals and postliberals in the American context. Torrance offers us a way beyond the critical reductionism of liberal theology and the doctrinal defensiveness of evangelicals in *The Trinitarian Faith*.[15] On the doctrine of the Trinity, Torrance masterfully re-presents the theological substance of the Nicene theologians within the framework of the best heritage of modern theology. Additionally, the publication of the papers presented at the Consultations between Orthodox and Reformed Churchmen and Theologians during the years 1979, 1981 and 1983 demonstrates that Torrance has been a leading light in these meetings (the final form of the theological documents bears the stamp of his influence).[16] This could only have been possible because of his official recognition and acceptance by the Greek Orthodox Church as a theologian of Orthodox theology.

By presenting Torrance I am not at all slighting the important contributions of Jüngel,[17] Moltmann,[18] Pannenberg[19] and Jenson[20] on the Protestant side, or Rahner,[21] Congar,[22] von Balthasar,[23] Kasper,[24] LaCugna,[25] Lossky[26] and Zizioulas[27] on the Catholic[28] and Orthodox side. Unfortunately, among evangelicals no substantial contributions to the renewal of trinitarian theology have yet emerged. In the West most Christians have a long way to go toward the renewal of trinitarian theology and worship.

In a world where the confrontation of religions represents the real battleground for Christianity, any discussion of God's sole means of salvation for the nations through God the Son will have to be preceded by a presentation of the truth of God the Father and God the Spirit in inseparable unity with him. Unfortunately, many of the evangelical and Protestant discussions of the Trinity presuppose too much about the firmness of theological understanding or its regulative nature over the rest of Christian doctrine. These discussions are often typified by methodological questions that engulf the proper exposition of trinitarian truth. The need to establish fully developed theological treatments of the doctrine of the Trinity is very great indeed.

The Trinity and the Heart of Christianity

Torrance has brought out the essential relationship between revelation and salvation when they are grounded in the knowledge of the triune God. We see this when he states, "The basic decision taken at Nicaea made it clear that the eternal relation between the Father and the Son in the Godhead was regarded in the Church as the supreme truth upon which everything else in the Gospel depends. Jesus Christ is himself the content of God's unique self-revelation to mankind."[29] His contribution has been to awaken us to the trinitarian substance of our Christian faith. *Mia ousia, treis hypostaseis* is that view of God received from Athanasius,[30] Gregory Nazianzen[31] and Cyril of Jerusalem.[32] For God is known in his triune nature only insofar as Jesus and the Holy Spirit, working toward our salvation, guide us to the Father. Both are *homoousios* ("one being") with the Father; they are coeternal with him and therefore share the same divine nature.

Torrance reassures both evangelicals and postliberals, for whom original Scripture and one version or other of its proper *sensus literalis* are at stake, of the Nicene Fathers' conviction that they brought nothing new to the faith but were, by the contemporaneous work of the Holy Spirit, giving needful clarification for the church's understanding.[33] This knowledge of God, which is received and comprehended by faith, necessarily results in the worship of God. This worship stems from the realization that the believer has been enfolded in a personal relation by the love of God. The love of God has an interpersonal richness that is prior to the creation itself. And yet out of this richness flows the love of the Three for the creation and desire for its final redemption. Jesus Christ is the final manifestation of the redeeming love of the Father, Son and Holy Spirit, who are always working out of the inseparable unity of their being, reaching us who are sinners and awakening in us new life.

In all of this, Torrance has always emphasized the ineffability of the Holy Trinity so that we do not underestimate the radical limits of our own ability to know this

God beyond what has been revealed through Jesus Christ and his apostles.[34] Torrance avers, "We have found in these centuries a continuing tradition characterised by a deep intertwining of faith and godliness, understanding and worship, under the creative impact of the primary evangelical convictions imprinted upon the mind of the Church in its commitment to God's self-revelation through the incarnate Son and in the Holy Spirit."[35]

The reliability of Scripture is the great presupposition of the theologians of the Christian faith, and whatever refinements in methodology we may recommend, we acknowledge this basis as our own. Torrance received his methodology from Athanasius's *godliness* and *precision*.[36] Theology, for all of its situatedness in particular cultures and their philosophical thought-forms, has often not been given its due as the product of the living faith of the church. Theology is much more a question of receiving, understanding and applying revelation than unearthing the truth or creatively reinterpreting it. Nicaea then becomes for Torrance the great summation of a process of understanding rooted in godliness of faith and the faithfulness in precision required of its theologians. The Christian doctrine of God, the Triune One, is actually the apprehending of God and never the real comprehending of God.[37] This is the classic principle of *lex orandi, lex credendi* at work.

The Nicene Confession, far from some abstraction or static construction of divine truth, presents the truth of the Trinity in the form of soteriology through a simple summary of the gospel employing key Johannine and Pauline terms. Obviously, *homoousion* is not biblical terminology but was adopted as a proper exposition of Jesus' words "I and the Father are one" (Jn 10:30). Although we are attentive to the clarifications of other great Christian confessions, there is a sense in which they all are unfoldings of the basic deposit of Nicaea. Indeed, as we survey the theological literature that takes Nicaea seriously, it is striking how often its statements are viewed as unsurpassable. Even the centuries-old controversy over the *filioque* ("and the Son") may find its resolution in this wake of awareness.[38]

Torrance, on the other hand, denies a simplistic biblicism with the terms *accuracy* and *precision*. For the Scriptures direct us to the truths of God, not merely present them. Torrance continues,

> This means that we have to decide what we ourselves say of the truth under the direction of the biblical statements, and how we are to formulate our statements in such a way that they are established as true through their adequacy to the truth itself. This involves what Athanasius called "freedom of religious discourse" on the basis of the Holy Scriptures when we pass beyond what they literally say to the truth of God which they convey, and seek to express that as accurately and precisely as we can. And we dare not do that except in the most cautious and reverent way and with much prayer.[39]

What the postliberal is likely seeking in terms of a type of consistent discourse is presented here. But what the evangelical is seeking in terms of contact with the reality of God is also present. Neither is content with simplistic biblicism. Perhaps

Torrance offers some real aid at this point toward the convergence of the two communities of theologians in a common critical realism that respects the primary concerns of both sides through intensification of doctrinal understanding afforded by him.

This compatibility of theological interests is probably well expressed in Torrance's melding together of the christological sources of theology: "Nicene theology . . . is both a 'Christology from below,' and a 'Christology from above,' since our knowledge of Christ as the incarnate Son and our knowledge of God the Father interpenetrate each other, arise together and regulate each other."[40] When the direction of theological reflection is guided by a unifying orientation in the two natures of Christ, referring beyond themselves to the triune nature of God, the complementarity of the evangelical and postliberal can perhaps come forcefully to the fore. As strongly as Protestants of both traditions have emphasized Christ, we must remember that our knowledge of him is always also trinitarian. As Athanasius says, "The Form of the Godhead of the Father is the *Being* of the Son."[41]

In all of this, the question of the critical thinking that became a criterion for liberal theology is absolutely relegated to secondary status. The common confession that Jesus Christ, made known by Scripture, is the real and true Word of God and thus is a real word from God must first of all criticize us rather than the other way around. As Torrance emphasizes,

> Jesus Christ is the *arche*, the Origin or Principle, of all our knowledge of God, and of what he has done and continues to do in the universe, so that it is in terms of the relation of Jesus the incarnate Son to the Father, that we have to work out a Christian understanding of the creation. It is the Fatherhood of God, revealed in the Son, that determines how we are to understand God as Almighty Creator, and not the other way round. It was through thinking out the inner relation of the incarnation to the creation that early Christian theology so transformed the foundations of Greek philosophy, science and culture, that it laid the original basis on which the great enterprise of empirico-theoretical science now rests.[42]

In *Trinitarian Perspectives: Toward Doctrinal Agreement*, Torrance begins, "It is upon our knowledge of the Father, the Son and the Holy Spirit, One God, Three Persons, that all Christian faith and worship depend, and from it that they take their essential orientation and significance."[43] Whatever may be the details of theologizing regarding the fullness and application of this principle, this is the direction of the Spirit in our time. He goes on to say that this direction provides "ground for deep doctrinal agreement that cuts beneath and behind the historical divisions in the Church between East and West, Catholic and evangelical, and [points] the way forward for firmly based ecumenical agreement in other areas of traditional disagreement behind which Churches have traditionally barricaded themselves."[44]

After tracing some outstanding features of Calvin's doctrine of the Trinity, Torrance comments on the agreement between the Orthodox and Reformed churches on the Holy Trinity.[45]

> We confess together the evangelical and ancient Faith of the Catholic Church in *"the uncreated, consubstantial and coeternal Trinity,"* promulgated by the Councils of Nicaea (A.D. 325) and Constantinople (A.D. 381). *"This is the Faith of our baptism that teaches us to believe in the Name of the Father, of the Son and of the Holy Spirit. According to this Faith there is one Godhead, Power and Being of the Father, of the Son, and of the Holy Spirit, equal in Honour, Majesty and eternal Sovereignty in three most perfect Subsistences (ἐν τρισὶ τελειοτάσεσιν ὑποστάσεσιν), that is, in three perfect Persons (ἤγουν τρισὶ τελείοις προσώποις)"* (*Ep. Syn. Constantinopolitanae* A.D. 382).[46]

In Torrance's concluding chapter, which offers his commentary on the statement, there is this helpful remark on hermeneutics: "It became clear that biblical and theological terms are to be interpreted and employed in the light of the divine realities to which they refer, and not the other way round, for terms are not prior to realities but realities come first."[47] Further, in tracing the original exposition of the doctrine of the Trinity to Epiphanius, he shows how the unity of God is not ensured by the monarchy of the Father (as Basil and Gregory Nazianzen thought) but by the whole Trinity. The eternal equality and *monarchia* of the Three was to be confessed: "Unity in Trinity and Trinity in Unity, One Godhead of the Father, Son and Holy Spirit."[48]

Finally, to ground the transcendent yet dynamically personal view of God the Trinity, Torrance brings out the concept of "the mutual indwelling of the Father, the Son and the Holy Spirit in one another." From Athanasius through Hilary of Poitiers and Basil, the term *perichoresis* was used to indicate "mutual movement as well as mutual indwelling . . . between the three divine Persons, in which their differentiating properties instead of separating them actually serve their oneness with one another." And by the Holy Spirit, other creatures are drawn into the communion of God with us.[49]

There are still many questions about the triune God we teach: the pathos of God, the equality and relational subordination of Son and Spirit, the meaning of divine person, the problem of gender-specific language, its relation to religious pluralism, and the relation of time and eternity. Torrance's work will still serve well in regard to these matters. Recent works by Ted Peters[50] and especially John Thompson[51] have offered very helpful introductions to these problems. Evangelicals have a responsibility to enter the discussion on the trinitarian doctrine of God with all their energy. It would be a terrible irony if, while resisting the dilution of the gospel, evangelicals missed the opportunity to participate in the church's own renewal in the central reality of the gospel: the God of love who has revealed himself as Father, Son and Holy Spirit.

The reality of the present dialogue between evangelicals and postliberals is an indicator of evangelical willingness to refine its own understanding and articulation of Christian truth. Evangelicals should always stand by Scripture, but they can also recognize that, on another front, the positive knowledge of God should share in this priority. The priority of the doctrine of God in his revelation stands alongside the doctrine of revelation in God.

Differences

By way of closing this essay, I wish to state my sensitivity to the differences of theological interest that separate postliberals and evangelicals. While there is a turning in the same direction to the triune God of Scripture and Christian doctrine, there are significant sensibilities that divide us. I will illuminate what I mean by reference to narrative theology and the classic ethical priority of liberal theologians.

This is exemplified by one of the leading postliberals, and a student of Frei's, William Placher. In *Narratives of a Vulnerable God* Placher presents some difficulties not only for evangelical thinkers but also for many orthodox theologians of the Catholic tradition. My difficulties do not reside primarily in what he says about God—there is much that surpasses the minimalism of the past decades—but in what he does not say. Beginning with a critical standpoint toward all ideologies of power, Placher rightly opposes all forms of Christianity that make their beds with political ideologies. But this oppositional agenda tends to limit theological statement too much. No doubt there needs to be a healthy suspicion about the association between the exultant language of Christian worship and the oppression perpetrated by "Christian" empires of the recent past. Like the ideological critique that serves to establish Placher's presuppositional base, narrative hermeneutics are also employed in a way that resists emerging from the narrative to the faithful summaries of doctrine and to the full exposition of the highly differentiated relations of the triune God to the world of creatures.

Quite apart from the great debate over the impassibility of God, where Placher has recommended passibility,[52] he presents us with a discussion that turns away from the cultural mainstream of the Christian tradition. As a Baptist, I have no problem with this, but I fear that the result of the turning away still leaves insufficient room for the fullness of the truth of the gospel. Quite rightly, Placher condemns the pathetic equations of God with civic deities as abominations, but his theological discourse is so shaped by the critique of the injustices of triumphalist "Christian" culture that the wealth of revelational truth in Scripture is restricted in its expression. As the critique comes to expression, the book is shaped by concern for the sufferings that false worshipers inflict on the helpless and weak. Placher then contends that only a God of passibility can speak to the contemporary situation. Does this mean that divine impassibility is a kind of "prison" for the person of God? Is vulnerability the only way in which proper Christian theology should communicate the "perfection of loving freedom"[53] of the divine Trinity?

It is quite proper to critique theological language as to its adequacy relative to biblical revelation. But the narrative approach to theology, a new form of biblical theology, is even more removed from the classic terminology and interests of doctrinal theology than the former. To bring the concept of divine immutability under scrutiny without resurrecting the rest of the issues from classic Christian theology is to work with too few instruments of theological exposition. The result is affirmations about God, perhaps even in his vulnerability, which are too restricted to the situational interests of the interpreter. If Placher and other postliberals would continue the work of recovering the classic Christian themes as Frei observed of Barth, considerable advance would be evident. This of course holds true for evangelicals as well, who also are guided far too much by their situational interests.

Paraphrasing Frei, Placher avers, "In Christian theology the story is the meaning of the doctrine."[54] This is only partly true, since the relation between doctrine and story is reversible. This is what is meant by the coherence of Christian theology. But even if our first statement is identical with this quote, we must hasten to add that real relation to God is the outcome of the story.

And from there we must necessarily press on to the full recovery of Christian doctrine and Scripture in the life of the church. We come to recognize afresh that Nicaea is both story and doctrine, summarized in a form that inspires worship and proclamation. Surely this will entail a profound renewal of fruitful debate among ourselves as Christians, and of evangelizing dialogue with the members of the world's religious communities. This very well could become an antidote to the doctrinal minimalism of the recent past and a source of a more just and compassionate witness to Christian faith.

13
TRUE
AFFECTIONS
Biblical Narrative
& Evangelical Spirituality

Henry H. Knight III

T he heart of evangelicalism," says Stanley J. Grenz, "lies in its vision of
the Christian life. It is a religious experience couched in theological categories."[1] Grenz argues that evangelicalism is best understood in terms
of spirituality and only secondarily as a set of doctrinal distinctives.[2]

There is certainly an increased interest in evangelical spirituality, marked by a
returning to historic sources. Examples abound: Alister McGrath on the Protestant
Reformers, J. I. Packer on Puritanism, Steven Land on Pentecostalism, William Abraham and myself on Wesley.[3] This new interest in spirituality is not universally
welcomed. McGrath notes a "tension . . . between those who define evangelicalism
primarily with reference to explicitly theological propositions and those who emphasize the individual experience of faith and personal holiness."[4] Some like McGrath
see an "organic relationship" between theology and spirituality, preventing the
former from becoming mere "abstract speculation about God" and the latter "from
degenerating into a human centered quest."[5] Others, like Grenz and Abraham, want
(to paraphrase Abraham) to relativize formal theology and subordinate it to spiritual
renewal.[6]

In light of this tension and the proposal of some to ground theology in spirituality,
does this evangelical recovery of spirituality indicate a corresponding shift in what
George Lindbeck calls the "theological theories of religion and doctrine"?[7] More

particularly, is this a move away from the model of "cognitive" propositional orthodoxy toward another of Lindbeck's models, and, if so, which one? The language of
experience or spirituality as the defining feature of evangelicalism sounds superficially like the "experiential-expressive" model. There is perhaps the fear that advocates of the centrality of spirituality—including Wesleyans such as myself—will take
evangelicalism down a slippery Schleiermachian slope.

To allay that fear, I want to offer an account of the Christian life which insists,
in contrast to "experiential-expressive" theology, on *distinctive* Christian experience
and spirituality through a contemporary recovery of the religious affections. This
I take to be central to the theology of Jonathan Edwards and John Wesley, and
compatible with the intent of contemporary evangelical writings on spirituality.

After describing the affections, I will show how postliberal insights concerning
narrative and community are helpful for an evangelical spirituality based on the
affections. Thus a recovery of evangelical spirituality may move evangelicals in a
Lindbeckian "cultural-linguistic" direction.

However, in the third section I will argue that the concern for truth claims characteristic of the "cognitive" model cannot be abandoned by evangelicals. Evangelical
appropriation of the insights of postliberal narrative theology will require a consideration of how the biblical story of God is "true."

The Distinctive Spirituality of Christian Affections
"True religion," said Jonathan Edwards, "chiefly consists in holy affections."[8] For
John Wesley, true religion was none "other than love: the love of God and of all
mankind."[9] For all their differences, the two dominant theologians of the eighteenth-century evangelical revival were united in understanding Christianity as a
religion of the heart, expressed in terms of affections. Edwards's *A Treatise on Religious
Affections* was a defense of the awakening against its rationalist critics as well as
offering criteria to distinguish true affections from religious enthusiasm. Wesley
published an abridged version of Edwards's treatise in England and, like Edwards,
understood the Christian fruit of the Spirit as affections or "holy tempers."[10]

In their use of the language of affections, Edwards and Wesley were advancing
a theological anthropology that was in tension with the emerging intellectualistic
anthropology of the Enlightenment. The Enlightenment assumed a conflict between
reason and "the passions" over the control of the will, with emotion playing the
negative role. As we shall see, an affection-based anthropology insists, in contrast,
on the intrinsic relationship between truth and human emotions.

Contemporary theologians have sought to recover the affections as an alternative
to the passion-reason conflict bequeathed to us by the Enlightenment. Don E. Saliers
wants to revive the word *affection* from "the shoddiness of current English usage"
(where it usually means "passing sentiment"), because it would avoid problems
connected with the term *emotion*.[11] Robert C. Roberts prefers the awkward but apt
term *emotion-disposition* and argues in terms reminiscent of Edwards: "Whatever else

Christianity may be, it is a set of emotions. It is love of God and neighbor, grief about one's own waywardness, joy in the merciful salvation of our God, gratitude, hope, and peace."[12] Roberts offers a typology of fruit of the Spirit as emotion-dispositions, styles and strengths, of which the emotions are the "most central traits of Christian spirituality."[13]

The central feature of religious affections is that they are, at one and the same time, dispositional, relational and interpretive of the world. As we shall see, it is this set of characteristics that distinguish the affections from an "experiential-expressive" way of talking about experience.

To say that affections are dispositions points to their character as deep, abiding emotions of the heart. They make us the kind of persons we are and provide the reasons and motives for our actions. They are not, for example, feelings (or "feeling states") that come and go; rather, they are abiding and persisting elements of a person's character.

The distinction between abiding affections and passing feelings is important. One may, for example, be leading an essentially selfish life and narrowly escape death. At the moment of escape one may "feel" thankful. Yet one could continue to live a life characterized by ingratitude. On the other hand, one might be living a life of gratitude, in which life itself is seen as a gift of God. One might not "feel" thankful at the moment, yet remain a thankful person. Of course if one *never* felt thankful, it would raise questions about whether one actually had a grateful character. But the distinction remains: *feeling* an emotion is not necessarily the same thing as *having* an emotion.

As dispositions, affections incline us to act in certain ways. If we are loving persons, then we will seek to do works of love. For Wesley and Edwards, Christian affections must bear fruit in the life that is lived if they are to be considered valid. True affections in fact *are* fruitful.

Affections are at the same time relational: they are evoked by certain "objects," which in turn qualify and shape the affections. In words of Saliers, the "particularity of the Christian affection has to do with the objects toward which they are directed."[14] One does not simply hope; one hopes for something or in someone. The promise of the kingdom of God evokes hope; the content or shape of that hope is determined by the kingdom, which is its object, and manifested in a way of life. Thus the "essential feature of the order among Christian emotions is that they take God and God's acts as their object and their ground."[15]

We can see how their objects form and shape distinctive affections by examining love as an emotion. To love God is not the same as to love one's neighbor. Wesley, for example, sees love of God as characterized by gratitude and praise, and love of neighbor by benevolence. Roberts argues that while compassion is central to our love for our neighbor, it would be an inappropriate description of our love for God.[16] In contrast to both of these affections, love of money is different still, characterized by greed or covetousness and leading to a very different way of life.

It is this feature of the affections that sharply distinguishes them from the "experiential-expressive" model. Such models understand religious language as a symbolic expression of a deeper religious experience. There is, in other words, a prior experience of God, which is then expressed in language.

Because the affections are formed and shaped by their object, the direction here is the reverse: one encounters God "objectively," as an Other, by way of language; that encounter evokes, forms and shapes the affections. Thus Christian affections are not a subspecies of general religious experience; rather, they are distinctive. Christian experience is not the same as, say, Hindu experience, and each leads to distinctive ways of life and ways of seeing the world.

This brings us to the third aspect of the affections: they are ways of seeing the world. Saliers notes that while particular "affections are what they are by virtue of their objects and the characteristic roles they play in the pattern of our thought and behavior," the affections taken together denote a way of understanding the world—they "always combine evaluative knowledge of the world and self-awareness."[17] Roberts sees Christian emotions as "construals" of the world in light of the Christian story: to "experience peace with God," for example, "is to see God as a reconciled enemy."[18]

This evaluative role of the affections implies a linkage between emotion and reason. The Enlightenment assumption, in which the stormy, unpredictable emotions are said to come over us and cloud the otherwise clear, precise conceptual work of reason, is at best only partially accurate. Instead, as Saliers argues, there is a "conceptual link between the central emotions in prayer and the way of regarding, assessing, and judging the world and the things therein."[19]

Indeed, because they are ways of seeing the world, affections serve as rational justification for our various actions. If asked, "Why did you feed that hungry child?" you might respond, "Because I had compassion for her," in which case your compassion is the justification for your action. In terms of the Christian story, such compassion is an appropriate or reasonable emotion, an accurate depiction of the situation. In contrast, hatred or disgust for a starving child would be irrational, as it would violate the truthfulness of the story of God in Jesus Christ.

Thus affections are not only evaluations of the world, but they in turn can be evaluated as to their faithfulness to the reality depicted by Christianity. To fail to have compassion for a starving child is fundamentally to misunderstand the situation as seen from the perspective of God.

The Narrative Shape of Christian Community
Having described the dispositional, relational and evaluative aspects of the affections as a way of understanding what it means to be a Christian, we can now turn our attention to the context within which those affections are evoked, formed and shaped. Let me begin with my own Wesleyan tradition.

John Wesley understood that the great purpose of God in human salvation was to restore the imago Dei, which had become totally corrupted. God's gracious acts in the atonement and through the Holy Spirit are designed both to enable us to enter into a relationship with God and to invite us into that relationship. Through our grace-enabled participation in a relationship with God, we grow in the Christian affections, most especially in love of God and neighbor. The imago Dei is restored when God's love fills our hearts and becomes our central motivating disposition (or "holy temper," as Wesley would say).[20]

The central arena in which this relationship is lived out Wesley called the means of grace. These included spiritual disciplines such as searching Scripture, prayer, the Eucharist, fasting and Christian conference, as well as acts of mercy to one's neighbor. It is through these that the love of God is primarily received, and we in turn respond in faith, love, gratitude and obedience. Early Methodists attended weekly class meetings and were held accountable to these spiritual disciplines.

Wesley's pattern of spiritual discipline is not much different from that of his Puritan and Pietist predecessors. It is also an anticipation of the recovery of spiritual disciplines among evangelicals, as represented by writers such as Richard Foster, Dallas Willard and James Houston.[21]

The significance of these disciplines for the affections has to do with their relational character. It is the object of the affections that determines their "shape." God is the object of the Christian affections—but who is this God? We know who God is from God's revelation, most centrally in Jesus Christ. In other words, we know God because God's promise and character have been revealed to us in the story of God's creating and redemptive activity. As Saliers puts it, Christian "emotions are connected with specific teachings about God and the world."[22] This is what makes them distinctively Christian.

It is this feature of the affections that provides a linkage to Lindbeck's cultural-linguistic model, in which "the nature of experience and its relation to expression and communication are construed quite differently" from the way they are in an "experiential-expressive" model.[23] Instead of a universal primordial religious experience coming to expression in a variety of culturally related religious forms, the cultural-linguistic model understands "the means of communication and expression as a precondition . . . for the possibility of experience."[24] That is, each religion has a distinctive language and set of practices that enable its participants to have a distinctive experience of God.

At the same time, the cultural-linguistic model replaces the cognitive models' emphasis on propositional truth with a comprehensive story that structures "all dimensions of existence" and serves as a "medium in which one moves, a set of skills that one employs in living one's life."[25] "The primary knowledge," says Lindbeck, "is not *about* the religion . . . but rather *how* to be religious"—that is, "how to feel, act, and think in conformity with a religious tradition."[26]

Among contemporary evangelical theologians, Stanley Grenz has most thoroughly embraced a cultural-linguistic approach, though not uncritically. Grenz seeks to move evangelicalism away from an emphasis on autonomous individualism by way of a renewed appreciation for Christian community.[27] Constituted in its ongoing life by the Holy Spirit through the biblical narrative, the community "provides a constellation of symbols and concepts which its members employ in order to understand their lives and experiences of the world and within which they experience their world."[28]

Similarly, Clark Pinnock has emphasized the role of biblical narrative in the Christian community. The "essence of the gospel," says Pinnock, "is the biblically narrated epic of salvation through Jesus Christ."[29] The story creates a "universe of meaning we inhabit by faith" and "supplies the interpretive framework in which we live and by which we understand what reality is."[30]

What is significant in all of this for a spirituality centered on the affections is the distinctive nature of Christian community. Shaped by the biblical narrative, the community is where the story of salvation is experienced anew through Scripture, the Eucharist, prayers, hymns and other practices, as well as lived out in discipleship. Through our participation in community, the biblical narrative forms and shapes our affections by providing descriptive access to the history, character and promises of God. Because our relationship with God is lived out within such a community, it does not consist of some free-floating set of experiences but is governed and shaped by the biblical narrative itself.

The Truthfulness of Biblical Narrative

So far I have argued that when evangelical spirituality is understood in terms of the Christian affections, it avoids the danger of subjective experientialism. Instead of insulating evangelical theology from spirituality by way of a propositional rationalism, theology can more appropriately be understood as inextricably related to spirituality, because that spirituality is formed within a community whose life is shaped by the biblical narrative.

Of course, this will not satisfy those evangelicals who remain loyal to a cognitive-propositional approach. They would perhaps agree with Carl F. H. Henry, who criticized narrative theology for suspending "the question of ontological truth and historical factuality," offering "no objective criterion for distinguishing truth from error and fact from fiction."[31]

Yet such concerns are not limited to ardent propositionalists. Donald Bloesch, an evangelical critic of rationalist propositionalism, echoes Henry's concerns. Bloesch takes Lindbeck and other narrative theologians to task for failing "to give due recognition" to Karl Barth's "firm insistence on the historical basis of the Christian faith" or his concern to "set forth ontological truth claims."[32] Likewise, Mark Wallace argues that Barth "sets forth a theological realism at odds with Lindbeck's . . . understanding of theology" because Barth believes "that church language, if true, corresponds to objective reality."[33]

To put it quite simply, evangelical theology, given its commitment to the inspiration and authority of Scripture, insists that biblical narrative be understood as making truth claims about God, the world and God's actions in history. This is why Grenz and Pinnock critically appropriate the cultural-linguistic model with the question of truth in mind. Grenz notes with approval that "evangelical propositionalism capsules" the "fundamental insight" that our "faith is tied to the truth content of a divine revelation that has been objectively disclosed."[34] Pinnock describes the gospel story as a "eucatastrophe that is at once historical and mythical," making "a claim upon every one, and it is at the same time factual and also alive with existential promise."[35]

One postliberal who has tried to take seriously the issue of truth is William Placher, who understands Christian theology to be making "a claim about an emerging pattern" in the lives of people and "the world around them."[36] While made from a Christian perspective and rooted in the Bible, this pattern involves universal truth claims concerning past events, present realities and future expectations.[37] Both the story of Christ and the larger story of salvation history enable Christians to interpret the world and live faithfully within it. While not able to prove these claims according to universally acceptable criteria, Christians nonetheless "want to claim that these really *are* the patterns of reality."[38]

It is this denial of a "universal standard of rationality" and the insistence that "all argument operates within some particular tradition"[39] which does most to set a cultural-linguistic approach apart from the rationalist propositionalism of evangelicals like Henry. This may also account for the reticence or ambiguity of many postliberals on the question of truth. But, as Placher notes, it is important to distinguish "between claims about *truth* and claims about *justification*";[40] locating the latter within a particular cultural-linguistic context precludes neither making universal truth claims nor communicating those claims to those in other contexts.

What is being denied by evangelical proponents of a cultural-linguistic approach is that there are universal objective criteria for assessing truth claims, and with that the requirement that a truth claim must of necessity be propositional. Rather, the locus of truth claims is ultimately in the biblical narrative of God, which takes specific form in a variety of literary genres. Such genres as narratives, psalms and parables, as well as the metaphors and other imagery they contain, are divinely inspired and do make truth claims, but in ways different from the more straightforward language of propositions. Thus while avoiding on one hand the error of asserting contextless universal criteria for truth, evangelicals at the same time seek to avoid a purely functional understanding of truth.

Far from being unsatisfactory, narrative and metaphor have certain advantages in enabling us to truthfully know God, both cognitively and experientially. First, consider the claim by Bloesch that "the dogma of revelation is the story of salvation—but as interpreted by the Spirit of God to the church. We can grasp it only as we are grasped by it."[41] Narrative and metaphor as divinely given language are admirably suited for this purpose. Because this language is not simply propositional, it depicts God and God's activity more indirectly, through story and imagery. This makes clear the derivative nature of our theology, preventing us from thinking we have somehow grasped God through our human reason. Rather, through the Holy Spirit we are grasped by the story, drawn into it and transformed by it. Rightly understood, narrative and metaphor are actually congruent with Bloesch's concern that language about God be understood neither as univocal nor as equivocal, but as analogical, given by grace alone and truthful precisely because it is limited and indirect.[42]

Second, narrative and metaphor are also generative of meaning. As Pinnock notes, the "Bible is rich in symbolic and metaphorical language"[43] which "contains a great deal of tacit and implied meaning."[44] "It opens up to us realms of awareness not easily made accessible by discursive speech. Its meaning cannot easily be nailed down, and its value is more one of putting us in touch with truth that cannot be captured easily and of giving rise to thought and reflection."[45]

Pinnock goes on to describe the biblical text as "a piece of literature" that is "available for fresh interpretation without end."[46] Because the text has a definite original meaning, it "cannot just mean anything we want it to, but it does open up a field of possible meanings, not one."[47] It is this characteristic that makes Scripture an admirable tool of the Holy Spirit in enabling us to grow in the knowledge and love of God as we live with Scripture over time.

Understood in these two ways, biblical narrative and metaphor are in service to a realist, rather than an idealist, epistemology—that is, Christians believe they truthfully refer to God and the world. It is, however, a critical realism that recognizes the limitations of human language and at the same time the possibilities of that language when used by the Spirit to enable us to know God.[48]

We have seen how the practices of the Christian community and most especially biblical narrative provide a context for a relationship with God in which distinctively Christian affections are enabled to form and develop. Because the Christian claim is that this narrative truthfully reflects the character, purposes and activity of God, the affections resulting from participating in this story are not simply a cultural variant of a more general religious experience. Rather, the Christian affections themselves reflect something of the life of the one true God who was revealed in Jesus Christ and anticipate in the present the life of the eschatological kingdom to come.

14
THE NATURE
OF CONVERSION

How the Rhetoric of Worldview Philosophy Can Betray Evangelicals

Gregory A. Clark

Thomas said to him, "Lord, we don't know where you are going,
so how can we know the way?"
Jesus answered, "I am the way and the truth and the life.
No one comes to the Father except through me."
(Jn 14:5-6)

Hans Frei, in his essay "Theology, Philosophy and Christian Self-Description," defines philosophical foundationalism as follows:

Philosophy may be regarded as being a foundational discipline which, rather than giving us information, provides us with the criteria of meaning and certainty, coherence as well as truth, in any arena of human reflection. In other words, the rules of correct thought are invariant and all-fields-encompassing. In the light of its foundational status, philosophy articulates what may at any time and anywhere count as meaningful language, genuine thought, and real knowledge. And theology, given its long but also dubious standing in the academy, is a prime candidate for philosophical scrutiny.[1]

This image of philosophy achieves its classical expression in Descartes, who uses the same method and criteria for knowledge in all disciplines and who uses philosophy to establish the grounds of certainty from which all other disciplines (mathematics, physics, chemistry, etc.) sprout.

Frei classifies Carl F. H. Henry with David Tracy because Henry insists that theology have a philosophical foundation.[2] Frei himself is not at all friendly to this position, claiming that it cannot deal successfully with the real, historical sense of

Scripture. By reducing scriptural and theological language to philosophical terminology, Henry and Tracy, Frei says, settle for an account of Christianity dictated by a foreign frame of reference. Since Henry represents the American evangelical tradition and Frei is classified with postliberal theologians, any rapprochement between evangelicals and postliberals must address the relation of philosophy and theology and the implications of this relation for understanding the Bible.

Evangelicals must begin by answering two questions: Does Frei accurately capture evangelical thought when he claims that it looks to philosophy for a foundation? If so, does this relation to philosophy prevent evangelicals from recognizing a literal sense in Scripture or providing a viable self-description of their faith?

I will argue that Frei is correct on both counts. Specifically, when evangelicals articulate their faith in terms of worldviews, they make philosophy foundational to their theology, and this philosophy prevents them from grasping the literal message of Scripture. In order to show this, I will first argue that the rhetoric of worldviews belongs to the domain of philosophy. After this point, my argument could proceed in one of two different ways. The first way belongs to the order of philosophy. It would (1) claim that Christianity is committed to a set of philosophical claims and then (2) show that worldview philosophy implicitly contradicts these claims. If the argument were successful, it would force one's philosophical opponents into logical contradiction.

Though such an argument would be fruitful, this is not the procedure that I will employ. I am not (and Frei is not) concerned with whether evangelicalism is *philosophically* tenable or with whether it meets a set of criteria dictated by philosophy. The question concerns whether evangelicalism remains faithful to Scripture. My question is whether we can faithfully incorporate worldview philosophy into the internal description of the Christian life. Rather than transpose Christianity into a philosophical key, I will try to uncover the movement of the spirit implicit in worldview philosophy. I will show that (1) worldview philosophy is committed to a form of spirituality and that (2) this form of spirituality is different from that of Christian spirituality. This procedure is a "phenomenology of the spirit" and will take the form of a meditation. My conclusion will not force evangelicals who use worldview language into a logical contradiction, but it will reveal two different forms of life, two different movements of the spirit.

Philosophy and the Concept of Worldviewness[3]

A concept is more than a word and more than a timeless definition isolated from a universe of discourse. A concept is a tool. By creating new concepts, a philosopher can make one set of problems obsolete and create a new set of problems. A concept consists in the relations that it draws between one set of ideas and the barriers it presents to connecting other sets of ideas. To fully appreciate a concept, one must understand the problem to which it responds, the work that it performs and the cluster of other concepts to which it is tied.

The concept of worldviewness differs from the concept of any one particular worldview or any collection of particular worldviews. A list of worldviews does not reveal the idea of worldviewness. One can easily catalog examples of what are today called "worldviews": naturalism, subjective idealism, objective idealism, deism, nihilism, existentialism, theism, secular humanism, the New Age, etc. But what is the concept of worldviewness? To speak like a Platonist, what do all these share that allows us to group them together *as* worldviews? What principle will determine whether something counts as a worldview or not? What is the intentional definition of the set of all worldviews?

The idea of "worldviewness" emerges to solve a set of problems in epistemology. The solution to these problems establishes connections to other ideas which in turn lead to their own problems. As such, "worldviewness" is a philosophical concept. More specifically, the idea of a "worldview" has its natural home in the field of post-Kantian philosophy. I will show this by following two paths, first looking at evangelical uses of "thinking worldviewishly" and then tracing the history of the concept of "worldview."

Evangelicals and worldviews. This question—"What is the concept worldviewness?"—will be more accessible if we first ask, "Why talk in terms of worldviews?" or "What work does worldview talk accomplish?" A survey of contemporary evangelical writers such as James Sire, Arthur Holmes, Brian Walsh, Richard Middleton and Ronald Nash[4] will show that they believe "thinking worldviewishly" can be useful for apologetic purposes. That is, evangelical worldview philosophers claim that Christianity is (or implies) a worldview, that this worldview is true and that thinking worldviewishly can help justify the belief that the Christian worldview is true.

In this regard, evangelicals seek to distinguish themselves from liberals who, they claim, sacrifice the truth claims of Christianity to those of the modern world. For example, James Orr takes up worldview language for "the rational vindication" of "the Christian view of the world."[5] Perhaps Orr only intends to show that Christianity is not *irrational*, though this would be less than rational vindication. Arthur F. Holmes too is "convinced . . . that the most persuasive case for Christianity lies in the overall coherence and human relevance of its worldview."[6]

On the other hand, worldview language also allows evangelicals to take account of other perspectives, a concern that goes to the very core of American evangelical faith. Evangelicalism distinguishes itself from its fundamentalist origins by its commitment to engage with the dominant culture and with other cultures. This requires that evangelicals work out their theology while explicitly reflecting on culture and competing claims about reality. Worldview thinking seems to provide the resources for this task. Thus a dominant stimulus for thinking "worldviewishly" is pluralism. Worldview thinking provides a metaperspective or a formal position that can mediate between competing "ways of seeing."

It is worth noting that this concern with perspectives outside the church transforms the church's self-understanding of its faith. Holmes's work on the Christian worldview has the merit of making this aspect explicit. A viable Christianity will understand its worldview as one of many worldviews. An inattentiveness to others' worldviews Holmes calls "fideism." Fideism is "a refusal to take seriously the plurality of alternatives; . . . it refuses to weigh conflicting claims. And as a result it is difficult to keep it from mere credulity."[7] On this reading, *sectarian* and *irrational* are redundant terms.

The apologetic aims and the concern with pluralism come together in the desire of worldview thinkers to transform culture. Any preface of a book espousing evangelical worldview thought will confirm this conclusion. Walsh and Middleton are disappointed that "Christianity is ineffective in shaping our public life." They hope that "Christianity may receive social and cultural embodiment."[8] Carl F. H. Henry is concerned that evangelical theology, while preserving the "timeless biblical heritage," also engage with contemporary developments. Holmes encourages evangelicals to address "secular, naturalistic humanism that approaches human existence without the theistic basis for human values on which Western culture was built."[9]

From the perspective of evangelicals, worldview thought provides an ear by which evangelicals can listen to other worldviews in a way that the dogmatism of fundamentalism cannot. It also gives a voice with which they can argue for the truth of their own worldview, a voice that skepticism concerning dogma does not allow to liberalism.

The ear and voice of worldview thought shows itself as the ear and voice of philosophy by the way these evangelicals try to distance themselves from fundamentalist apologetics. For example, why don't evangelicals adopt the strategy, say, of Josh McDowell's *Evidence That Demands a Verdict?*[10] Why not just claim that Christianity is true, present evidences that it is true and claim that anyone who looks at the facts in an unbiased manner will see that (evangelical) Christianity is true? The answer is clear. Worldview philosophers do not embrace McDowell's approach because they cannot accept the *epistemology* of commonsense realism that McDowell's apologetic assumes. If worldview thinking has an epistemology definite enough to rule out other epistemologies, then it embodies and is determined by some other philosophy or philosophies.

We can be more definite than this, however. What philosophy in particular does worldview thinking assume? What exactly is the disagreement with commonsense realism? According to worldview philosophers, one will not come to see the truth of Christianity simply by collecting together a series of facts or "evidences." People, worldview philosophers say, see the world differently. What counts as evidence will look one way to someone with one worldview, and another way to someone with another worldview. Coming to see the truth of Christianity is a matter not simply of considering objective historical data but also of examining the categories of understanding or the conceptual scheme that the subject brings to the data. The claim that the data conform to the structure of our own mind is, if Kant is to be believed, a new insight of Kant's. Worldview philosophers, then, accept some form of Kant's Copernican revolution, while McDowell and commonsense realists do not. Thus prior to Kant's Copernican revolution, the concept of worldviewness could not exist.

What is the structure of worldviewness? A survey of evangelical worldview philosophers would show a general agreement that a worldview consists of (1) a set of beliefs or judgments that are (2) pretheoretical or presupposed by all other beliefs and experiences, that (3) form a web or an internally coherent system and that (4) actively determine how we see the world and how we respond to it. This structure is most easily interpreted as belonging to a knowing subject.

The History of the Concept of Worldviewness

I now turn to the second path by which to determine whether and how worldview thinking is philosophically determined—the history of the concept of worldviewness. This is a legitimate line of inquiry. While tracing the history of a concept will not produce a timeless definition, it does constitute a well-established philosophical move. The history of a concept can reveal the soil from which a concept grew, the various uses for which a concept has been employed and the effects of employing it. The history of concepts is particularly important for concepts that people apply to themselves. Whereas the realm of nature is what it is without knowing anything about itself, the manner in which humans think of themselves determines, at least partially, who we are. The history of a concept, then, can uncover the sort of difficulties in self-reflection that led someone to formulate a concept, and also reveal the effects that the new concept had on the form of human subjectivity.

Furthermore, James Orr, writing in 1893, established a precedent for inquiring into the history of the idea of worldviewness. Orr complained that the idea of worldviewness remained too vague to use with a great deal of confidence. People often reduce disagreements to differences in worldviews, he noted, but "how entirely is there wanting a clear and intelligible, universally valid notion of the word ['worldview'] itself!"[11] Without a clarification of the concept of worldviewness, worldview philosophy simply pushes disagreements back into an even darker and more difficult arena. In order to clarify the idea of worldviewness, Orr suggests that we should trace its history. Thus establishing the history of the concept of worldviewness is both legitimate and important.

Orr realized in 1893 that the "history of the term [Weltanschauung] has yet to be written,"[12] and one hundred years later his observation is still true. Nevertheless, a few historical observations will be helpful.

Given our overview of evangelical worldview philosophers, it will come as no surprise that both Orr and Martin Heidegger agree that the notion of worldviewness first becomes possible with the work of Kant.[13] Heidegger points out that Weltanschauung or worldview "is not a translation from Greek, say, or Latin. There is no such expression as kosmotheoria. The word 'Weltanschauung' is of specifically German coinage; it was in fact coined within philosophy."[14] According to Heidegger, Kant first uses the word in his *Critique of Judgment*, referring to an intuition of the world as given to the senses.[15]

Following Heidegger's claim, let us explain how, according to Kant, we intuit the world through the senses. Kant insists that sense experience is a construct. On one side, we bring the forms of space and time to experience. We do not *derive* our notions of space and time from experience, for all our experiencing and reasoning about the world *presuppose* them. They are introduced before reflection, and they remain functional without reason coming in to prop them up. On the other side, the world contributes the content of our experience. Sense experience, then, is a composition of objective data presented by the world and the pure forms of intuition contributed by the mind. We cannot know what the world is like apart from or prior to our experience, outside the forms of space and time. We always perceive the external world as in space, not because it actually is in space and we perceive space along with other things, but because our minds are programmed to order the external world spatially. Likewise, all our experiences are structured by time, because we bring the form of time to all of our experiences. To change the metaphor, space and time are like lenses *through which* we see. Our worldview, in the Kantian sense, incorporates both objective and subjective elements.

One might reasonably ask, "How does Kant know this?" That is, how does Kant know that space and time are forms that we bring to experience rather than content that we derive from experience? Kant establishes this distinction between form and content on the basis of what is and is not necessary and universal. Knowledge that we derived from experience can be confirmed or falsified by further experience. Because no further experience could falsify something that everyone necessarily believes, that which is necessary and universal cannot be derived from experience. For example, one will never have a nonspatial experience of the external world. Thus, for Kant, the structures of the human mind are necessary for all rational creatures.

What problem does Kant's so-called Copernican revolution attempt to solve? First, the Copernican revolution is attempting to refute the skepticism of Hume's empiricism. It is trying to show that knowledge is possible because not all knowledge is a posteriori. We have knowledge of experience with the aid of the forms of intuition, and we can even reflect on these forms themselves. On the other hand, it is trying to temper the dogmatism of the rationalists by circumscribing the domain in which knowledge is possible. The subject contributes the forms of intuition. This fact does not make them arbitrary in any way. Rather, the subjectivity of the forms of intuition marks the limits of human knowledge.

How is human knowledge limited? Experience and knowledge are limited to phenomena. We cannot know what the world is like apart from or prior to our experience, outside the forms of space and time. The noumenal world is closed to us. The distinction between the form and the content of our knowledge makes us acutely aware of the distance between our own knowledge and the way things are in themselves. This has two implications. If metaphysical knowledge means knowledge of the noumena, then Kant's position implies a metaphysical skepticism. Further, if "truth" is a correspondence between appearance and reality or an adequation of the idea to the object, it is impossible to say whether the phenomena or judgments about the phenomena are "true." In fact, because "truth" is a notion that applies only within the realm of the phenomena, this is an inadmissible question.[16]

Kant calls the claim that our view of the world does correspond to the things in themselves "an idle hypothesis." Because one cannot get outside one's self to compare one's experience to the noumenal world, one can neither prove nor disprove the claim. However, the claim itself shows little appreciation for how the Copernican revolution creates a barrier between experience and things in themselves. To summarize, the concept of a worldview offers a solution to the epistemological problems of empirical skepticism and dogmatic rationalism, but it also makes it very difficult to talk about truth in terms of a correspondence between the idea and the thing.

A history of the concept of worldviewness would have to follow the history of German idealism through J. G. Fichte, F. W. J. von Schelling and G. W. F. Hegel. They introduce at least two modifications in the idea of a worldview. First, a worldview operates not at the level of the sense intuition but at the level of intelligence. A worldview is the product of an active but unconscious operation of intelligence and provides a way of interpreting what is given in sense intuition. Second, while these thinkers will maintain the distinction between form and content, this distinction is no longer tied to necessity and universality. That is to say, humans are capable of producing a plurality of worldviews. Individuals have different worldviews, and worldviews are differentiated historically and by people groups. The post-Kantian notion of "worldview," then, is inherently pluralistic. On the other hand, all humans necessarily have some worldview. Thus the idea of worldviewness remains purely formal in the Kantian sense of the word.[17]

Wilhelm Dilthey turned to worldview philosophy because the diversity of philosophical opinions all claiming the status of universal truths disturbed him. This, it seemed to him, would lead to skepticism. He proposes, instead, that we historicize these philosophical positions, that we understand them as expressing, at a propositional level, views of life that emerge within history. Thus he distinguishes naturalism, subjective idealism and objective idealism as worldviews. In every form these take, however, they are historically determined and thus limited and relative. Worldviews do compete with one another and come into conflict, but while a particular worldview may be dominant for some time, no worldview is ultimately defeated. A worldview will always emerge again in another form. Finally, the category of "truth" does not apply to a worldview. One cannot even ask the question of whether a worldview is true.

A history of the concept of worldviewness would then need to trace the idea of worldviewness through nineteenth-century studies of religion. Scholars adopted the idea of worldviews in this domain because it allowed them to grasp religion as a human phenomenon, as a way of organizing human experience, and to compare the various organizational principles of those religions, all without raising the question of whether any particular religion was true or false.

James Orr seems to have picked up the term from Albrecht Ritschl, and Abraham Kuyper may have picked it up from Orr.[18] Contemporary evangelicals, the descendants of Orr, Kuyper and Henry, use the term to accomplish much the same work that Kant and his successors used it for—to mediate between (a different form of) skepticism and an uncritical dogmatism, and to address pluralism. They insist that everyone necessarily has some worldview, thereby accepting the Kantian distinction between form and content. Finally, when they introduce their notion of "worldview," they invariably use the German *Weltanschauung* in the course of their explanations, thereby acknowledging the German paternity of their perspective.

Contemporary evangelical worldview philosophers differ from their predecessors most clearly only in wishing to argue that the Christian worldview is true. However, they have realized that "true" cannot mean a correspondence between a worldview and reality. For this reason, they flee to a different definition of truth; truth is now "coherence." The coherence theory of truth, which receives its classical expression from the idealist philosopher F. H. Bradley, claims that "a belief is justified by virtue of its coherence within the entire body of what one knows and believes."[19] Thus a worldview can be evaluated by testing to see if it is a comprehensive, coherent unity. That is to say, a viable worldview should be self-consistent and unified as well as encompass all of life. Only on this basis is it conceivable to claim that "the most persuasive case for Christianity lies in the overall coherence and human relevance of its worldview."[20]

If contemporary evangelicals wish to use the term in a different sense, they have the responsibility of *distancing* their idea from the history of the term *Weltanschauung*. Further, they must make clear how their use of the term and its history differs from that of German idealism. Even then, while evangelical worldview philosophy may free itself from German idealism, their idea of a worldview would still remain philosophical. So long as evangelicals use the language of worldviews to make Christianity intelligible and plausible, they express their faith through the medium of philosophy. Thus Frei's claim that evangelicals rest their theology on a philosophical foundation is true of evangelicals who speak the language of worldviews.

A Philosophical Excursus

In apologetics one sometimes hears the claim that Christians must draw on the resources of philosophy in order to present the faith to those who make different basic assumptions and do not recognize the authority of Scripture. The reasoning behind this claim goes something like this: Theology uses Scripture, or special revelation, as an authority. This authority is not accepted by all people. Those who do not accept the authority of Scripture will find the arguments of theology unconvincing. Philosophy appeals only to natural reason, which all persons possess in principle. Thus the proofs of philosophy should be convincing to all. This way of thinking about the difference and relation between theology and philosophy may easily lead to thinking of philosophy as a foundation for, or something presupposed by, theology.[21]

Given this assumption about the need for a philosophical foundation, it is worth pointing out that many, perhaps most, philosophers no longer find this picture of philosophy convincing. Many other papers in this volume note the postmodern and postliberal criticisms of appealing to philosophy for a foundation. The later part of this paper will be more intelligible if I also indicate some implications of these criticisms for the relation between philosophy in general and theology.

It has become almost a cliché to say that philosophy is not presuppositionless. Philosophy assumes a tradition, certain forms of expression, social practices and a community that make it possible. If this is true, then philosophy does not offer a neutral or universal language or a "natural reason" common to all rational inquirers. Philosophy represents a particular tradition with a specific access to truth. Likewise, theology is rooted in the traditions and practices of the church. Truth itself emerges only in the context of communities.

In what sense, then, is the community of philosophers prior to other communities? Its priority cannot be established by some supposed presuppositionless or universal standpoint. To insist that one philosophize prior to practicing theology or that one establish philosophical hermeneutical principles prior to doing biblical exegesis means that one ought to interpret one tradition only through another tradition. This would be difficult to justify. Philosophy's priority, likewise, does not consist in its privileged access to notions like "truth." If Jesus is the truth, then it would seem that faith and theology relate to truth in a more genuine fashion than does philosophy.

Further, all disciplines, and not only philosophy, are capable of calling their presuppositions into question; all disciplines are capable of categorical inquiry.[22] Still, philosophy does and should question its own assumptions. Philosophy's ability to question its own self opens for reexamination the tradition and the community which has typically been regarded as "philosophical." This makes it possible for philosophy to engage with feminism and multiculturalism and thereby to reconsider the philosophical canon and those practices that philosophers consider philosophical. Postmodernism transforms philosophy by criticizing narrowly conceived views of reason (including natural reason) and then expanding what can count as "proper" philosophy.

In the interest of keeping philosophy self-critical, let us ask, Does philosophy make theological presuppositions? Jean-Luc Marion is only the most recent of a long tradition of French philosophers to argue that it does.[23] For example, the first question philosophy asks about God is "Does he exist?" This beginning assumes that God's first name is "Being" rather than, say, "Goodness." This assumption allows philosophy to approach God in a purely intellectual manner. However, if God's first name is "Goodness," the situation is different. To say that something is "good" is to say that it is valuable, admirable and to be imitated. It is to say that you personally value it. If this is true in a limited way in the created order, it is even more true for the one who is "Good" in an unqualified sense. To acknowledge that "God is Good," and to have any hint at what that means, requires that one love God. In asking first whether God exists, philosophy has taken a position on the order of divine names, and this position is the proper subject of theology.

Let us ask the question in other terms. Are the philosophical community and its tradition essentially related to the community of Christian faith? Again, it seems that they are. For example, Michael J. Buckley's *At the Origins of Modern Atheism* argues that the question of the existence of God and the possibility of atheism was constituted as a *philosophical* problem by a set of decisions made by theologians.[24]

When the philosophical community becomes aware of its theological presuppositions and of its rather hostile relations to the community of faith, it has begun to be self-critical. Philosophy, then, is capable of questioning its presuppositions and of relating to theology and to the church differently from the way it has in its past. First, philosophical self-criticism can free theology from its philosophical captivity. Christian theology need not uncritically model itself on philosophical reason. That is, it is possible for Christian theology to become more than slightly modified Kantianism, Hegelianism, Marxism, existentialism or process philosophy. Christianity has the opportunity to make its own genuine contribution to philosophy because it need no longer live within the dichotomy of faith and reason. Philosophy is a form of faith, and Christianity is a way of reasoning.

Second, it becomes possible for philosophy to welcome Christianity. This means that philosophy could be opened up to the sources and content of the Christian faith. A reflection on the Gospel of John and on Jesus' confrontation with those in power can be as reflective and as properly "philosophical" (in a now expanded sense of the word *philosophy*) as are meditations on Plato's *Apology* and Socrates' confrontation with various citizens in Athenian democracy. That is, philosophy should now be open to the Bible as a collection of texts illustrating serious *philosophical* reflection, and to be a Christian philosopher will be bound up with thinking with and out of that tradition that has faithfully and rigorously drawn on the categories and stories of Scripture. Scripture can lead us to places the Greeks never went, and back to places from which some of our ancestors fled.

The welcome that philosophy extends to theology extends not only to the sources and content of faithful reflection but also to its form. One way to criticize conventional philosophical forms may be to set its content in opposition to its form, as does Alasdair MacIntyre when he criticizes the genre of the lecture in his Gifford Lectures.[25] One may also simply engage in an alternate practice, presumably a practice appropriate to the content of one's philosophy. For the Christian, the practices that Christian philosophy presupposes may include, or even be identified with, prayer, meditation, celebrating the Eucharist, feeding the poor, healing the sick, casting out demons, preaching a sermon and confession. Christians have traditionally worked out their reflections on the nature of the God they worship and their understanding of truth in these contexts, rather than in essays or papers delivered at conferences.

Postmodernism makes it impossible to distinguish sharply between philosophy and nonphilosophy. Thus one cannot distinguish Christian philosophy from theology. The proper goal of Christian philosophy is, then, Christian description of Christian experience.[26] This conception of philosophy undermines the theologically motivated claim that theology must look to philosophy for its foundations, and, specifically, that worldview philosophy can provide foundations for evangelical articulations of the faith.

Phenomenology of the Spirit

One can argue about whether philosophy provides a foundation for other disciplines on traditional philosophical grounds, as does postmodern philosophy. Frei's project, however, does not rest on philosophical claims. Frei charges that resting one's theology on a philosophical foundation will lead one away from what he calls the real, historical sense of Scripture. Thus evangelicals may successfully defend philosophical foundationalism, but if Frei is correct about its implications for reading Scripture, they have won a bitter victory. Specifically, if worldview philosophy prevents us from understanding the literal sense of Scripture, worldview philosophy betrays evangelicals who espouse it.

I wish to argue that this, Frei's second charge, also sticks to evangelical worldview philosophers. In order to show this, I will first remind my readers that philosophy itself is a form of spirituality (or a process of conversion). Spirituality, then, encompasses both philosophy and Christianity and can provide a formal model to compare them. Second, I will turn to a particular Scripture passage and show that the spiritual life that makes this passage intelligible is incommensurable with the spiritual life of worldview philosophy.

Philosophy, spirituality and formal models. From its origins in ancient Greece, philosophy has always been, and has always known itself to be, a form of spirituality. Only on this basis could it come into conflict with some aspects of Homer's epic poems and various cultic practices. By "spirituality" or one's "spiritual life" I mean one's turning and moving toward truth or supreme goodness, one's orientation toward that which satisfies our intellect and gives happiness. The spiritual life will take different forms, according to what people identify as "truth" or "the supreme good." It will also vary with the resources one has to move along toward the goal.

Philosophy expresses and shapes the life of the spirit because it concerns itself with the nature of truth and goodness, and it offers the tools to approach them. Plato formulates the spiritual life of the philosopher most clearly in the analogy of the cave in the *Republic*. Besides offering a theory of knowledge and of reality, the cave analogy is both a theory of education and a description of what the entire *Republic* enacts. The cave analogy, then, offers us a picture of the movement in the spiritual life of the philosopher. Philosophy is that life. Philosophy is not primarily the thematization of that life, but a *manner* or a *how* of life; it is a process of continual education, transformation and conversion.

Let me say this again: philosophy is a form of life that the cave analogy identifies with the act of conversion and subsequent transformation in the pursuit of knowledge and the Good; the primary locus of philosophy is not in its discourse but in the life of its practitioners.[27] Further, in the Platonic allegory this philosophical life is the process of coming to see and understand. By forcing the entire body to stand up, to turn around and to ascend out of the cave, the eyes will suffer much pain, but will also be put in conditions that enable them to see truth. Philosophy produces some conversion in its practitioners by which they come to see or understand what they had not seen or understood before.

The cave analogy can be taken as a formal model to describe the form of conversion and life encouraged and expressed by various philosophies. Philosophies will vary with their different understandings of truth and the different resources used to reach truth. Different philosophies can be distinguished by the different forms of conversion which they claim to produce. By comparing what one converts from, what one converts to and the stages of conversion, we can individuate different forms of life. This formal description of the spiritual life of the philosopher will allow me to determine and compare the nature of the experience provided in worldview philosophy and in (part of) the Gospel of John.

The literal sense of Scripture. In his *Types of Christian Theology*, Frei considers how philosophical foundationalists read Scripture, addressing writers like Kant, Gordon Kaufmann and David Tracy. In the work of these theologians, the real or historical sense of Scripture gets translated into philosophical analyses of one's own experience. Tracy reads the parables as offering "a possible mode-of-being-in-the-world," or as presenting us with an "existential possibility." Jesus, according to Tracy, is "a most powerful symbol."

Frei does not explicitly argue his thesis against evangelicals, however. Since Frei does not provide an analysis of how a worldview philosopher reads Scripture, I will provide my own. My analysis has three guiding principles.

First, I have narrowed my focus to a particular Scripture—to Jesus' reply to Thomas that he is "the way and the truth and the life." We have access to the literal sense of this passage, I will suggest, through Thomas's own conversion.

Second, I insist that worldview philosophy itself does not provide me with the resources necessary to understand this Scripture. If I can show that Thomas's conversion and the meaning of "I am . . . the truth" evades the worldview philosopher, then I can conclude that this form of philosophical foundationalism prevents one from grasping the literal sense of Scripture.

Third, my guiding question is "How do we experience truth?" or "How is truth made accessible to us?" This is an appropriate question to ask of this passage because it concerns truth. I am assuming that the nature of truth and the way in which truth reveals itself determine one another. Scripture makes truth accessible to us in some way. But philosophy too claims to have a special relation to truth. Does philosophy give us our most primordial access to truth?

The nature of truth, our access to truth and the form of our spiritual lives are all at stake in the reading of this passage. While one might pursue this question through traditional philosophical forms, I will adopt the form of a meditation.

Meditation 1. It is the Last Supper. Jesus gives a piece of bread to Judas Iscariot, who then quickly departs. Scripture says, in one short sentence: "And it was night."

Judas winds his way through the darkened streets of Jerusalem, moving, quite deliberately, toward the ruling authorities, to the betrayal of Jesus and to his own death. Jesus, in the Upper Room, speaks words to his disciples that they cannot now understand, but that will become important in the coming days.

"My children, I will be with you only a little longer" (Jn 13:33).

"A new command I give you: Love one another" (Jn 13:34).

"Do not let your hearts be troubled. Trust in God; trust also in me" (Jn 14:1).

Then the passage above: "I am the way and the truth and the life" (Jn 14:6).

Jesus is going away, and the disciples want to know how to get there. They hope not to get lost on dark streets. We can understand why Jesus says "I am the way," even if we do not understand very fully what this means.

Jesus will soon die—and be resurrected. We can understand why Jesus says "I am the life," even if we do not understand that statement very well either. This sentence sends us back to the prologue of the Gospel: "In him was life, and that life was the light of men. The light shines in the darkness, but the darkness has not understood it" (Jn 1:4-5). And it was night.

But why does Jesus say "I am the truth"?

Before this question I fall silent. My silence, however, is not the silence that all mortal flesh keeps before God. It is the silence of a mind that understands each word but cannot grasp the sentence as a whole. My silence in the face of this question reveals a mind that has been numbed. Jesus quotes Isaiah to those such as myself:

You will be ever hearing but never understanding;
    you will be ever seeing but never perceiving.
For this people's heart has become calloused;
    they hardly hear with their ears,
    and they have closed their eyes.
Otherwise they might see with their eyes,
    hear with their ears,
    understand with their hearts,
    and turn, and I would heal them. (Mt 13:14-15)

How can my eyes be opened, my ears made keen and my heart attentive? How can I be healed? How does philosophy enable me to see, hear or understand? Can worldview philosophy bring me to that place where I can see that Jesus is truth, or at least describe the process by which I might come to that place?

Conversion in worldview philosophy. Since philosophy is a way of being oriented toward the truth, worldview philosophy also embodies a spiritual life. It offers a way of turning from darkness to light. It should heal my sight and my deafness. What, then, does worldview philosophy convert one from?

Our cave prisoner, in this case, will be someone as yet uninitiated to worldview philosophy. This is, perhaps, a first-year college student who was raised in a protective and conservative Protestant environment. She has been exposed only to one brand of Christianity and thinks that the fundamentalism of her parents is quite sufficient. Further, she is most probably a naive realist, or perhaps a scientific realist. That is, she believes that the world is pretty much as she experiences it, or perhaps it is pretty much as the natural sciences tell her it is. In any case, the darkness of the cave represents fideism and lack of exposure to critical philosophy.

How will the worldview philosopher begin to free his charge? First, the philosopher will parade the pluralism of other cultures, other religions and even other Christian beliefs before his student. This pluralism is like loosening the chains, and is not yet a turning point or a departure from the cave. Pluralism itself does not lead one out of the cave. For after seeing the variety of options, the student may remain dogmatic and assert that other opinions are simply wrong.

The worldview philosopher (to lead the student out of her dogmatism) must provide a definite interpretation of this pluralism. In other words, the worldview philosopher must master this pluralism, impose an interpretation on the variety of perspectives and circumscribe them as "worldviews." At the second stage, then, the worldview philosopher will turn the gaze of his student away from the diversity of cultures and toward the origin or source of those cultures—to the human conceived as a subject, as a producer of values and of religions. The subject provides the conditions for the possibility of culture in all its varieties. Third, the worldview philosopher will point out that one has access to the "real" world only through the culture, which is itself grounded in the subject. The realization of the unbridgeable gap between appearance and reality is essential to the spiritual formation of any worldview philosopher. The structure of a worldview, then, is such that what we grasp is not the "real" world but the world as it appears to (and as it is grounded in) the subject.

Once the student comes to see that other views cannot simply be dismissed, she will no doubt feel confused, lost and perhaps even blinded. This is a common experience among first-year philosophy students.

When the education process is complete, what does worldview philosophy convert one to? At the pinnacle of the philosophical experience, the student, having now become a full-fledged worldview philosopher, occupies a choice seat in the theater of the collective subjectivity of humankind. Across the stage of this theater she can observe a parade of worldviews. If our philosopher has a historical bent, she may discern some story in this parade. If she has a more logical or epistemological inclination, she may compare various worldviews on the basis of their internal consistency and comprehensiveness.

How will Christianity appear in this spectacle? Christianity shows itself only if it is forced to wear the poorly fitting robes of a worldview and is compelled to display itself in this theater. The internal logic of worldview philosophy requires that one conceive of Christianity as a worldview and that Scripture presents it as a world-view, that the Scriptures are "a worldview book."[28] Christianity can then appear only as one among many and as competing with other worldviews.

How will conversion to Christianity look to a worldview philosopher? When someone converts to Christianity, the worldview philosopher assures us, she exchanges one worldview for another.[29] If the convert is aware that Christianity is a worldview, she will be neither dogmatic nor fideistic, for worldview philosophy will keep before her mind an unbridgeable gulf between the worldview and reality. She will not suppose that her worldview corresponds with reality, but merely that it is the most consistent and comprehensive one she has found so far.

How does Jesus appear to a worldview philosopher? Does Jesus appear at all? Jesus is not a worldview. The Scriptures do not lead us to Jesus, but to a Christian worldview. Jesus would have to be a person who held a worldview, or perhaps gave expression to a worldview. What, then, does Jesus mean when he says "I am the way and the truth and the life"? It seems as if Jesus is guilty of a category mistake, for only *worldviews* provide normative outlooks on life that allow us to find our way through the world. It is the Christian worldview that promises salvation. Surely Jesus meant to say, "My worldview offers the way and the truth and the life." This *must* be what he meant if Christianity is a worldview and conversion to Christianity is a conversion to a Christian worldview.

This conclusion pulls me up short. I began my meditation keenly aware of my inability to hear Jesus' words "I am the truth." Worldview philosophy has just shown itself as the possible origin of my deafness, because it can see or hear Jesus only if he conforms to the image presented by worldview philosophy. This conversion, then, cannot be a conversion from one worldview to another. To hear Jesus' own words will require a conversion from worldview philosophy to Jesus.

Meditation 2. Perhaps I will find how my ears can be opened by returning to my meditation on the Gospel of John. Jesus' words "I am the way and the truth and the life" respond to a question put to him by Thomas: "Lord, we don't know where you are going, so how can we know the way?" (Jn 14:5). It is to Thomas that Jesus speaks, and it is Thomas who does not understand.

This is not the first time that Thomas speaks in the Gospel of John. He was introduced earlier, and under similar circumstances. During the previous winter, Jesus had gone up to Jerusalem for the Feast of the Dedication. He had made some claims that sounded blasphemous to those with a theistic worldview, and had nearly gotten himself stoned. Subsequently, Jesus and his disciples withdrew across the Jordan. Shortly thereafter, Jesus' friend Lazarus, who lived near Jerusalem, died. Jesus announced his intention to go to Lazarus and raise him from the dead, and then added, "For your sake I am glad I was not there, so that you may believe." Then Thomas speaks: "Let us also go, that we may die with him" (Jn 11:15-16).

From the standpoint prior to the resurrection of Lazarus, Thomas's perspective is fully comprehensible and perhaps even praiseworthy. Thomas is one of the Twelve, chosen by Jesus himself. If we may use the language, he has a theistic worldview. Further, he is willing to die with Jesus.

On the other hand, it is equally obvious that Thomas has not really seen or heard Jesus at all, in spite of the fact that Jesus is directly in front of him. Even after Jesus says that going to Bethany will make believers out of the disciples, Thomas fully expects that a mob will lynch Jesus, and perhaps those who follow him or defend him as well. When Thomas says, "Let us also go, that we may die with him," he reveals the nature of his blindness and deafness. Where Jesus walks forward in light toward life, Thomas looks ahead and sees only death, or, what is perhaps the same thing, he does not see at all, and so he stumbles. Thomas is a disciple and he is willing to die with Jesus, but he does not believe Jesus' words and he does not know the one whom he follows. The challenges to Thomas are not alternate nontheistic worldviews, but death and darkness and unbelief.

When Thomas says in the Upper Room, "We don't know where you are going, so how can we know the way?" he reveals that he still does not understand; he demonstrates that death and darkness and unbelief still hold him captive.

The third speech we have from Thomas occurs in the Upper Room, after the resurrection but still before he had seen Jesus: "Unless I see the nail marks in his hands and put my finger where the nails were, and put my hand into his side, I will not believe it" (Jn 20:25). Thomas's insistence that he see and touch Jesus before he believe states a simple truism. In point of fact, Thomas has not yet believed because even while Jesus was among them, he was not able to either see or touch Jesus. The problem is not with the absence of Jesus but with Thomas's eyes and ears that see and hear only death, even when life has shattered death.

And then, a week later, when Thomas is with the other disciples, Jesus appears. To all those disciples, whose lives were nearly shattered by his death, he says, "Peace be with you" (Jn 20:26). He turns his eyes on Thomas . . . What does Thomas see? What is he thinking in that moment? What does he feel as the gaze of Jesus falls on him? Jesus speaks to Thomas, showing that Jesus had been among them even a week earlier when Thomas had voiced his lack of belief, that he had seen and heard Thomas long before Thomas ever heard or saw Jesus: "Put your finger here; see my hands. Reach out your hand and put it into my side. Stop doubting and believe" (Jn 20:27).

Did Thomas do it? Did he still want to do it? Did he want to touch his Lord, this one who had conquered death, now that he had seen Jesus for the first time? By what light did Thomas now see? We do not know. It does not matter. *Before* he did any of these things, Thomas had already been converted. Thomas was not able to predict the form his own conversion would take. In the act of conversion, the subject is not master nor even the actor. Thomas's response is not that of intellectual assent, but of worship: "My Lord and my God!" (Jn 20:28).

In this moment, has Thomas seen that Jesus is truth? When Thomas exclaims, "My Lord and my God!" he knows that he addresses the One whose name is truth (Is 65:16). When he cries out, "My Lord and my God!" he addresses the One who established the covenant with Abraham. This is the God whose word is true, and who establishes all else that is reliable. This God is true in that he is trustworthy and good. "Trust in God; trust also in me." Jesus will not give us a stone when we ask for bread, or a scorpion when we ask for a fish, or death when he has promised life.

Conclusion

Thomas has been converted. This does not mean that I too have been transformed, but I do see more now than I had at the beginning of this paper. By considering the philosophical life as the life of conversion or a form of spirituality, and contrasting the forms of conversion offered by worldview philosophy with the Gospel of John, I have shown how far worldview philosophy remains from the gospel narrative. Worldview philosophy brings its practitioners out of fideism and naiveté, while Scripture points us to One who can bring us out of death, darkness, unbelief and falsity. Followers of Christ oppose these spiritual powers rather than other world-views. At the center of the conversion to Christianity stands the encounter with the crucified and resurrected Jesus, the One with whom we die and who is the guarantee of our resurrection. Conversion in worldview philosophy culminates in gaining admission to a theater of worldviews. When one converts to Jesus, one has a sense that nothing is more real than this One who wrecked the gates of hell, whereas in worldview philosophy one is keenly aware of the distance between one's worldview and reality. Coming into contact with Jesus inspires worship, gives us access to the very mind of God and provides enough confidence to endure martyrdom, while worldview philosophy brings us out of dogmatism but has tendencies toward skepticism. Conversion within Christianity, then, is quite different from conversion in worldview philosophy.

These contrasts have a different force from traditional philosophical proofs. I have not, for example, demonstrated that worldview philosophy and Christianity are logically contradictory. Still, if my descriptions of the experience of living in the universe of worldview philosophy and of the conversion to Jesus have any validity, they constitute a major objection to any conflation of the two. The different forms of conversion indicate that worldview philosophy and Christianity represent different forms of spiritual life.

If evangelicals try to articulate their faith through worldviews, or allow worldview philosophy to define notions like "truth" and "rationality," Frei is surely correct about their reading of Scripture. Scripture becomes a "worldview book," and Jesus is simply the initiator or fullest expression of a worldview. This fails to do justice to the real, historical Jesus and to Jesus' presence among us now. The best case for Christianity, then, is not the coherence and comprehensiveness of its worldview. Jesus himself is the most persuasive case for Christianity. If Christianity is true, it is only because Jesus himself is truth, and Christianity has some relation to Jesus.

Evangelicals are generally better than their philosophy. At some point in their writings, all evangelical worldview philosophers will acknowledge that Jesus himself is truth, and that conversion is an encounter with Jesus rather than the adoption of another worldview. When they do so, however, they cease to operate within the constraints of worldview philosophy.

The language of worldviews is quite effective both pedagogically and as a way to engage people to think about their faith. However, the language of worldviews can only take one so far. At a certain point in the discussion, if a person is to convert to Christianity, one must stop using the language of worldviews and begin using the language of the church. One must abandon argument and risk prayer. This step is not a step within worldview philosophy, but a step outside of it.

How does one know when to take that step? Worldview philosophy cannot provide guidance here. If a student takes worldview philosophy more seriously than does the teacher, the student will not follow. From a philosophical perspective, the student would be acting properly.

Thus the contrasts suggest that if a Christian is searching for a formal model by which to compare various philosophical positions, John's model of conversion is preferable to that of worldview philosophy. The language of conversion has such a long tradition in the Christian tradition that no leap outside of that language is required. Further, the language of conversion makes it clearer than worldview philosophy that one's life is at stake, not just one's beliefs or presuppositions. To use the Platonic imagery, one does not emerge from the cave as an eyeball; the entire body must ascend. Conversion requires that our desires—our loves and our hates—change.

From a Christian perspective, this is possible only when we realize that God has first loved us and most fully expressed this in the death and resurrection of Jesus. Indeed, if Jesus speaks truly, then the church shows Jesus to the dominant culture not when it learns to speak rationally but when it loves, when it shows that it has been converted. The love of wisdom, *philosophia*, is properly the life of the church responding to God's love for it.[30]

Part VI
PUTTING
THE POSTLIBERAL
MODEL TO WORK

15
ATONEMENT &
THE HERMENEUTICS
OF INTRATEXTUAL
SOCIAL EMBODIMENT

George Lindbeck

T he atonement is discussed in this essay as an illustration of the thesis that premodern hermeneutics better accommodates differences without disunity than is possible in modern modes of interpretation, whether liberal or conservative. In the light of this and other considerations, it is argued that the retrieval of classical hermeneutics in a form suitable to the present is both possible and desirable.

Formal questions of interpretation, it will be noticed, are in the forefront, and the theologically substantive issue of how to preach the cross of Christ is in the background. This, however, is not a judgment of relative importance. For Christians, the reason for reflecting on hermeneutical problems is in order to better embody and proclaim the good news of Jesus' atoning death, which together with the resurrection is central to the gospel.

In presenting a preliminary sketch of the argument, as I shall now do, brevity requires the use of neologisms which will only later be explained, but I hope that the general drift will be apparent. The first section advances reasons for the priority of practice. It follows from this priority that premodern scriptural interpretation in its classical patristic and Reformation forms is to be taken seriously as a guide to contemporary Bible reading, and that theology as an academic discipline is concerned first of all with the description of the normative "grammar" of the faith.

The second part outlines an understanding of historic practice as a hermeneutics of "intratextual social or ecclesial embodiment." Our ancestors in the faith communally embodied the intratextually discerned biblical world in different social, cultural and intellectual situations (or, alternatively expressed, they absorbed other worlds into the world of the text) by means of intratextual "performance interpretations."[1] These performance interpretations could on occasion be radically different and yet all be acknowledged as authentic scriptural words of God accommodated to different contexts.

The third part of this essay looks briefly at how this description accounts for the unity despite diversity and diversity despite unity of historic atonement teachings. It is argued that an intratextual hermeneutics of embodiment is descriptively adequate as far as the past is concerned.

Part four deals with the changed contemporary situation. It was once dogma (in practice even if not theory) for the vast majority of Christians that Christ's death saves, even though none of the diverse and sometimes irreconcilable explanations or theories of how or why this is so were dogmatized.[2] Now, however, the atonement itself has fallen into disrepute among many who profess the Christian name, while those for whom Christ's death continues to be soteriologically crucial tend on the whole to insist on some particular theory of how or why. One major benefit of retrieving an intratextual hermeneutics of social or ecclesial embodiment, so I suggest, is the help it provides in overcoming this and similar polarizations.

Part 1. The Priority of Practice

The priority of practice to theory is an academic shibboleth these days, but is honored more in the breach than the observance, perhaps especially in biblical studies. If this priority were granted, hermeneutical theory would be descriptive. Investigators would look at the communal traditions of the first-order use of the Bible in worship, preaching, piety and life (and also in theology in its more kerygmatic or proclamatory modes). They would then seek to find the second-order concepts and theories which make maximum sense of these actual practices. Perhaps the most obvious analogy is to the linguistic study of the grammar of natural languages. In both instances, the test of theory is whether the distinctions between acceptable and unacceptable usage it mandates fit the consensus intuitions of competent speakers of the natural or biblical language. (This procedure breaks down, to be sure, when there is disagreement over the criteria of competence—but more of that later.)

Premodern Christians for the most part practiced scriptural interpretation rather than discussed it, but when they did turn to method, their approach was on the whole what we have indicated: descriptive rather than prescriptive. Beginning with Irenaeus's discussion of the difference between "catholic" and "gnostic" hermeneutics, premoderns formulated low-level generalizations about the rule of faith which should guide scriptural interpretation, and from Origen on there are discussions of what we would now call the literary features of the Bible, especially its literal and spiritual senses. In contrast to this, the last several centuries have seen a tendency for interpretation (on both right and left) to start with doctrines of inspiration and revelation, while in our day, structuralist, Marxist, Freudian and deconstructionist critical theories have been added to the agenda. Reflective interpreters have treated practice as the application of theory, while unreflective ones have tended to lapse into enthusiasm, on the one hand, or the parroting of pat formulas, on the other. There are, however, both theological and nontheological reasons for thinking that this modern priority of theory to practice is a mistake.

One theological warrant for giving priority to practice is confidence that the Holy Spirit guides the church into the truth. If one believes this is so, one will think that the burden of proof rests on those who deny that the Christian mainstream has on the whole and in the long run rightly discerned God's word in Scripture. Historic mainstream interpretation should be given the benefit of the doubt. If a given way of understanding Scripture has long been fruitful, we have reason to believe that it is God's word to his people.

This does not mean, however, that it is always and everywhere what God wants them to hear. It may be such only at some times and places. Even on the level of what is communally, not to mention individually, normative, different messages may be conveyed by the same scriptural words. The command to love one another has radically different behavioral entailments for spouses and siblings, and for parent-child relations.

Augustine and Calvin talked frequently of God accommodating his words to our frailty and weakness, and Luther again and again warns his readers to make sure before obeying a scriptural command that the command is addressed to them. Scripture makes clear that God accommodates also to social and political situations that are, as theologians once habitually phrased it, against his ordaining though not his permissive will. In 1 Samuel 8, you recall, he mandated the monarchy as the proper form of government for Israel, but this was a reluctant decision contingent upon Israel's lack of trust in him regarding its perilous international situation. The monarchy as a time-bound political arrangement was only temporary, and yet as long as it lasted it was mandatory, a God-established rule. Christians have in practice often similarly treated their biblical interpretations (whether or not dealing with ecclesiastical polity) as divinely authorized, and yet also acknowledged that they are not for all times, places or people. (In theory, to be sure, they have rarely been equally flexible, with the result that it has at times been theologically difficult to allow for obviously necessary changes.)

Consensus, it next needs to be noted, does not guarantee that God's word has been heard. Think, for example, of how the church as a whole has allowed the sexism and master-slave attitudes of the world to eviscerate Galatians 3:28 of much of its meaning throughout most of Christian history. Yet such instances do not invalidate the general principle. Consensus traditions of false interpretation are for the most part customary rather than reflective, traditions of unthinking acquiescence to what everyone takes for granted rather than traditions of continuing argument and decision. Alasdair MacIntyre's characterization of tradition as an extended argument as to what constitutes the tradition[3] implies that christological and trinitarian orthodoxy but not patriarchy belong to the traditional Christian consensus. The first two have been argued, but the third has not.

Not all consensus errors, however, can be described as unthinking capitulation to cultural pressures. Sometimes, it seems, the church as a whole has misheard God's biblical word when it was not inattentive but struggling to listen. A mainstream interpretive consensus can be drastically wrong in the sense of never and nowhere having been Spirit-guided. Supersessionist anti-Judaism, for example, is an instance where the Gentile church (and in this sense, to be sure, not the church as a whole) has reflectively and argumentatively misread Paul, especially Romans 9—11, for close to two thousand years. Fortunately, supersessionism never became formally dogmatic in any major tradition, yet it is no exaggeration to say that the great majority of Christians, not excepting the theologians whom we most honor as our ancestors in the faith, have at this point heard the voice of the devil quoting Scripture when they thought they were listening to God. Charitable reading, in short, must not be uncritical.

And yet, to return to our starting point, those who believe in God's guidance of the church will first seek to hear God's word in the community's interpretations. It is only with fear and trembling and when conscience is compelled by Scripture itself that they will reject a reflective consensus as one that God never ordained (although, of course, they will believe that he permits it for his unfathomable purposes just as he permitted Israel's rejection of the Messiah according to St. Paul). Charitable reading has its limits, but it is not to be abandoned.

The next point to consider is that descriptive interpretive theory goes hand in hand with charitable reading. Both depend on the confidence that because God does not leave himself without witnesses in the church even when it is unfaithful, the *consensus fidelium* (which includes the consent of the faithful remnant)[4] is evidence, even if not infallible evidence, that the Spirit is at work.[5] It is thus on the level of practice, the first-order use of Scripture in life and thought, that the Spirit primarily guides.

That is why theory that is obedient to the Spirit seeks to be descriptive. It does not presume to improve on Spirit-guided practice, but rather seeks to identify and correct errors by first-order interpretation's own implicit standards. Its role is the secondary one of testing the spirits. Theory of the kind contemporary academic theology is capable of producing can be useful to the church, but only if it remembers that its primary task is corrective rather than constructive. The best professional theologians, like the best professors of literature, are those who have the humility, empathy and skill to describe and assess in a helpful manner the work of those whose inspiration may greatly exceed their own.

Whatever one thinks of these theological warrants for theory as description, they have been mostly ignored in recent centuries. Theological conservatives and liberals alike have been influenced by modern notions of reason according to which theory should guide practice, conscious method replaces skill, and artificial languages such as Esperanto are judged superior to natural ones. Modern romanticism did not help. Instead of broadening the narrow Enlightenment understanding of reason, it accepted the rationalistic dichotomy between feeling, instinct and emotion, on the one hand, and rationality on the other, and simply inverted the evaluative index: the nonrational or irrational is now to be preferred to the rational. To rely on the Spirit's guidance and the priority of practice was in this context to capitulate to the untestable interpretive disorder of enthusiasts and *Schwärmer*. The reaction of the intellectually concerned on both the theological right and left was to exalt theory and reduce practice to mere application. All parties ignored premodern interpretation.[6]

It is only in this century, to continue with the story, that the intellectual balance has begun to shift. There is irony in this: twentieth-century scholars of literature, themselves often unbelievers, have helped open the eyes of long-blind theologians such as myself to the insightfulness and possible continued viability of premodern modes of biblical interpretation.[7] We now find it easier to recognize what we should have seen all along—the pneumatological grounding of the priority of practice. Yet this shift in nontheological opinion is an occasion rather than reason for the corresponding theological change. The nontheological warrants that I shall now mention are auxiliary, rather than foundational, to the theological ones.

Some of these warrants go back as far as Aristotle, who insisted in his *Ethics* that those unpracticed in virtue do not recognize even theoretically what virtue is. Such premodern insights have in recent times been deepened and extended by Wittgenstein and many others. We now know that they apply also in such abstractly rational realms as formal logic and mathematics.

Some of us of my generation were first awakened from our Enlightenment slumbers (if I may be allowed the oxymoron) by Michael Polanyi's emphasis on the role of the tacit dimension in knowledge, the knowing *how* to do things, which vastly exceeds knowing *what* we are doing.[8] He is the original source, if I recall correctly, of the often repeated example of bicycle riding. If we first had to learn what balancing skills are required for the physical action by mastering the complex mathematical equations that most adequately (though still only very partially) represent them, we would still be falling off our training bikes. The same is true in the sciences and other intellectual disciplines. In these activities also the skills required greatly surpass the grasp of methodological theory. Lastly, the second-order descriptions that sometimes aid in acquiring competence are crudely pictorial rather than mathematically precise. They are, one could say, metaphorical rather than literal. And this is true of intellectual as well as physical skills.

In summary, the theory that is relevant to practice is not first learned and then applied, but rather is chiefly useful as part of an ongoing process of guarding against and correcting errors while we are engaged in practice. Thus the nontheological case for the priority of practice reaches conclusions parallel to the theological one.

Part 2: Descriptive Theory

In starting this essay, as I have done, with a theoretical apologia for the priority of practice and for keeping theory descriptive, I have not been practicing what I preach. I should have begun by practicing the description of practice. But the ignorance and suspicion of classic Bible reading are so immense—perhaps because we confuse it with what we know from our grandparents—that it seemed best first to raise doubts about our modern prejudices.

That these prejudices persist even among scholars is, however, understandable. Our ancestors in the faith, as I have already mentioned in passing, were not much given to theorizing, and what little they said on the topic did not do justice to their interpretive practice. As is true of most skilled practitioners in any trade, their self-descriptions are at times simply wrong. They knew how to interpret at times without knowing what they were doing.

It sounds pretentious, but we now have the tools to do better if we use them rightly. Twentieth-century linguistics, philosophy of language, literary studies, descriptive (as contrasted with explanatory cultural) anthropology, ethnology and sociology have given us previously unavailable conceptual tools for describing how texts and readers interact. Intratextuality and the hermeneutics of social embodiment have been influenced by these developments, and they lend themselves to our descriptive purposes better than any other currently widespread approaches. They do not exclude the premodern descriptions of scriptural interpretation, which borrowed from classical rhetoric and philosophy, but incorporate them into contemporary theoretical frameworks. (Perhaps this is the point at which to note that the use of nonbiblical concepts in descriptive theology is inescapable. Scripture does not describe itself: it is overwhelmingly first- rather than second-order discourse.)

Karl Barth wrote a famous early essay called "The Strange New World of the Bible."[9] For most Christians through most of Christian history, however, this world was neither new nor strange. Once they entered it, they experienced it as the world in which they lived, which was embodied in their communities and churches, and which absorbed all other worlds. As a contemporary sociologist of knowledge influenced by literary theorists might put it, they inscribed in Scripture the socially constructed reality they inhabited. In the process of doing this, they distorted the biblical world, sometimes egregiously, but nevertheless it was the scriptural text that structured their cosmos, their communities and their self-descriptions as saints and sinners, saved or damned.

The interpretive practice that corresponds to this experience is a hermeneutics of intratextual social or ecclesial embodiment. It is intratextual in a double sense: first, Scripture is interpreted in the light of Scripture, and the biblical canon is read as a single interglossing whole; and second, all reality is interpreted in this same scriptural light—the biblical world absorbs all other worlds. One can also speak of light as absorbed into that which it irradiates: it is embodied or enacted. This last aspect, embodiment, it should be noted, is the condition for what I first mentioned, for the absorbing of other worlds. To the degree that Scripture is the embedded guide for the social construction of reality, the universe itself is perceived, as Calvin put it, through scriptural lenses or spectacles. Less metaphorically expressed, Christians use the Bible's stories, images, categories and concepts to interpret all that is.[10]

Further, if use largely determines meaning, as we constantly hear these days, then we must say that to interpret the Bible is to use it to interpret other things. The strictly intratextual meaning of the cross, for example, is indefinite or vague (in Charles Peirce's sense of the term) until it is completed by such social-ritual-experiential enactments as taking up the cross, or bearing the cross, or being baptized into Christ's death so that we might rise with him. Wayne Meeks (I have borrowed "the hermeneutics of social embodiment" from the title of one of his articles) puts it this way: to ascertain the sense of a text "entails the competence to act, to use, to embody" in particular social settings "the universe rendered or signalled by the text." Thus "the hermeneutical circle is not completed until it finds a fitting social setting."[11]

A theological way of making the same point is to say that the Bible exists for the sake of the church. This is why in this essay I speak of ecclesial as well as social embodiment. The purpose of the Old and New Testaments is the formation of peoples who live in accordance with God's commands and promises and embody his will for the world. The church, we recall, is the body of Christ. The Bible, from this perspective, is a tool or collection of tools for the upbuilding of the body. Rightly to interpret in this context is not to describe these tools (as the overwhelming bulk of biblical scholars have done and continue to do), but to learn to use them for the formation of Christian community in the unprecedented circumstances (and therefore with the unprecedented meanings) with which the church is constantly confronted. We discern the new light that God has yet to break forth from his Word, as the Puritan divine put it, not so much by focusing on Scripture as by focusing through it.

Yet though glasses are for seeing, they need at times to be ground and cleaned. Similarly, though the Bible's meaning is completed in its use, the transparency of the lens is crucial. The lens, according to historic tradition, is what I have called the intratextual sense.[12] Intratextual or text-immanent meaning is constituted by the text, not by something outside of it such as Marxist, Freudian or Nietzschean causal or genealogical explanations in terms of economic, psychological or power factors. Nor is it only extratextual explanatory frameworks such as I have just listed which are irrelevant to determining the sense of the text. Also excluded are historically reconstructed referents, (human) authorial intention and extratextually known ideas presumed to be present in the text allegorically or otherwise.

The identity and character of the biblical God, to give just one example, is known from his role in biblical stories and in the other scriptural materials in which he plays a part, not from human religiosity in general, nor from philosophical arguments, nor from his putative origins in patriarchal or nomadic ways of life, nor from oedipal projections such as Freud describes, nor even sometimes from what a particular biblical redactor or speaker (such as Caiaphas in John 11:51) intended to say about that God. This does not deny that we project our ideas into the Bible and then think these are part of the immanent or intratextual meaning, but when reading intratextually, we struggle against this reflex instead of consciously employing extratextual meanings as hermeneutical keys.[13]

Second, the meaning that was ultimately crucial for the tradition was that which texts had in the context of the entire canon, not in isolation. The imprecatory Psalms, for example, were read in the light of Jesus' God. So deeply entrenched were such habits of interpretation that the plea in Psalm 137 that God dash the Babylonians' children against the stones was automatically heard as a prayer that our own nascent "Babylonian" sins be extirpated in their infancy.

The Bible can be read intratextually and canonically, however, in a variety of ways. One may search, as did the Calvinist divines at Westminster, for an intratextual system of propositionally understood doctrines; or, as was true of the biblical theology movement of a generation ago, for the concepts within the text; or, following Paul Ricoeur, for the symbolisms in the text that signal possible ways-of-being in the world in front of the text.

Of these three modes of interpretation, perhaps only Westminster was successfully both intratextual and canonical, but none focused on the kind of immanent or intratextual meaning that has been central for most Christians most of the time. On the popular level even until now and for theologians until after the Reformation, the intratextual biblical world was structured primarily not by biblical propositions, concepts or symbols (of which there are an abundance), but by narrative of two kinds: first, the metanarrative or cosmic tale stretching from Genesis to Revelation which told of the universe's creation and consummation, and second, the more intramundane and realistically told stories of God's chosen ones centering and culminating in Jesus Christ. His story was the hermeneutical key to the whole. Both the frame and the center were narrational.

Conjoined with narration, it next needs to be noted, was figuration. Figural reading was the glue that held the canon together, centering it in Christ, and enabled the intratextual biblical world to move out of the text and, through its social embodiment, to absorb all other worlds.

Both aspects are illustrated by what the tradition called the spiritual senses of Scripture. The past is typologically anticipated in Christ, the antitype; the present time between incarnation and eschaton is tropologically shaped by Christ, the prototype; and the promised future is the anagogical foreshadowing of Christ's return in glory so that God may be all in all (1 Cor 15:28). Thus in this biblical world, one word or one reality may have an indeterminate number of meanings: the sacrifice of the Passover lamb is antitypically fulfilled on the cross, which, in turn, is endlessly troped in the lives of those who follow Christ and, third, is anagogically signaled in the coming again of the Lamb slain from the foundation of the world. All three

senses played a part in welding the intratextual world of the canon into a metaphorical interglossing unity of cosmic comprehensiveness, but the tropological sense is
for our topic of special importance, because it is this that chiefly functioned applic-
atively in the embodiment of the faith in social reality by the absorbing of other
worlds. By it in particular, though not to the exclusion of the other senses, each age,
each culture and each individual in his or her special circumstances could be addressed directly by God speaking in and through Scripture.

Yet the changing and multivocal meanings of the various scriptural words did not
lead to chaos. They were all anchored in the literal sense, as careful thinkers such
as Thomas Aquinas took pains to emphasize, and above all in the central story of
Jesus. This is the one part of the Bible, as Hans Frei powerfully argued,[14] regarding
which all mainstream Christian traditions have always taken the literal sense to be,
as the Jewish literary critic Erich Auerbach put it, realistic narrative. The accounts
of the Passion so clearly fit this genre that even radical biblical scholars at their
pseudohistorical allegorizing worst have generally been wary of substituting critical
reconstructions for the actual tale of Christ's death. In any case, to the degree
Christians agree on construing the story of Jesus realistically, they have a usable
criterion for all biblical interpretation (which, to be sure, they have not always used).
Whatever coheres with the Gospel recitals of Jesus' Spirit-guided enactment of his
identity as God's Messiah is a possible interpretation, a possible scriptural word from
God, and whatever does not cohere is to be rejected. This is a powerful touchstone
for differentiating between allowable and unallowable construals, but there are also
other criteria that must be noted.

The two that are important for our purposes in this essay are formal and therefore variable: they lack the concreteness of the story of Jesus in its realistic narrative
construal and can thus be filled with diverse content. One of these two criteria has
already been mentioned: faithfulness to the text—making sense of the actual words
of Scripture that are being interpreted. Yet, as has also been noted, differing or
opposing construals can be textually faithful depending on what the interpreter
takes to be the primary subject matter, whether propositional, narrative, conceptual
or symbolic. All of these genres are biblical, but the Bible does not tell us *verbis expressis*
which is primary. This is a point that now needs to be expanded.

In making this expansion, I am dependent on David Kelsey's notion of *discrimen*[15]
as well as Nicholas Wolterstorff's already mentioned "performance interpretation."
They might have reservations about the use I make of their ideas, but that does not
lessen my debt. The difference between primarily narrative and primarily propositional construals of Scripture, to go back to that contrast, can be compared to
different traditions of performance of a drama, to the difference between, for example, classic, romantic and Freudian ways of performing Hamlet. There are many
performances within each of these interpretive traditions, and these may vary greatly in textual fidelity. One may thus have textually good and textually bad enactments of both a romantic and a Freudian Hamlet.[16] It is the textually most faithful

renditions of each of these different types of Hamlet—those that carry through
their diverse interpretations most consistently and make the most sense of Shakespeare's words, each in its own terms—that are likely to be most obviously irreconcilable.

Similarly, the Westminster Confession can be viewed as a trinitarian and christologically orthodox propositional performance of scriptural interpretation which is
particularly sharply opposed at crucial points to an equally textually faithful trini-
tarian-christocentric narrative-figural one (of which Luther provides at least partial
examples). It appears that faithfulness to the biblical text even in combination with
trinitarian and christological orthodoxy does not exclude contradictory performance
interpretations.

The number of possible contradictory performance interpretations is reduced
when there is agreement on what is the structurally primary subject matter. Treating narrative as primary, for example, has historically excluded both the supralap-
sarian affirmation of limited atonement and the fundamentalist views of inerrancy
which have sometimes flourished in propositional approaches. Yet the possibilities
of contradiction are not eliminated. Neither the narrative biblical world together
with its figural accompaniments nor, even more obviously, propositionalism can
specify what is the right interpretation, the actual biblical Word of God, for particular contexts, for definite times, places, audiences and cultures. The intratextual
meaning needs to be completed, but whether it has been acceptably completed
cannot be adequately tested by simply the two criteria of textual faithfulness and
christological coherence in conjunction with agreement on the primary subject matter of Scripture.

A third, pragmatic criterion can also be invoked; and for this, as Charles Peirce,
father of American pragmatism, liked to say, we have the highest authority, the
words of Jesus, "By their fruits ye shall know them." How to define "fruits," to be
sure, differs between interpretive approaches. The very notion of "success" changes
as one moves from one tradition of performance interpretations to another in
Shakespearean drama or Christian Scripture. The pragmatic criterion must therefore be formulated in terms of some particular approach. What this formulation is
in the case of an intratextual hermeneutics of social embodiment seems obvious:
when other criteria are not decisive, the interpretation that seems most likely in
these particular circumstances to serve the upbuilding of the community of faith in
its God-willed witness to the world is the one to be preferred.

This criterion, needless to say, does not abolish conflict. Debates over what Christians should do here and now about pacifism, just war theory, abortion or divorce
will not be settled. Beyond the three criteria is the Spirit's guidance, but the Holy
Spirit bloweth where it listeth and we do not know beforehand what God will judge
to be fruitful. Gamaliel's advice to the Sanhedrin is also often applicable to Christians: wait and see whether such and such is of God (Acts 5:38-39). There are other
times, however, when risks must be taken and decisions made between apparently

incompatible interpretations of Scripture, each of which seems to its advocates to fit the three criteria. In order to test the usefulness of our description of interpretive practice in dealing with these problems, we need a good illustration, and atonement teaching in both past and present is the one I have chosen.

Part 3: Atonement in the Past—Variety
The most obvious reason for choosing the atonement as our test case is the importance for Christian faith of the saving work of Christ accomplished by his death on the cross. That death is the center of the center: it is central to the central narrative. Just as the gospel story is prefigured in the Old Testament and presupposed in the epistles and Revelation, so the accounts of Jesus' birth and ministry lead up to the crucifixion, and the crucifixion gives meaning to what follows. It is as the Crucified One that Jesus rose, ascended, abides with us now and will come again. It is possible to separate the person from the work of Christ only if one thinks in nonnarrative terms; but if one thinks narrationally, one can never ask Duns Scotus's question of whether the Son would have become incarnate even if there had been no fall into sin and therefore no atoning work. In the Gospel accounts, accommodated to human understanding as they are, person and work coincide. It is through Jesus' saving work that his personal identity as fully human yet Son of God becomes manifest. You will recall that in the fourth Gospel the first public confession of Jesus as Son of God comes from the centurion at the foot of the cross.

In view of this inseparability of person and work, it is not surprising that the atonement, despite great differences in representation, has not been a distinct subject of controversy leading to dogmatic decisions in any of the major traditions. The affirmations about Christ's person incorporated in the trinitarian and christological creeds have been sufficient to set the guidelines for acceptable atonement teachings. What was decisive for church fellowship was *that* the cross is necessary for salvation, not the explanation of *how* or *why*.

More fully stated, the universal saving import of the cross was well assured, it seemed, if the one who suffered on it was himself God the Son, coequal with the Father, who, as the unbroken tradition down through the Reformation maintained, died in his human nature on the tree. So portentous an event must have inconceivably magnificent consequences—ultimately the transformation of the cosmos, a new heaven and a new earth. One might argue that some of the explanations of how or why that death is saving were mistaken or deficient, but one did not accuse others of heresy as long as the affirmation that the world could not otherwise be saved (except, to introduce a scholastic quibble, *potentia absoluta* though not *ordinata*) was firmly maintained. It was because this was implicitly recognized that none of the major traditions either formally dogmatized or anathematized any particular theory of the atonement. None was the only right one, and none was simply wrong.

This pluralism of interpretations is another less substantive but formally important reason for choosing the atonement as our test case. Pluralism combined with importance vividly poses the question of how diversity did not rupture unity, flexibility did not destroy firmness, and relevance did not exclude abiding authority. Yet the description of interpretive practice which I have sketched seems to make these combinations comprehensible.

We do not have time for anything more than caricatures and pat formulas in describing this pluralism of atonement teachings, but the readership of this book has for the most part the historical knowledge needed to make the necessary emendations in my oversimplified account. The passion story as summarized, for example, in the Emmaus incident tells of a Jew whose disciples had hoped he was the Messiah, but they came to understand after the resurrection vindicated his messiahship that it was right and proper (that is, in accordance with Scripture) that God's chosen one should "suffer these things and then enter his glory" (Lk 24:26).

The mostly scriptural materials that they used to picture the saving significance of Christ's death fall, roughly speaking, into two main groups. The first consists of the liberation images that depict human beings in bondage. Evil is something that we undergo rather than undertake. Jesus is the conqueror of the demons that hold men and women captive. Death is a personified power, the last enemy whose destruction will usher in the subjection of all things to the Son and the Father.

Then, second, there are the reconciliation images that focus on human complicity in evil. Liberation is not enough, for what is needed is reconciliation with God. The focus is on Jesus' death and his blood poured out as a sacrifice for sin. Death in this context is not the unjust captor of humanity but the wages of sin, not the enemy of God but sin's consequence which God imposes, the consequence of turning away from life. Insofar as external evil powers cause human suffering, they do so as the servants of God, not as enemies.

These two ways of depicting Christ's saving work, that of liberation and of reconciliation, that of Christ the victor and Christ the victim, are present side by side in the New Testament in unrelieved tension, sometimes even in the same or adjacent sentences (as in Col 2:13-15). This, however, does not reflect a passion for paradox. Rather, the clusters of images serve as interpretations of the narratives, and narrative tensions are not paradoxical (or much less contradictory) except when transposed into putatively primary rather than properly interpretive images or concepts. This is a benign transmutation as long as one remembers that the meaning of the concepts and images is in this context inseparable from the story, and thus avoids the essentialist mistake of supposing that the meaning of the story is better expressed in the images or concepts. It is the narratives, we recall, that primarily identify and characterize the biblical God and through which we have access to Jesus Christ as personal agent. That is why images and concepts, liberation and reconciliation, are to be understood by means of the stories, not the other way around.

There is perhaps no period of later church history, however, in which the priority of the story was fully maintained. Already in the patristic period one of the two sets of images, that of liberation, began to dominate, with the result that the story of Christ's saving work was increasingly retold in terms of his victorious struggle unto death against demonic powers. Sacrifice, to be sure, was not denied, but it tended to be understood more and more metaphorically, while the liberation language was taken literally. It could scarcely have been otherwise in the devil-ridden world of late antiquity. Turning the minor New Testament motif of Christ's conquering the demons by his death into a major theme was the understandable and perhaps indispensable means of absorbing that ancient world into the biblical one and thereby transforming it. Liberationist atonement teaching was both a condition and a consequence of the embodiment of Christian faith in late Roman and Greek culture and society.

It was not until the eleventh century and only in the West that the primarily liberation understanding of the atonement collapsed and was replaced by interpretations for which vicarious sacrifice was central and the crucified Christ was first of all victim, not victor. The two main ways of understanding this vicarious sacrifice of Christ as victim are, to retrace familiar paths, Anselm's satisfaction theory and, on the other hand, a punitive or penal substitution view. This substitutionary understanding was in part an offshoot of Anselm's work, despite his strong opposition to it. Anselm emphatically insisted that it would be contrary to God's justice for the innocent Jesus to bear the punishment that sinners deserve. Rather, the Son's loving obedience in becoming man (and inevitably being murdered in a world as wicked as ours) infinitely outweighs or compensates for the damage, grave though this be, that our sinfulness has inflicted on God's good creation. God cannot punish those who flee to Christ for mercy, because that would spoil the Christ-wrought beauty now irradiating the universe and making it a far, far better place than it would ever have been without Christ's coming and inevitable death.

This is not the place to describe in detail the intellectual world in which Anselm lived and in which he was a leader. Suffice it to say that a passion for the newly rediscovered logic or dialectic of the ancients was part of the atmosphere—curiously enough, a monastic atmosphere—that he breathed. Socially, on the other hand, it was a feudal world (a point much exaggerated, it seems to me, in most discussions of his satisfaction theory). More important was the devotional and liturgical context of increasing penitentialism and of Christ-and-cross centered eucharistic piety. Suffice it to say that Anselm's satisfaction theory was an admirable instrument for absorbing, transforming and adjusting the faith to these various worlds, and in its penal substitution offshoots, it was at the heart of grassroots Christian vitality among Protestants as well as Catholics in the West down to modern times.

Yet despite its power to transform (and adapt to) pagan Latin and Germanic cultures with their different forms of very un-Greek legalism, it has also been vigorously opposed and repudiated. The educated classes with their often humanistic sensibilities have regarded satisfaction with incomprehension and penal substitution with repulsion. Already in the generation after Anselm, Peter Abelard advanced an alternative generally known as the subjective moral influence theory of atonement. When linked with a high Christology, this has been a powerful component of all Western atonement teaching. Its explanation of the necessity of Christ's death for salvation is that only the voluntary and uttermost self-giving for us of a wholly innocent human being who is also God could move our hearts, sinful as they are, to saving repentance and love. Without a high Christology and a strong doctrine of grace, however, the moral influence view degenerates into a Pelagianism for which Christ is important chiefly as an example of self-sacrificing love, which human beings have the strength and goodness to imitate if only they will to do so. Yet there are also circumstances and cultural worlds in which contemplation of the sufferings of the innocent Christ has nourished trust and love of the Crucified, not self-righteousness.

Enough has been said, I hope, to remind you of the flexibility combined with determination of historic practice in absorbing and becoming embodied in vastly different cultural and intellectual worlds. Each theory of atonement functioned as a distinct—sometimes irreconcilably distinct—performance interpretation of the significance of Christ's death. Yet the differences were not church-dividing. God speaks particular words in particular settings to his people by means of the Bible, but not in such a way as to break the bonds of brotherly and sisterly affection.

There are, so I have suggested, three conditions for this unity despite difference. First, the text of the drama remained self-identical no matter how varied the interpretations. Second, all the interpretations of the work of Christ were variations on an intratextual and canonically unified hermeneutic of social embodiment constrained by a single set of guidelines, the trinitarian and christological creeds. Thus the common text read within the parameters of the common dogmatic guidelines about God and Christ's person projected a common biblical world within which culturally and historically diverse outlooks and experiences could be interpreted. The third condition for unity despite difference is the pragmatic criterion for identifying which among the possible interpretations is God's word for the particular situation. Different though they were, all the major atonement theories have functioned when well-used to promote trust and love in recognizably the same Jesus as Immanuel, God with us. Unity in the faith was thus maintained. Westerners and Easterners, Roman Catholics and Protestants have never anathematized each other because of differences over Christ's saving work.

This, then, is a notable illustration, so it would seem, of the strength of the description of historic hermeneutics which I have sketched. It provides the best available account of the relevance combined with authority, the contextualization combined with unity, of the varied interpretations of biblical atonement in the Christian past.

Part 4: Atonement in the Present—Crises
The crisis that concerns us in this discussion of contemporary atonement teaching

is particularly severe in the historically Christian West. Medieval Anselmian out-looks are being abandoned, and nothing of comparable effectiveness is taking their place. The patristic soteriologies prevalent in Eastern Orthodoxy are not to the same degree a subject of controversy, and in any case, discussing their present status would require a second essay. As for the Christians of the younger churches in the so-called Third World, they for the most part seem content with the Anselmianism they received from the missionaries. Perhaps this will not continue to be the case, but for the present, the crisis is in the West.

As has already been mentioned, the most common way of speaking of the atone-ment among both Protestants and Catholics ever since the Middle Ages has been a penal substitution version (and distortion) of Anselm's satisfaction theory. Christ was punished in the place of sinners, and those who truly accept this merciful exchange escape the penalty. Love of Jesus and of neighbor was nourished by this understanding of the atonement for hundreds of years. It was at the center of Catholic devotion as well as Protestant pietism and revivalism, and it helped inspire immense missionary efforts and reform movements, not least Wilberforce's oppo-sition to the slave trade and Finney's advocacy of abolition (although, to be sure, many who shared their soteriology disagreed with their activism).

Now, however, penal substitution as well as other ways of emphasizing the cross as the means by which sins are forgiven is receding in importance. Such teachings survive chiefly among Roman Catholic traditionalists and Protestant conservative evangelicals. Even among the latter, however, the centrality of the cross is said by some to be weakening. There are self-described evangelicals who make much of conversion experiences, being born again and accepting Jesus as personal Savior, and who also freely use such language as "a high five for Jesus" or "five ways to prop up your ego whenever it loses pressure." It is hard to see how such talk can be reconciled with what was once considered central to any definition of evangelicalism, "a zeal to proclaim the gospel of salvation from sin through the atoning work of Christ."[17] Therapy seems to be triumphing over the passion, and feeling good over being forgiven.

What seems to an outside observer such as myself to be happening in conservative evangelicalism is unmistakably evident in so-called mainline churches. I am not thinking at this point of liberal Protestants. The centrality of the cross had vanished from their churches already in the nineteenth century, even at the grassroots level. For them, in H. Richard Niebuhr's famous words, "a God without wrath brought men and women without sin into a Kingdom without judgment through the min-istration of a Christ without the cross."[18] But even in traditions that profess to remain fully committed to the historic trinitarian and christological dogmas, such as Roman Catholicism and my own Lutheranism, the cross has quite suddenly faded from preaching and piety in the last few decades. Not long ago I received a letter from a pastor who was comparing sermons now and, say, thirty years ago. In one sentence he summed up the difference: "We preachers [now] avoid or ignore the gospel metaphor that employs the picture of vicarious sacrifice and blood atonement."

That by itself need not be worrisome. As we earlier observed, great shifts in the conceptualization and pictorialization of the atonement have taken place in the past. But this time, nothing seems to be replacing what is disappearing. No alternative love-evoking way of using the biblical materials to proclaim Christ's death as that by which human beings are saved seems to be developing.

I shall later have more to say about this lacuna, but first a word about the causes of the change. These are on one level easy to identify. Our increasingly feel-good therapeutic culture is antithetical to talk of the cross. Nor is it difficult to suggest plausible reasons for this cultural shift. One need not be a Marxist to point, for example, to economic factors: a late capitalist consumerist society such as ours depends on promoting self-indulgence. When one adds to such considerations the dreadful misuse of atonement motifs to tell battered women or members of oppressed races that they should go like Jesus as lambs to the slaughter, it becomes easy to understand the widespread revulsion against historic atonement teaching.

A more puzzling feature of this development as it has affected professedly confessional churches in the recent past is that it has happened silently: there has been little audible resistance or protest. Yet this aspect can also be explained. In the confessionally Reformational and mainstream Roman Catholic circles with which I am best acquainted, reputable theologians were not interested in defending Western penitentialism and vicarious sacrifice in either their popular penal substitution or their more Anselmian satisfaction forms.

Gustav Aulen's book *Christus Victor* (London: SPCK, 1931) is less than fully reliable on Anselm and Luther, but it rightly made my generation of theological students intensely aware that what we had learned about the atonement in Sunday school and confirmation class was based on a theory that had not existed for the first millennium of Christian history and that even in the West, to which it was largely confined, had not been central in the atonement teachings of some of the greatest theologians such as Luther and, in a different way, Aquinas. As for penal substitution, the major thinkers who use the motif, such as Calvin, are well aware that it is not the scripturally primary way of thinking of the saving significance of Christ's death. Those who saw history this way were not in a position to protest the demise of popular atonement teaching and were, for the most part, not inclined to do so. We were often as repelled by penitentialism as were antidoctrinal liberals, and we had learned, we believed, that the atonement could be better understood in other ways without loss of biblical substance.

Thus through the influence of Aulen and others, it is widely proposed to replace the medieval Western emphasis on Christ as victim with the patristic stress on Christ as victor. The cross, it is said, is best proclaimed in conjunction with the resurrection as the place where Christ triumphs over death and the devil and liberates "those who all their lives were held in slavery [to sin] by their fear of death"

(Heb 2:15). This picture of Christ not primarily as sacrificial Lamb but as the One who conquers cosmic evil through selfless suffering on our behalf was still powerful in the sixteenth-century Reformation: consider, for example, its role in Luther's "A Mighty Fortress Is Our God." In our day, however, it seems to have little emotional resonance for most people. Some have suggested that it seems too "mythical" to modern men and women, even if they happen also to be what are pejoratively called biblicistic fundamentalists.

What has most often happened to the *Christus Victor* motif of Jesus triumphing on the cross is that it has come to be understood in revelational rather than soteriological terms. Darkness is paradoxically conquered in Christ's crucifixion. This above all is the event that reveals the depths of God's being and love. It is the supreme demonstration that strength is made perfect in weakness. In a revelational context, however, where salvation is construed as first of all being grasped by the truth, it is perhaps inevitable that Christ is encountered chiefly as Model to be imitated rather than Savior to be trusted. To be saved is to be so joined to Christ as to share in his vulnerability to human suffering and oppression. Most of the many theologies of the cross that proliferate in our day (including those influenced by liberation theology) seem to fit this pattern. In them, not only does revelation subsume soteriology but, so the Reformers would say, law absorbs gospel. This is what happens when the crucified God is first of all the prototype of authentic human existence, so that it is by being prototype that Jesus Christ is Savior.

From a traditional perspective, the error here is in the reversal of the order: Jesus is not first Example and then Savior, but the other way around. He is trusted and loved as the One who saves from sin, death and the devil, and it is from this trust and love that there arises the longing to be like him in his life and death. Theologies of the cross that stress the *imitatio Christi* have their place, but that place is not with atonement but with what Calvinists call the third use of the law.

In summary, theological as well as cultural changes help account for the present situation. Mainstream proponents of confessional orthodoxy and neo-orthodoxy joined with liberals they accused of capitulating to modernity in repudiating old-fashioned Western atonement penitentialism. As a result, there have been few theologically reputable continuators of Anselmic doctrine in mainline churches. This helps explain why such teachings have receded so swiftly and, for the most part, silently in a single generation. Among recognized alarm ringers there were none who tolled the bell.

The consequence is crisis, for nothing has filled the vacuum on the grassroots level. It seems self-evident to most Christians who have interiorized the faith that love of Jesus best flourishes when it is believed that he died that sinners might live (or, emphasizing the Reformation *pro nobis*, that you might live, and I might live, and all humankind might live) and that without his freely offered and utterly agonizing death, none of this would and will happen. For all human beings, from primitive cave dwellers to future star trekkers, there is no more powerfully love-evoking conviction[19] than the belief that one exists only because an identifiable person voluntarily sacrificed his or her life on one's behalf.

But in the case of Jesus, devotion to the One to whom one owes one's life has cosmic scope and force. It is the triune, sovereign Creator and Ruler of the universe who so loves sinners that he did not spare himself (for the incarnate Son in trinitarian outlook is no less fully Godself than is the Father and the Spirit). It is "very God of very God" who in the incarnation is the fullest possible eruption into our history of the infinite mystery that surrounds all our beginnings and ends. This Jesus, in the words of Hebrews, is the "express image of [God's] person, . . . upholding all things by the word of his power" (1:3 KJV), and yet it is he who, in enacting who the Father is, suffered a maximally painful and shameful death for you personally, and for me personally, and for everyone personally so that we might live, and all might live.

Not many Christians down through the centuries have lived these convictions with deep intensity, but those who have are a major source of whatever glimmers of Christlikeness have shone amidst the sins of Christendom. These lovers of Jesus are much of the leaven in the lump, the faithful remnant, the salt that saves the church from insipidity. Love of Jesus has been the angelic light in which many a devilish deed has been disguised, but on the other hand, will not the salt lose its savor where no one teaches and no one learns to love Jesus as the One who surrendered his totally innocent and infinitely precious life for you and for me? If the root withers, how in the long run can there be fruit? Without the atonement-centered love of Jesus, where will one find communities that nourish heroic yet selfless love of God and neighbor? From where will come our Bonhoeffers and our Mother Teresas?

Such considerations make it seem self-evident to many that interiorizing the message of Christ's atoning death is a necessary condition for Christian vitality. Without this message there can be no passing of the pragmatic test, "by their fruits you shall know them," and thus even by the world's standards crisis is inescapable.

In considering this crisis, however, we need to remember that the atonement message, though necessary, is not a sufficient condition for overflowing fruits of faith and works of love. There are ways of preaching that message which foster a narrow love of a little Jesus. The history of the church is full of such distortions, and while these are by no means only in the West, it is there that most of us are chiefly aware of them. Cross-centered medieval piety and later Protestant conversionism affirmed that there is no forgiveness of sins apart from Christ's death on the cross, and yet also often fell into the Pelagian trap of speaking as if the reception of that forgiveness were made possible only through one's own ethical, religious or emotional good works. For Luther, we recall, the loving empathy for Christ's sufferings that the devout were urged to cultivate was in reality a form of idolatrous works righteousness: it was one's own feelings one adored by attributing them to Jesus.

Yet distorted though cross-focused devotion can be, it is nevertheless important. The cure is to reform, not abolish it. That is what the Reformers sought to do by reshaping the tortured Jesusology of their day, and what we must attempt with the sweet-Jesus (or, sometimes, Jesus-the-Liberator) sentimentality of ours.

One additional warning is in order. It will be recalled that when praxis is primary, the role of theology or doctrine is to guide the enactment of God's saving work in the ordinary means of grace, in communal worship, life and action. Thus the communication of the reality of the atonement and trust in that reality may exist without the doctrine. Where practice is in order, faith and love in the crucified Lord may flourish even in the midst of grave deficiencies in second-order teaching, but faith and love wither despite purity of doctrine when worship, life and action are corrupt. Doctrinal guidelines can be communally crucial especially in crises such as were confronted at Augsburg or Barmen, but there are occasions when creedless churches, even liberal ones, better promote justifying faith than those seemingly well buttressed with orthodoxy. These are banalities, but they do remind us that the reality of the atonement may be efficaciously at work in communal service, fellowship and worship even where it is absent in preaching and theology.

Yet though we may be as blind as was Elijah to thousands who have not bowed the knee to Baal, that does not deny that sound teaching may now be in short supply just as it was then. The theology that may be helpful, if the first part of this essay is correct, is the kind that seeks to discern and describe the logic or grammar of Christian communal discourse in past and present. The aim is the critical and constructive correction of what is inconsistent, first with scriptural norms and second with effective proclamation in contemporary contexts.

Effective proclamation requires adaptation to varied audiences and situations, but this takes place very differently when the approach is classically descriptive (or "dogmatic") rather than basically apologetic, as in most modern theology. In the first case, nonbiblical discourse is translated into scriptural conceptualities, whereas in the second, translation moves in the opposite direction. As was illustrated in the third part of this essay in reference to the variety of past interpretations of atonement, a classical hermeneutics of social embodiment absorbs changing cultural and historical worlds into the world of the Bible: it makes the varying social, cultural and intellectual milieus of believing communities biblically intelligible. The apologetic approach, in contrast, does the reverse. It seeks to render scriptural language intelligible by transposing it into contemporary thought forms. At its most extreme, the world absorbs the Bible: it supplies the framework within which Holy Writ is understood rather than the other way around.

The only way to escape this apologetic trap, it seems, is by the retrieval of something like premodern hermeneutics. This must be done, needless to say, in a form capable of dealing with current problems of absorbing the contemporary world. There can, for example, be no rejection of historical-critical biblical studies, but these become auxiliary to literary-canonical readings in which narrative (especially realistic narrative à la Erich Auerbach and Hans Frei) is primary. The discussion of atonement could flourish mightily within such a classical hermeneutical framework.

The outcome of such a flourishing cannot be specified in advance. To absorb nonbiblical worlds into the biblical one is a communal enterprise in which, as I have emphasized, the role of theology of the academic variety is corrective rather than constructive. Yet the retrieval of classical hermeneutics of the kind this essay has described cannot help but have formal consequences.

One consequence is that the orthodoxy of a hermeneutically classical theology in the modern context of historical awareness and cultural diversity cannot help but be generous. Its practitioners will know, as their ancestors in the faith could not know, of the variety of biblically legitimate ways of proclaiming the saving power of Christ's death in the church's past. They will be open to new ways of telling one and the same story of redemption in unprecedented settings, and at the same time they will have resources in tradition as well as Scripture for distinguishing between fruitful and unfruitful retellings. The truth that God speaks differently to his people in different situations through one and same scriptural words is self-evident from the perspective of a critically retrieved understanding of premodern hermeneutics. Thus the message of the cross becomes for the generously orthodox a magnet drawing together Christians from different traditions in brotherly and sisterly affection.

This essay has tried to sketch a paradigm shift that paradoxically moves both backward and forward to take us beyond the liberal-conservative polarities of the last several hundred years. The shift, if it occurs, will develop at first in isolated oases, but its influence will spread by osmosis. The process may take generations, but insofar as the connections between faith in Christ's self-giving death with the love of Jesus, God and neighbor become lived realities, the atonement will again be central, perhaps more than ever, of Christian vitality and, far more than in the past, of unity. The clouds promising these blessings are on the horizon, and the time has come to pray, prepare and rejoice in the hope of the treasures they bear.[20]

16
A HOMILY
Jill Peláez Baumgaertner

On the evening of that day, the first day of the week, the doors being shut where the disciples were, for fear of the Jews, Jesus came and stood among them and said to them, "Peace be with you." When he had said this, he showed them his hands and his side. Then the disciples were glad when they saw the Lord. Jesus said to them again, "Peace be with you. As the Father has sent me, even so I send you." And when he had said this, he breathed on them, and said to them, "Receive the Holy Spirit. If you forgive the sins of any, they are forgiven; if you retain the sins of any, they are retained."

Now Thomas, one of the twelve, called the Twin, was not with them when Jesus came. So the other disciples told him, "We have seen the Lord." But he said to them, "Unless I see in his hands the print of the nails, and place my finger in the mark of the nails, and place my hand in his side, I will not believe."

Eight days later, his disciples were again in the house, and Thomas was with them. The doors were shut, but Jesus came and stood among them, and said, "Peace be with you." Then he said to Thomas, "Put your finger here, and see my hands; and put out your hand, and place it in my side; do not be faithless, but believing." Thomas answered him, "My Lord and my God!" Jesus said to him, "Have you believed because you have seen me? Blessed are those who have not seen and yet believe."

Now Jesus did many other signs in the presence of the disciples, which are not written in this book; but these are written that you may believe that Jesus is the Christ, the Son of God, and that believing you may have life in his name.
(Jn 20:19-30 RSV)

I n December of 1993 at the annual convention of the Modern Language Association in Toronto, I attended the presidential forum entitled "Amo, Amas, Amat . . . Literature." The president of MLA had invited four scholars to speak, each of whom was well-known for his or her aggressive voice in one of the current predominant areas of literary theory. Jonathan Culler, knight errant of deconstructionist theory, sat at the table facing the grand ballroom filled with MLA members. "Amo, Amas, Amat . . . Literature." Would he actually claim to love literature, he whose theory went about deconstructing it?

When he rose to speak, I was reminded of O. E. Parker from Flannery O'Connor's short story "Parker's Back." Parker is mystified by his attraction to the very plain and bony Sarah Ruth. He is, to quote from the first paragraph, "embarrassed and ashamed of himself." Jonathan Culler prefaced his remarks with disclaimers. He was going to talk about a piece of literature he had memorized during his college years. He was embarrassed, he said, that he was attracted to a poem with such a sentimental topic, the resurrection. But he had memorized the poem years before, and it had been in his head ever since, for some mystifying reason.

He then proceeded to quote from memory Gerard Manley Hopkins's poems "The Leaden Echo" and "The Golden Echo." It was clear that the Hound of Heaven was at work in the most unlikely place—the soul of a deconstructionist—at an MLA convention. One felt in listening to Culler that the only parts of his faith that were still alive were his doubt and his memory of something long ago and far away, something almost romantic in its impossibilities.

In the short space I have been allotted to address the Gospel lesson for the second Sunday of Easter, I feel that I have been given permission by the very topic of this conference to allow the story of Thomas to actually create my reading of the story of Jonathan Culler at the MLA.

I am reminded of another of Flannery O'Connor's stories, in which a criminal, the Misfit, complains to a woman he is about to shoot:

> Jesus was the only One that ever raised the dead and He shouldn't have done it. He thrown everything off balance. If He did what He said, then it's nothing for you to do but throw away everything and follow Him, and if He didn't, then it's nothing for you to do but enjoy the few minutes you got left the best way you can—by killing somebody or burning down his house or doing some other meanness to him.

The grandmother he is about to kill says, "Maybe He didn't raise the dead," and the Misfit answers, "I wasn't there so I can't say He didn't. I wisht I had of been there. It ain't right I wasn't there because if I had of been there I would of known. Listen lady, if I had of been there I would of known and I wouldn't be like I am now."

How odd that the Misfit's doubt has—at its center—belief. "If I had of been there I would of known and I wouldn't be like I am now."

The grandmother spouts pious clichés to the Misfit in an attempt to flatter him and to save her skin. The Misfit does not resort to the dishonesty of clichéd language. He speaks the truth. In belief? Yes. In doubt? Yes.

Now don't misunderstand me. The Misfit is about as close to an antihero as you can get. But this we can say for him: he does not fall into the sort of laziness that kills so much human discourse. He does not fall into the familiar and invisible grammar which so often forms the language of the pulpit. Nor does he display the kind of deadly self-consciousness that so often makes religious expression feel so unauthentic. You know what I mean: the hint of a hint that the *person* telling the story is at the center of the story, preaching Christian principles because they happen to coincide with her own—doing anything but facing the cross, because to do that is to risk losing one's self.

In the story of Thomas as related in the Gospel of John, Christ gently chides Thomas for his doubt, but Christ also comes to him and satisfies his need to see and to touch. Remember that Jesus appeared first to the other disciples and showed them his hands and his side, and only then does the text say that they "were glad when they saw the Lord." They, too, *needed* to see. They also had heard and had doubted. And as soon as they saw, Christ was able to become the story in all of its fullness. Without his appearance, without their personal experience of the resurrection, what would have happened to them? Would they have remained confused behind closed doors, growing more cynical through the years, uncertain about exactly what their responsibilities were? Would they have drifted into bitterness and self-pity? Would this have seeped into their story of Christ and the purported resurrection which they had heard of but not themselves seen? Would they have preached with the same conviction?

So it isn't only Thomas. It is all of the disciples who needed to see and hear for themselves.

And that is what stories do for us who cannot put our hands in his side. Stories create the environment for the imagination to work. And no one who lacks imagination can have faith.

There is something about story that is so necessary and so satisfying that even the most ordinarily prosaically uncreative and dull persons begin to weave stories as soon as they fall asleep. In fact, that state of deepest REM sleep, the stage of sleep associated with dreaming, is essential if one is to avoid the critical effects of sleep deprivation. Our deepest need for rest is, evidently, intimately linked to our need for the narratives of dreams. The need for story is as basic as our need for water. It is downright physiological.

I am going to be so bold as to say that the strength of Scripture lies in its presentation as story. But it presents us—two thousand years after the death and resurrection of Christ—with a peculiar set of problems. Sometimes stories are so familiar that they are invisible. Last week a student in my senior seminar confessed to me that even though she had spent years going to church, attending and leading Bible studies, and reading Scripture daily, she had not really understood what the gospel was until she read a novel by Frederick Buechner that I had assigned as an answer and challenge to Michel Foucault. She asked, "Why couldn't I just get it straight from Scripture? Why do I need to read a novel in order to see God's truth?" My answer was that it is sometimes difficult to read Scripture as story and to receive revelation from it as story—because as we read we are concentrating so much on what we want to find or what we think we should find that it blinds us to the surprises of the text.

How wonderfully ironic it is that the protagonist in the Frederick Buechner novel that my student was reading (the first part of *The Book of Bebb*) finds himself reading the Gospel of Nicodemus from the Apocrypha. Why? He is fascinated by it because it is *unfamiliar*. In other words, he is able to read it as a narrative, which he, for one reason or another, felt prohibited from doing with the canonical books.

Here is the problem: because it is orthodox belief to accept the scandal of the cross, we treat is as if it were not scandalous. I return to Flannery O'Connor, who said, "For the hard of hearing you have to shout. For the blind you must draw large and startling figures." Our vision is clouded, our hearing is faint. We must, like Thomas, actually finger Christ's wounds before we believe. We can't, of course, literally do that. But we can participate imaginatively in narration, which makes it real for us.

And so O'Connor writes odd and offensive stories to make us see the scandal of the cross. There is no story more offensive than "The River," about a child who is baptized in a river he returns to later and drowns in, in his attempt to get to the kingdom of God. After all, he heard the preacher say the kingdom of God was in the river's baptismal waters, so, he thought, why not just enter the water and go under for good? This story about the baptism of a child and the death of a child strips baptism down to its core, ridding it of any possibility of a sentimentalized reading. There is no baby in a beautiful lace dress. There is no fancy reception with champagne punch afterward. What we have at the end is a dead child. If you are offended and outraged, you should be.

What O'Connor is doing is focusing on the truth. And she is using the cross as her standard. Not the sentimentalized version on Hallmark Easter cards, but the instrument of death for murderers, thieves, criminals and political enemies. For the King of the Universe. Ugly, violent, grotesque. We tend to forget what it meant originally. We have made it into art. We have encrusted it with jewels and covered it with gold. We have taken Christ off from it. We hang it from holes in our ears. We have trivialized it.

And O'Connor wants to remind us that first—before anything else—the cross is a scandal because it is a symbol of our attempts to kill God. And that is only a part of the story. The other part is that he let us do it. He let us kill him. *That* is what we are wearing around our necks. An electric chair, if you will. An electric chair that points beyond itself to something else. But first and foremost it is an electric chair where someone has been executed.

Of course, unless we happen to be Enoch or Elijah, we are, every one of us, living with a death sentence. Yes, death has been conquered, but we still have to cross that River. Like the child in O'Connor's story, we still have to go under the water to get to the kingdom of God.

So did Christ die? Yes. Is he alive? Yes. Will we die? Yes. Has death been overthrown? Yes. Does Thomas doubt? Yes. Does Thomas believe? Yes.

There are those who want a clearer message and a stronger example than the one that Thomas provides. In Kurt Vonnegut's novel *Slaughterhouse Five*, Billy Pilgrim is told about a book called *The Gospel from Outer Space*, in which the author has rewritten the crucifixion.

> The visitor from outer space made a gift to Earth of a new Gospel. In it, Jesus really was a nobody, and a pain in the neck to a lot of people with better connections than he had. He still got to say all the lovely and puzzling things he said in the other Gospels.

So the people amused themselves one day by nailing him to a cross and planting the cross in the ground. There couldn't possibly be repercussions, the lynchers thought. The reader would have to think that, too, since the new Gospel hammered home again and again what a nobody Jesus was.

And then, just before the nobody died, the heavens opened up, and there was thunder and lightning. The voice of God came crashing down. He told the people that he was adopting the bum as his son, giving him the full powers and privileges of The Son of the Creator of the Universe throughout all eternity. God said this: *From this moment on, he will punish horribly anybody who torments a bum who has no connections!*

Notice that this gospel contains no paradox. This God gives a clear message and responds with immediate justice. There is no waiting. There is also no resurrection.

At the end of O'Connor's story "Parker's Back," there is a remarkable scene. Parker has just had the face of Christ tattooed on his back as a rather original present to his wife. But when she sees it, she picks up a broom and begins to beat him until welts appear.

And where is God? Where is God during this unfair, painful, unjust suffering? He is embedded in Parker's flesh. He is color, design, pattern, unity—receiving the welts on Parker's back as Parker is receiving them. Here is the Word made flesh. God in the flesh on Parker's back. God taking the welts with us. God dying with the child under the water. God knowing pain and suffering it as we have suffered it. God experiencing all we read about in our morning papers: God taking the bullet in the brain. God, a Fed, crushed under the bombed-out building. God losing his leg under the train. God, the baby the mother throws out the window of the tenement building.

God on the cross wondering why God is so silent: "God, my God, why have you forsaken me?"

Chaos, turmoil in the heavens and on earth, suffering, persecution, hatred—this is what one finds in all of the Gospel descriptions of Christ's crucifixion. Yet *in the midst* of these terrors, Christ reveals himself to the thieves hanging next to him and tells one of them that today he will be with him in Paradise.

Violence. Revelation. Faith. Doubt. Life. Death. Uncomfortable combinations for those who would prefer, as O'Connor says in one of her letters, to think of faith as a "big electric blanket, when of course it is the cross." Parker discovers that life with Jesus on his back will not be comfortable.

Even though nothing can separate us from the love of God, still the kingdom of God is not a nuclear-free zone. It comes to us in a gashed side and punctured palms and invites us into the wounds themselves. In fact, then and only then do we really begin to believe.

17
A PANEL DISCUSSION
Lindbeck, Hunsinger, McGrath & Fackre

O n the final morning of the conference at which the papers in this volume were presented, the four keynote speakers (George Lindbeck, George Hunsinger, Gabriel Fackre and Alister McGrath) gathered for a panel discussion. What follows is an edited transcript of the conversation assessing the conference.

George Lindbeck: I have six points. First of all, it struck me as this conference proceeded that comparing postliberals and evangelicals is very much like comparing apples and oranges. Postliberals happen to be a collection of individuals engaged in what scientists call a research program, whereas evangelicals are members of communities, institutions, movements that are historically associated with inerrancy controversies on the one hand and conversionist revivalism on the other. At least in North America, I think that would be a fair characterization of evangelicalism.

Second, the particular research program that postliberals are engaged in can be characterized as an attempt to recover premodern scriptural interpretation in contemporary form. "Premodern" means three things. It means before modern foundationalism. Another thing that premodern here means is before scriptural reading was molded and distorted, in many cases, by the inerrancy and inspiration controversies. In other words, postliberalism is agnostic about these controversies and positions that come out of them, just as premodern scriptural interpretation was. Finally, premodern means before modern individualism. The individualism of conversionist revivalism tended in various ways to modify the classical tradition of Scripture reading. To speak of individualism in this context means that postliberalism tries to divorce itself from the antiecclesial, the anti- or low-sacramental and the anti- or noncreedal ways of reading Scripture that have prevailed on the modern evangelical side.

The contemporary aspect of the postliberal research program is the acceptance of biblical criticism, but placing it in a very subordinate role as far as the theologically significant reading of Scripture is concerned.

The third overall point is that this postliberal research program overlaps, to some extent, with goals that an increasing number of evangelicals have. These would include the renewal of evangelicalism, in Alister McGrath's terms, a recovery of the Christian heritage—especially the Reformation heritage. If you are going to talk about the postliberals being concerned about recovering heritage, I suppose you would say that most of them want to recover both the Reformation and Catholic heritages.

My fourth point is that, looked at from this perspective, the complaint voiced a number of times about the lack of substantive theological work on the postliberal side is misplaced. It's misplaced because the research program is one regarding methods of reading Scripture, not specifically regarding the development of any single theological outlook. If I do theology (and I have done a fair amount of substantive theology), it's Lutheran theology in the Lutheran confessional tradition. For George Hunsinger it's in the Reformed confessional tradition.

The fifth point is that from the postliberal point of view, the question that arises for evangelicals is, How many of the modern distinctives of evangelicalism can evangelicals omit in their attempt to recover the fullness of the Christian heritage as it developed in the premodern period? In this regard I find myself very far to the right, theologically, of most evangelicals. I knew this before, but I became more conscious of it at this conference. I'm much more creedal than most of the people here. I place more emphasis on creeds, confessions and dogmas. I'm sacramentally realistic in a way that free church people are not. I have a much higher ecclesiology than most of the people here. So for me it's not at all a dialogue between the left and the right. It's much more complicated than that.

The last point that I'd like to make, which in some ways is the most important to me, is that it's understandable that my name should come up with numbing frequency in this conference. I happen to have introduced into the public domain the word *postliberal*, though I didn't intend to name a research program or a movement. And I happen to be, I suppose, the senior living member of the group that is willing to call itself postliberal. But if you're going to talk about the decisive figure in this particular research program, it's clearly Hans Frei by a very large margin. He is the major figure. But because it's a research program in a rather limited area, a methodological research program, Hans Frei doesn't have disciples. There is no school of theology that is a Freian school of theology. What we are is a group of collaborators in a common research program that may or may not have a promising future. I'm sure that the goal has a promising future. But the question is whether or not our particular way of trying to recover the premodern heritage of Scripture reading in contemporary form will succeed wholly over the long run.

George Hunsinger: First, there is a danger here of getting ourselves into a situation where the more things change, the more they remain the same. We've heard a lot at this conference about foundationalism and antifoundationalism. We've heard about semiotic and nonsemiotic systems—a lot of technical, philosophical and sociological terminology. It's good to know this terminology. It's good to be able to use it, but this is a relative good. It's even a lesser good. And if this kind of thing takes off and takes over, it will defeat what all of us are most concerned about. So I make a plea here especially to the evangelicals. If *you* start using technical jargon at the expense of what we've been calling first-order discourse (i.e., the ordinary language of the church), what's going to happen to us poor postliberals?

In this regard, I would like to comment on the distinction between first-order and second-order discourse. I see a danger in the way this distinction has sometimes been used. I would like to suggest that this be seen as a merely relative distinction. No statement is entirely first-order or second-order. Any statement somehow is making both moves at one time—sometimes predominantly or almost exclusively one way, sometimes almost exclusively the other. Think for example of what Karl Barth is doing in the *Church Dogmatics.* Is that first-order discourse or second-order discourse? It changes from place to place. Sometimes you actually get personal address in a very Kierkegaardian sense, and other times he's making rather technical moves. But the one is never very far from the other. Hans Frei used to talk about how Barth is teaching us to rediscover a language and relearn it simply by immersing ourselves in it. This first-order or second-order distinction can get out of hand, and we don't want to pit the discourses against one another. We don't want to say, for example, that we hear only second-order discourse from the podium and only first-order discourse from the pulpit. We would be bewitching ourselves in the way that Wittgenstein warned us against if we let the distinction function for us in a dichotomized way.

So I would urge that along with becoming methodologically sophisticated and mastering these external languages, we keep them under theological control. To those who are theologians I would say, immerse yourself in the work of at least one great theologian. Barth is not for everyone here, I'm sorry to say. So immerse yourself in Calvin. Immerse yourself in Luther. Immerse yourself in Aquinas or Augustine. Of course, any of these theologians will have some kind of technical apparatus. But it's deeply embedded in another form of discourse, which is where it finally belongs. It needs to be used more provisionally and eclectically than it will be if we set that external language up independently and then constantly use it as a norm that controls and validates our theology (which is what happens in theological liberalism).

One last point along these lines: I'm very encouraged by what I have heard at this conference. In preparing for it I read some things about Bernard Ramm and his book *After Fundamentalism.* I came across a quotation from James Daane of Fuller Seminary, saying that it will take generations before Karl Barth gets over the bad press he has had in the evangelical community. But this conference shows that it's not taking generations, and that's enormously encouraging.

Gabriel Fackre: My comments are under the general heading "Reading the Minutes of the Last Meeting." I was helped greatly by Hal Knight's paper saying that issues faced today between postliberals and evangelicals may have their roots in Jonathan Edwards and John Wesley. I think it's helpful in a number of ways to read these past minutes of the Christian tradition.

For example, one key issue between us is the conception of this master metaphor "story." Back in the Reformation debates, the polarity was between the "assent of the mind"—belief—and the "trust of the heart"—faith. And most of the great theologians insisted these two belong together, that faith is both *assensus* and *fiducia*, both the head and the heart, both assertions and affect. And I think of story in those terms. I don't think that story is counterposed to doctrine or propositions. These are inextricable. So when you say in the language of the church, "The Word was made flesh and dwelt among us," you're making not only an act of commitment and trust of the heart but also an assertion that this is the way the world works. When you say, "There is the second person of the Trinity who became one of us," you move from the (first-order) language of the church to the (second-order) language of Chalcedon. But both languages entail assertion. They're not only affective, or narrative, and they're not only rules of discourse. What's a proposition? A proposition is an assertion about states of affairs to which the response has to be yes or no. So I think there are assertions embedded in narrative.

That's learning from the old debates on *fiducia* and *assensus*. Another learning from the past is how ecclesial traditions shape the conversation about what postliberalism is, about what evangelicalism is and how the two converge or diverge. For example, there are different kinds of postliberals. George Lindbeck has said flat out how much of a Lutheran and evangelical catholic he is. And George Hunsinger comes at postliberalism from the Reformed tradition. I really think the difference between the Reformed and the Lutheran sensibility is a difference over *finitum capax infiniti*, whether or not the finite is capable of receiving the infinite. Lutherans believe it is. God is in solidarity with us in Christ and in the Eucharist.

The Reformed tradition instead stresses *finitum non capax infiniti*. It is wary of the domestication of God in the Eucharist. So you have Calvin's spiritual real presence but somehow not the same consubstantiality that the Lutherans stress. When I hear George Lindbeck talking about his interpretation of postliberalism, I hear a Lutheran version of it, in which God is enfleshed in Christ. That enfleshment continues in community and its sacramental, liturgical and confessional life. That's a Lutheran version of postliberalism. On the other hand, I often hear a Barthian Hunsinger holding a little bit of reserve about this. And then in comes Stanley Hauerwas, who depends on John Howard Yoder's Anabaptist reading of postliberalism, and you get yet another dimension. In evangelicalism, meanwhile, we have the dispute between David Wells and Clark Pinnock, which is really a replay of the Calvinist-Arminian debate, now in a new and interesting form. So it helps me to think of ecclesial traditions as informing these matters.

My final observation about remembering the minutes of the last meeting relates to something that Miroslav Volf spoke about in his paper. I have in mind the struggle in the nineteenth and twentieth centuries with the hermeneuticians of suspicion (Marx and Freud and Nietzsche). I read that engagement through the eyes of Reinhold Niebuhr, who drew on Marx and Freud and Nietzsche but did it from within the language and faith of the gospel. So he appropriated these traditions and said that's really a way of talking about sin and finitude. That's how these secular commentators can remind us, in this discussion between evangelicals and postliberals, that there are historical matrices; this isn't just a debate among ideas. There are social, political, economic factors—finitude and sin—at work in these two traditions. And we ought to be more aware of them.

Finally, we haven't said much in these three days about Bosnia and Oklahoma City and the O. J. Simpson trial. I think we worry about the liberal tendencies to rush to incorporate issues of justice and peace in matters of theology. We're wary of being trapped into letting the world's agenda reformulate the faith. But the Lord Jesus Christ rules over the marketplace and the courthouse as well as the soul and the church. Something of what we have been saying ought to have implications for the marketplace and the counting house and the judge's chamber.

Alister McGrath: I find George Lindbeck's categorization of postliberalism as a research program very helpful. Going back and reappropriating the premodern is something from which evangelicals can learn. There are treasures waiting to be retrieved and reappropriated—such as Edwards, the Wesleys, Calvin and Luther. The Reformation itself in one sense can be seen as going behind the medieval period to rediscover parts of the patristic heritage. And perhaps we as evangelicals can begin to go behind modernity and rediscover a wealth of things that we've overlooked in our tradition. I think writers like Thomas Oden are encouraging us to do this. In this light the strategy of seeing postliberalism as a methodology is actually very helpful and has caused me to revise my estimation of it.

But I think, as Jeffrey Stout once said, that talking about methodology is like clearing your throat. You can only do it for so long until you lose your audience. In the end, I think that we will want to know where postliberalism goes, where this research program will take us. It is right to ask what happens when we start applying these methods. In one sense it is premature for me to try to anticipate where it might go. But I can raise two issues that I think evangelicals will want to discuss as this conversation goes on.

One of them is the whole issue of revelation and authority. In making this point I don't want you to see me as necessarily critiquing postliberals. I'm saying that it is an area of divergence between evangelicals and postliberals. Further exploration and discussion would be both helpful and appropriate.

The other issue is something that we haven't really touched on at all. It has to do with evangelism. Certainly evangelicals see the active proclamation of the gospel as integral to our understanding of Christianity. One question for future discussion is whether or not postliberalism will enable us to evangelize in that it enables us to understand the way in which religions function. But does such an understanding actively enable us to commend Christianity to others? What is the motivation for evangelism in this context? What is it about the Christian story that commends it above other stories?

Panel Interaction

Gabriel Fackre: George [Lindbeck], I'd be interested in your responding to Alister's comment because as I read your views on *fides ex auditu*, I saw that for you hearing the word has soteric import, which suggests that there may be grounds in your theology for the importance of evangelism. Is that a fair statement?

George Lindbeck: This presents the question of how one understands evangelism in a more ecclesial sacramental setting in contrast to—not necessarily in opposition to—a more conversionist and revivalistic setting. I spent seventeen years of my life in China, growing up as the child of missionaries. I have been reminded frequently of the Chinese situation, which as I experienced it was very much like that of the early church. In the first three centuries of the Christian era evangelism took place because people wanted to associate themselves with this community of Christians that they found attractive. Years of catechesis preceded baptism. In China it took years and years, as the Chinese themselves would later say, for them to absorb the language, the understanding ("the worldview," to use abstract Christian terms) that enabled their minds to become conformed to the mind of Christ well enough for them to begin thinking like Christians. That's a very different kind of evangelism from the evangelism that grew up in nominally Christian cultures such as those in the West. So any differences we have on evangelism are not strictly postliberal versus evangelical at all. It is rather a matter of how we as Christians ought to evangelize now in the West, caught as we are in the middle of an agonizing transition from Christendom to post-Christendom.

George Hunsinger: Professor Lindbeck's bringing up China reminds me of the difference between Hudson Taylor and Timothy Richard as missionaries to China. I think part of the postliberal sensibility would be to try to embrace both of them rather than to polarize and make us choose. As individuals we might have to choose whether we want to go one way or another, but each path is commendable and necessary in its own way and not everyone can do everything. So let a hundred flowers bloom.

I think of the book by William Hutchinson, *Errands to the World*, which is a study of the English-speaking missionary movement. The final chapter focuses on some differences between John Stott on the one hand and Lesslie Newbigin on the other. My sympathies are generally with Newbigin on matters that seem to separate them. But I don't see why that should keep me from a very agreeable appreciation of someone like John Stott. Evangelicals seem to be the ones who want to turn this into an either-or. It's better not to make it a forced option, better to see it all as somehow perhaps in God's inscrutable providence, something that different communities are given to work at simultaneously and somewhat antagonistically, but all finally moving toward the same goal.

Gabriel Fackre: I want to stay on this one more inch: Does the proclamation of the gospel, whether by word or sacrament, in community or proclamation, have soteric weight for the postliberal research project? Or is it something else? I think that's what Alister was pressing, and I thought, George, that your comments on *fides ex auditu* and the Lutheran emphasis on hearing the word in order to have saving faith would represent a convergence here.

George Lindbeck: I misunderstood your question, Gabe. There's a very interesting conceptual problem, not to say a deeply critical Christian kerygmatic problem, of how to combine this genuine hope for the salvation of all without in any way dogmatically asserting that it's going to happen, of combining it with the *fides ex auditu* emphasis on the proclamation of the word and explicit decision for Christ. And I don't want to pursue that question now. If you want to identify it as the challenge to postliberals, that's all right with me, but I think it's not a challenge distinctively to postliberals.

Alister McGrath: Here the issue that we're trying to explore relates to what I see as an aspect of the postliberal enterprise. Let me put it this way: what reasons might I give for saying to, for example, a Muslim, that I believe that the community, the narrative, within which I stand has merit over his or hers? That kind of issue would certainly be of interest to evangelicals.

George Lindbeck: That clarifies the problem, Alister, and the slogan that has become popular among postliberals is the slogan of ad hoc apologetics. There is no general answer to your question. Normally, those who turn to Christ consider Christianity as a live option after other options have collapsed. One doesn't argue people to faith—we would agree with that, as you indicated in your paper. Why Christianity rather than another faith? The answer depends on the character of the questioner and the character of the questions he or she raises. In regard to some Muslims you might say, Look, this is why I recommend Christ rather than Muhammad to you. To other Muslims you might present a different set of reasons. As Hans Frei expressed it, there is no single logic of coming [to faith]. There is a logic of belief. There is a structure of Christian faith. But the ways in which God calls us through the Holy Spirit to come to believe are so varied that you cannot possibly make generalizations. I would add: people are inevitably committed to working within a given conceptual cultural language system. We Christians think, look and argue from within the faith. There's no way of getting outside the faith to objectively compare different options. Why follow Christ rather than someone else? I find myself thinking very much along the epistemological lines of Alasdair MacIntyre.

After the panelists fielded questions from the floor, Professor Lindbeck offered a final comment.

I have not expressed fully enough my enormous gratitude for this conference. I will also say that if the sort of research program represented by postliberalism has a real future as a communal enterprise of the church, it's more likely to be carried on by evangelicals than anyone else.

Notes

Chapter 1: The Nature of Confession/Phillips & Okholm

[1]C. Stephen Evans, "Can the New Jesus Save Us?" *Books and Culture* 1, no. 2 (November/December 1995): 6.

[2]Betty J. Eadie, *Embraced by the Light* (Placerville, Calif.: Gold Leaf, 1992).

[3]Jaroslav Pelikan, *Jesus Through the Centuries: His Place in the History of Culture* (New Haven, Conn.: Yale University Press, 1985).

[4]Carl F. H. Henry, *Gods of This Age, or God of the Ages?* (Nashville: Broadman & Holman, 1994); Os Guinness and John Seel, eds., *No God but God: Breaking with the Idols of Our Age* (Chicago: Moody Press, 1992); Michael Scott Horton, ed., *Power Religion: The Selling Out of the Evangelical Church?* (Chicago: Moody Press, 1992); David F. Wells, *No Place for Truth: Or, Whatever Happened to Evangelical Theology?* (Grand Rapids, Mich.: Eerdmans, 1993); David F. Wells, *God in the Wasteland: The Reality of Truth in a World of Fading Dreams* (Grand Rapids, Mich.: Eerdmans, 1994).

[5]James Davison Hunter, *Evangelicalism: The Coming Generation* (Chicago: University of Chicago Press, 1987), pp. 34-40, 150-54, 180-86; James Davison Hunter, *American Evangelicalism: Conservative Religion and the Quandary of Modernity* (New Brunswick, N.J.: Rutgers University Press, 1983), pp. 84-91; Wells, *No Place for Truth*.

[6]Stanley Grenz proposes a "threefold norm" for theology, one being the "thought-forms of the historical-cultural context in which the contemporary people of God seek to speak, live, and act." Stanley J. Grenz, *Theology for the Community of God* (Nashville: Broadman & Holman, 1994), p. 21; see also pp. 25-26. For a similar expression, see Stanley J. Grenz, *Revisioning Evangelical Theology: A Fresh Agenda for the 21st Century* (Downers Grove, Ill.: InterVarsity Press, 1993), pp. 93, 97-101.

These statements cannot be explained as careless speech. Some of Grenz's substantial theological proposals explicitly employ the "thought-forms of the historical-cultural context" as a norm: "Our assertions concerning the Bible's inspiration and complete trustworthiness are themselves faith declarations which as such must be set aside during the search for the historical basis for the Christian assertion of Jesus' deity" (Grenz, *Theology for the Community*, p. 264).

Nor is this move limited to the Enlightenment West. Some descendants of evangelical missions are now openly advocating a revisionist methodology in theology. See Osadolar Imasogie, *Guidelines for Christian Theology in Africa* (Achimota, Ghana: African Christian Press,

1983). This publication by an evangelical press advocates and applies David Tracy's theological method to the African scene.

[7]Because popular Christianity is "too quickly denigrated by many Christian intellectuals," Richard J. Mouw wrote *Consulting the Faithful: What Christian Intellectuals Can Learn from Popular Religion* (Grand Rapids, Mich.: Eerdmans, 1994), pp. 9-10.

[8]J. Gresham Machen, *Christianity and Liberalism* (Grand Rapids, Mich.: Eerdmans, 1923), p. 105.

[9]See Donald W. McCullough, *The Trivialization of God* (Colorado Springs, Colo.: NavPress, 1995).

[10]Harry Emerson Fosdick, "The Church Must Go Beyond Modernism," in *Sermons in American History: Selected Issues in the American Pulpit, 1630-1967*, ed. Dewitte Holland (Nashville: Abingdon, 1971), p. 340.

[11]Sallie McFague, "An Epilogue: The Christian Paradigm," in *Christian Theology: An Introduction to Its Traditions and Tasks*, ed. Peter C. Hodgson and Robert H. King, 2nd ed. (Philadelphia: Fortress, 1985), p. 381.

[12]Karl Barth, *Church Dogmatics* 2/1, trans. T. H. L. Parker et al. (Edinburgh: T & T Clark, 1957), pp. 163ff.

[13]For some fresh examples of this distortion among conservatives, see John H. Sailhamer, *Introduction to Old Testament Theology: A Canonical Approach* (Grand Rapids, Mich.: Zondervan, 1995), pp. 79-83.

[14]Hans W. Frei, *The Eclipse of Biblical Narrative: A Study of Eighteenth and Nineteenth Century Hermeneutics* (New Haven, Conn.: Yale University Press, 1974), p. 130.

[15]Lesslie Newbigin, *The Gospel in a Pluralist Society* (Grand Rapids, Mich.: Eerdmans, 1989), pp. 42-44. Compare Thomas S. Kuhn, *The Structure of Scientific Revolutions*, 2nd ed. (Chicago: University of Chicago Press, 1970).

[16]This is Auerbach's phrase; he deeply influenced Frei. Erich Auerbach, *Mimesis: The Representation of Reality in Western Literature* (Princeton, N.J.: Princeton University Press, 1953), pp. 14-15.

[17]George A. Lindbeck, *The Nature of Doctrine: Religion and Theology in a Postliberal Age* (Philadelphia: Westminster Press, 1984), p. 132.

[18]Ibid., p. 128.

[19]Ibid., p. 132.

[20]Lindbeck in this volume, p. 239.

[21]Note the parallels in Anthony C. Thiselton, *New Horizons in Hermeneutics: The Theory and Practice of Transforming Biblical Reading* (Grand Rapids, Mich.: Zondervan, 1992), pp. 377-93, 592; and Alister McGrath, *The Genesis of Doctrine: A Study in the Foundations of Doctrinal Criticism* (Oxford: Basil Blackwell, 1990), pp. 192-93. Recall Augustine's hermeneutic of *caritas* in *On Christian Doctrine*.

[22]Nicholas P. Wolterstorff, *What New Haven and Grand Rapids Have to Say to Each Other*, Stob Lectures of Calvin College and Calvin Theological Seminary (Grand Rapids, Mich.: Calvin College, 1993), p. 2.

[23]Carl F. H. Henry, "Narrative Theology: An Evangelical Appraisal," *Trinity Journal* 9 (Spring 1987): 19; see also p. 13. Henry charges that narrative theology fails to guarantee a link between the narrative and factual events to which the narrative refers.

[24]Hans Frei, "Response to 'Narrative Theology: An Evangelical Appraisal,' " *Trinity Journal* 9 (Spring 1987): 23-24. Very helpful is the article by George Hunsinger, "Afterword: Hans Frei as Theologian," in *Theology and Narrative: Selected Essays*, ed. George Hunsinger and William C. Placher (New York: Oxford University Press, 1993), p. 265 n. 13.

²⁵Ironically, those indebted most to the Enlightenment assumption of a universally comprehensive objective truth often cannot understand a nonfoundationalist's argument.

²⁶Roger E. Olson, "Whales and Elephants: Both God's Creatures, but Can They Meet? Evangelicals and Liberals in Dialogue," presidential address to the American Theological Society, Chicago, April 15, 1994; "Evangelicals and Postliberals: Where Can They Meet?" paper delivered at the Wheaton Theology Conference, Wheaton, Ill., April 19, 1995; "Postconservative Evangelicals Greet the Postmodern Age," *The Christian Century*, May 3, 1995, pp. 480-83.

²⁷Grenz, *Revisioning Evangelical Theology*, p. 78.

²⁸Ibid., p. 103; Grenz, *Theology for the Community*, pp. 21-26, 264, 328-41. The subtitles of their recent books reflect their own substantive proposals: Stanley J. Grenz, *Revisioning Evangelical Theology: A Fresh Agenda for the 21st Century*; Clark H. Pinnock and Robert C. Brow, *Unbounded Love: A Good News Theology for the 21st Century* (Downers Grove, Ill.: InterVarsity Press, 1994).

²⁹See Grenz, *Revisioning Evangelical Theology*, p. 98.

³⁰Pinnock and Brow, *Unbounded Love*, pp. 8-9, 63-66, 70-77, 99-110; Clark H. Pinnock, *A Wideness in God's Mercy: The Finality of Jesus Christ in a World of Religions* (Grand Rapids, Mich.: Zondervan, 1992), pp. 37-40; Clark H. Pinnock et al., *The Openness of God: A Biblical Challenge to the Traditional Understanding of God* (Downers Grove, Ill.: InterVarsity Press, 1994). Roger Olson raises a similar question more indirectly in "Postconservative Evangelicals," pp. 480-83. At times it appears that Pinnock's polemic simply reflects his attempt to gain a hearing. But the persistence of his dismissive attitude suggests a subtle yet resurgent Arminian dogmatism.

³¹See Sailhamer, *Introduction to Old Testament Theology*, p. 70: "The task of biblical theology is to allow the fixed reality of the narrative world to shape and inform our understanding of the real world, not the other way around." Alister McGrath's popular works on theology have the same goal. For example, see *Understanding Doctrine: What It Is—and Why It Matters* (Grand Rapids, Mich.: Zondervan, 1990), and *Understanding Jesus: Who Jesus Christ Is and Why He Matters* (Grand Rapids, Mich.: Zondervan, 1987).

³²Guinness and Seel, eds., *No God but God*, pp. 19-20, 189-203, 213-14; Alister McGrath, *Evangelicalism and the Future of Christianity* (Downers Grove, Ill.: InterVarsity Press, 1995), pp. 114-17; Wells, *No Place for Truth*, pp. 127-36; *God in the Wasteland*. Note Lindbeck's telling insight: "The impossibility of effective catechesis in the present situation is partly the result of the implicit assumption that knowledge of a few tag ends of religious language is knowledge of the religion (although no one would make this assumption about Latin)" (*Nature of Doctrine*, p. 133).

Postconservatives generally dismiss Wells's indictment and prescription as "a new manifestation of the kind of conservative, premodern evangelical theology to which Grenz and Pinnock seek to provide an alternative" (Olson, "Whales and Elephants," p. 15 n. 38).

³³See Sailhamer, *Introduction to Old Testament Theology*; Kevin Vanhoozer, *Biblical Narrative in the Philosophy of Paul Ricoeur: A Study in Hermeneutics and Philosophy* (New York: Cambridge University Press, 1990); Alister McGrath, *The Genesis of Doctrine: A Study in the Foundations of Doctrinal Criticism* (Oxford: Basil Blackwell, 1990).

³⁴Wilson in this volume, p. 159.

³⁵See Mark Noll, *The Scandal of the Evangelical Mind* (Grand Rapids, Mich.: Eerdmans, 1995).

Chapter 2: An Evangelical Evaluation of Postliberalism/McGrath

¹Writings that illustrate this approach include Hans Frei, *The Identity of Jesus Christ* (Philadelphia: Fortress, 1975); Paul Holmer, *The Grammar of Faith* (New York: Harper & Row, 1978);

David Kelsey, *The Uses of Scripture in Recent Theology* (Philadelphia: Fortress, 1975); David Kelsey, "The Bible and Christian Theology," *Journal of the American Academy of Religion* 48 (1980): 358-402; George Lindbeck, *The Nature of Doctrine: Religion and Theology in a Postliberal Age* (Philadelphia: Westminster Press, 1984).

[2]A point noted by Brevard Childs, *The New Testament as Canon* (Philadelphia: Fortress, 1984), p. 541.

[3]See Stanley Hauerwas, *Against the Nations* (Minneapolis: Winston, 1985), as well his *A Community of Character: Toward a Constructive Christian Social Ethic* (Notre Dame, Ind.: University of Notre Dame Press, 1981); William C. Placher, *Unapologetic Theology: A Christian Voice in a Pluralistic Conversation* (Louisville, Ky.: Westminster/John Knox, 1989); Ronald E. Thiemann, *Revelation and Theology: The Gospel as Narrated Promise* (Notre Dame, Ind.: University of Notre Dame Press, 1985).

[4]For a general overview, see William C. Placher, "Postliberal Theology," in *The Modern Theologians*, ed. D. F. Ford, 2 vols. (Cambridge, Mass.: Blackwell, 1989), 2:115-28; Sheila Greeve Davaney and Delwin Brown, "Postliberalism," in *The Blackwell Encyclopaedia of Modern Christian Thought*, ed. Alister E. McGrath (Cambridge, Mass.: Blackwell, 1993), pp. 453-56.

[5]William C. Placher, "Paul Ricoeur and Postliberal Theology: A Conflict of Interpretations," *Modern Theology* 4 (1987): 35-52.

[6]See Alasdair MacIntyre, *After Virtue*, 2nd ed. (Notre Dame, Ind.: University of Notre Dame Press, 1984). For perceptive readings of this text and its program, see Richard J. Bernstein, "Nietzsche or Aristotle? Reflections on Alasdair MacIntyre's *After Virtue*," *Soundings* 67 (1984): 14-15; L. Gregory Jones, "Alasdair MacIntyre on Narrative, Community and the Moral Life," *Modern Theology* 4 (1987): 53-69.

[7]On the theological aspects, see D. Z. Phillips, *Faith After Foundationalism* (London: Routledge, 1988). For the more general phenomenon, see Stephen Crook, *Modernist Radicalism and Its Aftermath: Foundationalism and Anti-foundationalism in Radical Social Theory* (London: Routledge, 1991); John E. Thiel, *Nonfoundationalism* (Minneapolis: Fortress, 1994).

[8]Mary Midgley, *Beast and Man* (New York: Meridian, 1980), p. 306.

[9]This point is made, although in different ways, in Holmer, *Grammar of Faith;* Frei, *Eclipse of Biblical Narrative;* and Lindbeck, *Nature of Doctrine.*

[10]Lindbeck, *Nature of Doctrine*, p. 129.

[11]I think it is fair to point out that postliberal writers are not themselves entirely free from such dependence on extrabiblical foundations. For example, in his *Nature of Doctrine*, George Lindbeck clearly depends on the kind of cultural analysis provided by Clifford Geertz, as in his major essay "The Religion as a Cultural System," in *The Religious Situation*, ed. D. R. Cutler (Boston: Beacon, 1968), pp. 639-88. In his *Community of Character*, Stanley Hauerwas seems to rely on the analysis of Yves Simon regarding "political authority," as stated in *Philosophy of Democratic Government* (Chicago: University of Chicago Press, 1951).

[12]For a useful study, see C. Stephen Evans, *Subjectivity and Religious Belief* (Grand Rapids, Mich.: Christian University Press, 1976).

[13]Lindbeck, *Nature of Doctrine*, p. 32.

[14]Ibid., p. 23.

[15]Ibid., p. 17.

[16]See the useful analysis of William P. Alston, "Christian Experience and Christian Belief," in *Faith and Rationality: Reason and Belief in God*, ed. Alvin Plantinga and Nicholas Wolterstorff (Notre Dame, Ind.: University of Notre Dame Press, 1983), pp. 103-34.

[17]Spiegler, *Eternal Covenant*, pp. 136-56.

[18]Bernard Lonergan, *Philosophy of God and Theology* (Philadelphia: Westminster Press, 1973), p. 50.

19It must be noted at this point that Lonergan is heavily dependent on the somewhat questionable conclusions (e.g., that the "higher religions" derive from the same common core experience of transcendence) of the Chicago writer Friedrich Heiler.

20For additional considerations, see Alister McGrath, *A Passion for Truth: The Intellectual Coherence of Evangelicalism* (Downers Grove, Ill.: InterVarsity Press, 1996).

21Stanley Hauerwas and William H. Willimon, *Resident Aliens: Life in the Christian Colony* (Nashville: Abingdon, 1989), p. 18.

22The use of this Wittgensteinian term is significant: see Paul Holmer, "Wittgenstein: Saying and Showing," *Neue Zeitschrift für systematische Theologie und Religionsphilosophie* 33 (1980): 222-35.

23Holmer, *Grammar of Faith*, p. 23.

24Lindbeck, *Nature of Doctrine*, p. 16.

25Ibid., p. 21. This would certainly correspond to the popular stereotype of evangelicalism, although I would not have expected to find such wooden stereotypes in this work.

26It might also reasonably be pointed out that it pays inadequate attention to what it means to suggest that religious claims are "cognitive" in the first place; an excellent discussion of this point (published too late to be available to Lindbeck) may be found in James Kellenberger, *Cognitivity of Religion: Three Views* (London: Macmillan, 1985).

27Lindbeck, *Nature of Doctrine*, p. 47. But compare the concessions on pp. 80, 105.

28A point noted by Brian A. Gerrish in "The Nature of Doctrine," *Journal of Religion* 68 (1988): 87-92, especially pp. 87-88.

29On this, see J. M. Parent, "La notion de dogme au XIIIe siècle," in *Etude d'histoire litteraire et doctrinaire du XIIIe siècle* (Paris, 1932), pp. 141-63.

30Gillian R. Evans, *Alan of Lille: The Frontiers of Theology in the Later Twelfth Century* (Cambridge: Cambridge University Press, 1983), pp. 64-80.

31For example, see Bede's careful discussion of various different modes and levels of representation, *tropoi* (such as metaphor, catachresis, metalepsis, anadiplosis and metonymia) and *schememata* (such as anaphora, prolepsis and zeugma). Bede, *De schematibus et tropis*, MPL 90.175A-B.

32For example, see Evans, *Alan of Lille*, pp. 33-36. A recent work that attempts a similar clarification of the word *God* is Theodore W. Jennings, *Beyond Theism: A Grammar of God-Language* (New York: Oxford University Press, 1985), especially pp. 59-74.

33For an exploration of the relation between cognitive statements and experience, see Alister E. McGrath, "Theology and Experience: Reflections on Cognitive and Experiential Approaches to Theology," *European Journal of Theology* 2 (1993): 65-74.

34Lindbeck makes a related point in connection with Hamlet and Denmark: *Nature of Doctrine*, p. 65.

35C. S. Lewis, *Surprised by Joy* (London: Collins, 1959), p. 17. It is, of course, debatable whether this is the experience Longfellow had intended to convey; this question, however, lies beyond the present study.

36For this point in relation to the writings of Schillebeeckx, see L. Dupré, "Experience and Interpretation: A Philosophical Reflection on Schillebeeckx' *Jesus* and *Christ*," *Theological Studies* 43 (1982): 30-51.

37A point stressed by John R. Carnes in *Axiomatics and Dogmatics* (Belfast: Christian Journals, 1982), pp. 10-15; see also the earlier study of Norbert R. Hanson, *Perception and Discovery* (San Francisco: Freeman and Cooper, 1969), as well as his *Observation and Explanation* (New York: Harper & Row, 1971).

38Gerhard Ebeling, "Die Klage über das Erfahrungsdefizit in der Theologie als Frage nach ihrer Sache," in *Wort und Glaube III* (Tübingen: Mohr, 1975), pp. 3-28.

[39]See Eberhard Jüngel, *God as the Mystery of the World* (Edinburgh: T & T Clark, 1983), p. 32.

[40]Clifford Geertz, "Religion as a Cultural System," in *The Religious Situation*, ed. D. R. Cutler (Boston: Beacon, 1968), pp. 639-88.

[41]It would seem that Lindbeck's philosophical stances must be related to the long-standing English-language debate concerning "Wittgensteinian fideism": see Kai Nielsen, "Wittgensteinian Fideism," *Philosophy* 42 (1967): 191-209. The continuing use of this term has been severely criticized by Kerr, *Theology After Wittgenstein*, pp. 28-31. It is one of the many merits of Lindbeck's work to attempt to respond to Wittgenstein, both in the rejection of "cognitive" models of doctrine and in the affirmation of the value of a "cultural-linguistic" approach.

[42]See Lindbeck, *Nature of Doctrine*, pp. 32-41; quote on p. 33.

[43]Ibid., p. 65.

[44]For Hans Frei's discussion of the relation of "fact-likeness" to "factuality," see Frei, *Eclipse of Biblical Narrative*, p. 187.

[45]Lindbeck, *Nature of Doctrine*, p. 114. Lindbeck argues that an "extratextual" approach characterizes the propositionalist and experiential-expressive approach. For further discussion of this point, see T. W. Tilley, "Incommensurability, Intratextuality and Fideism," *Modern Theology* 5 (1989): 87-111.

[46]Holmer, *Grammar of Faith*, p. 203.

[47]Ibid., p. 20.

[48]F. D. E. Schleiermacher, *Brief Outline of the Study of Theology* (Richmond, Va.: John Knox, 1966), p. 71.

[49]Lindbeck, *Nature of Doctrine*, p. 106. See also pp. 66-67.

[50]On this point, see D. Z. Phillips, "Lindbeck's Audience," *Modern Theology* 4 (1988): 133-54.

[51]Lindbeck, *Nature of Doctrine*, p. 65. For views similar to Lindbeck's, yet articulated from an evangelical perspective, see Stanley J. Grenz, *Revisioning Evangelical Theology* (Downers Grove, Ill.: InterVarsity Press, 1993), p. 15; Clark Pinnock, *Tracking the Maze* (San Francisco: Harper & Row, 1990), p. 186.

[52]Bruce D. Marshall, "Aquinas as a Postliberal Theologian," *The Thomist* 53 (1984): 353-401. See also his "Absorbing the World: Christianity and the Universe of Truths," in *Theology and Dialogue: Essays in Conversation with George Lindbeck*, ed. Bruce D. Marshall (Notre Dame, Ind.: University of Notre Dame Press, 1990), pp. 69-102.

[53]Lindbeck, *Nature of Doctrine*, p. 19.

[54]Ibid., pp. 92-96.

[55]Ibid., p. 94. For the suggestion that Lindbeck is not merely dependent on Bernard Lonergan at this point but actually misunderstands him, see Stephen Williams, "Lindbeck's Regulative Christology," *Modern Theology* 4 (1988): 173-86.

[56]As pointed out by Williams, "Lindbeck's Regulative Christology," p. 178.

[57]Rowan Williams, "Trinity and Revelation," *Modern Theology* 2 (1986): 197-212.

[58]See Alister E. McGrath, *The Making of Modern German Christology*, 2nd ed. (Grand Rapids, Mich.: Zondervan, 1994), pp. 145-98.

[59]Ronald Thiemann would appear to represent a critic of this approach, at least in respect of the referent of theological language. Focusing on the concept of "promise," Thiemann argues that the character of the gospel as promise points to a reality beyond the world of human language, and points to the realm of eschatology as the sphere in which questions of "truth" or "reference" are ultimately resolved. See his *Revelation and Theology*, pp. 153-56.

[60]For example, see Alister E. McGrath, *Evangelicalism and the Future of Christianity* (London:

Hodder & Stoughton, 1994/Downers Grove, Ill.: InterVarsity Press, 1995).

61See the sophisticated "critical realist" approach to Scripture developed by N. T. Wright, *Christian Origins and the Question of God*, vol. 1 of *The New Testament and the People of God* (London: S.P.C.K., 1992), pp. 47-80.

62Hauerwas, *Community of Character*, p. 56.

63Ibid., pp. 65-66. Note that Hauerwas is not denying that Scripture may be used and interpreted in other spheres; he is simply pointing out that the *proper* sphere for such use and interpretation is the life of the church.

64See the helpful discussion in John Sykes, "Narrative Accounts of Biblical Authority: The Need for a Doctrine of Revelation," *Modern Theology* 5 (1989): 327-42; L. Gregory Jones, "A Response to Sykes: Revelation and the Practices of Interpreting Scripture," *Modern Theology* 5 (1989): 343-48.

65Carl F. H. Henry, "Theology and Biblical Authority: A Review Article," *Journal of the Evangelical Theological Society* 19 (1976): 315-23.

66For a survey of evangelical opinion on this issue, see Kern Robert Trembath, *Evangelical Theories of Biblical Inspiration* (New York: Oxford University Press, 1987).

67For the issues that lie behind my formulation, see Brevard Childs, *Biblical Theology in Crisis* (Philadelphia: Westminster Press, 1970), p. 102; Frei, *Eclipse of Biblical Narrative*, p. 133.

68The best (and probably the most sympathetic) analysis is to be found in George Hunsinger, "Hans Frei as Theologian: The Quest for a Generous Orthodoxy," *Modern Theology* 8 (1992): 103-28. Note especially the extended discussion at note 13, pp. 124-26.

69Ibid., p. 123.

70For the argument, see *Eclipse of Biblical Narrative*, p. 315.

71See Wolfhart Pannenberg, *Jesus—God and Man* (Philadelphia: Westminster Press, 1968). For reflections on Pannenberg's methodological analysis, see Alister E. McGrath, "Christology and Soteriology: A Response to Wolfhart Pannenberg's Critique of the Soteriological Approach to Christology," *Theologische Zeitschrift* 42 (1986): 222-36.

72A. B. Ritschl, *The Christian Doctrine of Justification and Reconciliation* (Edinburgh: T & T Clark, 1900), 3:591.

73Ibid., p. 465.

74See the excellent analysis in Stefan Scheld, *Die Christologie Emil Brunners* (Wiesbaden: Franz Steiner, 1981), especially pp. 111-15.

75For this phrase, see Frei, *Identity of Jesus Christ*, p. 4.

76Ibid., p. 56.

77For the phrase, see ibid., p. 143.

78See Ernst Käsemann, "Blind Alleys in the Jesus of History Controversy," in *New Testament Questions of Today* (London: SCM Press, 1969), pp. 23-66; Joachim Jeremias, *New Testament Theology* (London: SCM Press, 1975), vol. 1; Günther Bornkamm, *Jesus of Nazareth* (London: Hodder & Stoughton, 1960); Reinhard Slenczka, *Geschichtlichkeit und Personsein Jesu Christi* (Göttingen: Vandenhoeck & Ruprecht, 1967).

79See McGrath, *Making of Modern German Christology*, pp. 145-98, and references therein.

80See Wolfgang Grieve, "Jesus und Glaube: Das Problem der Christologie Gerhard Ebelings," *Kerygma und Dogma* 22 (1976): 163-80.

81For an analysis, see David V. Way, *The Lordship of Christ: Ernst Käsemann's Interpretation of Paul's Theology* (Oxford: Clarendon, 1991).

82For a survey of related issues, see Douglas Jacobsen and Frederick Schmidt, "Behind Orthodoxy and Beyond It: Recent Developments in Evangelical Christology," *Scottish Journal of Theology* 45 (1993): 515-41.

[83]A point stressed to me by George Lindbeck during the 1995 Wheaton Theology Conference, which focused on evangelical-postliberal dialogue, held at Wheaton College, Illinois.

[84]This paper draws on material previously published in my work *Passion for Truth*. I gratefully acknowledge the importance of the 1995 Evangelical-Postliberal Dialogue at the Wheaton Theology Conference in shaping the views expressed in that publication and this article.

Chapter 3: Theology, Meaning & Power/Volf

[1]Jeffrey Stout, *Ethics After Babel: The Language of Morals and Their Discontents* (Boston: Beacon, 1988), p. 163.

[2]Ibid.

[3]George Lindbeck, *The Nature of Doctrine: Religion and Theology in a Postliberal Age* (Philadelphia: Westminster Press, 1984), p. 135.

[4]Among numerous other studies on Lindbeck's *Nature of Doctrine* see the discussions of his work in *Modern Theology* 4 (February 1988); *The Thomist* 49 (1985): 393-472; Frederic B. Burnham, ed., *Postmodern Theology: Christian Faith in a Pluralist World* (New York: Harper & Row, 1989); Bruce D. Marshall, ed., *Theology and Dialogue: Essays in Conversation with George Lindbeck* (Notre Dame, Ind.: University of Notre Dame Press, 1990).

[5]My primary interest in Lindbeck's methodological proposal is along the axis "theology-church-world"; I want to examine its bearing on public theology. His methodological proposal as well as his other work has another significant axis: "theology-church-churches"; indeed, his proposal is explicitly intended as a contribution to ecumenical theology. I will deal with the ecumenical aspects of his work only as they bear directly on the public theology.

[6]Nicholas Wolterstorff, *What New Haven and Grand Rapids Have to Say to Each Other*, Stob Lectures of Calvin College and Calvin Theological Seminary (Grand Rapids, Mich.: Calvin College, 1993), p. 2.

[7]Lindbeck, *Nature of Doctrine*, p. 118.

[8]Friedrich Schleiermacher, *On Religion: Speeches to Its Cultured Despisers*, trans. John Owen (New York: Harper & Row, 1958), p. 1.

[9]I am using *translation* in this paper not simply in the sense of restating the Christian message in a different language and cultural idiom, as does Lamin Sanneh in *Translating the Message: The Missionary Impact on Culture* (Maryknoll, N.Y.: Orbis, 1989), but in the sense of recasting the Christian message in the framework of what is plausible within a given culture. This, I think, is the way Lindbeck uses the term when discussing the nature of modern theology.

[10]George Lindbeck, "Scripture, Consensus and Community," in *Biblical Interpretation in Crisis: The Ratzinger Conference on Bible and Church*, ed. Richard John Neuhaus (Grand Rapids, Mich.: Eerdmans, 1989), p. 87; Lindbeck, *Nature of Doctrine*, p. 130.

[11]Ibid., p. 128.

[12]David H. Kelsey, "Church Discourse and Public Realm," in *Theology and Dialogue*, ed. Bruce Marshall (Notre Dame, Ind.: University of Notre Dame Press, 1990), pp. 12-18.

[13]Rowan D. Williams, "Postmodern Theology and the Judgment of the World," in *Postmodern Theology*, ed. Frederic Burnham (New York: Harper & Row, 1989), p. 92.

[14]Søren Kierkegaard, *Fear and Trembling and the Sickness unto Death*, trans. Walter Lowrie (Princeton, N.J.: Princeton University Press, 1954), pp. 26-37.

[15]Lindbeck, *Nature of Doctrine*, p. 117.

[16]George Lindbeck, "Barth and Textuality," *Theology Today* 43 (1986): 371.

[17]Lindbeck, *Nature of Doctrine*, p. 83.

[18]Ibid., p. 59.

[19]Ibid., p. 30.

[20]Walter Kasper, "Postmodern Dogmatics: Toward a Renewed Discussion of Foundations in North America," *Communio* 17 (1990): 186.

[21]Friedrich Schleiermacher, *The Christian Faith*, trans. H. R. Mackintosh and J. S. Stewart (Philadelphia: Fortress, 1976), p. 2.

[22]Karl Barth, *Church Dogmatics* 1/1, trans. G. W. Bromiley, ed. G. W. Bromiley and T. F. Torrance (Edinburgh: T & T Clark, 1975), p. 42. On this question, see Lyle D. Dabney, "Otherwise Engaged in the Spirit: A First Theology for a Twenty-first Century," in *The Future of Theology*, ed. Miroslav Volf et al. (Grand Rapids, Mich.: Eerdmans, 1996).

[23]Lindbeck, *Nature of Doctrine*, pp. 114-15.

[24]Clifford Geertz, *The Interpretation of Culture: Selected Essays* (New York: Basic Books, 1973), pp. 110, 119, 122.

[25]Ibid., p. 119.

[26]Ibid.

[27]Ibid., p. 122.

[28]Talal Asad, "Anthropological Conceptions of Religion: Reflections on Geertz," *Man* 18 (February 1983): 250.

[29]David J. Bryant has underscored an inconsistency in the postliberal program: although postliberals "recognize the historicity of human understanding, they do not always consistently accept the implications of this recognition" for the interpretation of the biblical story. See his "Christian Identity and Historical Change: Postliberals and Historicity," *Journal of Religion* 73 (1993): 31-41.

[30]Jean-François Lyotard, *The Postmodern Condition: A Report on Knowledge*, trans. Geoff Bennington and Brian Massumi (Minneapolis: University of Minnesota Press, 1984), p. 15.

[31]Lindbeck, *Nature of Doctrine*, p. 33.

[32]Ibid., p. 82.

[33]Ibid.

[34]Though it contains a message that addresses and challenges all cultures, the textual world of the Bible is not acultural. Yet it does always remain not only partly outside our own culture but also partly outside our own being as Christians.

[35]Lindbeck, *Nature of Doctrine*, p. 33.

[36]Ibid.

[37]Ibid., p. 62.

[38]James J. Buckley, "Doctrine in Diaspora," *The Thomist* 45 (1985): 449. Because the analogy of religion to languages controls the analogy to cultures, it would be more appropriate to call the model Lindbeck proposes "linguistic-cultural" than "cultural-linguistic," which is Lindbeck's preferred way of designating it. See Lindbeck, *Nature of Doctrine*, p. 39.

[39]Lindbeck, *Nature of Doctrine*, pp. 27-28, n. 16; Geertz, *Interpretation of Culture*, p. 125.

[40]Geertz, *Interpretation of Culture*, pp. 144-45.

[41]Lindbeck, *Nature of Doctrine*, p. 62.

[42]Talal Asad, "Anthropology and the Analysis of Ideology," *Man* 14 (April 1979): 618.

[43]If we accept a Geertzian reading of Lindbeck, then the picture of the blimp has a strong sense of "language of faith" as "a system of discursive and nondiscursive symbols" existing (in Geertzian terms) as an extrinsic source of information and doing the job of "linking motivation and action and providing an ultimate legitimation for basic patterns of thought, feeling, and behavior uniquely characteristic of a given community." See Geertz, *Interpretation of Culture*, p. 92; Lindbeck, *Nature of Doctrine*, p. 62. If we give Lindbeck a Wittgensteinian reading, then things look somewhat different. In this case we could not say even for

analytic purposes of symbols that they are "extrinsic sources of information" providing "a blueprint or template in terms of which processes external to themselves can be given a definite form," as Geertz says of cultural patterns in general and of religion in particular. See Geertz, *Interpretation of Culture*, p. 92. Rather than being a blueprint independent of social practices, the "language of religion" would then be the flip side of particular "forms of life"; the patterning would then not go from language to forms of life, but language-cum-forms of life would be seen as social practice. Yet even in this case the problem of the blimp remains, only the blimp is no longer "a system of symbols" but a "network of practices." See Ludwig Wittgenstein, *Philosophical Investigations*, 3rd ed., trans. G. E. M. Ascombe (New York: Macmillan, 1953), p. 23.

[44]It would pay to study carefully the issue of agency in relation to religion as cultural-linguistic system in Lindbeck's proposal. Who or what is doing all these wonderful things Lindbeck says the Christian "cultural-linguistic system" is doing? The answer to this question is not always clear in Lindbeck. Is the system itself doing the doing? Would that not be like saying that "hammer is hitting nails" (as Richard Heyduck suggested in personal correspondence)? Do people use the system? If they do, they must be more than the system. What defines the people—the Christians—who can put the system to use?

[45]Michel Foucault, *Power/Knowledge: Selected Interviews and Other Writings, 1972-1977*, trans. Colin Gordon et al. (New York: Pantheon, 1980), p. 114; Michel Foucault, "Afterword: The Subject and Power," in *Michel Foucault: Beyond Structuralism and Hermeneutic*, ed. Hubert L. Dreyfus and Paul Rabinow, 2nd ed. (Chicago: University of Chicago Press, 1982), pp. 208-26.

[46]Foucault, *Power/Knowledge*, p. 115.

[47]For further elaboration of the notion of "relations of force" that I presuppose in the following discussion, see below the section entitled "Power."

[48]Making a point similar to the one I wish to make here, though in a different way, Geoffrey Wainwright has noted that a "linguistic-cultural" model of Christian faith "won't do in the case of the (relative) *origins* of a religious tradition." Mary's "fiat at Luke 1:38 and the humanity of Christ as an active organ of the redemption surely imply a co-constitutive role (responsive, of course) for human *experience* in the *foundation* of the Christian tradition." Geoffrey Wainwright, "Ecumenical Dimensions of George Lindbeck's 'Nature of Doctrine,' " *Modern Theology* 4 (February 1988): 124.

[49]Geertz, *Interpretation of Culture*, p. 5.

[50]Asad, "Anthropological Conceptions of Religion," 237.

[51]On the negative side, people are often pressured in many ways to become Christians, and the power of the "Christian story" is sometimes established and maintained by the power of the "sword."

[52]Lindbeck, *Nature of Doctrine*, p. 35.

[53]Ibid.

[54]Ibid., p. 51.

[55]Ibid., p. 65.

[56]Ibid., p. 66.

[57]Ibid., p. 64.

[58]Ibid., p. 67.

[59]Bruce D. Marshall, "Aquinas as Postliberal Theologian," *The Thomist* 53 (1989): 364.

[60]George Lindbeck, "Response to Bruce Marshall," *The Thomist* 53 (1989): 403.

[61]As I read *Nature of Doctrine*, Lindbeck is not simply claiming that nonperformance (*Christus est Dominus* as a battle cry of a Crusader) makes a religious utterance intrasystemically false,

as Bruce Marshall suggests, but that it makes it also ontologically false. Lindbeck clearly states that a religious utterance acquires "the propositional truth of ontological correspondence only insofar as it is a performance . . . which helps create that correspondence" (*Nature of Doctrine*, p. 65).

[62]Geertz, *Interpretation of Culture*, p. 131.

[63]Ibid., p. 98.

[64]Ibid., p. 131.

[65]Kasper, "Postmodern Dogmatics," p. 189.

[66]Foucault, *Power/Knowledge*, p. 131.

[67]Michel Foucault, *Language, Counter-Memory, Practice: Selected Essays and Interviews*, trans. Donald F. Bouchard and Sherry Simon (Ithaca, N.Y.: Cornell University Press, 1977), p. 225.

[68]Ibid., p. 141.

[69]Ibid., p. 142.

[70]Ibid., p. 98.

[71]Talal Asad, *Genealogies of Religion: Discipline and Reasons of Power in Christianity and Islam* (Baltimore: Johns Hopkins University Press, 1993), p. 50.

[72]Ibid., p. 53.

[73]Peter L. Berger, *The Heretical Imperative: Contemporary Possibilities of Religious Affirmation* (Garden City, N.Y.: Anchor/Doubleday, 1979), pp. 17ff.

[74]Wolterstorff, *What New Haven and Grand Rapids Have to Say*, p. 45.

[75]Lindbeck, *Nature of Doctrine*, p. 39.

[76]John Howard Yoder, "How H. Richard Niebuhr Reasoned: A Critique of *Christ and Culture*," in *Authentic Transformation: A New Vision of Christ and Culture*, ed. John Howard Yoder et al. (Nashville: Abingdon, 1995), pp. 1-74.

[77]Ibid., p. 38.

[78]Lindbeck, *Nature of Doctrine*, p. 56.

[79]George Lindbeck, "The Church's Mission to a Postmodern Culture," in *Postmodern Theology*, ed. Frederic Burnham (New York: Harper & Row, 1989), p. 55.

[80]Ibid., p. 47.

[81]Ibid., pp. 54-55.

[82]Niklas Luhmann, "Paradigm Lost: Über die ethische Reflexion der Moral: Rede anlässlich der Verleihung des Hegel-Preises 1989," in *Paradigm Lost: Über die ethische Reflexion der Moral*, ed. Niklas Luhmann and Robert Spaemann (Frankfurt: Suhrkamp, 1991), pp. 23ff.

[83]Robert Bellah, "Christian Faithfulness in a Pluralist World," in *Postmodern Theology*, ed. Frederic Burnham (New York: Harper & Row, 1989), p. 89.

[84]Stephen Toulmin, *Cosmopolis: The Hidden Agenda of Modernity* (New York: Free Press, 1990), pp. 184, 193.

[85]Ibid., p. 192.

[86]For helpful comments on previous versions of this paper I am greatly indebted to professors Robert Cathey, Philip Clayton and Robert H. Gundry, to the members of the Fuller Restaurant Group (in particular, professors Judith Gundry-Volf and Nancey Murphy) and to my research assistant, Richard Heyduck.

Chapter 4: Are Postliberals Necessarily Antirealists?/Hensley

[1]Mark Ellingsen goes so far as to argue that metaphysical realism is one of the central, identifying features of evangelical theology. See his "Common Sense Realism: The Cutting Edge of Evangelical Identity," *Dialog* 24 (Summer 1985): 197-205. Richard Lints, in his

recent work on evangelical theology, articulates this characteristic methodological tendency of evangelicalism as the "realism principle." See his book *The Fabric of Theology: A Prolegomenon to Evangelical Theology* (Grand Rapids, Mich.: Eerdmans, 1993), especially pp. 20-28.

[2]George Lindbeck, *The Nature of Doctrine: Religion and Theology in a Postliberal Age* (Philadelphia: Westminster Press, 1984).

[3]Donald G. Bloesch, *A Theology of Word and Spirit: Authority and Method in Theology* (Downers Grove, Ill.: InterVarsity Press, 1992), pp. 17, 30.

[4]Donald G. Bloesch, *Holy Scripture: Revelation, Inspiration and Interpretation* (Downers Grove, Ill.: InterVarsity Press, 1994), pp. 211-12.

[5]Ibid., p. 215.

[6]Bloesch, *Theology of Word and Spirit*, p. 133.

[7]Thomas Morris, introduction to *Philosophy and the Christian Faith*, ed. Thomas Morris (Notre Dame, Ind.: University of Notre Dame Press, 1988), pp. 6-7.

[8]Alister McGrath, *The Genesis of Doctrine: A Study in the Foundation of Doctrinal Criticism* (Oxford: Blackwell, 1990), pp. 29, 31.

[9]This antirealist reading of Lindbeck is in no way unique to evangelical assessments of his work; in fact, this reading of Lindbeck's theology is shared by many of his nonevangelical critics. See, for example, Ian Barbour, *Religion in an Age of Science* (London: SCM Press, 1990), 1:14-16; Brevard Childs, *The New Testament as Canon: An Introduction* (Philadelphia: Fortress, 1984), pp. 541-46, and his *Biblical Theology of the Old and New Testaments* (Minneapolis: Fortress, 1993), pp. 21-22; C. John Sommerville, "Is Religion a Language Game? A Real World Critique of the Cultural-Linguistic Theory," *Theology Today* 51 (1995): 594-99; and, possibly the most sustained critique of the metaphysics of postliberalism, Mark Wallace, *The Second Naiveté: Barth, Ricoeur and the New Yale Theology* (Macon, Ga.: Mercer University Press, 1990), especially pp. 104-10.

[10]In much of what follows I am indebted to Nicholas Wolterstorff's work on the realism-antirealism debate. See the following: "Realism vs. Anti-realism," in *Realism: Proceedings and Addresses of the American Catholic Philosophical Association*, ed. D. Dahlstrom (Washington, D.C.: American Catholic Philosophical Association, 1984), pp. 182-205; "Are Concept-Users World-Makers?" in *Metaphysics*, vol. 1 of *Philosophical Perspectives*, ed. James Tomberlin (Atascadero, Calif.: Ridgeview, 1987), pp. 233-67.

[11]Hilary Putnam, *Reason, Truth and History* (Cambridge: Cambridge University Press, 1981), p. 52. Nelson Goodman, another influential antirealist, states this antirealist view as follows: "Identification rests upon organization into entities and kinds. . . . Identity or constancy in a world is identity with respect to what is within that world as organized [by our concepts]." See his *Ways of Worldmaking* (Indianapolis: Hackett, 1978), p. 8.

[12]Hilary Putnam, *Realism and Reason* (Cambridge: Cambridge University Press, 1983), p. 230.

[13]Nelson Goodman likewise distinguishes his antirealism or "irrealism" from idealism when he lyrically states, "The realist will resist the conclusion that there is no world; the idealist will resist the conclusion that all conflicting versions describe different worlds. As for me, I find these views equally delightful and equally deplorable—for, after all, the difference between them is purely conventional!" See his *Of Mind and Other Matters* (Cambridge, Mass.: Harvard University Press, 1984), pp. 43-44.

[14]Hilary Putnam, *The Many Faces of Realism* (LaSalle, Ill.: Open Court, 1987), p. 7. Strictly speaking, Putnam calls his metaphysical view "internal realism" or "pragmatic realism," but he clearly opposes all traditional forms of metaphysical realism. Thus his "internal realism" can be justifiably classified as a type of metaphysical antirealism. See, for example, his *Many Faces of Realism*, p. 17.

¹⁵Alvin Plantinga, "How to Be an Anti-realist," in *Addresses and Proceedings of the American Philosophical Association*, 1983, p. 48.

¹⁶Wolterstorff, "Are Concept-Users World-Makers?" pp. 237-39.

¹⁷See, for example, Goodman, "On Starmaking," in *Of Mind and Other Matters*, pp. 39-44.

¹⁸Similarly Wolterstorff understands the "core of metaphysical anti-realism" to be the following claim: "For any proposition P, only relative to some conceptual scheme is it the case that P is true or false"; see "The World Ready-Made," chapter two of his forthcoming book *Presence and Praxis*. This is what I will later characterize as alethic antirealism, yet conceptual antirealism can be stated in similar fashion: for any entity or kind of entity, only relative to some conceptual scheme is it the case that that entity or kind of entity exists.

¹⁹Putnam, *Realism and Reason*, p. 230. See also his *Many Faces of Realism*, pp. 33, 36.

²⁰In other words, I am interpreting conceptual antirealism to be a species of *conceptual relativism*. Conceptual relativism, as characterized by Donald Davidson, is the view that "reality itself is relative to a scheme: what counts as real in one system may not in another." See his now classic article "On the Very Idea of a Conceptual Scheme," *Proceedings and Addresses of the American Philosophical Association* 47 (1973-1974): 5-20. I quote from p. 5.

²¹As Goodman states, "Whatever can be said truly of a world is dependent on the saying—not that whatever we say is true but that whatever we say truly (or otherwise present rightly) is nevertheless informed by and relative to the language or other symbol system we use." See his *Of Mind and Other Matters*, p. 41.

²²Richard Rorty, "Pragmatism, Relativism and Irrationalism," in *Consequences of Pragmatism* (Minneapolis: University of Minnesota Press, 1982), p. 166.

²³Lindbeck, *Nature of Doctrine*, p. 117.

²⁴Ibid., p. 84.

²⁵Ibid., p. 69.

²⁶Ibid., p. 10.

²⁷Ibid., pp. 120-21.

²⁸Ibid., p. 118.

²⁹Lindbeck states that religions such as Christianity "are the lenses through which human beings see and respond to their changing worlds, or the media in which they formulate their descriptions." See ibid., p. 83.

³⁰Ibid., p. 117.

³¹Ibid., p. 33.

³²Ibid., p. 131.

³³Elsewhere Lindbeck similarly states, "Religion, whatever else it may be or do, provides an overarching integrating and legitimating frame of reference for the socially constructed worlds that human beings inhabit" (ibid., p. 27, n. 10).

³⁴He states, "The *sense* of what is real or unreal is in large part socially constructed" (ibid., p. 63, emphasis mine). Reality itself is not socially or conceptually constructed, just our conceptual takes of it.

³⁵"Reality *as meaningful signs* is wholly constituted in any individual occurrence by [its] intratextuality, by [its] place, so to speak, in a story" (ibid., p. 114, emphasis mine).

³⁶I am indebted to Nicholas Wolterstorff for this helpful analogy.

³⁷Lindbeck, *Nature of Doctrine*, p. 69.

³⁸See, for example, ibid., pp. 19, 80, 106. Lindbeck specifies various first-order uses of doctrinal statements: "For Christian theological purposes, that sentence [i.e., 'Christ is Lord'] becomes a first-order proposition capable (so nonidealists would say) of making

ontological truth claims only as it is used in the activities of adoration, proclamation, obedience, promise-hearing, and promise-keeping which shape individuals and communities into conformity to the mind of Christ" (ibid., p. 68). He adds that such statements "acquire enough referential specificity to have first-order or ontological truth or falsity only in determinate settings, and this rarely if ever happens on the pages of theological treatises or in the course of doctrinal discussions."

[39]Ibid., p. 80.

[40]In other words, this distinction is fundamental to his entire project in *Nature of Doctrine*—the project of explaining the "ecumenical problematic" or how it is "possible for doctrines that once contradicted each other to be reconciled and yet retain their identity . . . how doctrines can be both firm and flexible, both abiding and adaptable" (ibid., pp. 78-79).

[41]In fact, Lindbeck emphasizes the importance of this first-order use of doctrinal statements in religion when he states that "a religion's truth claims are often of the utmost importance to it (as in the case of Christianity)," even though the grammar or "inner logic" of a religion determine the kinds of truth claims that the religion can make; see ibid., p. 35.

[42]There are more detailed treatments of Lindbeck's account of truth already in print. See, for example, Bruce D. Marshall, "Absorbing the World: Christianity and the Universe of Truths," in *Theology and Dialogue: Essays in Conversation with George Lindbeck*, ed. Bruce D. Marshall (Notre Dame, Ind.: University of Notre Dame Press, 1990), pp. 69-102; and, more recently, Bruce D. Marshall, " 'We Shall Bear the Image of the Man of Heaven': Theology and the Concept of Truth," *Modern Theology* 11 (January 1995): 93-117.

[43]He states, "There is nothing in the cultural-linguistic approach that requires the rejection (or acceptance) of the epistemological realism and correspondence theology of truth" (*Nature of Doctrine*, pp. 68-69).

[44]See, for example, ibid., pp. 64 and 47, respectively.

[45]Ibid., p. 48.

[46]Ibid., pp. 51 and 67.

[47]Ibid., p. 65.

[48]Lindbeck's commitments to antifoundationalism, while operative throughout *Nature of Doctrine*, are made clear on pp. 130-32. See also his article "Theologische Methode und Wissenschaftstheorie," *Theologische Revue* 74 (1978): 267-80. This article, to the best of my knowledge, has never been published in English.

[49]See René Descartes, "Meditations on First Philosophy," in *The Philosophical Writings of Descartes*, vol. 2, trans. J. Cottingham, R. Stoothoff and D. Murdock (Cambridge: Cambridge University Press, 1985).

[50]For more on this close association of epistemological foundationalism and metaphysical realism in modernity, see John Searle, "Rationality and Realism: What Is at Stake?" *Daedalus: Journal of the American Academy of Arts and Sciences* 122 (Fall 1993): 55-83.

[51]Richard Rorty is an excellent example of this "postmodern" trend. See, for example, "The World Well Lost," *Journal of Philosophy* 69 (1972): 649-66, especially pp. 662-63; and *Philosophy and the Mirror of Nature* (Princeton, N.J.: Princeton University Press, 1979), especially pp. 273-311.

[52]For more on the debate between foundationalism and anti- or nonfoundationalism and its subsequent impact on theology, see John Theil, *Nonfoundationalism* (Minneapolis: Fortress, 1994).

[53]Some might question the coherence of an antifoundationalist realism. Yet unfortunately, while demonstrating its coherence is an interesting and much-needed project, it lies outside

the scope of this essay. For the purposes of this essay, I am claiming minimally that there is no *prima facie* incoherence in combining the two views. What has been taken as a necessary connection between realism and foundationalism, on the one hand, and antirealism and antifoundationalism, on the other, is merely an accidental rather than necessary connection in the history of modern philosophy. For instance, the eighteenth-century Scottish philosopher Thomas Reid is an excellent example of an antifoundationalist, realist thinker. See Reid's *Inquiry and Essays*, ed. Ronald Beanblossom and Keith Lehrer (Indianapolis: Hackett, 1983).

⁵⁴I would like to thank David Kelsey, George Lindbeck and the Yale Symposium for the Philosophy of Religion for their critical and helpful comments on an earlier version of this paper.

Chapter 5: How Firm a Foundation/Clapp

¹Richard R. Topping, "The Anti-foundationalist Challenge to Evangelical Apologetics," *Evangelical Quarterly* 63, no. 1 (1991): 45-60 (quote from p. 45). Helpful overviews of foundationalism can be found in Jonathan Dancy, *Introduction to Contemporary Epistemology* (Oxford: Blackwell, 1985), and John E. Thiel, *Nonfoundationalism* (Minneapolis: Fortress, 1994).

²Jeffrey Stout, *The Flight from Authority* (Notre Dame, Ind.: University of Notre Dame Press, 1981), p. 46. A more detailed account of the historical situation and its results is offered in the first two chapters of Stephen Toulmin, *Cosmopolis* (Chicago: University of Chicago Press, 1990), pp. 1-87.

³Lorraine Daston, "Baconian Facts, Academic Civility and the Prehistory of Objectivity," in *Rethinking Objectivity*, ed. Allan Megill (Durham, N.C.: Duke University Press, 1994), pp. 52-53.

⁴Stephen Toulmin, *The Uses of Argument* (Cambridge: Cambridge University Press, 1958), pp. 249, 127. Descartes is quite explicit about mathematics's appeal and influence on his work. In the first chapter of his *Discourse on Method*, he comments, "Above all I enjoyed mathematics, because of the certainty and self-evidence of its reasonings," and "I was astonished that on such firm and solid foundations nothing more exalted had been built." In the second chapter he explains that since "only the mathematicians have been able to arrive at proofs, that is to say, certain and evident reasons, I had no doubt that it was by the same things which they had examined that I should begin." And in chapter five he writes, "I have always remained firm in my resolution . . . not to accept anything as being true which did not seem to me more clear and certain than had previously the demonstrations of the geometers" (*Discourse on Method*, trans. F. E. Sutcliffe [London: Penguin, 1986], pp. 31, 41-42, 61).

⁵Stanley Hauerwas has pointed out to me that *individual* was a term first used in mathematics, to denote a "free-standing entity."

⁶George M. Marsden, *Fundamentalism and American Culture* (New York: Oxford University Press, 1980), p. 111. For more on the influence of Scottish Common Sense Realism, see pp. 14-16 and 109-18, and Marsden's "The Collapse of American Evangelical Academia," in *Faith and Rationality*, ed. Alvin Plantinga and Nicholas Wolterstorff (Notre Dame, Ind.: University of Notre Dame Press, 1983), pp. 219-64.

⁷Marsden, *Fundamentalism*, p. 111.

⁸Ibid., pp. 111, 112.

⁹One of the central points of this paper is that words and their truth mean nothing apart from the communal contexts in which they are used. In that spirit, I hope it is clear that I am aware that the word *foundationalism* hardly has a single, univocal meaning. Thus there

are some important Christian thinkers, perhaps most notably Alvin Plantinga and William Alston, who call themselves foundationalists but are certainly not foundationalists of the sort worried over through these pages.

[10]Toulmin, *Uses of Argument*, p. 183.

[11]Ibid., p. 218.

[12]I take this example from David S. Cunningham, who clearly fared better in algebra than I did. See his *Faithful Persuasion: In Aid of a Rhetoric of Christian Theology* (Notre Dame, Ind.: University of Notre Dame Press, 1991), pp. 152, 154.

[13]Ronald Nash, *Faith and Reason* (Grand Rapids, Mich.: Zondervan, 1988), pp. 23, 26, 28, 23, 30.

[14]I know Ron Nash to possess a sense of humor. Accordingly, the smoking metaphor is an attempt to clarify a tendency among some evangelicals—maybe "funly," as a friend of mine often says. It is not intended to mock or disrespect Professor Nash.

[15]Nash, *Faith*, pp. 38-39.

[16]Ibid., p. 55.

[17]Quoted in ibid., p. 57.

[18]In a book powerfully pertinent to the contention of this essay as a whole, David Cunningham notes, "Most of our arguments take place precisely because we have no general agreement about the rules of the game; and the absence of such universally accepted conventions makes persuasion essential." See his *Faithful Persuasion*, p. 154.

[19]Nash, *Faith*, p. 63.

[20]Ibid., pp. 65-66.

[21]Kenneth S. Kantzer, "Unity and Diversity in Evangelical Faith," in *The Evangelicals*, ed. David F. Wells and John D. Woodbridge (Grand Rapids, Mich.: Baker Book House, 1977), p. 80.

[22]See Nancey Murphy, *Reasoning and Rhetoric in Religion* (Valley Forge, Penn.: Trinity Press International, 1994); McClendon and Smith, *Convictions*, pp. 106-7.

[23]Stanley Hauerwas, "No Enemy, No Christianity: Preaching Between 'Worlds,'" unpublished paper, p. 17; later published in an edited form, "Preaching As Though We Had Enemies," *First Things*, May 1995, pp. 45-49.

[24]I have borrowed William Placher's phrase from his *Unapologetic Theology: A Christian Voice in a Pluralistic Conversation* (Louisville, Ky.: Westminster/John Knox, 1989). He explains that in recent decades "the search for universal starting points and standards for rationality" has come under crippling critical fire. Dialogue need no longer "await universally acceptable starting points" before beginning. "We could admit that of course we all stand within traditions and can never achieve an 'objective' point of view." Given these conditions, and since Christianity "cannot criticize our culture very effectively if it has already accepted many of the assumptions of that culture," it may be that the time has come for a more particular, explicit and "unapologetic" theology (p. 12).

[25]"Yet," he continues, "this does not reduce the choice between different frameworks to whim or chance. . . . The norms of reasonableness are too rich and subtle to be adequately specified in any general theory of reason or knowledge. These norms, to repeat a point often made in this book, are like the rules of depth grammar, which linguists search for and may at times approximate but never grasp." See *The Nature of Doctrine: Religion and Theology in a Postliberal Age* (Philadelphia: Westminster Press, 1984), p. 130. Cogent arguments that Lindbeck's account of truth is compatible with the mainstream of Christian tradition have been made by one of his former students, Bruce D. Marshall, in "Aquinas as Postliberal Theologian," *The Thomist* 53 (1984): 353-401 (to which Lindbeck responds [pp. 403-6] affirmatively that "Marshall has explained the view of truth which I had in mind

better than I explained it myself" [p. 406]), and "Absorbing the World: Christianity and the Universe of Truths," in *Theology and Dialogue: Essays in Conversation with George Lindbeck*, ed. Bruce D. Marshall (Notre Dame, Ind.: University of Notre Dame Press, 1990), pp. 69-102.

26Kantzer, "Unity and Diversity," p. 71. Contrast this with Nancey Murphy's candid admission that though she considers Christianity historically and ontologically true, "no system fulfills all of these criteria [of epistemological persuasion] perfectly. We always have some inconsistencies and a great deal of incoherence in our networks of belief." She also observes, "No one working with a holist account of knowledge is likely to argue for absolutism" (*Reasoning and Rhetoric in Religion*, pp. 257, 263).

27In terms compatible with the criticisms I offer here of Nash, Kantzer, Piper and Grudem, Richard R. Topping critiques the foundationalist apologetics of evangelicals Carl F. H. Henry and Stuart Hackett. See his "Anti-foundationalist Challenge to Evangelical Apologetics."

28John Piper and Wayne Grudem, "An Overview of General Concerns: Questions and Answers," in *Recovering Biblical Manhood and Womanhood*, ed. John Piper and Wayne Grudem (Wheaton, Ill.: Crossway, 1991), pp. 84-85.

29See Toulmin, *Uses of Argument*, p. 235. Relativism as the inversion of foundationalism often draws remark. See, for example, Nancey Murphy, "Textual Relativism, Philosophy of Language and the Baptist Vision," in *Theology Without Foundations*, ed. Stanley Hauerwas, Nancey Murphy and Mark Nation (Nashville: Abingdon, 1994), pp. 268-69; and Ian S. Markham, *Plurality and Christian Ethics* (Cambridge: Cambridge University Press, 1994), p. 142-43.

30For a lucid discussion of these holistic epistemological rules, see Murphy, *Reasoning and Rhetoric in Religion*, particularly pp. 256-57.

31See Alasdair MacIntyre, *Whose Justice? Which Rationality?* (Notre Dame, Ind.: University of Notre Dame Press, 1988), pp. 349-88.

32Likewise, of course, we may be changed and our faith enriched in the same relationship. Or, though we hardly expect it, we cannot deny the possibility that our faith may be shattered in the relationship. I paraphrase here, in my own Christian and theological terms, the summary of persuasion on nonobjectivist grounds presented by Barbara Herrnstein Smith in "The Unquiet Judge: Activism Without Objectivism in Laws and Politics," in *Rethinking Objectivity*, ed. Allan Megill (Durham, N.C.: Duke University Press, 1994), p. 301.

33In this regard I am friendly to Cunningham's description of theology. Seen rhetorically, he writes, theology recognizes that its task "is to persuade others to thought and action. Such persuasion will be unable to operate in a value free, individualistic mode; it must take account of the moral presuppositions of both speaker and audience, as well as the 'material concerns, resources, and strategies in the present situation' " (*Faithful Persuasion*, p. 36).

34George Parkin Grant, *English-Speaking Justice* (Notre Dame, Ind.: University of Notre Dame Press, 1985), p. 102.

35For critical surveys of liberalism, see Ronald Beiner, *What's the Matter with Liberalism?* (Berkeley: University of California Press, 1992); H. Jefferson Powell, *The Moral Tradition of American Constitutionalism* (Durham, N.C.: Duke University Press, 1993); and Robert Booth Fowler, *Unconventional Partners: Religion and Liberal Culture in the United States* (Grand Rapids, Mich.: Eerdmans, 1989).

36MacIntyre, *Whose Justice?* p. 335 (emphasis added).

37This is not to say there are no nonfoundationalist liberals. Nonfoundationalist liberalism differs from its foundationalist ancestor in that it does not, at least not as easily, appeal to universal and acultural norms. But it persists in idealizing individual freedom and eschewing any substantive common good. For nonfoundationalist defenses of liberalism, see Richard Rorty, *Contingency, Irony and Solidarity* (Cambridge: Cambridge University Press, 1989), and "The Priority of Democracy to Philosophy," in *Prospects for a Common Morality*, ed. Gene Outka and John P. Reeder Jr. (Princeton, N.J.: Princeton University Press, 1993), as well as Jeffrey Stout, *Ethics After Babel: The Language of Morals and Their Discontents* (Boston: Beacon, 1988), pp. 220-92.

[38]Stanley Fish, *There's No Such Thing as Free Speech and It's a Good Thing, Too* (New York: Oxford University Press, 1994), p. 16. I agree with Fish that liberalism is "basically a brief against belief and conviction," that it "is an incoherent notion born out of the correct insight that we will never [noneschatologically] see an end to these squabbles and that therefore we must do something, and the doing something is somehow to find a way to rise above the world of conviction, belief, passion. I simply don't think that's possible" (pp. 296, 298).

[39]For fine guidance on reading the Bible nonviolently and nonhegemonically, see J. Richard Middleton and Brian J. Walsh, *Truth Is Stranger Than It Used to Be: Biblical Faith in a Postmodern Age* (Downers Grove, Ill.: InterVarsity Press, 1995).

[40]John Howard Yoder, *The Royal Priesthood*, ed. Michael Cartwright (Grand Rapids, Mich.: Eerdmans, 1994), pp. 112-13.

[41]These last two sentences paraphrase Hauerwas, "No Enemy, No Christianity," pp. 3, 4.

[42]Yoder, *Royal Priesthood*, p. 373.

[43]I am grateful for the draft readings and criticism of this essay by Kelly James Clark, Stanley Hauerwas, Philip Kenneson, Nancey Murphy, Tim Peebles, James Sire and Brian Walsh. Whatever its remaining faults, it has been much improved through their generosity and intelligence.

Chapter 6: The Alleged Incorrigibility of Postliberal Theology/Kenneson

[1]My own sense is that the way I view theology could be categorized as falling within the postliberal camp, if indeed such a camp exists. While I make frequent reference to George Lindbeck's writings in what follows and would be quick to acknowledge that my own way of thinking has been greatly influenced by him on these subjects, I in no way pretend to be a faithful expositor of his proposals. As a result, if one finds the following proposals inadequate or incoherent, one should not necessarily attribute those shortcomings to Lindbeck's seminal insights. On the question of whether I am an evangelical, a category no less contested than that of postliberal, I leave other people to judge.

[2]George A. Lindbeck, *The Nature of Doctrine: Religion and Theology in a Postliberal Age* (Philadelphia: Westminster Press, 1984), pp. 47-48.

[3]Ibid., p. 35.

[4]Ibid., p. 117.

[5]Ibid., p. 118.

[6]Mark Corner, review in *Modern Theology* 3 (October 1986): 112; Corner is referring to Lindbeck, *Nature of Doctrine*, p. 101.

[7]Corner, review, p. 113.

[8]James Gustafson, "The Sectarian Temptation: Reflections on Theology, the Church and the University," *Proceedings of the Catholic Theological Society* 40 (1985): 85-86.

[9]Ibid., pp. 87, 88.

[10]Ibid., p. 90.

[11]In making this distinction I am indebted to Bruce D. Marshall, who makes a similar point in his fine essay "Absorbing the World: Christianity and the Universe of Truths," in

Theology and Dialogue: Essays in Conversation with George Lindbeck, ed. Bruce D. Marshall (Notre Dame, Indiana: University of Notre Dame Press, 1990), especially pp. 82-90.

[12]Part of the confusion stems from what I take to be misreadings of Wittgenstein's comments about language games and forms of life. Given the examples that Wittgenstein offers of the former, it's hard to imagine that his work could be used to sanction the idea that "Christianity" would qualify as a language game.

[13]Gustafson, "Sectarian Temptation," pp. 91-92.

[14]Ibid., p. 91.

[15]Stanley Fish, "Change," in *Doing What Comes Naturally: Change, Rhetoric and the Practice of Theory in Literary and Legal Studies* (Durham, N.C.: Duke University Press, 1989), p. 148.

[16]On the parallels between the prohibitions of Acts 15 and of Leviticus 18—19, see Raymond E. Brown and John P. Meier, *Antioch and Rome: New Testament Cradles of Catholic Christianity* (New York: Paulist, 1983), p. 3.

[17]Fish, "Change," p. 148.

[18]Ibid., p. 150.

[19]While there is no room to pursue the point here, I think other examples from the history of the church abound. For example, certain forgotten "nonliteral" readings of Genesis have been recovered largely as a result of the impetus of contemporary science. Perhaps certain lessons that the church has learned or might learn from the civil rights movement, the women's movement, the environmental movement and even the contemporary emphasis on multiculturalism could be helpfully conceptualized by distinguishing between the impetus for change and the "internal" reasons given for that change.

[20]It seems to me that the Barmen Declaration offers a pertinent reminder at this point: "Jesus Christ, as he is attested for us in Holy Scripture, is the one Word of God which we have to hear and which we have to trust and obey in life and in death. We reject the false doctrine, as though the Church could and would have to acknowledge as a source of its proclamation, apart from and besides this one Word of God, still other events and powers, figures and truths, as God's revelation."

[21]Gustafson, "Sectarian Temptation," pp. 90-91. In another context he gives a further example of what he has in mind: "Theologians and ethicians have shown remarkable myopia in not taking into account the inferences that can be reasonably drawn from some of the most secure knowledge we have of the creation of the universe, the evolution of species, and the likely end of the planet as we know it." See James M. Gustafson, *Ethics from a Theocentric Perspective* (Chicago: University of Chicago Press, 1981), 1:97.

[22]Ibid., pp. 144-45.

[23]John Milbank, *Theology and Social Theory: Beyond Secular Reason* (Oxford: Blackwell, 1990), p. 388 (original emphasis).

[24]Ibid., p. 249.

[25]Lindbeck, *Nature of Doctrine*, p. 131.

[26]Ibid.

[27]This is not to suggest that this gives the church some decisive advantage or leverage that could then be used to sponsor triumphalism. Rather, Milbank himself would likely be the first to remind us that there is no neutral standpoint from which to judge who tells the most comprehensive and adequate story; this too is a matter of judgment made from within particular communities. Perhaps this recognition is also behind Lindbeck's following comment: "The Bible itself, as becomes clear when it is interpreted historically, holds that God works redemptively outside the Church as well as within it, and that Christians must therefore respect and be ready to learn from non-Christians and to adopt 'dialogue' rather

than 'proselytism' as the appropriate form of witness. Such attitudes in both their Jewish and Christian form are compatible with the conviction that the truth to which one's own community is elected to testify is the final revelation which will endure until the end of time." See "The Sectarian Future of the Church," in *The God Experience: Essays in Hope*, ed. Joseph P. Whelan (New York: Paulist, 1971), p. 230.

[28]J. Richard Middleton and Brian Walsh, "Facing the Postmodern Scalpel: Can the Christian Faith Withstand Deconstruction?" in *Christian Apologetics in the Postmodern World*, ed. Timothy R. Phillips and Dennis L. Okholm (Downers Grove, Ill.: InterVarsity Press, 1995), pp. 131-54.

[29]Jeffrey Stout, *After Babel: The Languages of Morals and Their Discontents* (Boston: Beacon, 1988), p. 301.

[30]I owe a special debt to George Hunsinger and A. K. M. Adam for their insightful criticisms of an earlier draft of this essay. For those interested in a more detailed examination of contemporary debates about sectarianism, of which this essay forms a small part, see my forthcoming *Beyond Sectarianism: A Postliberal Reappraisal of Church and World*, Christian Mission and Modern Culture Series (Trinity Press International).

Chapter 7: Relativism, Fideism & the Promise of Postliberalism/Clark

[1]Thomas S. Kuhn, *The Structure of Scientific Revolutions*, 2nd ed. enlarged, International Encyclopedia of Unified Science 2/2 (Chicago: University of Chicago Press, 1970).

[2]Paolo Rossi, "Hermeticism, Rationality and the Scientific Revolution," in *Reason, Experiment and Mysticism in the Scientific Revolution*, ed. M. L. Righini Bonelli and William R. Shea (New York: Science History, 1975), p. 271.

[3]*Fideism* is difficult to define because the word is used as an epithet. I mean by fideism the view that religious claims are not in any way defensible by recourse to facts, that knowledge about God is inaccessible to normal human experience and reflection. Fideism stands at the end of a continuum. At the opposite end of that continuum is a strong rationalism which says that human experience and thinking can demonstrate truths about God (i.e., that he exists). Some will use the words *fideism* and *rationalism* for positions that are in the middle of this continuum. I think it better to call these moderate views *soft fideism* and *soft rationalism*. My concern in this essay is with the stronger form of fideism. I use the word *fideism* (or strong fideism) to describe that position.

[4]Stanley Hauerwas, *Truthfulness and Tragedy: Further Investigations in Christian Ethics* (Notre Dame, Ind.: University of Notre Dame Press, 1977), p. 34.

[5]Paul Lauritzen, "Is 'Narrative' Really a Panacea? The Use of 'Narrative' in the Work of Metz and Hauerwas," *Journal of Religion*, 1987, p. 322.

[6]A helpful though dated essay is Gabriel Fackre, "Narrative Theology: An Overview," *Interpretation* 37 (1983): 340-52. This entire issue of *Interpretation* discusses narrative.

[7]Gary L. Comstock, "Two Types of Narrative Theology," *Journal of the American Academy of Religion* 55 (1987): 688.

[8]George A. Lindbeck, *The Nature of Doctrine: Religion and Theology in a Postliberal Age* (Philadelphia: Westminster Press, 1984).

[9]Ibid., pp. 9-18. Doctrine and theology are different: "There can be great variety in the theological explanation, communication, and defense of the faith within a framework of communal doctrinal agreement" (p. 76).

[10]The recent discussion of theistic science presses the point that Christians in the sciences need not accept arbitrary naturalistic limitations on their scientific thinking. Of course in the operational sciences (which investigate how nature functions on its own), resorting to

divine interventions as explanations *merely because no good natural explanation is available* amounts to a God-of-the-gaps strategy. But it is perfectly acceptable in historical/forensic sciences (which seek to reconstruct past singular events from present clues) to claim that divine action explains a certain phenomenon (say, a Jewish rabbi's rising from the dead) when positive evidence supports that explanation. See J. P. Moreland, ed., *The Creation Hypothesis: Scientific Evidence for an Intelligent Designer* (Downers Grove, Ill.: InterVarsity Press, 1994).

[11]Compatibilism in this context means that God's will is so all-persuasive that he can foreordain all events. God can even foreordain human free actions without negating that freedom. God's almightiness means he can bring about a world where humans always freely do his predetermined will.

[12]Many Arminians reject compatibilism partly because it entangles Christians in grave difficulties on the problem of evil. If God can "sovereignly bring it about such that I freely do his will," as a Calvinist says regarding God's work at conversion, what is God doing as I live the Christian life? Suppose I lie to cover up my own laziness. Is God "sovereignly bringing it about such that I freely do his will"? If not, why does he act so differently in sanctification from the way he does in regeneration? If so, is my sin God's will? Compatibilism eliminates recourse to the free will defense as a response to the problem of evil and thereby makes it difficult to see why God acts as he does in my life.

[13]Barth writes, for example, "Theology must, of course, give an account of this history [of God's deeds] by presenting and discussing human perceptions, concepts, formulations of human language. But it does this appropriately only when it *follows* the living God in those unfolding historical events in which he is God." Karl Barth, *Evangelical Theology: An Introduction*, trans. Grover Foley (Grand Rapids, Mich.: Eerdmans, 1963), p. 9.

[14]"For those who are steeped in [the canonical writings], no world is more real than the ones they create. A scriptural world is thus able to absorb the universe" (Lindbeck, *Nature of Doctrine*, p. 117).

[15]Terrence W. Tilley warns that Lindbeck should clarify his point. A person reading an ancient text must understand it in connection to her world: "Lindbeck is surely correct to say that understanding a text 'in its own terms' requires no reference to 'extratextual,' e.g., Freudian, analyses of those texts. . . . But concretely for a reader to understand a text in any terms, those terms must be accessible in the reader's world" ("Incommensurability, Intratextuality and Fideism," *Modern Theology* 5 [1989]: 98).

[16]Augustine *De Trinitate* 12.22-25; 13.24-25; 14.1-3.

[17]Lindbeck writes, "In thus inverting the relation of the internal and external dimensions of religion, linguistic and cultural approaches resemble cognitivist theories for which external (i.e., propositionally statable) beliefs are primary, but without the intellectualism of the latter. A comprehensive scheme or story used to structure all dimensions of existence is not primarily a set of propositions to be believed, but is rather the medium in which one moves, a set of skills that one employs in living one's life. Its vocabulary of symbols and its syntax may be used for many purposes, only one of which is the formulation of statements about reality. Thus while a religion's truth claims are often of the utmost importance to it (as in the case of Christianity), it is, nevertheless, the conceptual vocabulary and the syntax or inner logic which determine the kinds of truth claims the religion can make. The cognitive aspect, while often important, is not primary" (Lindbeck, *Nature of Doctrine*, p. 35).

[18]This shows the poverty of the negativity and legalism so prevalent in evangelical and fundamentalist ethical preaching and teaching. Too many think that the rationale of "Thou

shalt not commit adultery" is to keep us pure from sexual sin. But that is not the point. As good as sexual purity may be, the point of the seventh commandment is first and foremost to love one's spouse! The *no*, as Barth would say, is based on a much more fundamental *yes*. The negative approach to Christian living seems to entail that total inactivity would foster the zenith of spirituality—as though getting a frontal lobotomy and locking oneself in a closet would *really* lead to the holy life. To refrain from intercourse with your neighbor's husband is good. But loving your own husband passionately is the real point of the rule.

[19]See, for example, Michael Root, "Truth, Relativism and Postliberal Theology," *Dialog* 25 (1986): 175-80; Alan Padgett, "Review of *The Nature of Doctrine*, by George A. Lindbeck," *TSF Bulletin*, January-February 1985, p. 31; Charles M. Wood, "Review of *The Nature of Doctrine*, by George A. Lindbeck," *Religious Studies Review* 11 (July 1985): 235-40; Timothy P. Jackson, "Review of *The Nature of Doctrine*, by George A. Lindbeck," *Religious Studies Review* 11 (July 1985): 240-45; Tilley, "Incommensurability, Intratextuality and Fideism," p. 109.

[20]Kuhn, *Structure of Scientific Revolutions*, p. 148.

[21]One softer definition of incommensurability: "There is no 'third paradigm' into which [two paradigms] can be translated without remainder or equivocation for the purpose of providing standards for measuring them against each other" (Tilley, "Incommensurability, Intratextuality and Fideism," p. 89).

[22]Donald Davidson, "On the Very Idea of a Conceptual Scheme," *Proceedings and Addresses of the American Philosophical Association* 47 (1973-1974): 5-20.

[23]Keith E. Yandell, *Christianity and Philosophy* (Grand Rapids, Mich.: Eerdmans, 1984), pp. 140-48.

[24]Maurice Mandelbaum, "Subjective, Objective and Conceptual Relativisms," *The Monist* 62 (1979): 405.

[25]Bernard Williams, "Auto-da-Fe: Consequences of Pragmatism," in *Reading Rorty: Critical Responses to Philosophy and the Mirror of Nature (and Beyond)*, ed. Alan R. Malachowski (Cambridge, Mass.: Blackwell, 1990), p. 29.

[26]Faced with this dilemma, some relativists posit a second order or category of statements that are *about* language. In this view, only first-order language *within* frameworks is relative to the framework, while second-order language *about* frameworks transcends them. First-order (ontological) statements are perspective dependent, but second-order (metalogical or metalinguistic) statements—which refer only to statements and not to real states of affairs—are not. See Mark B. Okrent, "Relativism, Context and Truth," *The Monist* 67 (1984): 351-52, 356-57. This move evades the self-referential criticism. But it also moves away from strong relativism and fideism. For one thing, it appears that these second-order statements (which refer directly to first-order propositions) will imply indirectly other framework-transcending first-order propositions that are about reality. For instance, the second-order claim "All knowledge is relative to linguistically based perspectives" entails statements that describe reality. It entails first-order propositions like "All human minds are subject to rational flaws," "The world process is the sort of thing that is captured by human language only imperfectly," and so on.

[27]Lindbeck, *Nature of Doctrine*, p. 128.

[28]Ibid., p. 130.

[29]Ibid., p. 10.

[30]Ibid., p. 11.

[31]Lindbeck writes: "What is innovative about the present proposal is that this becomes the only job that doctrines do in their role as church teachings." Then he adds, "This is not

to suggest that other functions of doctrinal formulations are unimportant" (ibid., p. 19). The operative phrase is "in their role as church teachings."

[32]Ronald F. Thiemann, *Revelation and Theology: The Gospel as Narrated Promise* (Notre Dame, Ind.: University of Notre Dame Press, 1985), p. 61.

[33]Carl F. H. Henry, "Narrative Theology: An Evangelical Appraisal," *Trinity Journal* 8 (1987): 12-13, 19. Leon Uris's novel *Exodus* profoundly shaped the movement called Zionism. Is the Bible realistic fiction of that sort? (p. 8).

[34]Hans Frei, "Response to 'Narrative Theology: An Evangelical Appraisal,' " *Trinity Journal* 8 (1987): 23-24.

[35]William C. Placher, *Unapologetic Theology: A Christian Voice in a Pluralistic Conversation* (Louisville, Ky.: Westminster/John Knox, 1989), pp. 165-66.

[36]Comstock, "Two Types of Narrative Theology," p. 688.

[37]Epistemic foundationalism includes many subtypes. See Timm Triplett, "Recent Work on Foundationalism," *American Philosophical Quarterly* 27 (1990): 93-116.

[38]Self-evident beliefs are immediately obvious as soon as someone understands them. Incorrigible beliefs are not correctable.

[39]Timm Triplett, "Reason and Belief in God," in *Faith and Rationality: Reason and Belief in God*, ed. Alvin Plantinga and Nicholas Wolterstorff (Notre Dame, Ind.: University of Notre Dame Press, 1983), pp. 59-61.

[40]A very helpful introduction to the details of Reformed epistemology is Kelly James Clark, *Return to Reason: A Critique of Enlightenment Evidentialism and a Defense of Reason and Belief in God* (Grand Rapids, Mich.: Eerdmans, 1990).

[41]This approach might also be called soft rationalism. See Rod Sykes, "Soft Rationalism," *International Journal for the Philosophy of Religion*, 1977, pp. 51-66; William J. Abraham, "Soft Rationalism," in *An Introduction to the Philosophy of Religion* (Englewood Cliffs, N.J.: Prentice-Hall, 1985), pp. 98-113.

[42]Robert Audi, *Belief, Justification and Knowledge: An Introduction to Epistemology* (Belmont, Calif.: Wadsworth, 1988), p. 98. See also his *The Structure of Justification* (Cambridge: Cambridge University Press, 1993), pp. 117-64.

[43]For a competent introduction to various kinds of coherentism, along with a discussion of their benefits and problems, see Audi, *Belief, Justification and Knowledge*, pp. 87-98.

[44]Patricia Waugh, ed., *Postmodernism: A Reader* (London: Edward Arnold, 1992), p. 5.

[45]Carl Raschke, "Theology, Hermeneutics and the Shattering of Foundations," *Encounter* 43 (1982): 402.

[46]Waugh, *Postmodernism*, p. 6.

[47]Lindbeck, *Nature of Doctrine*, p. 129.

[48]Ibid.

[49]I argue for an audience-sensitive apologetic strategy in *Dialogical Apologetics: A Person-Centered Approach to Christian Defense* (Grand Rapids, Mich.: Baker Book House, 1993).

[50]Lindbeck, *Nature of Doctrine*, p. 130-31.

[51]Paul J. Griffiths argues, "The empirical part of the cultural relativist's thesis is at least very dubious; it just isn't clear that as a matter of fact the criteria for rationality and truth are so different from culture to culture. I would argue that, as far as Indian Buddhism and Anglo American analytical philosophy are concerned, they are close to identical" ("Philosophizing Across Cultures: Or, How to Argue with a Buddhist," *Criterion* 26 [1987]: 13).

[52]Lindbeck, *Nature of Doctrine*, p. 130.

[53]I see this conclusion as entirely consistent with our discussion of the Henry-Frei dialogue referenced above. When pressed, Frei did not want to deny the historicity of Christian

claims about the resurrection, but he did resist Henry's desire to couch that historicity in modernist terms.

Chapter 8: Narrative/Fackre

1George Lindbeck, "Scripture, Consensus and Community," in *Biblical Interpretation in Crisis*, ed. Richard John Neuhaus (Grand Rapids, Mich.: Eerdmans, 1989), p. 75.

2Ronald Thiemann, *Revelation and Theology: The Gospel as Narrative Promise* (Notre Dame, Ind.: University of Notre Dame Press, 1985), p. 99.

3Carl Henry, *God, Revelation and Authority* (Waco, Tex.: Word Books, 1979), 4:468.

4Thiemann, *Revelation and Theology*, pp. 100-101.

5Keith Nickle and Timothy F. Lull, eds., *A Common Calling: The Witness of Our Reformation Churches in North America Today* (Minneapolis: Augsburg/Fortress, 1993).

6Walter Brueggemann, *Texts Under Negotiation: The Bible and Postmodern Imagination* (Minneapolis: Fortress, 1993), pp. 108, 70. See also William Placher (one whom we would expect to be sympathetic to the current conversation and its commonalities), *Narratives of a Vulnerable God* (Louisville, Ky.: Westminster/John Knox, 1994).

7Phrase attributed to John Robinson.

8Phrase attributed to Søren Kierkegaard.

9Alister McGrath, *Evangelicalism and the Future of Christianity* (Downers Grove, Ill.: InterVarsity Press, 1995), p. 65.

10For an elaboration of these themes in John 14:6, see my *Authority: Scripture in the Church for the World*, vol. 2 of *The Christian Story* (Grand Rapids, Mich.: Eerdmans, 1987), pp. 160-240.

11McGrath, *Evangelicalism and the Future*, p. 66.

12Hans W. Frei, " 'Narrative' in Christian and Modern Reading," in *Theology and Dialogue*, ed. Bruce D. Marshall (Notre Dame, Ind.: University of Notre Dame Press, 1990), pp. 150-51.

13Hans W. Frei, *The Identity of Jesus Christ: The Hermeneutical Bases of Dogmatic Theology* (Philadelphia: Fortress, 1975).

14Thiemann, *Revelation and Theology*, pp. 112-40.

15McGrath, *Evangelicalism and the Future*, p. 61.

16For a discussion of the varied theories of inspiration and interpretation among evangelicals see my *Ecumenical Faith in Evangelical Perspective* (Grand Rapids, Mich.: Eerdmans, 1993), pp. 3-20.

17George A. Lindbeck, "The Church's Mission in a Postmodern Culture," in *Postmodern Theology: Christian Faith in a Pluralist World*, ed. Frederic B. Burnham (New York: Harper & Row, 1989), p. 55.

18Bruce D. Marshall, "Aquinas as Postliberal Theologian," *The Thomist* 55 (July 1989): 353-402; George Lindbeck, "Response to Bruce Marshall," pp. 402-6 in the same issue.

19Bruce D. Marshall, "Absorbing the World," in *Theology and Dialogue*, ed. Bruce D. Marshall (Notre Dame, Ind.: University of Notre Dame Press, 1990), pp. 72-73.

20Karl Barth, *Karl Barth's Tabletalk*, recorded and ed. John Godsey (Richmond, Va.: John Knox, n.d.), p. 26.

21Ibid.

22Fackre, *Ecumenical Faith*, pp. 157-340.

23Does Lindbeck's incorporation of personal commitments in his coherence theory of truth reflect this Lutheran sensibility? Only when an assertion ("Christ is Lord," for example) coheres with a life of personal self-emptying, in contrast to assaultive aggression, is it "true." Only when it is true *for me* as a personal appropriation of the way of Christ is it true at all. Another example is Lindbeck's Lutheran insistence on the importance of a personal faith that comes only *ex auditu*, and thus his "postmortem" soteriological view for those who have not made such an act of personal faith. See Lindbeck, *Nature of Doctrine*, pp. 55-72. See also John Sanders, *No Other Name* (Grand Rapids, Mich.: Eerdmans, 1992), pp. 200-205.

[24]David Wells, *No Place for Truth* (Grand Rapids, Mich.: Eerdmans, 1993), p. 173.

[25]The hegemony of personal experience can lead in many directions. One is the temptation to allow contemporary experience, including political, economic and social experience, to write the evangelical agenda, as in the phenomenon of the Religious Right—the thesis of my *The Religious Right and Christian Faith* (Grand Rapids, Mich.: Eerdmans, 1983).

[26]Mark I. Wallace, "The New Yale Theology," *Christian Scholar's Review* 17 (December 1987): 167.

[27]As in the evangelical scholarship of N. T. Wright and Anthony Thiselton, historical-critical and literary-critical work that presupposes the covenant with Noah, so the writer argues in an SBL Chicago 1994 paper, "The Bible, the Spirit and the Community."

Chapter 9: What Can Evangelicals & Postliberals Learn from Each Other?/Hunsinger
[1]Hans Küng, *The Church* (New York: Sheed and Ward, 1967), p. 442.
[2]Ibid.
[3]Hans W. Frei, *Types of Christian Theology* (New Haven, Conn.: Yale University Press, 1992), p. 84.
[4]Jack Rogers and Donald McKim, *The Authority and Interpretation of the Bible: A Historical Approach* (San Francisco: Harper & Row, 1979).
[5]Richard B. Gaffin Jr., "Old Amsterdam and Inerrancy?" *Westminster Theological Journal* 44 (1982): 250-89; 45 (1983): 219-72.
[6]As a movement within Anglo-Saxon Christianity, however, evangelicalism is best understood as arising in the early eighteenth century. See David W. Bebbington, *Evangelicalism in Modern Britain: A History from the 1730s to the 1980s* (Grand Rapids, Mich.: Baker Book House, 1989).
[7]Carl F. H. Henry, "Narrative Theology: An Evangelical Appraisal," *Trinity Journal* 8 n.s. (1987): 3-19, on p. 5.
[8]Ibid., p. 15.
[9]Ibid., p. 4.
[10]Ibid., p. 9.
[11]Ibid., p. 10.
[12]Quoted by Henry, ibid., p. 15. Although I do not mean to equate narrative theology with postliberal theology, they are closely enough related that what Fackre says of the one applies equally to the other.
[13]Ibid., p. 15.
[14]Ibid., pp. 8, 9, 19.
[15]Ibid., p. 19.
[16]See, however, Robert Letham, "Is Evangelicalism Christian?" *Evangelical Quarterly* 67 (1995): 3-16. Letham not only offers an illuminating account of distinctive "evangelical" characteristics but also uses it to explain why evangelicalism has become increasingly fragmented.
[17]It is not clear that all who call themselves "evangelicals" would be willing to subscribe to these ecumenical standards, and in general I would regard this as a serious problem. On the other hand, most such dissenting evangelicals would probably be willing to rule out the kinds of theological positions that these ecumenical standards are designed to rule out. Even among those who might somehow want to endorse a position that is ruled out, however, it would not always be easy (though sometimes it would) from a postliberal point

of view to reject the endorsed position out of hand. For an incisive discussion of this and related matters, see Letham, "Is Evangelicalism Christian?" (see n. 14).

[18]Henry, "Narrative Theology," p. 18.

[19]Perhaps as another indication of his worry about "subjectivism," Henry strangely misreads Frei's narrative analysis of the Gospels as proposing a merely "linguistic" or "literary" presence of God. "Narrative hermeneutics removes from the interpretative process any text-transcendent referent and clouds the narrative's relationship to a divine reality not exhausted by literary presence" (ibid., p. 13). Does God really speak to us through his Word as Calvin taught, Henry asks, or not? "Narrative exegesis is misguided if it leaves problematical the divine authority of its message and its revelatory identity and fails over and above literary affirmation to indicate an adequate test for truth" (p. 13). It is not enough to stay at the level of literary analysis. Frei (along with Brevard Childs) is said to correlate the biblical text with "God's linguistic presence"—a category that has no conceivable bearing on any fair reading of Frei (or for that matter, of Childs). See ibid., pp. 7, 9. Henry seems to think, oddly, that if "historical events are not per se a medium of revelation," then God's only mode of presence must be "literary" (ibid., p. 7). Frei speaks of God's "presence" in relation to Scripture as "mysterious," but never as "literary." See Frei, *The Identity of Jesus Christ* (Philadelphia: Fortress, 1975). There seems to be no good reason to think that Frei viewed the relationship between Word and Spirit fundamentally differently from Calvin.

[20]Ibid., p. 12.

[21]Ibid.

[22]Ibid., p. 9.

[23]Ibid., p. 6.

[24]Ibid.

[25]Ibid.

[26]Ibid., p. 13.

[27]Ibid.

[28]Ibid.

[29]Ibid., p. 8.

[30]Ibid., p. 12.

[31]Ibid.

[32]Ibid, p. 11.

[33]Ibid.

[34]Ibid.

[35]Ibid., p. 12.

[36]This positive move may, in turn, take one of several forms. It may simply argue that the case for historical factuality is *one* plausible position among others. Or it may take the stronger form that historical factuality is *more* plausible than any other position. Or it may take the still stronger form that historical factuality is the *only* plausible position and that all other possibilities are implausible. If I am not mistaken, Henry seems to gravitate toward the latter position.

[37]Ibid., p. 5, italics added.

[38]Ibid., p. 8.

[39]Ibid., p. 3.

[40]Ibid., pp. 13, 14.

[41]Ibid., p. 14.

[42]Ibid.

[43]Ibid., p. 19.

[44]Hans W. Frei, "Response to 'Narrative Theology: An Evangelical Proposal,' " in *Theology and Narrative: Selected Essays,* ed. George Hunsinger and William C. Placher (New York: Oxford University Press, 1993), pp. 207-12, quote on pp. 207-8. Reprinted from *Trinity Journal* 8 n.s. (1987): 21-24.

[45]Frei, "Response," p. 208.

[46]Ibid.

[47]Frei, "Remarks in Connection with a Theological Proposal," in *Theology and Narrative,* pp. 26-44, quote on p. 32.

[48]Frei, "Response," p. 208.

[49]Henry, "Is the Bible Literally True?" in *God, Revelation and Authority* (Waco, Tex.: Word, 1979), 4:103-28. See especially the remarks about metaphor on pp. 109, 113, 120, and about stories on pp. 105-8.

[50]Frei, *Identity of Jesus Christ,* p. 151; compare p. 103.

[51]Ibid., p. 51.

[52]For a further account see George Hunsinger, "Afterword: Hans Frei as Theologian," in Frei, *Theology and Narrative,* pp. 235-70, especially pp. 265-68.

[53]Frei, *Identity of Jesus Christ,* pp. 48, 132, 141.

[54]Ibid., p. 151; compare 103.

[55]Ibid., p. 152.

[56]Ibid., p. 157; compare p. 147.

[57]Frei, "Response," p. 210; see n. 42.

[58]Ibid.

[59]Ibid. Whereas Henry seems to make the question of performance a function of cognitive truth, George Lindbeck seems to move in the opposite direction. "The *only* way to assert the truth is to do something about it.... It is *only* through the performatory use of religious utterances that they acquire propositional force" (Lindbeck, *The Nature of Doctrine* [Philadelphia: Westminster Press, 1984], p. 66, italics added). Although Frei agrees with Lindbeck that the cognitive and performative aspects of truth are interrelated, he does not follow him in making the one a function of the other. In "Epilogue: George Lindbeck and *The Nature of Doctrine,*" Frei differentiates himself from Lindbeck by giving qualified support to those whom he describes as "moderate propositionalists." Moderate propositionalism seems to be the idea that the cognitive and performative aspects of truth are deeply interrelated and inseparable while also being relatively autonomous and distinct, so that in principle neither has precedence over the other (though in practice either one may assume precedence, depending on the situation). See Bruce D. Marshall, ed., *Theology and Dialogue: Essays in Conversation with George Lindbeck* (Notre Dame, Ind.: University of Notre Dame Press, 1990), pp. 278-79.

[60]Frei, *Identity of Jesus Christ,* pp. 140-41.

[61]Frei, "Response," p. 209.

[62]Ibid.

[63]Ibid.

[64]For Henry's argument against analogical reference, and for univocal reference, see "Is the Bible Literally True?" See especially p. 118.

[65]Frei, "Response," p. 209.

[66]Ibid., p. 211.

[67]Ibid., p. 210.

[68]Ibid., p. 211.

[69]Ibid.

[70]Ibid., p. 210.

[71]Ibid.

[72]Abraham Kuyper, *Principles of Sacred Theology* (Grand Rapids, Mich.: Eerdmans, 1954), p. 474. Quoted in Richard B. Gaffin Jr., "Old Amsterdam and Inerrancy? Part 1," *Westminster Theological Journal* 44 (1982): 256-57.

[73]Kuyper, *Principles*, p. 480; quoted in Gaffin, "Old Amsterdam and Inerrancy? Part 1," p. 257. For a somewhat similar view, see David H. Kelsey, *The Uses of Scripture in Recent Theology* (Philadelphia: Fortress, 1975), p. 103.

[74]Henry, "The Lost Unity of the Bible," in *God, Revelation and Authority*, 4:456; see n. 49 above.

[75]Henry, "The Unity of Divine Revelation," in *God, Revelation and Authority* (Waco, Tex.: Word, 1976), 2:74.

[76]Kuyper, *Principles*, p. 477; quoted in Gaffin, "Old Amsterdam and Inerrancy? Part 1," p. 255.

[77]Gaffin, ibid.

[78]George Lindbeck, "Scripture, Consensus and Community," in *Biblical Interpretation in Crisis*, ed. Richard John Neuhaus (Grand Rapids, Mich.: Eerdmans, 1989), p. 83.

[79]See the belated and underdeveloped reference in Henry, "Lost Unity," pp. 468-69.

[80]Henry, "Unity of Divine Revelation," pp. 74-75.

[81]Ibid., p. 74. See also "Lost Unity," p. 469.

[82]Gaffin, "Old Amsterdam and Inerrancy? Part 1," p. 278; compare p. 276.

[83]Ibid.

[84]Ibid, pp. 288-89.

[85]Ibid., p. 281.

[86]Herman Bavinck, *Gereformeerde dogmatiek*, 4 vols., 6th ed. (orig. 1895-1901; Kampen: J. H. Kok, 1976), 1:356; quoted in Richard B. Gaffin Jr., "Old Amsterdam and Inerrancy? Part 2," *Westminster Theological Journal* 45 (1983): 229.

[87]Bavinck, *Gereformeerde dogmatiek*, pp. 361ff.; quoted in Gaffin, ibid., p. 231.

[88]Bavinck, *Gereformeerde dogmatiek*, pp. 546ff.; quoted in Gaffin, ibid., p. 259.

[89]Gaffin, ibid., p. 269.

[90]Gaffin, "Old Amsterdam and Inerrancy? Part 1," p. 272; compare p. 284.

[91]Kuyper, *Dictaten dogmatiek*, vol. 2 (1.66; Grand Rapids, Mich.: J. B. Hulst, n.d.); quoted in Gaffin, ibid., pp. 271-72.

[92]John Calvin, *A Harmony of the Gospels: Matthew, Mark and Luke*, vol. 2 of *Calvin's Commentaries* (Grand Rapids, Mich.: Eerdmans, 1972), p. 55 (on Lk 8:19); cited by William C. Placher, *Narratives of a Vulnerable God* (Louisville, Ky.: Westminster/John Knox, 1994), p. 7.

[93]Calvin, *A Harmony of the Gospels: Matthew, Mark and Luke*, vol. 1 of *Calvin's Commentaries* (Grand Rapids, Mich.: Eerdmans, 1972), p. 139 (on Mt 4:5); cited by Placher, *Narratives*, p. 7.

[94]Perhaps it might also be mentioned here for the sake of future discussion that from a postliberal point of view, American evangelicals have typically been at least as excessive (and with consequences no less unfortunate for the progress of the gospel) in committing themselves to the pathologies of American nationalism and militarism as they have in encumbering themselves with the excesses of modern epistemology. The common thread in both cases, if I may say so, seems to have something to do with a lack of Christian self-confidence, an inordinate, or insufficiently self-critical, desire for external validation, and an aversion (in practice) to the theology of the cross.

[95]Alister E. McGrath, *Christian Theology: An Introduction* (Oxford: Blackwell, 1994).

[96]John R. W. Stott, *The Cross of Christ* (Downers Grove, Ill.: InterVarsity Press, 1986), p. 7.

[97]Ibid.

[98]Ibid.; see pt. 4, "Living Under the Cross."

[99]In making this observation, I am using the term *evangelical* in the somewhat peculiar sense it has acquired in the English-speaking world over the last 250 years or so. A more generous (and more descriptively apt) usage would widen its scope to include theologians often neglected, excluded or castigated by self-described "evangelicals"—theologians like Thomas F. Torrance, Eberhard Jüngel and Robert W. Jenson, each of whose work I would regard as distinguished.

[100]Lindbeck, "Scripture, Consensus and Community," p. 98.

[101]Ibid.

[102]It may not be amiss to indicate that I don't think there is necessarily a tight fit between one's views of historical criticism and the continuum I am seeking to establish. The continuum pertains to the relationship between *signum* and *res* in Holy Scripture. What the theologians on my continuum all share is a belief that this relationship is positive, though not univocal. The rejection of univocity separates them from someone like Henry, just as the affirmation of adequate and reliable reference separates them from modernist skeptics. Not everyone who accepts historical criticism believes that it undermines adequate reference or significant (although there may be disagreements about just what constitutes the *res*). The issue that determines the continuum is not whether one accepts the relative validity of modern historical criticism (about which Calvin of course knew nothing, and toward which Kuyper and Bavinck were largely negative, though not without some ambivalence). The issue is whether one affirms the texts of Holy Scripture as inspired, authoritative and sufficient vehicles of reference to their relevant subject matter (about which the likes of Frei and Lindbeck agree with the rest).

Chapter 10: Toward a New Evangelical Paradigm of Biblical Authority/Wilson

[1]For references, see John Warwick Montgomery, ed., *God's Inerrant Word: An International Symposium on the Trustworthiness of Scripture* (Minneapolis: Bethany Fellowship, 1973).

[2]Harold Lindsell, *Battle for the Bible* (Grand Rapids, Mich.: Zondervan, 1976).

[3]Robert H. Gundry, *Matthew: A Commentary on His Literary and Theological Art* (Grand Rapids, Mich.: Eerdmans, 1982).

[4]Jack Rogers and Donald K. McKim, *The Authority and Interpretation of the Bible: An Historical Approach* (San Francisco: Harper & Row, 1979); James M. Boice, *Does Inerrancy Matter?* (Oakland, Calif.: International Council on Biblical Inerrancy, 1979); Earl D. Radmacher and Robert D. Preus, *Hermeneutics, Inerrancy and the Bible: Papers from ICBI Summit II* (Grand Rapids, Mich.: Academie/Zondervan, 1984); Kenneth S. Kantzer, *Applying the Scriptures* (Grand Rapids, Mich.: Academie/Zondervan, 1987).

[5]F. Leroy Forlines, *Systematics: A Study of the Christian System of Life and Thought* (Nashville: Randall House, 1975).

[6]John R. W. Stott, *The Contemporary Christian* (Downers Grove, Ill.: InterVarsity Press, 1992), back cover.

[7]George Lindbeck, *The Nature of Doctrine: Religion and Theology in a Postliberal Age* (Philadelphia: Westminster Press, 1984).

[8]Ibid., p. 18.

[9]My account here overlaps with that of Stanley Hauerwas, "The Moral Authority of Scripture," in *A Community of Character: Toward a Constructive Christian Social Ethic* (Notre Dame, Ind.: University of Notre Dame Press, 1981), pp. 53-71.

[10]Since most evangelical theology has been bound to a foundationalist epistemology, this discussion may cause some discomfort. But evangelical theology does not need this kind

of foundationalism. For further discussion of these matters, see the essay by Rodney Clapp in this volume and the essays in Stanley Hauerwas, Nancey Murphy and Mark Nation, eds., *Theology Without Foundations: Religious Practice and the Future of Theological Truth* (Nashville: Abingdon, 1994).

[11]W. V. O. Quine with Joseph Ullian, *The Web of Belief* (New York: Random House, 1970).

[12]Richard Rorty, *Philosophy and the Mirror of Nature* (Princeton, N.J.: Princeton University Press, 1979).

[13]For a description of the foundation of the gospel that does not depend on a foundationalist epistemology, see my *Theology as Cultural Critique: The Work of Julian Hartt* (Macon, Ga.: Mercer University Press, forthcoming).

[14]An admirable example of this approach may be found in Donald G. Bloesch, *Holy Scripture: Revelation, Inspiration and Interpretation* (Downers Grove, Ill.: InterVarsity Press, 1994), although I do not have Bloesch's account directly in view in what follows.

[15]Nicholas Lash, "Performing the Scriptures," in *Theology on the Way to Emmaus* (London: SCM Press, 1986), pp. 37-46; see also Stephen E. Fowl and L. Gregory Jones, *Reading in Communion: Scripture and Ethics in Christian Life* (Grand Rapids, Mich.: Eerdmans, 1991).

[16]Sean Hand, ed., *The Levinas Reader* (Oxford: Blackwell, 1989), and Richard Rorty, *Objectivity, Relativism and Truth* (Cambridge: Cambridge University Press, 1991). As Wes Avram noted at the Wheaton Theology Conference, I am not a pure follower of Levinas or Rorty because I want to retain a chastened epistemology and a robust doctrine of revelation. My point is that we often obscure the conviction that God's revelation is both "truth and command." See my further explication of this in "The Gospel as Revelation in Julian N. Hartt," *Journal of Religion* 72 (October 1992): 549-59.

[17]Lindbeck, *Nature of Doctrine*, pp. 30-45.

[18]This is particularly important to note because although formal evangelical theology has tended to follow Lindbeck's cognitive-propositionalist type, popular evangelical faith tends to be experiential-expressivist.

[19]Here let me register a warning for evangelicals (like me) who are appropriating Lindbeck's work. Lindbeck's work requires a robust ecclesiology—which he is currently developing. Evangelicalism, as a movement that crosses ecclesiastical boundaries, has been notoriously lacking in ecclesiology. Can one have an ecclesiology that pleases Episcopalians, Baptists, Presbyterians, Pentecostals and others who make up the evangelical movement? I am not sure.

[20]Fowl and Jones, *Reading in Communion*, pp. 14-21.

[21]John Howard Yoder, "The Hermeneutics of Peoplehood: A Protestant Perspective," in *The Priestly Kingdom: Social Ethics as Gospel* (Notre Dame, Ind.: University of Notre Dame Press, 1984), pp. 15-45.

[22]Lash, "What Might Martyrdom Mean?" in ibid., p. 79.

[23]Bloesch, *Holy Scripture*.

[24]See Fowl and Jones, *Reading in Communion*, chap. 5, for some guidance here.

[25]Lindbeck, *Nature of Doctrine*, p. 118. See also Bruce D. Marshall, "Absorbing the World: Christianity and the Universe of Truths," in *Theology and Dialogue: Essays in Conversation with George Lindbeck*, ed. Bruce D. Marshall (Notre Dame, Ind.: University of Notre Dame Press, 1990), pp. 69-102.

[26]Hans Frei, *Types of Christian Theology* (New Haven, Conn.: Yale University Press, 1992).

[27]Lindbeck, *Nature of Doctrine*, p. 118.

[28]My point here is not that all Christians should practice nonviolence, but that all Christian practices must be rooted in an account of Jesus Christ and are interpretations of the world.

[29]Julian N. Hartt, *Theological Method and Imagination* (New York: Seabury Press, 1977), p. 254. For development of this claim, see my "Gospel as Revelation" and *Theology as Cultural Critique*.

Chapter 11: Toward a *Sensus Fidelium* for an Evangelical Church/Freeman

[1]James W. McClendon Jr., *Systematic Theology: Ethics* (Nashville: Abingdon, 1986), p. 27.

[2]By identifying myself as a baptist I also accept the label of evangelical. Some have argued that in strict historical terms (big B) Baptists are not evangelicals because the two groups have different histories. But in broad theological terms (e.g., conversionist spirituality, biblical authority and evangelistic strategy) baptists (of both upper and lower cases) *are* evangelicals. For a careful discussion of the question see James Leo Garrett Jr., E. Glenn Hinson and James E. Tull, *Are Southern Baptists "Evangelical"?* (Macon, Ga.: Mercer University Press, 1983).

[3]Jon D. Levenson describes how applicants to graduate studies in religion typically provide a "conversion narrative" that describes how they came to accept the historical-critical method and to abandon biblical inerrancy, in "The Bible: Unexamined Commitments of Criticism," *First Things*, February 1993, p. 24.

[4]Krister Stendahl, "Biblical Theology, Contemporary," in *Interpreter's Dictionary of the Bible*, ed. George Buttrick (Nashville: Abingdon, 1962), 1:418-32.

[5]A historical-critical reading of the texts required that *the meaning* (that is, what it meant) must account for the kind of fulfillment that prophet himself envisioned in the post-exilic community (such as a king or a prophet like Moses). Thus a christological reading was precluded from being *the meaning* and should be understood as an ascribed interpretation.

[6]George Lindbeck, "Scripture, Consensus and Community," in *Biblical Interpretation in Crisis*, ed. Richard John Neuhaus (Grand Rapids, Mich.: Eerdmans, 1988), p. 85.

[7]Ibid., p. 87.

[8]The suggestion was made by Stanley Hauerwas, and he graciously followed through by helping to guide the project as an outside reader on the dissertation committee. See Curtis W. Freeman, "Reading St. Augustine's *City of God* as a Narrative Theology," Ph.D. dissertation, Baylor University, 1990.

[9]James W. McClendon Jr. makes this distinction wonderfully clear in his essay "A New Way to Read the Bible," Collins Lecture, Houston Baptist University, March 16, 1995.

[10]Gilbert K. Chesterton, *Orthodoxy* (New York: Dodd, Mead, 1908; reprint New York: Doubleday, 1990), pp. 9-12.

[11]For an excellent discussion of the conservative-liberal consensus against ancient allegory see William S. Babcock, review of *Allegorical Readers and Cultural Revision in Ancient Alexandria* by David Dawson, *Modern Theology* 9 (July 1993): 299-301.

[12]For a fuller account of this argument see my essay "The 'Eclipse' of Spiritual Exegesis: Biblical Interpretation from the Reformation to Modernity," *Southwestern Journal of Theology* 35 (Summer 1993): 21-28.

[13]Gabriel Fackre calls for an "evangelical catholicity" drawing from Philip Schaff, who gave currency to the phrase, in *Ecumenical Faith in Evangelical Perspective* (Grand Rapids, Mich.: Eerdmans, 1993), pp. 71-88. For examples of how the notion of catholicity is appropriated here see also James W. McClendon Jr. and John Howard Yoder, "Christian Identity in Ecumenical Perspective," *Journal of Ecumenical Studies* 27 (Summer 1990): 561-80; Curtis W. Freeman, "A Confession for Catholic Baptists," *Ties That Bind: Life Together in the Baptist Vision*, ed. Gary A. Furr and Curtis W. Freeman (Macon, Ga.: Smyth and Helwys, 1994), pp. 83-

97.

[14]Stanley M. Hauerwas, "The Church as God's New Language," in *Christian Existence Today* (Durham, N.C.: Labyrinth, 1988), pp. 47-65.

[15]See, for example, Richard Rorty, *Philosophy and the Mirror of Nature* (Princeton, N.J.: Princeton University Press, 1979), for a devastating critique of Enlightenment epistemology and foundationalist ontology; and Alasdair MacIntyre, *Whose Justice? Which Rationality?* (Notre Dame, Ind.: University of Notre Dame Press, 1988), for a rigorous refutation of modernity's claim to a tradition-independent morality and rationality. Jerry H. Gill (*On Knowing God: New Directions for the Future of Theology* [Philadelphia: Westminster Press, 1981]) and Lesslie Newbigin (*Foolishness to the Greeks: The Gospel and Western Culture* [Grand Rapids, Mich.: Eerdmans, 1986]) are two evangelicals who acknowledge the failure of the Enlightenment project.

[16]I borrow a line from Percy Bysshe Shelley's classic poem "Ozymandias."

[17]Thomas Oden, "On Not Whoring After the Spirit of the Age," in *No God but God*, ed. Os Guinness and John Seel (Chicago: Moody Press, 1992), p. 195.

[18]George A. Lindbeck, *The Nature of Doctrine: Religion and Theology in a Postliberal Age* (Philadelphia: Westminster Press, 1984), p. 118.

[19]Karl Barth, *The Word of God and the Word of Man*, trans. Douglas Horton (New York: Harper Torchbooks, 1956), p. 41.

[20]Lindbeck, *Nature of Doctrine*, 114.

[21]Hans Frei was keenly aware of the historicist danger that confuses biblical realism (the history-likeness of the text) with ostensive referents to historical events, in *The Eclipse of Biblical Narrative* (New Haven, Conn.: Yale University Press, 1974), p. 27.

[22]Robert Yarbrough, "The Bible in a Post-liberal Church: Review of *Unleashing the Scripture: Freeing the Bible from Captivity to America*, by Stanley Hauerwas, and *Texts Under Negotiation: The Bible and Postmodern Imagination*, by Walter Brueggemann," *Christianity Today*, April 25, 1994, pp. 52-53.

[23]Barth, "An Introductory Essay," in Ludwig Feuerbach, *The Essence of Christianity*, by trans. George Eliot (New York: Harper Torchbooks, 1957).

[24]Bill J. Leonard, "Southern Baptists and Conversion: An Evangelical Sacramentalism," in *Ties That Bind*, pp. 16-17; and W. Loyd Allen, "Spiritual Discernment, the Community and Baptists," in *Ties That Bind*, pp. 118-19. I do not wish to depreciate "the hour I first believed" of conversionist theology. I have simply attempted to call attention to the modern notion of the individual that became wedded to revivalism.

[25]Charles Blanchard, quoted in George M. Marsden, *Fundamentalism and American Culture* (New York: Oxford University Press, 1980), pp. 219-20. For a more detailed examination of the fundamentalist commitment to the Enlightenment notions of objectivity and autonomy in biblical interpretation see Stanley Hauerwas, *Unleashing the Scriptures: Freeing the Bible From Captivity to America* (Nashville: Abingdon, 1993), pp. 29-38.

[26]Hauerwas makes this comparison between Benjamin Jowett and modern biblical criticism in *Unleashing the Scripture*, pp. 33-34.

[27]See, for example, Billy Graham's sermon "Why God Allows Suffering and War," in which he intones the phrase "the Bible says" in almost a mantralike fashion, in *Twenty Centuries of Great Preaching*, ed. Clyde E. Fant Jr. and William M. Pinson Jr. (Waco, Tex.: Word, 1971), 12:312-20.

[28]Robert P. Roth, *Story and Reality: An Essay on Truth* (Grand Rapids, Mich.: Eerdmans, 1973), p. 66.

[29]Hans W. Frei, *Types of Christian Theology*, ed. George Hunsinger and William C. Placher (New

Haven, Conn.: Yale University Press, 1992), p. 24.

[30]Frei, *The Eclipse of Biblical Narrative* (New Haven, Conn.: Yale University Press, 1974), pp. 10, 134, 324; and Lindbeck, "The Bible as Realistic Narrative," *Journal of Ecumenical Studies* 17 (Winter 1980): 85.

[31]The movement on the continuum from the evangelical end toward the liberal pole (historical-critical) can be traced in the theology of Clark Pinnock. His early attempts to apply the theology of biblical inerrancy exhibit the assumptions of evangelical hermeneutics—for example, *A Defense of Biblical Infallibility* (Philadelphia: Presbyterian & Reformed, 1967) and *Biblical Revelation: The Foundation of Christian Theology* (Chicago: Moody Press, 1971). His later work admittedly attempts to nuance inerrancy in the direction of historical-critical assumptions—for example, *The Scripture Principle* (San Francisco: Harper & Row, 1984) and "Climbing out of a Swamp: The Evangelical Struggle to Understand Creation Texts," *Interpretation* 43 (April 1989): 143-55. Pinnock admits that his later view is a mediating position between modernism (liberalism) and traditionalism (fundamentalism) in *"The Scripture Principle* Reviewed," *SBC Today*, May 1986, pp. 6-7.

[32]Although it is impossible to project too much at the present time, there is an emerging postconservative mood in evangelical theology that is exploring, among other matters, how to read Scripture beyond the liberal-conservative assumptions of modernity. See Roger E. Olson, "Postconservative Evangelicals Greet the Postmodern Age," *The Christian Century*, May 3, 1995, pp. 480-83.

[33]McClendon, *Ethics*, p. 33.

[34]Walter Brueggemann attempts to blend spirit and imagination in what he calls the construals of evangelical imagination that are gospel-bearing narrations of a counterworld—that is, a world that is counter to the rival imaginative construals of secularity—in *Texts Under Negotiation: The Bible and Postmodern Imagination* (Philadelphia: Fortress, 1993).

[35]Abraham Joshua Heschel, quoted in *A Guide to Prayer*, ed. Reuben P. Job and Norman Shawchuck (Nashville: Upper Room, 1983), p. 35.

[36]Karl Barth, "The Strange New World of the Bible," in *The Word of God and the Word of Man*.

[37]Jean Leclercq, *The Love of Learning and the Desire for God*, trans. Catharine Misrahi (1961; reprint New York: Fordham University Press, 1982), pp. 2-3.

[38]Ibid., p. 3.

[39]Arnoul of Boheriss *Speculum monachorum* 1, quoted in Leclercq, *Love of Learning*, p. 73. Augustine also uses the image of Scripture as a fountain wherein "each man for himself may draw the truth he can attain," in *Confessions* 12.27.37: *The Confessions of St. Augustine*, ed. John K. Ryan (New York: Image/Doubleday, 1960), p. 328. Thus Augustine argues that no one can approach Scripture with *the meaning*. Rather, he suggests that "the one God has adapted the sacred writings to many men's interpretations, wherein will be seen things true and also diverse" (*Confessions* 12.31.42, p. 332).

[40]Leclercq, *Love of Learning*, pp. 72-73, and Jean Leclercq, "Lectio Divina," *Worship*, May 1984, pp. 239-48. For helpful discussions of contemporary uses of the *lectio* method see M. Robert Mulholland Jr., *Invitation to a Journey* (Downers Grove, Ill.: InterVarsity Press, 1993), pp. 112-15; M. Robert Mulholland, "Spiritual Reading of Scripture," *Weavings*, December 1988, pp. 26-32; Gabriel O'Donnell, "Reading for Holiness: *Lectio Divina*," in *Spiritual Traditions for the Contemporary Church*, ed. Robin Mass and Gabriel O'Donnell (Nashville: Abingdon, 1990), pp. 45-54.

[41]Bernard of Clairvaux, sermon 85 on the *Canticles*, in *Late Medieval Mysticism*, ed. Ray C. Petry (Philadelphia: Westminster Press, 1957), pp. 74-78.

[42]For a careful discussion of this approach in contemporary literary theory see Stanley Fish,

"How I Stopped Worrying and Learned to Love Interpretation," introduction to *Is There a Text in This Class?* (Cambridge, Mass.: Harvard University Press, 1980), pp. 1-17. In addition to demonstrating the relationship between Fish's reader response theory and catholic hermeneutics, Hauerwas shows how the Protestant doctrine of *sola scriptura* as a distortion of and departure from the catholic understanding of Scripture is a heresy rather than a help in the church (Hauerwas, "Stanley Fish, the Pope and the Bible," in *Unleashing the Scripture*, pp. 19-28).

43Lindbeck, "Scripture, Consensus and Community," p. 87.

44Geoffrey Wainwright, *Eucharist and Eschatology* (New York: Oxford University Press, 1981), pp. 64-68.

45The language of the Lord's Supper as a "remembering sign" belongs to James W. McClendon Jr. in *Systematic Theology: Doctrine* (Nashville: Abingdon, 1994), pp. 382, 400-406.

46Nicholas Lash, *Theology on the Way to Emmaus* (London: SCM Press, 1986), p. 42.

47Martin Kuske, *The Old Testament as the Book of Christ: An Appraisal of Bonhoeffer's Interpretation*, trans. S. T. Kimbrough Jr. (Philadelphia: Westminster Press, 1976).

48Dietrich Bonhoeffer, *Life Together*, trans. John W. Doberstein (New York: Harper & Row, 1954), p. 45.

49Ibid., p. 46.

50I am following the excellent summaries of Williams by McClendon in *Doctrine*, pp. 482-87, and Alan Simpson, *Puritanism in Old and New England* (Chicago: University of Chicago Press, 1955), pp. 46-50. See the Williams-Cotton correspondence in H. Leon McBeth, *A Sourcebook for Baptist Heritage* (Nashville: Broadman, 1990), pp. 85-90.

51McClendon, *Doctrine*, 487.

52Lindbeck, *Nature of Doctrine*, 64.

53Richard Kieckhefer, "Imitators of Christ: Sainthood in the Christian Tradition," in Richard Kieckhefer and George D. Bond, *Sainthood: Its Manifestations in World Religions* (Berkeley: University of California Press, 1987), p. 3.

54Frederick Buechner, *Wishful Thinking*, rev. ed. (San Francisco: Harper, 1993), s.v. "saint," p. 102. James McClendon has cautioned me that the New Testament sense of *hagioi* might be better conveyed as "the faithful" rather than "the saints." He is surely right that such a translation better emphasizes the collectivity of holiness over against a distorted individualistic notion of sainthood. However, as I have reminded him, the Protestant sense of *hagioi* as "the faithful" can all too easily be flattened out so that the emphasis on "the *exemplary* faithful" gets lost. In this flattened account the operative phrase becomes "brothers and sisters it seems to me."

55Anne Tyler, *Saint Maybe* (New York: Ivy Books, 1991), p. 138.

56Ibid., p. 291.

57David Hugh Farmer, *The Oxford Dictionary of the Saints*, 3rd ed. (New York: Oxford University Press, 1992), pp. xx-xxi.

58James W. McClendon Jr., *Biography as Theology* (Nashville: Abingdon, 1974), pp. 209-10.

59Robert Wilken, "The Lives of the Saints and the Pursuit of Virtue," *First Things*, December 1990, p. 45.

60Karl Rahner, *The Theology of the Spiritual Life*, vol. 3 of *Theological Investigations*, trans. Karl-H. Kruger and Boniface Kruger (Baltimore: Helicon, 1967), p. 100.

61Augustine *Confessions* 5.13.23, p. 130.

62Ibid. 5.14.24-25, pp. 131-32.

63Athanasius *On the Incarnation of the Word of God* 57.1-3, in *Nicene and Post-Nicene Fathers of the Christian Church*, 2nd series (Grand Rapids, Mich.: Eerdmans, 1978), 4:67. See Hauerwas,

Unleashing the Scripture, pp. 37-38.
64Augustine *Confessions* 8.12.29, p. 202.
65Ibid. 9.6.14, p. 214.
66Hauerwas, *Unleashing the Scripture*, p. 15.
67Cited by Christopher Hill, *A Turbulent, Seditious and Factious People: John Bunyan and His Church* (Oxford: Oxford University Press, 1988), p. 125. Hill's account of the Civil War and the revolution of seventeenth-century England demonstrates the political sedition that was inherent within the theology of the Baptists and other dissenting groups.
68John Howard Yoder, "The Hermeneutics of Peoplehood," in *The Priestly Kingdom: Social Ethics as Gospel* (Notre Dame, Ind.: University of Notre Dame Press, 1984), p. 22.
69Stanley Hauerwas often levels this criticism against modern Baptists.
70Yoder, *Priestly Kingdom*, p. 28-34.
71Chesterton, *Orthodoxy*, p. 20.
72Yoder, *Priestly Kingdom*, p. 45.

Chapter 12: The Contemporary Renewal of Trinitarian Theology/Richardson
1Indeed, Vatican II, Orthodox and classic Protestant creeds and confessions of faith all explicitly or implicitly declare the inerrancy or infallibility of Scripture, the propositional nature of biblical teaching and the reality of those things to which the teachings refer.
2Mark Noll, Cornelius Plantinga Jr. and David Wells, "Evangelical Theology Today," *Theology Today* 51 (January 1995): 495-507.
3Alister McGrath, *Evangelicalism and the Future of Christianity* (Downers Grove, Ill.: InterVarsity Press, 1995).
4Avery Dulles, *The Craft of Theology: From Symbol to System* (New York: Crossroad, 1992).
5Ibid., p. 193.
6See the document *Evangelicals and Catholics Together*.
7Albert C. Outler, "Toward a Postliberal Hermeneutics," *Theology Today* 42 (1985): 281-91, quotation from p. 284.
8Ibid., pp. 286, 291.
9Hans Frei, *Types of Christian Theology*, ed. George Hunsinger and William Placher (New Haven, Conn.: Yale University Press, 1992).
10Ibid., p. 158.
11George Hunsinger, *How to Read Karl Barth: The Shape of His Theology* (New York: Oxford University Press, 1991). Hunsinger dedicates this work to his mentor, Hans Frei.
12Mark Heim, ed., *Faith to Creed: Ecumenical Perspectives on the Affirmation of the Apostolic Faith in the Fourth Century* (Grand Rapids, Mich.: Eerdmans, 1991).
13Significant exposition extends throughout the *Church Dogmatics* 1/1, 2/1-2, 4/1; the questions about whether Barth is in the end monarchian (Moltmann) or whether he has lost the proper distinction between the immanent and economic Trinity (Molnar) require a careful rereading to uncover that Barth has not succumbed to resolutions that would do violence to the doctrine. Barth in fact maintains the reality of divine persons in inseparable relation along with the oneness of the divine nature.
14See Colin Gunton, *The Promise of Trinitarian Theology* (Edinburgh: T & T Clark, 1991), and his Bampton Lectures of 1992, *The One, the Three and the Many: God, Creation and the Culture of Modernity* (Cambridge: Cambridge University Press, 1993).
15Thomas F. Torrance, *The Trinitarian Faith: The Evangelical Theology of the Ancient Catholic Church* (Edinburgh: T & T Clark, 1988); compare my *Trinitarian Reality: The Interrelation of Uncreated and Created Being in the Thought of Thomas Forsyth Torrance*, published dissertation of the Uni-

versity of Basel, 1993; see Torrance's contribution to the discussion of trinitarian language, "The Christian Apprehension of God the Father," in *Speaking the Christian God: The Holy Trinity and the Challenge of Feminism*, ed. Alvin F. Kimel Jr. (Grand Rapids, Mich.: Eerdmans, 1992), pp. 120-43.

[16]Thomas F. Torrance, ed., *Theological Dialogue Between Orthodox and Reformed Churches*, 2 vols. (Edinburgh: Scottish Academic Press, 1985-1993).

[17]Eberhard Jüngel, *The Doctrine of the Trinity: God's Being Is in Becoming* (Grand Rapids, Mich.: Eerdmans, 1976.)

[18]Jürgen Moltmann, *The Trinity and the Kingdom* (San Francisco: Harper & Row, 1981).

[19]Wolfhart Pannenberg, *Systematic Theology*, vol. 1., trans. Geoffrey W. Bromiley (Grand Rapids, Mich.: Eerdmans, 1988).

[20]Robert W. Jenson, *The Triune Identity: God According to the Gospel* (Philadelphia: Fortress, 1982).

[21]Karl Rahner, *The Trinity* (New York: Herder, 1970).

[22]Yves Congar, *I Believe in the Holy Spirit*, 3 vols. (New York: Seabury Press, 1983).

[23]Hans Urs von Balthasar, *The Glory of the Lord: A Theological Aesthetics*, ed. John Riches, trans. Andrew Louth et al. (San Francisco: Ignatius, 1984-1991).

[24]Walter Kasper, *The God of Jesus Christ* (New York: Crossroad, 1986).

[25]Catherine Mowry LaCugna, *God for Us: The Trinity and the Christian Life* (San Francisco: Harper, 1991).

[26]Vladimir Lossky, *The Mystical Theology of the Eastern Church* (London: Clarke, 1957).

[27]John D. Zizioulas, *Being as Communion: Studies in Personhood and the Church* (Crestwood, N.Y.: St. Vladimir's, 1985).

[28]Compare the outstanding introduction by Edmund Hill, recent translator of St. Augustine's *The Trinity* (Brooklyn: New City, 1991), pp. 18-59.

[29]Torrance, *Trinitarian Faith*, p. 3.

[30]Athanasius, *Select Works and Letters: Nicene and Post-Nicene Fathers*, vol. 4., ed. Philip Schaff and Henry Wace (Peabody, Mass.: Hendrickson, 1994).

[31]Gregory Nazianzen, *Select Orations and Letters*, in *Nicene and Post-Nicene Fathers*, vol. 7, ed. Philip Schaff and Henry Wace (Peabody, Mass.: Hendrickson, 1994).

[32]Cyril of Jerusalem, *Catechetical Lecture*, in *Nicene and Post-Nicene Fathers*, vol. 7, ed. Philip Schaff and Henry Wace (Peabody, Mass.: Hendrickson, 1994).

[33]Ibid., p. 15.

[34]Torrance, *Theological Dialogue*, 1:83.

[35]Torrance, *Trinitarian Faith*, p. 44.

[36]Ibid., p. 49.

[37]Ibid., p. 53.

[38]The Western Church added this term intending to safeguard the affirmation of the coequality of the Son with the Father by saying that the Spirit also proceeded from the Son. But this violated Scripture; the Father is the sole originator of the Spirit, according to John's Gospel. In the West, this is becoming more widely recognized and very likely will result in a return to the original form of the confession.

[39]Ibid., p. 57.

[40]Ibid., p. 60.

[41]Ibid., p. 63, quoting *Contra Arianos* 3.3, 6; italics are Torrance's.

[42]Ibid., p. 7.

[43]Thomas F. Torrance, *Trinitarian Perspectives: Toward Doctrinal Agreement* (Edinburgh: T & T Clark, 1994), p. 4.

[44]Ibid., p. 5.

⁴⁵Ibid., chaps. 2-3; see also Philip Butin, *Revelation, Redemption and Response: Calvin's Trinitarian Understanding of the Divine-Human Relationship* (New York: Oxford University Press, 1995).

⁴⁶Ibid., p. 115; compare Torrance, *Dialogue,* 2:219.

⁴⁷Torrance, *Dialogue,* p. 129; Torrance cites Athanasius *Contra Arianos* 2.3; *De decretis* 10-11.

⁴⁸Torrance, *Dialogue,* p. 139; Torrance is quoting from Epiphanius *Adversus haereses* 62.3.

⁴⁹Torrance, *Dialogue,* pp. 139, 141.

⁵⁰Ted Peters, *God as Trinity* (Louisville, Ky.: Westminster/John Knox, 1993).

⁵¹John Thompson, *Modern Trinitarian Perspectives* (New York: Oxford University Press, 1994).

⁵²See William Placher, *Narratives of a Vulnerable God* (Louisville, Ky.: Westminster/John Knox, 1994). Placher dismisses Pelikan's estimation of the essential presupposition of the impassibility of God in Christology.

⁵³Ibid., p.19.

⁵⁴Ibid., p. 40.

Chapter 13: True Affections/Knight

¹Stanley J. Grenz, *Revisioning Evangelical Theology: A New Theology for the 21st Century* (Downers Grove, Ill.: InterVarsity Press, 1993), p. 58.

²Ibid., p. 38-39.

³Alister E. McGrath, *Spirituality in an Age of Change: Rediscovering the Spirit of the Reformers* (Grand Rapids, Mich.: Zondervan, 1994); J. I. Packer, *A Quest for Godliness: The Puritan Vision of the Christian Life* (Wheaton, Ill.: Crossway, 1990); Steven J. Land, *Pentecostal Spirituality: A Passion for the Kingdom* (Sheffield, U.K.: Sheffield Academic Press, 1993); William J. Abraham, *The Coming Great Revival* (San Francisco: Harper & Row, 1984); and my *The Presence of God in the Christian Life: John Wesley and the Means of Grace* (Metuchen, N.J.: Scarecrow, 1992).

⁴Alister E. McGrath, *Evangelicalism and the Future of Christianity* (Downers Grove, Ill.: InterVarsity Press, 1995), p. 120. David F. Wells has also made a case for the interrelationship of spirituality and theology in *No Place for Truth: Or, Whatever Happened to Evangelical Theology?* (Grand Rapids, Mich.: Eerdmans, 1993), pp. 98-101. I share his concern for the eclipse of an authoritative confession by managerial and therapeutic technique, privatized and centered on the self (p. 101). Also we have in common a desire to recover a lost spirituality "that is centrally moral in its nature because God is centrally holy in his being" (p. 100). However, my approach to this is somewhat different. In particular, I am proposing through the affections a more integrated view of heart, life and mind, and a greater understanding of Scripture not only as the primary authority for theological reflection, but even more as an environment within which we dwell and through which the Spirit shapes the Christian life.

⁵McGrath, *Evangelicalism and the Future,* p. 136.

⁶Abraham, *Coming Great Revival,* p. 53.

⁷George A. Lindbeck, *The Nature of Doctrine* (Philadelphia: Westminster Press, 1984), p. 16.

⁸Jonathan Edwards, *A Treatise on Religious Affections* (Grand Rapids, Mich.: Baker Book House, 1982), p. 11.

⁹John Wesley, "An Earnest Appeal to Men of Reason and Religion," in *The Works of John Wesley,* ed. Frank Baker (Oxford: Oxford University Press, 1975), 11:45.

¹⁰On this see Gregory Scott Clapper, *John Wesley on Religious Affections* (Metuchen, N.J.: Scarecrow, 1989).

¹¹Don E. Saliers, *The Soul in Paraphrase: Prayer and the Religious Affections* (New York: Seabury Press, 1980; reprinted by the Order of Saint Luke), p. 7.

¹²Robert C. Roberts, *Spirituality and Human Emotion* (Grand Rapids, Mich.: Eerdmans, 1982),

p. 1; see a similar quote in Saliers, *Soul in Paraphrase*, p. 11.

[13]Robert C. Roberts, *The Strengths of a Christian* (Philadelphia: Westminster Press, 1984), p. 23.

[14]Saliers, *Soul in Paraphrase*, p. 12.

[15]Ibid., p. 13.

[16]Roberts, *Spirituality*, pp. 109-10.

[17]Saliers, *Soul in Paraphrase*, p. 7.

[18]Roberts, *Spirituality*, pp. 20-21.

[19]Saliers, *Soul in Paraphrase*, p. 46.

[20]Randy L. Maddox, *Responsible Grace* (Nashville: Abingdon, 1984), p. 69.

[21]Richard J. Foster, *Celebration of Discipline: The Path to Spiritual Growth* (San Francisco: Harper & Row, 1978); Dallas Willard, *The Spirit of the Disciplines: Understanding How God Changes Lives* (San Francisco: Harper & Row, 1988); James Houston, *The Transforming Friendship: A Guide to Prayer* (Oxford: Lion, 1989).

[22]Saliers, *Soul in Paraphrase*, p. 13.

[23]Lindbeck, *Nature of Doctrine*, p. 35.

[24]Ibid.

[25]Ibid, p. 36.

[26]Ibid.

[27]Grenz, *Revisioning Evangelical Theology*, p. 73.

[28]Ibid., pp. 77-78.

[29]Clark H. Pinnock, *Tracking the Maze* (San Francisco: Harper & Row, 1990), p. 154.

[30]Ibid., p. 159.

[31]Carl F. H. Henry, "Narrative Theology: An Evangelical Appraisal," *Trinity Journal* 8 (Spring 1987): 19.

[32]Donald G. Bloesch, *A Theology of Word and Spirit: Authority and Method in Theology* (Downers Grove, Ill.: InterVarsity Press, 1992), p. 30.

[33]Mark I. Wallace, "The New Yale Theology," *Christian Scholar's Review* 17 (December 1987): 170.

[34]Grenz, *Revisioning Evangelical Theology*, p. 72.

[35]Pinnock, *Tracking the Maze*, p. 153.

[36]William C. Placher, *Unapologetic Theology: A Christian Voice in a Pluralistic Conversation* (Louisville, Ky.: Westminster/John Knox, 1989), p. 126.

[37]Ibid.

[38]Ibid, p. 128.

[39]Ibid., p. 121.

[40]Ibid.

[41]Bloesch, *Theology of Word and Spirit*, p. 122.

[42]Ibid., pp. 69-70; see also pp. 60-61.

[43]Clark H. Pinnock, *The Scripture Principle* (San Francisco: Harper & Row, 1984), p. 189.

[44]Ibid., p. 190.

[45]Ibid.

[46]Ibid., p. 191.

[47]Ibid., p. 193.

[48]For a defense of critical realism in relation to metaphor, see Janet Martin Soskice, *Metaphors and Religious Language* (Oxford: Clarendon, 1985).

Chapter 14: The Nature of Conversion/Clark

[1]Hans Frei, *Types of Christian Theology*, ed. George Hunsinger and William Placher (New

Haven, Conn.: Yale University Press, 1992), p. 20.

²Ibid., pp. 3, 24, 45.

³I feel I owe the reader an apology for employing such an awkward term as *worldviewness*. This term, however, seemed to be the easiest way to indicate that I am not talking about a particular worldview but of the very idea of a worldview.

⁴James W. Sire, *The Universe Next Door: A Basic World View Catalog* (Downers Grove, Ill.: InterVarsity Press, 1976); Arthur F. Holmes, *Contours of a Worldview* (Grand Rapids, Mich.: Eerdmans, 1983); Brian J. Walsh, "Worldviews, Modernity and the Task of Christian College Education," *Faculty Dialogue* 18 (Fall 1992): 13-35; Brian J. Walsh and J. Richard Middleton, *The Transforming Vision: Shaping a Christian World View* (Downers Grove, Ill.: InterVarsity Press, 1984); Ronald H. Nash, *Worldviews in Conflict: Choosing Christianity in a World of Ideas* (Grand Rapids, Mich.: Zondervan, 1992).

⁵James Orr, *The Christian View of God and the World* (Edinburgh: Andrew Elliot, 1893), p. 3.

⁶Holmes, *Contours of a Worldview*, p. viii.

⁷Ibid., p. 50.

⁸Walsh and Middleton, *Transforming Vision*, p. 9. The quotation comes from the foreword by Nicholas Wolterstorff.

⁹Holmes, *Contours of a Worldview*, p. vii.

¹⁰Josh McDowell, *Evidence That Demands a Verdict: Historical Evidences for the Christian Faith* (Campus Crusade for Christ, 1972).

¹¹Orr, *Christian View*, p. 43. Orr concurs with August Baur's "surprise that more has not been done for the elucidation of a term which has become one of the favorite terms of the day (a fact which had struck myself) in books professedly dealing with the terminology of philosophy and theology" (pp. 42-43). I owe a debt of gratitude to John Castelein for pointing me to James Orr's work on worldviews.

¹²Orr, *Christian View*, p. 42.

¹³Max Scheler claims that the "plastic expression 'Weltanschauung' [was] given to our language by that outstanding historian of the mind, Wilhelm von Humboldt." See *On the Eternal in Man* (London: SCM Press, 1960), p. 82.

¹⁴Martin Heidegger, *The Basic Problems of Phenomenology*, trans. Albert Hofstadter (Bloomington: Indiana University Press, 1988), p. 4.

¹⁵Martin Heidegger, *The Metaphysical Foundations of Logic*, trans. Michael Heim (Bloomington: Indiana University Press, 1992), p. 179; *Basic Problems of Phenomenology*, p. 4. I have not yet found the term *Weltanschauung* in Kant, and Heidegger does not provide any references. Heidegger and Orr disagree as to where one might find it in Kant. Orr speculates that the term originates with the "world-whole" (*Weltganz*), which is an Idea of Pure Reason and has no empirical content. Orr then makes a classical worldview move. He assumes that Kant is right, and imposes the Kantian structure on the entirety of history, arguing that, of course, people have had an idea of the world as a whole from "the dawn of reflection." It is first formulated in religion, and made explicit in philosophy. See Orr, *Christian View*, p. 5.

¹⁶Merold Westphal argues against this as an adequate interpretation of Kant, with the somewhat novel interpretation that God perceives the noumena for Kant and that, consequently, Kant preserves the traditional account of truth. My concern is only with traditional (more humanistic) interpretations of Kant, and then only insofar as these interpretations lead to worldview philosophy. See Merold Westphal, "Christian Philosophers and the Copernican Revolution," in *Christian Perspectives on Religious Knowledge*, ed. C. Stephen Evans and Merold Westphal (Grand Rapids, Mich.: Eerdmans, 1993).

[17]If one wanted to follow the order of philosophy that I suggested above, the argument would begin here. One would need to show that the idea of worldviewness introduces some content that is not necessary and universal, such as a metaphysic of subjectivity, and then show that this content conflicts with the philosophical commitments of Christianity.

[18]Abraham Kuyper, *Lectures on Calvinism* (Grand Rapids, Mich.: Eerdmans, 1953), p. 11, n. 1.

[19]Holmes, *Contours of a Worldview*, p. 51.

[20]Ibid., p. viii.

[21]The principle of distinction between philosophy and theology that operates here comes from theology. That is, philosophy and theology are here distinguished by the authorities to which they appeal, and these authorities are designated by the categories of special and general revelation or of aided and unaided reason. Both of these are theological rather than philosophical categories. If philosophy were to use these categories to define itself, it would rely on arguments and assumptions proper to the domain of theology.

[22]Jean-François Lyotard defines this as the postmodern condition. See *The Postmodern Condition: A Report on Knowledge*, trans. Geoff Bennington and Brian Massumi (Minneapolis: University of Minnesota Press, 1984), p. 81.

[23]Jean-Luc Marion, *Dieu sans l'être: Hors-texte* (Paris: Librairie Arthème Fayard, 1982). Or see its translation, *God Without Being*, trans. Thomas A. Carlson (Chicago: University of Chicago Press, 1991).

[24]Michael J. Buckley, *At the Origins of Modern Atheism* (New Haven, Conn.: Yale University Press, 1987).

[25]Alasdair MacIntyre, *Three Rival Versions of Moral Enquiry: Encyclopedia, Genealogy and Tradition* (Notre Dame, Ind.: University of Notre Dame Press, 1990).

[26]While I come at this from the perspective of phenomenology rather than from Barth or from the later Wittgenstein, I take it that Frei would classify this position as representing either his fourth or fifth type of theology.

[27]As Pierre Hadot writes in *Exercices spirituels et philosophie antique* (Paris: Études Augustiniennes, 1987), p. 181: "More and better than a theory of conversion, philosophy is itself essentially an act of conversion." See also A. D. Nock, *Conversion: The Old and the New in Religion from Alexander the Great to Augustine of Hippo* (Oxford: Clarendon, 1952); Martha C. Nussbaum, *The Therapy of Desire: Theory and Practice in Hellenistic Ethics* (Princeton, N.J.: Princeton University Press, 1994).

[28]Walsh, "Worldviews," p. 26.

[29]Walsh defines conversion as "the abandonment of one worldview for another" (ibid., p. 24).

[30]I acknowledge and thank Jim Sire, Ric Hudgens, Mary Doak, John Castelein, Rich Knopp, Tim Peebles, Syd Hielema, the Faculty Research Group at North Park College and participants in my North Park College, Spring 1995, "Heidegger's *Being and Time*" course for their illuminating and gracious responses to an earlier version of this paper.

Chapter 15: Atonement & the Hermeneutics of Intratextual Social Embodiment/Lindbeck

[1]These are, it should be noted, quite different from J. L. Austin's "performative utterances." For the analysis of performance interpretation which I shall use, I am indebted to a book by Nicholas Wolterstorff which I have been able to consult only in its prepublication form, *Divine Discourse: Philosophical Reflections on the Claim That God Speaks* (New York: Cambridge University Press, 1995).

[2]The understanding of dogma or doctrine (as well as of theology and classical biblical interpretation) presupposed in this essay is that developed in my *Nature of Doctrine* (Philadelphia: Westminster Press, 1984). The issues treated here, however, except for those in

part two ("Descriptive Theory"), are not dealt with in my previous publications.

[3]Alasdair MacIntyre, *After Virtue* (Notre Dame, Ind.: Notre Dame University Press, 1987), p. 207.

[4]The *consensus fidelium* is not to be confused with majority opinion nor with localized unanimity whose wider and enduring persuasiveness is uncertain. The consent that counts is that of the company of those whose lives cohere with the creed they profess, who are not swept about by every wind of doctrine and who are prepared to die rather than dishonor the Name.

[5]I should here add as an aside that lack of consensus is not evidence that the Spirit is *not* at work. When Christians are divided, beginning with Paul's conflicts with Peter in Antioch, with the spiritualizers in Corinth and with the Judaizers in Galatia, one party may be on God's side and the other not. Sometimes, to be sure, God is not with any of the disputing parties.

[6]From this perspective, what has come to be known as fundamentalist biblicism is a thoroughly modern phenomenon. It starts not with first-order scriptural interpretation but with theories of inspiration and inerrancy combined with a hermeneutical decision in favor of an unprecedented notion of the literal sense. Instead of the latter being, as Aquinas classically formulates the point, whatever the divine author intends to convey by such and such words (and this is ultimately to be discerned by reading these words within the context of the narrationally and typologically unified canon under the guidance of trinitarian and christological dogma and in reference to possibly varying situations with the result that multiple literal—that is, God-intended—senses are possible, some of which may be tropes if measured by ordinary usage), the literal sense is now identified as univocal, empirically and/or rationally propositional and syllogistically systematizable. Furthermore, anything in the Bible that can possibly be literally interpreted in the sense so defined must be thus interpreted. Clearly it is not biblical inerrancy that is distinctive in this outlook; for no believer who thinks of the literal sense as that which the divine author intends could possibly deny its lack of error. Rather, that which makes fundamentalism different from premodern interpretation is the hermeneutical decision in favor of an understanding of the literal sense, which was unknown before such modern thinkers as Descartes and Locke.

[7]The single best compendium of the kind of studies I have in mind is Robert Alter and Frank Kermode, eds., *The Literary Guide to the Bible* (Cambridge, Mass.: Harvard University Press, 1987), but Erich Auerbach's much earlier work as appropriated by Hans Frei in his notable *The Eclipse of Biblical Narrative* (New Haven, Conn.: Yale University Press, 1975) has been the theologically most influential work in this area for me, as for many others.

[8]Michael Polanyi, *Personal Knowledge* (Chicago: University of Chicago Press, 1958).

[9]I discuss this and related aspects of Barth's work in "Barth and Textuality," *Theology Today* 43 (1986): 361-76.

[10]For a more conceptually rigorous exposition of the ideas in this paragraph, see Bruce D. Marshall, "Absorbing the World: Christianity and World of Truths," in *Theology and Dialogue: Essays in Conversation with George Lindbeck*, ed. Bruce D. Marshall (Notre Dame, Ind.: Notre Dame University Press, 1990), pp. 69-102.

[11]Wayne Meeks, "The Hermeneutics of Social Embodiment," *Harvard Theological Review* (1986): 184-85, 183-84.

[12]This corresponds to what Nicholas Wolterstorff calls the "sense of the text" in *Divine Discourse.*

[13]This struggle also involves the effort to distinguish intratextual meanings from theological constructs even when the latter are biblically warranted or permissible. Adherents of

classical theism as represented by Aquinas, for example, may believe that their understanding of such divine attributes as omniscience and impassibility is biblically superior to that of, let us say, process theology, but it is nevertheless important for them to recognize that their conceptualizations are at best consistent with the intratextual meanings of these attributes in the biblical stories, and are neither identical to nor entailed by the latter. Thus other theological conceptualizations may also be scripturally allowable. Needless to say, it is as imperative from this perspective for process thinkers as for classical theists to distinguish their theological constructs from the ultimately normative intratextual meanings.

14Especially in the 1986 essay "The 'Literal Reading' of the Bible in the Christian Tradition: Does It Stretch or Will It Break?" reprinted in his posthumous *Theology and Narrative: Selected Essays* (New York: Oxford University Press, 1993), pp. 117-52.

15David Kelsey, *The Uses of Scripture in Recent Theology* (Philadelphia: Fortress, 1975), passim.

16Perhaps it should be noted that the kind of performance interpretations that I am envisioning are those that respect the "realistic narrative" dimension of Shakespeare's play. If so, the romantic, Freudian or classical hero would remain recognizably the same fundamentally Shakespearean Hamlet. The world of Shakespeare's drama, in other words, would absorb and redescribe romantic, classical and Freudian motifs much more than the other way around. If, in contrast, Hamlet were to be played as the dream of a patient in therapy, Freud's world would swallow that of Shakespeare's drama, much as various alien worlds swallow that of the Bible in, for example, gnostic, Mormon, Christian Science or Unification Church interpretations.

17The quotations are from Mark Noll, Cornelius Plantinga Jr. and David Wells, "Evangelical Theology Today," *Theology Today* 51 (January 1995): 503, 496.

18H. Richard Niebuhr, *The Kingdom of God in America* (1937; reprint New York: Harper, 1959), p. 193.

19It will be noted that in good Reformation fashion, I here make faith (that is, conviction and belief) that which is active in love, rather than formed by love.

20It should not be supposed that recent contributions to revitalized atonement teaching are entirely lacking. Karl Barth and Hans Urs von Balthasar, for example, have done much to advance the discussion by means of biblical interpretations that have some of the features for which this essay pleads. They fall short, however, of the flexibility combined with determinateness, the plurality combined with unity, of a full-fledged hermeneutics of social/ecclesial embodiment.

Contributors

Jill Peláez Baumgaertner is professor of English at Wheaton College. Her latest volume of poetry, *Leaving Eden* (White Eagle Coffee Store Press), was winner of the spring 1994 Poetry Chapbook Contest. She is poetry editor of *First Things* and the recipient of a Fulbright.

Rodney Clapp is academic and general books editor at InterVarsity Press. He has published essays in several periodicals, including *Christian Century, Christianity Today, Books and Culture* and *The Wall Street Journal*. His books include *Families at the Crossroads* (IVP) and the forthcoming *A Peculiar People: The Church as Culture in a Post-Christian Society* (IVP).

David Clark is professor of theology at Bethel Theological Seminary, St. Paul, Minnesota. His current research interests focus on evangelical theological prolegomena. His books include *Dialogical Apologetics* (Baker) and *Readings in Christian Ethics* (Baker).

Gregory A. Clark is assistant professor of philosophy at North Park College. He completed his Ph.D. at Loyola University (Chicago) in 1996 with a dissertation on Henri Bergson. His speciality is twentieth-century French philosophy, and he is currently working on the theory of attention in Bergson and Gabriel Marcel.

Gabriel Fackre is Abbot Professor of Christian Theology at Andover Newton Theological School. Widely published, he is coauthor of *What About Those Who Have Never Heard?* (IVP) and the author of *Ecumenical Faith in Evangelical Perspective* (Eerdmans) and the forthcoming *The Doctrine of Revelation: A Narrative Intepretation* (University of Edinburgh Press).

Curtis W. Freeman is associate professor of Christianity and philosophy at Houston Baptist University and the preaching minister of an inner-city congregation. He is coeditor of *Ties That Bind* (Smith and Helwys) and author of a forthcoming work on biblical interpretation (IVP).

Jeffrey Hensley is a doctoral candidate in theology at Yale University. His dissertation concerns Schleiermacher and Christology. He has been the recipient of a Pew Younger Scholar Award, the Paul Holmer Scholar Award and the Archibald Prize.

George Hunsinger is a member of the Center of Theological Inquiry. A leading interpreter of Karl Barth and Hans Frei, he has published works including *How to Read Karl Barth* (Oxford University Press). He is the coeditor of two posthumously published books by Hans Frei, *Theology and Narrative* (Oxford University Press) and *Types of Christian Theology* (Yale University Press).

Philip Kenneson is assistant professor of theology and philosophy at Milligan College. His Ph.D. is from Duke University, and he has written for *Modern Theology, The Asbury Theological Journal* and *Soundings*. He is a contributor to *Christian Apologetics in a Postmodern World* (IVP) and is at work on several projects in the theology of culture and ecclesiology.

Henry H. Knight III occupies the E. Stanley Jones Chair of Evangelism at St. Paul School of Theology. He earned his doctorate at Emory University and has published essays in *The Journal of Pentecostal Theology* and *The Evangelical Journal*.

George Lindbeck is professor emeritus at Yale Divinity School. He and his colleague, the late Hans Frei, were the founders of postliberal theology. His key works include *The Nature of Doctrine* (Westminster) and "Scripture, Consensus and Community," in *Biblical Interpretation in Crisis* (Eerdmans).

Alister E. McGrath is principal of Wycliffe Hall (Oxford University) and teaches theology both at Oxford and at Regent College (Vancouver, B.C.). His most important recent works include *Iustitia Dei: A History of the Christian Doctrine of Justification* (Cambridge University Press) and *A Passion for Truth: The Intellectual Coherence of Evangelicalism* (IVP).

Dennis L. Okholm is associate professor of theology at Wheaton College. His essays have appeared in *Christian Scholar's Review* and *The Proceedings of the American Benedictine Academy*. He is coeditor of *Christian Apologetics in a Postmodern World* (IVP) and *More Than One Way? Four Views on Salvation in a Pluralistic World* (Zondervan).

Timothy R. Phillips is associate professor of theology at Wheaton College. His essays have appeared in *Through No Fault of Their Own? The Fate of Those Who Have Never Heard* (Baker) and *Historians of the Christian Tradition* (Broadman and Holman). He is coeditor of *Christian Apologetics in a Postmodern World* (IVP) and *More Than One Way? Four Views on Salvation in a Pluralistic World* (Zondervan).

Kurt A. Richardson is associate professor of theology and ethics at Gordon-Conwell Theological Seminary. His research interests focus on the integration of theology, science and culture. He has published essays in *Zygon* and *Faith and Mission* and is completing a work on barbarism and contemporary culture (forthcoming, IVP).

Miroslav Volf is associate professor of systematic theology at Fuller Theological Seminary. His doctoral work was completed at Tübingen. His essays have appeared in *Zeitschrift fur Theologie und Kirche, Ex Auditu* and *The Calvin Journal of Theology*. He is the author of *Work in the Spirit: Toward a Theology of Work* (Oxford University Press).

Jonathan R. Wilson is assistant professor of religious studies at Westmont College. He has published essays in *Modern Theology, Journal of Religion* and *Crux*. His forthcoming books include *Theologian as Interpreter and Critic: Julian Hartt's Theology of Culture* (Mercer University Press) and a study of evangelical theology and the ethics of virtue (IVP).